Biblical Women and Jewish Daily Life in the Middle Ages

Jewish Culture and Contexts

Published in association with the Herbert D. Katz Center
for Advanced Judaic Studies of the University of Pennsylvania

SERIES EDITORS:

Shaul Magid, Francesca Trivellato, Steven Weitzman

A complete list of books in the series is available from the publisher.

Biblical Women
and Jewish Daily Life
in the Middle Ages

Elisheva Baumgarten

PENN

University of Pennsylvania Press
Philadelphia

Published by
University of Pennsylvania Press
Philadelphia, Pennsylvania 19104-4112
www.upenn.edu/pennpress

Printed in the United States of America on acid-free paper
10 9 8 7 6 5 4 3 2 1

Hardcover ISBN 9780812253580
Ebook ISBN 9780812297522

Library of Congress Cataloging-in-Publication Data
Names: Baumgarten, Elisheva, author.
Title: Biblical women and Jewish daily life in the Middle Ages / Elisheva Baumgarten.
Description: First edition. | Philadelphia : University of Pennsylvania Press, [2021] |
    Series: Jewish culture and contexts | Includes bibliographical references and index.
Identifiers: LCCN 2021033977 | ISBN 978-0-8122-5358-0 (hardcover)
Subjects: LCSH: Women in the Bible. | Women in Judaism —Europe —History —To 1500.
    | Bible. Old Testament —Criticism, interpretation, etc., Jewish —History —To 1500. |
    Bible —Influence —Medieval civilization. | Judaism —Europe —History —To 1500. |
    Jewish way of life —History —To 1500. | Jews —Europe —Social life and customs —To
    1500. | Jews —Europe —History —To 1500.
Classification: LCC BS1199.W7 B38 2021 | DDC 220.9/2082 —dc23
LC record available at https://lccn.loc.gov/2021033977

For my parents, Al and Rita Baumgarten

Contents

Introduction

This study seeks a point of entry into the everyday lives of medieval Jews who left no written record because they did not belong to the learned elite whose oeuvre has reached us. It uses the Bible—as read and interpreted by the Jews of medieval Ashkenaz—as a tool for social history. By exploring select narratives, with attention to particular figures, and their varied tellings (and retellings) as explanations and validations for ritual practice, this book presents case studies that provide access to the daily existence of Jews who lived in northern France and Germany, particularly within urban social milieux, where they lived among a Christian majority. These Jewish communities are broadly known as the Jews of Ashkenaz because of their shared customs and cultural commonalities. This book does not attempt to be a comprehensive study of the Bible or its medieval interpretations. Nor do I posit that the genres I analyze here—literature, art, exegesis, legal directives—mirror social practice. Rather, my goal is to examine Jewish medieval engagement with the Bible as a window on aspects of the daily lives and cultural mentalités of medieval Ashkenazic Jews in the High Middle Ages, with the working assumption that these sources contributed to shaping and conveying elements of their world. Throughout, I explore this as an avenue along which social historians may access the quotidian circumstances of people of the past, in this case, medieval Jews who left no written accounts of their beliefs and practices.

By concentrating on biblical heroines and the everyday practices that emerge from examining these figures and their portrayals,[1] I argue that the Bible and its medieval European interpretations are of unique value for illuminating commonplace religious praxis, the beliefs that Jewish women and men embraced, the narratives they circulated, and their cultural identities. I consider the analysis presented here as a development to further some of the ideas that I have set forth elsewhere, when I wrote that "practice was one means by which Jews preserved their uniqueness and further fostered a separate ethnic identity" and concluded by seeking a way to access "the vantage point of those who performed rituals rather than those who penned their descriptions."[2] In the pages that follow, I set the stage by presenting the Ashkenazic communal frameworks and sources that I examine in this study and outline the complex role of the Bible in medieval Jewish life: as an internal source that was discussed within Jewish communities; as an external source that was considered and interpreted by Christians in relation to their own practices; and as a shared source providing the underpinnings of medieval Jewish-Christian dialogue and polemics.

▇ The Medieval Communities of Ashkenaz: Integration and Distinction

The Jews of medieval Ashkenaz are often referred to collectively, despite the significant political, cultural, and social distinctions that differentiated them within this region. These communities are documented from the decades before 1000 CE, as is evident in the charters and mentions of their presence from this time in northern France, then in Germany, and finally in England after the Norman conquest. By the late Middle Ages, Jews from Ashkenaz dwelled in Central and Eastern Europe as well as in northern Italy.[3] The origins of these communities are debated. Some trace their roots to southern Italy and their arrival in northern Europe to the emigration of businessmen and scholars, such as the Kalonymus family.[4] Others attribute the development of the Jewish communities in northern Europe to a more general influx of Jews from the south. By the late eleventh century, communities had been established in a number of key cities, and many smaller towns included tiny Jewish populations comprised of several families. The large Jewish communities of Germany—such as Mainz, Speyer, and Worms, as well as Würzburg, Cologne, Erfurt, and others—were home to scholars and established business families.[5] In northern France, Champagne and Paris had become centers of Jewish learning and thriving trade, especially during the great fairs of that period.[6] Smaller communities usually operated as satellites of the more established ones, with whom they joined for significant events, such as holidays or burial. The communal authorities and rabbis in larger centers provided guidance and advice for their smaller neighboring communities, in general and when legal disputes arose.[7]

Throughout the region, scholars and businesspeople moved from one area to another. So, for example, in the eleventh and twelfth centuries, students from France journeyed to Germany to study; and during the late twelfth and thirteenth centuries, German students regularly frequented French yeshivas.[8] Merchants also traveled from city to city, and marriages took place between the different families and communities. No study has documented all of this movement, but even the biographies of specific figures indicate mobility and contact between different regions. This pattern provides one example of the way that, despite their differences, Jews in medieval Germany and northern France shared numerous traditions and practices. These commonalities include ritual and liturgical norms as well as common beliefs.[9]

The Jewish population and the number of Jewish settlements, both small and large, grew tremendously over the course of the twelfth and thirteenth centuries.[10] This growth was halted first by forced expulsions, then by the plague; by the mid-fourteenth century, Jewish geography had changed dramatically, due to large-scale migration southward to Provence and Spain and eastward to Poland. English Jews were expelled in 1290 and northern France ceased to be home to medieval Jewish communities by the late fourteenth century.[11] Nonetheless, various Jewish communities survived in the lands of the Holy Roman Empire through modern times.

The characteristics of Jewish life in medieval Ashkenaz have been the subject of significant scholarly interest during the past century and a half. The pendulum has swung between viewing Ashkenazic Jewry as an isolated group, forcibly and volitionally separated from the Christian milieux within which it lived, and considering medieval Ashkenazic Jews to be an integrated community that had an important role in the daily urban life of predominantly Christian medieval Europe. This book follows those who see medieval Ashkenazic Jews as simultaneously entangled in their surroundings and distinct from them.[12] In this study I both examine mutually held traditions and investigate how medieval Jews saw themselves as distinct and made tangible that differentiation.

Within the medieval European urban landscape, Jews and Christians were joined by many elements of daily life, as well as by the biblical text they shared. Living in close proximity, the Jews, as a religious minority, and the Christians, as both the majority and ruling class, came into frequent contact. Jews dwelled alongside Christians in the various neighborhoods of medieval cities, and the synagogue was often located close to the municipal center, main churches, and town hall. Jews thus were part of the fabric of medieval urban life. Through their involvement in local trade, they were often associated with specific Christians as neighbors and business partners. Much recent research has considered the integration or separation of Jews in relation to their Christian neighbors, but it often lumps all the Jews together rather than seeking variety within the Jewish community, or assumes that Jews consistently adapted understandings from their surroundings or rejected them rather than allowing for a combination of both strategies. In some cases, contrasting understandings of the same issue or story existed, with some Jews appropriating the Christian interpretation and other Jews understanding it in a distinctly Jewish manner. Sometimes Jewish exegetes and storytellers adapted a new interpretation, and sometimes they chose to adhere to traditional narratives. In this study there are certain instances where I suggest that Jews incorporated concepts from their surroundings and others where I demonstrate how they chose to intentionally contrast Christian interpretation. Only by examining and comparing medieval Jewish understandings to their Christian parallels, whether concerning the Bible or relating to other elements of daily life, can we better comprehend and contextualize their meanings.

The evidence for medieval Jewish life has largely been collected from the writings of the rabbinic elite, and scholarly literature and the focus has been on this educated stratum of medieval Jewish society, assuming that it reflected medieval Jewry as a whole. My goal, although in some cases it is difficult to attain, is to get beyond this elite and examine a larger segment of Jewish society, whose presence is certain but whose lives remain elusive. In this quest, I explore religious identity as a core element of Jewishness in medieval Europe. My primary aim is to broaden our recognition of the Jewish community beyond the rabbis. When possible I also distinguish between cohorts within medieval society, men and women, lettered and less educated.

Over the past decade documentation of medieval tombstones has demonstrated how few people were identified as learned or as rabbis. This affirms that the texts we consult regularly to access medieval Ashkenazic life can represent only a small fraction of that population's members. Admittedly, the difficulty of reaching beyond textual evidence is nearly insurmountable. I suggest three central strategies in this book to try to overcome these obstacles: the use of multiple genres of sources to understand specific biblical narratives and their relevance to medieval life; a focus on practice rather than ideology or belief; and the use of gender as a heuristic category. I will now introduce each of these strategies and their relevance to this study.

The Bible in Medieval Culture and Practice

The Hebrew Bible, or Old Testament, was central in the religious lives of medieval Jews and Christians. Although each culture had later texts that were accorded greater attention and higher stature—namely the rabbinic literature (also referred to as the Oral Torah) and subsequent writings for Jews, and the New Testament and patristic writings for Christians—the importance of the Bible (Old Testament) endured.[13] Much has been written about the place of the Bible in the Middle Ages, and much of this focuses on the erudite study of the Bible and, especially, on the role of the Bible in interreligious polemics.[14] The Bible served as the foundation of both Christian tolerance for the presence of Jews in Christian Europe as well as for Christian animosity toward the Jews in their midst.[15] This shared text was a key tool for contesting Jews and Judaism in theological disputes. It is fair to say that the Bible was a site around which Jews and Christians both cooperated with mutual dependence and clashed with dissonant interpretations to the greatest extent.[16] While some have suggested that the Christian "discovery" or increased awareness of the Talmud, especially in the thirteenth century, diminished the status of the Bible in Jewish-Christian polemics, it remained a constant throughout these debates.[17]

Within the more tightly framed field of Jewish studies, much attention has been devoted to medieval commentaries on the Bible. The period under consideration here was formative, particularly regarding the development of varying methods of biblical interpretation and schools that cultivated these respective approaches. So, too, close comparisons have been made between approaches to biblical study among European Jews and those practiced by their Christian counterparts. Scholars who specialize in the study of biblical exegesis have focused their attention almost exclusively on the authors and students of these commentaries, whether Jewish or Christian, and on the Bible as a written and read text.[18]

Analogously, seemingly following in the footsteps of medieval Jewish scholars and polemicists, modern scholars of social and cultural history have also sidelined the Bible, allowing talmudic literature and halakhah to take precedence. While no one doubts the presence of the Bible in medieval Jewish culture, the articles and multiple volumes devoted to medieval halakhah (another central project of the northern European High Middle Ages) point to a marked preference for mapping talmudic origins among modern scholars as well as their medieval forebears. High medieval scholars favored talmudic precedents over biblical evidence, and at times we can document their turn to the Bible only in the absence of suitable talmudic proof texts.[19] From this perspective, medieval Jewish authorities subordinated the Bible to halakhic literature, and modern scholarship has followed suit.[20] Although valuing the Talmud need not eclipse attention to Bible, within modern discussions of practical halakhah and in social historical research, the Bible is usually mentioned tangentially or as a symbol rather than as a topic that merits independent treatment.[21] Here, too, the Bible is first and foremost treated by scholars as a written source rather than one that was read or spoken aloud.

Two additional factors have also influenced this tendency in scholarship. First, as noted earlier, medieval Christians accused Jews of being the people of the Talmud, insinuating that they had lost their standing as biblical witnesses, and this notion of a gradual move away from the Bible was accepted by Amos Funkenstein, who in the mid-1970s used the scholastic literature preceding the Paris Talmud Trial of 1242 to corroborate this phenomenon. Even as other scholars demonstrated that the Bible remained at the core of Jewish-Christian polemics, Funkenstein's argument reinforced the already common inclination of research on the history of halakhah to discount the role of the Bible.[22] A second potential contributing factor to this pattern may have stemmed from an apparent reluctance on the part of modern scholars to accept that Jews and Christians not only differed in their interpretation of the Bible but also held many common views of this shared text. Jews and Christians discussed and argued about biblical traditions with one another, which led each group to refine their own interpretations.[23] This interdependence prompted some modern scholars to observe a closeness between Jews and Christians that contradicted their earlier understanding of two distinct traditions. Others preferred to underline divergent interpretations. Yet in most cases, few considered the Bible as a source for social-historical investigation.[24]

In contrast, I contend throughout this book that the Bible served not only as a foundation for medieval study and belief but also as a central element of liturgy and prayer or, put differently, of practice.[25] Among Jews, scriptural portions were regularly chanted during daytime prayer services (on the Sabbath, Mondays and Thursdays, the new moon, fasts and festivals) or alluded to and quoted in the daily and annual liturgy.[26] Jewish children studied the Bible as an integral component of rudimentary education. This was true for boys as well as girls. Even those who advocated a limited scope for girls' education recognized the importance of studying the Bible and its basic meaning.[27] Christians, like Jews, included biblical passages in their readings, and incorporated biblical figures and verses in their prayers and liturgies.[28] Christian children, like their Jewish neighbors, also were taught biblical stories from an early age. Members of both religions included biblical figures in their stories and wrote their names on amulets.[29]

Throughout most of the medieval period, the biblical text was read in a language that was not well understood by many of the members of either society: Hebrew for Jews, Latin for Christians. Not until the late medieval period were vernacular Bibles produced and disseminated.[30] Yet, throughout the Middle Ages, the Bible was conveyed through multiple alternative means. Artwork that depicted the Bible and illuminated Bibles were produced by Jews and Christians alike.[31] Churches were decorated with paintings and sculptures of biblical scenes. Street plays publicly retold embellished biblical tales.[32] Amulets petitioned biblical figures to heal and protect whoever wore them.[33] As a result the Bible was accessed by and accessible to many medieval Jews and Christians on a daily basis,[34] particularly in urban milieux.[35] Recent research on Christian societies in various fields incorporates evidence from a range of sources: The place of the Bible in early medieval legal culture has been treated rather extensively; scholars of gender have devoted attention to how biblical exegesis might inform historical knowledge of women's lives; sermons have been analyzed to identify the ideas that preachers shared to discuss with their congregations; and scholars of political thought have studied biblical kings and queens to augment their understanding of medieval monarchy.[36]

When medieval Jews and Christians discussed and referenced the Bible, they were engaging in interpretation, and sometimes proffering a highly sophisticated elucidation of the biblical text. Modern scholarship about medieval Jews and Christians has been concerned with understanding complex exegesis, and in light of its intricacy has perhaps been overly preoccupied with the extent to which ordinary people understood the prayers they recited, the pictures they saw, and the sermons they heard. As a result, scholars have often contended that the theological or intellectual underpinnings of the medieval texts that have reached us were beyond the grasp of the majority of their audience. In recent decades this premise has repeatedly been questioned and reexamined in historical studies of the Christian Middle Ages.[37] In turn the scholarly consensus has shifted to a far more inclusive view of "ordinary people's" familiarity with the Bible. Frans van Liere summarizes this reevaluation: "Contrary to the popular myth, ordinary Christians did have access to the contents of the Bible through numerous channels. Vernacular translations did exist in the Middle Ages. However, reading scripture in one's own language was far from the only way that medieval people came into contact with the contents of the Bible, for the medieval world was much more visual and oral in character than our own."[38]

These approaches have attempted to get beyond the limitations of the "top-down" texts and find ways to assess how the "laity" or a wide variety of medieval people understood religion, nature, and the world around them.[39] These methods, which have become normative in social-historical research concerning medieval Christians, are not yet commonplace in Jewish studies; however, this same process is beginning to take root in current scholarship on medieval Jewry. One scholar who addresses the question of what most Jews could comprehend in the field of Jewish liturgy is Susan Einbinder. The medieval liturgy was filled with complex poems (*piyutim*) that required tremendous erudition for full comprehension. The Bible was central in their composition and for comprehending them. These poems have been primarily studied as texts,[40] and other dimensions of their role in medieval society have often been neglected by not questioning how less erudite people understood them, and by assuming they sang them without understanding. Einbinder has challenged common academic conventions concerning these intricate compositions by stating: "For the medieval Jew, texts were only one strand of a densely textured experience. Many of these poems come down to us with indications that they were to be inserted in liturgical ceremonies for penitential fast days; some still supply the names of melodies (unfortunately lost) to which they would have been sung."[41] With these lines, written at the turn of this century, Einbinder recognized the "social life" of texts in a new way. Yet in the case of highly stylized poetry, she also wondered to what degree those who did not belong to erudite circles could engage with this poetry. She argued that these liturgical works would have left an impression on less educated listeners by way of repetition and melodic performance.[42]

I would like to take this argument a step further by building on the insights of Van Liere, Einbinder, and others. The Bible was in Hebrew, a language that was not generally used for casual interactions among medieval Jews; but unlike the terse constructions of liturgical poetry, it was composed in a language that young children learned and many could read and write, if in a rudimentary manner.[43] Moreover, the biblical accounts were told and retold together with traditional tales from the Talmud and midrash, not only in the context of liturgy and the annual cycle but also in story collections.[44] Biblical stories were also depicted in pictorial formats. While interpreting images required a certain level of specialized knowledge, these materials were nevertheless accessible to those who lacked formal education. Also, the names of biblical characters were mentioned on a daily basis by medieval Jews, for many of them bore these same names.[45] Tombstones sometimes compared the dead to biblical figures.[46]

One more important perspective on the Bible that medieval Jews and Christians shared merits attention: Neither group doubted the veracity of its content. Thus when citing the Bible, they were recounting events they considered real. In short, the Bible was alive in the medieval cultural imagination, and this commonly held belief provides another foundation for comparisons between Jews and Christians. What was the place of the Bible in their respective praxes? What was the broad social context in which these communities lived side by side? And what are the implications of this proximity for contested scriptural interpretations?

The association of medieval people with biblical figures has been extensively discussed in the context of scholarship on the Hebrew chronicles that were written to commemorate the First Crusades. In these writings, the authors repeatedly evoked specific biblical personages, comparing them with Jewish victims and protagonists during the Crusades. In this case, medieval Jews enlisted biblical events and actors as points of reference with explanatory power. For example, the calamity that befell the medieval German Jews was explained in relation to biblical scenarios, such as the selling of Joseph or the sin of the Golden Calf, and recalled biblical figures as models to be emulated.[47] Notably, Abraham and Isaac were mentioned when medieval Jews compared the slaughter of their own children to avoid coerced baptism to the ordeal endured by Isaac at his father's hands.

As Shalom Spiegel demonstrated over half a century ago, medieval Jews constructed an alternative to the narrative in Genesis. Rather than the biblical original, where an angel stops Abraham a moment before his sword wounds his son, this medieval version claimed that Abraham indeed killed Isaac, who was subsequently resuscitated by the angel, who stitched close the incision on his throat. Spiegel considered this a reflection of the medieval Ashkenazic mentality, in contrast to earlier traditions or those in other Jewish cultures.[48] Gerson Cohen's study of the mother and her seven sons yields a similar assessment.[49] In his analysis of the biblical foundations of select 1096 narratives, Jeremy Cohen also draws connections between medieval practice and the Bible.[50] Although these studies sought to interpret an exceptional mindset rather than everyday life, they provide a sense of what I hope to achieve here.

Everyday Practice and Religious Identity

A second foundation of this study is the importance of daily praxis for accessing the lives of all members of medieval Jewish communities, especially those who weren't part of the learned elite. I contend that everyday activities, no less than the religious principles and beliefs that are regularly explored by scholars, are of cardinal significance for understanding medieval Jewish mentalités. Put differently, religious identities were cultivated and solidified by mundane routines as much as by abstract beliefs. The effort to identify these activities in the spirit of what has been termed *Alltagsgeschichte* (or the "practice of everyday life"),[51] supports this investigation of a broader swath of the population within medieval Jewish communities, most of whom (if not all) regularly read or heard the Bible and were familiar with its content. The Bible and the physical environment were shared by Jews and Christians and, as such, prompted mutual negotiation and Jews' assertions of their distinction as a minority culture. These central factors laid the foundation for shared practices in Jewish-Christian interactions. The structures of both Christian urban societies and Jewish communal law shared biblical foundations, despite differences in their legal systems. When Jews and Christians interacted in commerce and courts of law, the Bible was a commonality, and its narratives provided a basis for practice. For example, when taking oaths in Christian settings, Jews included scriptural verses and swore upon a Pentateuch, recalling biblical transgressors such as Akhan, or Datan and Aviram.[52] My focus on the centrality of practice distinguishes this book from other studies, especially of late antiquity, such as Robert Gregg's *Shared Stories, Rival Tellings* and Jane Kanarek's *Biblical Narrative and the Formation of Rabbinic Law*, which discuss models of theoretical constructions rather than lived experience.[53] These works do not provide the kinds of vistas on social history that I seek to offer here as they analyze versions of the story or prescriptive texts whereas I seek the ways these text were used and referenced when describing daily interactions as well.

Another critical factor in this prioritization of practice relates to the place of halakhah in assessing the past. To date, while focusing on literature written by rabbis, Jewish studies scholars have often assumed that all Jews adhered to halakhic guidelines. Some scholars have even labeled evidence that suggests some Jews did not live according to halakhah as "deviance."[54] As a complement to this approach, which privileges halakhah, other scholars have characterized the collective self-image of medieval Ashkenazic Jewry as a "sacred community" (*kehillah kedoshah*).[55] I would distinguish these two positions from that undertaken in this volume. While medieval Jews certainly saw themselves as a distinct entity and valued their religious beliefs and identity, it is unlikely that they unanimously or uniformly strived to perform halakhic mandates. Much like today, Jewish communities in the past were diverse in nature. The chapters of this book each draw attention to the practices of Jews that rabbinic authorities described at times as those of "women or men who do not know" (Chapter 2) or attributed to "conversations of old women" (Chapter 5). By centering this inquiry on the Bible rather than halakhic literature, I hope to illuminate facets of medieval Jewish life that have not typically been within the purview of Jewish studies scholars.

Women, Gender, and Non-elites

My decision to place women at the heart of this study is rooted in my interest in community members who were unlikely to leave written records of their lives, namely the medieval Jews whom I describe as "beyond the elite."[56] Although women constituted more than half of non-elite Jewry, they were certainly not synonymous with this cohort. It may reasonably be asked: Why focus on women, and how and for whom might their experiences offer insights?

Writings by medieval Jewish (and Christian) men frame our understanding of medieval Jewish life. In broad strokes these texts are predominantly religious in nature: commentaries on the Bible and Talmud, as well as liturgy and literature that explicate customs and halakhah. All are produced by intellectually accomplished men and reflect their mindsets. Yet while a wide range of men participated in the scholarly enterprise by which all medieval Jewish culture has been assessed, they comprised only a small fraction of the medieval Jewish community. This dominance of educated leadership in extant documentation is typical of premodern societies. A growing scholarly interest in social history, with its emphasis on practice and everyday life, has opened new areas of inquiry in recent decades. These developments, compounded by the feminist revolution, have been catalysts for pioneering research of medieval Christianity.[57]

By comparison, in Jewish studies, intellectual history and the history of beliefs remain at the forefront, despite notable exceptions. These priorities stem from the sources written by Jews that have reached us; they are also reinforced by conceptualizations of Jewish history as a tale of religious devotion. Jewish texts infuse the quotidian with religious meaning, and a diverse representation within Jewish society can be identified within them. Yet in most studies today, "man" is a general category that encompasses humanity as a broad category, whereas "woman" signals a subset.

Using gender as a tool for exploring the members of medieval Jewish communities is just a beginning of a social-historical examination. While distinctions between men and women stand out more readily in the medieval texts, many additional differentiations are subtly hidden, even if they would have been readily apparent within medieval societies. Moreover, in some cases, these divisions were not either/or, and overlapping categories coexisted. For example, in medieval Ashkenaz being a scholar did not preclude participation in the merchant class or practicing a skilled profession. How then might the nuanced membership in the intellectual elite be understood? One way I have tried to resolve this tension is by using gender as an analytical tool. Since we can readily affirm that women were not included in the scholarly elite, gender differences can help us to delineate varying levels of scholarship and halakhic proficiency.

While it seems that virtually all Jewish men were taught to read the Bible, and male literacy is taken as a given, albeit with differing levels of proficiency, Jewish women's knowledge and literacy have been questioned and all but dismissed by some modern scholars. We lack descriptions of women being taught to read and instead find discussions of restricting certain forms of education, following ancient traditions on this issue.[58] However, despite the uncertainties regarding women's access to education and levels of literacy, we have evidence that women were taught the Bible and followed biblical stories, even as part of the weekly readings in synagogue.[59] As a result, despite many open questions concerning women's halakhic conversance and scholarly knowledge, the Bible is one area of Jewish literature where a threshold for literacy, even according to more traditional definitions but surely according to the definition provided here, may be expected.

Women's educational opportunities and, therefore, their intellectual underpinnings, were more limited than men's on both ideological and practical grounds precisely in part because their textual engagement was largely confined to the Bible, in contrast to the literary cache to which men were exposed, including Mishnah, Talmud, and other sources. For this reason, women's knowledge and beliefs can be considered a baseline Jewish cultural literacy. Attending to women's practice in this examination of how biblical imagery and narratives were harnessed to guide their understandings of the world around them, provides insight on the extent to which certain traditions were particular to a certain cohort or known throughout society. The study of medieval Jewish women also provides another angle for examining social hierarchies within this patriarchal culture. As we will see, the retelling of biblical stories exposes certain tensions that were inherent in these hierarchies while also leading to more nuanced knowledge of men and women's roles in daily life.

The Bible is a fitting source for studying women for an additional reason. The medieval reliance on stories as a pedagogical standard for girls and women offers further evidence for medieval assumptions about their character. As Anna Dronzek describes in her study of fifteenth-century conduct books for women, medieval authors believed that girls would learn most effectively if their lessons were related to the tangible world, since their "nature" was centered on their bodies. In some cases, guidance is prescribed through the mother's deliberate modeling of proper conduct. Dronzek explains:

> One implication of a mother teaching her daughter is that the
> mother is passing on knowledge gained through her own life experi-
> ence. This model of life experience presents moral lessons in a far
> more tangible way than authors use in most of the boys' literature.

The Knight accomplishes the same purpose by using examples of ideal women to illustrate each aspect of the good behavior he wants his daughters to learn.... He does not simply tell his daughters that they should act charitably; he sets before them the examples of how Rahab of Jericho, St. Anastatia, and St. Aragon Queen of France all prospered through their charitable deeds.[60]

Within this pedagogical context, examining the applications of biblical narratives in Jewish women's lives is congruent with medieval conventions, as is the special attention that I direct toward female biblical figures who were presented as role models, whether for emulation or simply for educational purposes.

Nevertheless, I am also interested in a wider circle of the community beyond women, including men and children. Thus the use of the term gender in this volume is intended to allow for comparison between men and women and to posit that women and less-educated men may be contrasted with the scholarly elite. At the same time, I am well aware that, however meaningful the distinction was between intellectuals and less-educated Jews in everyday medieval life, this remains a somewhat artificial designation, as both groups held common beliefs and told similar stories. Over the past decades, studies on popular culture in medieval Europe have demonstrated a shared substructure of beliefs among clergy and their communities, as well as among university professors and manual laborers.[61] Every stratum of society told stories, and, like material culture, the Bible was a resource that transcended status. In this book I am interested in collapsing the popular-elite dichotomy to some degree in order to examine the joint traditions rather than the scholarly ones. I consider the Bible and everyday practice to be useful vehicles for the pursuit of these purposes. This endeavor cannot be fully accomplished, and as such this study is only a foray in this direction; I do not claim to have fully achieved this goal.

Biblical Literacy

One key aspect of this study concerns the definition of "biblical literacy."[62] In this context, I follow current scholarship and use the phrase to indicate broad familiarity with the Bible through any available medium, rather than the strict ability to read the Bible in Hebrew, Yiddish, Latin, or any other specific language. As Jack Goody has argued, literacy does not displace orality, and those who cannot read may access the written word through other means.[63] If we accept that biblical literacy was more widespread than most scholars have previously asserted, far more members of the Jewish community become part of the story I seek to tell. Yet, to provide a check on this claim, none of the chapters in this study focuses solely on a biblical figure. In each case, a practice is analyzed that is connected to specific biblical figures. As defined here, biblical literacy assumes familiarity with the content of the Bible, especially its narratives, rather than the ability to read this text in Hebrew or any other language.[64] Current research on medieval stories (whether in the form of exempla, moral tales, or fabliaux), has persuasively demonstrated the rapid circulation of oral tales in the medieval world. While verbally transmitted narratives cannot be gathered, their traces abound, including imprints from biblical sources.[65] It is impossible to quantify the number of oral tales in circulation or the number of times a story was retold. Recent studies estimate that saints' tales were repeated hundreds of times, however, and it seems safe to assume that biblical stories were retold with even greater frequency.[66]

The long history of familiarity with the Bible and with biblical interpretations has caused historians (as opposed to folklorists) to shy away from analyzing biblical stories because they are so difficult to situate, both chronologically and geographically. In this regard, I find David Hopkin's formulations concerning "ecotypes" as a folkloric concept in service of historians most helpful.[67] In his scholarship on nineteenth-century French culture, Hopkin has rigorously sought to retrieve multiple voices by examining numerous genres, with particular attention to narratives. In *Voices of the People* (2012; building on his article "The Ecotype," 2010), Hopkin has suggested a historical quest for ecotypes, defined as variations on an international type that developed distinctive versions in particular cultural milieux as a result of their national, political, geographic, and historical conditions.[68] For folklorists, this concept has served as a key for investigating the dialectics of stability and change. Galit Hasan-Rokem's recent study of the Wandering Jew exemplifies such a folklorist approach.[69] Hopkin has also used the ecotype as a tool in historical research on what he calls "contact zones" where stories are retold and modified. The biblical narratives, too, are ecotypes that connect daily practice with culture. This is true not only for medieval Jews and Christians but also in other times and places, for example among African Americans in the American South in the nineteenth century.

The sheer power of stories is another factor that must be considered.[70] As Catherine Cubitt, a scholar of Anglo-Saxon England, observes, "Narrative, the way in which we tell stories and the stories we tell, plays a vital part in making sense of human experience."[71] Cubitt also notes, "Historians have tended to focus upon questions of orality and literacy in governmental administration and legal dealings, while amongst literary scholars, the most pressing questions have concerned the composition of Old English poetry and the nature of heroic verse."[72] Yet as Cubitt concludes, oral traditions and stories establish a foundation for all forms of cultural interaction. They were a constituent of what R. W. Southern has termed the "chattering atmosphere" of medieval society.[73]

Hopkin concludes that the content and style of telling stories "relate to the way real life problems [are] experienced by the populations that narrate them and at the same time they suggest strategies for dealing with these problems."[74] Scholarship by psychologists and anthropologists reinforces this approach, for they have demonstrated how stories provided a means for explaining and processing behavior and events in medieval times, as in current circumstances.[75] People learn by example, and the use of the Bible in the Middle Ages for this purpose is evident in a range of media, from sermons and exempla to liturgy and art. Thus they serve as well-suited vehicles for this study.

Another area of study from which I have benefited is that of legal studies. Scholars of late antiquity have investigated the relationship between biblical stories and Jewish law, seeking to understand how one influenced the other on a theoretical level.[76] These studies tend to prioritize the process of deriving scriptural authority for the law and draw heavily on the work of Robert Cover and others. Many scholars have dedicated significant energy to identifying the defining features of narrative and law, and to elucidating the implications for narrative studies, distinguishing between halakhah and *aggadah*, as well as other themes.[77] This literature also acknowledges significant overlap between the categories and, thus, the difficulties that disentangling them poses from a modern perspective.[78]

These studies inform my thinking, but two factors have led me in additional directions. First, by the medieval period, halakhic scholars no longer considered the quest for biblical antecedents of legal conventions a priority;[79] Second, given my interest in practice, some of these classifications are less pertinent to how stories operated in social and cultural discourse. Analysis of the meanings that biblical narratives and figures and their interpretations generated in daily life is not predicated on a precise determination of genre. A biblical source's ability to enrich everyday activities was not dependent on whether it originated in a narrative framework or a legal foundation; rather, its efficacy stemmed from its provision of an explanation or justification for those who observed the related practices.

My approach relies on recent scholarship related to historians' engagement with folklore and literature. Within the field of medieval studies, although narrative sources have long been indispensable for literary scholars, historians have been reluctant to incorporate them in their scholarship. Recently a growing number of scholars of Christian Europe have begun to explore the use of narrative texts for writing history.[80] They have noted that stories' popularity and widespread circulation are indicative of deep concerns and habits of medieval societies, rather than "mere" literary constructions, and often express complex negotiations of identity. Within Jewish studies, Eli Yassif and Rella Kushelevsky have reflected on this question from the perspective of literature and folklore. Robert Bonfil, Eli Yassif, Ivan Marcus, Elhanan Reiner, and Lucia Raspe have examined stories as reflections of cultural stances, usually regarding belief or, in Raspe's work, local traditions.[81] Moreover, the recurrent connections across genres between a biblical figure and a corresponding custom contributes to a more complex understanding of the mentalités of medieval Jews, for each format conveys its own register for reinterpretation.

Sources and Genres

In this study, I have sought to include sources from many types of literature in which biblical narratives are retold or referenced. By including genres that are frequently associated with distinct disciplinary approaches and considering them in relation to a shared theme, I hope that we can attain new perspectives on medieval life. Some chapters discuss liturgy and poetry, while others consider epitaphs, inscriptions, architecture, and illuminations. Stories, custom books, exegesis, halakhic handbooks (*sifrei mitzvot*), and responsa also offer key insights on how daily practices were explained and, at times, justified. I have sought out many visual depictions of the narratives I examine so as to reflect on what medieval Jews may have seen. I do this not as an art historian but as a scholar interested in assembling as many points of reference as possible. References to the Bible appear in all these sources, although not consistently. Sermonic material is notably absent from this survey. Delivered orally, notes prepared before or after their delivery have not been preserved in significant numbers.[82] So, too, I do not discuss kabbalistic treatments of biblical figures, as these are not sources that allow a discussion of social history, and I only briefly discuss magical texts.[83]

The multiplicity of genres, in some cases among texts that were composed by a single author, enables renewed consideration of the varying registers that coexisted in medieval culture (as with all cultures) and their presence in daily activities. I also consider early modern literature, with particular attention to Yiddish compositions: advice manuals and petitional prayers (*tekhinot*) written for women, as well as retellings of the Bible. I include this later material to underscore lines of continuity and to demonstrate both how ideas that originated in high medieval texts were reformulated and how women authors articulated their ideas at a time when their voices were (finally) being preserved. As recent scholarship has indicated, Yiddish should not be considered a language only for women, as men and women alike conducted their daily lives in Yiddish, and in this light, the evidence from early modern Europe can be seen as a window onto a broader segment of society.[84] This discussion of the early modern sources is meant to be preliminary rather than conclusive, as the early modern period is not at the focus of my work. Undoubtedly, a scholar more conversant in the contexts in which these texts were written will be able to do more with them than I have. Nevertheless, I hope the benefits of "looking ahead" will be evident.

The chapters of this book explore only those female biblical personages whom I located in exegesis and other discussions connected to specific practices or sets of practices, ranging from the obscure to the familiar.[85] As a result I have not attempted an exhaustive treatment of all female biblical figures. In some cases, despite a relative abundance of commentaries, I could not locate a link to a specific set of practices, as in the case of Queen Esther, who is the subject of collected medieval commentaries. Similarly, Ruth, Tamar, and Bathsheba appear in multiple commentaries, but they are not associated with a practice that lends itself to robust discussion. One noteworthy exception is Miriam, sister of Moses and Aaron, who has another dimension of significance because she shares her name with the Virgin Mary. Miriam has been studied from various scholarly perspectives: within Kabbalah (Arthur Green, Sharon Koren, Peter Schaefer); as related to funerary customs (Ephraim Shoham-Steiner); and in the context of water-drawing practices on Saturday evenings (Israel Ta-Shma, Shoham-Steiner, and, most recently, Inbar Gabay-Zada).[86] As I had no significant contributions to add to this literature, I reference this as relevant, without developing a chapter on Miriam.

The chapters of the book demonstrate the central role biblical figures played in practices that encompass many levels of daily life. The first two chapters of this volume look at Eve (Chapter 1) and the matriarchs (Chapter 2), figures who were related to the realms of daily activities traditionally associated with women's domestic responsibilities, namely marriage and motherhood. The chapters also discuss the place of these biblical narratives in communal collective memory and the ritual, annual, and life cycles.

The next two chapters focus on women's roles and activities in communal life. Chapter 3 examines Deborah and Jael and women's communal leadership. In hierarchal and patriarchal cultures, where the positions of judge, military leader, and combatant were typically associated with men, how were these ancient stories and their anomalous heroines received? I ask how these figures related to the responsibilities that Jewish women held and power struggles within medieval Jewish communities. My primary focus considers women as teachers, without relying on prescriptive literature alone but drawing from documents of practice along with prescriptive literature.

Chapter 4 centers on Abigail. I examine her biblical depiction as a woman who defied her husband and the retellings and interpretations that associate her with the financial independence and agency of women. On the one hand, these elucidations offer a view of how the medieval rabbis responded to challenges regarding their own judicial and educational authority as well as women's fiscal autonomy. On the other hand, they also display the limits of patriarchy, for women found agency and voice within the system.

Chapter 5 addresses a specifically medieval Ashkenazic concern—martyrdom (*Kiddush haShem*)—and its incorporation within the annual cycle and the daily activity of drawing water, an essential daily activity. This chapter also highlights the relevance of biblical tales to education and daily activities, and to women's roles in these settings. The book concludes with a singular example of biblical imagery and medieval Jewish women, the poem written by Eleazar b. Judah of Worms (d. 1138) after the death of his wife Dulcia (d. 1196), which was modeled on the poem that concludes the book of Proverbs, the "Woman of Valor." Eleazar's poetic elegy for his beloved wife, which draws from the Bible to expound on her virtues and daily activities, is well known to those who study medieval Jewish society. This poem illustrates the phenomenon this project seeks to highlight, in relation to an individual who lived during the medieval period, even as it underscores the very obstacle this study seeks to overcome: There may have been many women like Dulcia of Worms, but she uniquely received explicit praise in a medium that has been preserved for posterity. By returning to this well-known example after the studies that comprise this book, I hope that future research will take the diverse members of the medieval Jewish communities into consideration and strive to incorporate as many of them as possible in discussions of their lives and times.

Cultural Paradigms
Blessed like Eve

I

And God is like the prayer leader [*hazan*]: Just as the prayer
leader blesses the bride under the wedding canopy, so God
blessed Adam and his helper [Eve].

—Margins of a fourteenth-century *mahzor*

[May] you [be] at peace and accompanied by the beauty of
companionship
[May you know] eternal tranquility and a portal of hope
And [may (God)] plant joy and camaraderie between you
And may (God) bless you like Adam and Eve.

—*Mahzor Vitry*, wedding poem

A fourteenth-century commentary on the sixth wedding blessing—
which expresses a desire for the couple to be granted the bliss that
was given to man and woman in Eden—likens the one who recites
this prayer at the ceremony to God. Just as God blessed Adam and Eve, so too
the prayer leader (*hazan*) blesses this bride and groom under the wedding
canopy. Similarly, in many medieval wedding poems, one of which is quoted
in the second epigraph, Adam and Eve's mutual happiness is recounted. This
explanation underlines one medieval understanding of Adam and Eve, envisioned as having been blessed with love and companionship. As I will demonstrate in this chapter, this is but one aspect of the biblical story of creation
that resonated in medieval Ashkenaz. This chapter explores how medieval
Ashkenazic Jews considered Eve and called upon her in theory and in practice, building on rabbinic traditions while engaging contemporaneous challenges and concepts. I will argue that Eve was invoked to frame every stage of
the female life cycle, lending meaning and explanation to everyday practice,
widespread beliefs, the social order, and lived experience. Furthermore, I examine what medieval Jewish and Christian reworkings of these accounts
from Genesis teach us about religious similarities and differences in quotidian life.

The story of Eve was familiar to medieval Jews and Christians, the learned and unlearned alike. Among Jews, the creation narrative and the subsequent expulsion from Eden were read in synagogue and retold in midrashim as well as in less formally codified tales; they were the topics of sermons, of songs sung on the Sabbath, and of illuminations. Jewish traditions presented Eve, far more than Adam, as a multifaceted personage, with specific medieval complexities.[1] Medieval Christians also heard the story in church, and plays of Adam and Eve were among the most popular ones, often enacted outside the church.[2] Medieval Christian exegetes and popular versions of the story most often cast Eve as a negative figure who had been superseded as a cultural heroine by the Virgin Mary.[3] Yet a cardinal difference between Jews and Christians was their understanding not only of Eve but also of the event in which she had a large role, the theological understandings of the Fall. While both Jewish and Christian exegetes blamed Eve for the banishment from Eden, the implications of this biblical event for both religions were somewhat different. Eve and all women were defined through the understandings of these biblical events.

Both Jewish and Christian exegetes portrayed Eve as a wife and, by extension, a standard of womanhood.[4] When Jews invoked a wholly negative figure, they often referred to Lilith—according to Jewish tradition, the initial wife-consort of Adam—as a subversive foil to virtuous Eve.[5] Recent research has demonstrated that, although medieval Christians broadly cast Eve in negative terms, this depiction included nuances that merit attention.[6] In Jewish studies, few scholars have examined portrayals of Eve after late antiquity. In the pages that follow, I will outline characterizations of Eve in Jewish and Christian culture; although I will demonstrate affinities, I contend that the distinctions between the cultures remained robust.[7]

As the original wife and mother, Eve was referenced to explain and provide a model for the realities of birth, marriage, and death even as she was also seen as a typological "everywoman" who became the anchor for gender hierarchies and their social implications for Jews and Christians. Depending on the circumstance, Eve served as a model to be emulated or the culpable catalyst for the experiences in life with which medieval people had to deal, whether birth, marriage, or death. Thus I am contending that everyday womanhood was experienced and viewed via the lens of the biblical Eve.

As we shall see, Eve came to represent a range of values and ideas that addressed the messiness of daily life. For the ease of analysis, I have divided this chapter into three sections, although in reality competing understandings would not have been mutually exclusive, and medieval Jews were certainly aware of the complex views of Eve. The first part of the chapter focuses on Adam and Eve as agents of sin and objects of divine retribution via their expulsion from the Garden of Eden and, ultimately, their mortality. As such, they are treated as models for humanity. As I will demonstrate, Eve was predominantly considered liable for their sin, despite the shared culpability conveyed in the Bible and by some commentators. This imagery was closely linked to the ordinal depiction of their creation—where God first gives form to Adam alone, then Eve from Adam's rib—providing the foundational story for gender relations and hierarchy, which was used to justify stratified roles throughout society. From this perspective the biblical model set the precedent for daily life and relationships between men and women. At the same time, I will highlight a variety of voices that emerge from medieval evidence for the way rituals associated with Eve and her sin were viewed, seeking to identify dynamic and subversive understandings alongside consistent traditions of interpretation.

The second section examines a relatively minor but not unimportant role played by Eve in medieval Jewish discourse and practice. For medieval Jewry a portion of women's conjugal rights were traced back to the first biblical couple. Following late antique traditions, medieval rabbis expounded on the verse, "And she was the mother of all living" (Gen. 3:20), to offer instructions regarding the positive treatment of women. While there are few examples in this section, the reference to Eve as a prototype and the use of the biblical text as an explanation for prescribed conduct and legal rulings are important as they indicate both the importance attributed to the Bible and the relative dearth of other available prooftexts, including halakhic ones.

Finally, as evidenced in the marriage poem that opens this chapter, Adam and Eve were portrayed as an idealized couple who were married in heaven, shared love and companionship, and were commanded to procreate.[8] The story of creation and the "wedding" of this first couple served as a backdrop for the Jewish wedding ritual and aspirations for fertility in Jewish unions. In this way Adam and Eve personified gendered roles, conjugal relationships, and procreation on many levels, both practical and abstract. All medieval references to Eve stem from the book of Genesis, with particular verses associated with each mode of interpretation. Therefore, each section of this chapter begins with a discussion of those relevant biblical verses and then moves to their application in everyday life. Throughout the chapter I also note the common and contrasting traditions about Eve that were held by medieval Jews and Christians, respectively, concluding with an overview of these perspectives.

■ Sin, Punishment, and Hierarchies

The association of sin and punishment with Adam and Eve is inherent in the biblical text itself. Each was subject to divine discipline after eating from the Tree of Life. Concerning Eve, the Bible states: "I will make most severe your pangs in childbearing. In pain you shall bear children, yet your urge shall be for your husband and he shall rule over you" (Gen. 3:17–18). Medieval commentators saw this as the lot of all women. Some emphasized this point when discussing how Eve might have averted this outcome. They note that she had but one option: If she did not give birth, she would not suffer pain. These same commentators acknowledge the impossibility of such an escape, since the punishment concludes by declaring women's subservience to men.[9]

The sentence imposed on Adam could equally have been interpreted as a symbol for the future of all humanity. However, Jewish and Christian commentaries alike placed far greater emphasis on women's pain during childbirth and their domination by men. The Bible continues: "In the sweat of your face you shall eat bread, till you return unto the ground; for out of it you were taken; for dust you are, and unto dust you shall return" (Gen. 3:19). Although the need for toil and the eventuality of death both stem from God's words to Adam, there is little discussion of his punishment in the medieval texts. Admittedly, Jewish commentators sometimes referred to death as "Adam's curse,"[10] and his deeds and punishment are cited to clarify various blessings and practices, but none of these compare in frequency or intensity to the connection made between Eve, women, childbirth, and death.[11]

Despite an understanding of punishment shared by Jews and Christians, there were some theological distinctions between the way the two religions understood the responsibility for the sin. Christian scholars tended to focus on Eve as responsible for the Fall—it was she who ate first from the Tree of Life—whereas Adam was held responsible for the sin and death. This approach is especially prominent in the writings of Thomas Aquinas (d. 1274), who follows a late antique tradition and explains this division of responsibility as the result of the power of men.[12] Making Adam responsible for sin and death reinforced the gender hierarchy between men and women.[13] Similar sentiments emerge from other Christian commentaries, from late antiquity through the High Middle Ages. Augustine (d. 430) set the tone by stating that women were inferior to men and singling out their reproductive capacity as their sole redeeming quality.[14] Medieval legal theorists further interpreted the narratives in Genesis as a basis for legal norms. For example, several thirteenth- and fourteenth-century commentaries explain that "a woman . . . should not have [juridical] power . . . because she is not made in the image of God; rather, man is the image and glory of God and woman ought to be subject to man and, as it were, like his servant, since man rules over [lit., is the head of] woman and not the other way about."[15]

Medieval Jewish texts tended to shift more of the weight of the blame to Eve, highlighting the distinction between Adam's and Eve's lots and by extension between men and women. One Jewish commentator explained the biblical verse from Exodus (19:3), "Thus you shall say to the House of Jacob, and tell the children of Israel," by using the traditional explanation that "House of Jacob" signifies "the women" and that women are mentioned first due to Eve's part in the couple's sin (*het Adam veHava*).[16] Furthermore, although Adam is mentioned first in this reference—regarding the sin of Adam and Eve—its author focuses on women's culpability, for they are daughters of Eve. Other commentaries convey a similar sentiment, albeit in a different context. Judah b. Samuel (d. 1217, Germany) observed that, while men are not all subject to physical toil, certainly not agricultural labor, all women endure pain in childbirth: "This curse is only realized among those who work the land but it does not apply to kings or nobles. By contrast, 'In sorrow you shall bear children' is the lot of all women because the woman sinned, and she caused [Adam] to sin; therefore, her punishment [lit., curse] is greater."[17] In other words Eve is seen more as "everywoman" than Adam as "everyman."

While Jews and Christians would have agreed with regard to the hierarchy between men and women, few medieval Ashkenazic commentators interpreted women in the role of "helper" (*ezer*, according to Gen. 2) as "servant," an interpretation proffered by Christian exegetes following Augustine. Nevertheless, a number of medieval Jewish commentators include a similar remark—asserting that any man who engages in tasks that women usually perform, such as weaving, cannot be trusted to give testimony, much like women's testimony cannot be admitted.[18] Many Jewish commentators describe women as their husbands' helpers and contrast male-female roles among humans to those among animals, highlighting the companionship and complementarity between men and women over stark subordination.[19] This is not to say that Jewish men did not view women as subordinate to them, but the difference in tone is noteworthy.

The tendency to absolve or at least understate Adam's culpability is evident in other Jewish texts as well. *Sefer Nizzahon Yashan* (late thirteenth-century France) depicts a Jew arguing with Christians about original sin, the Christian lesson derived from the story of Adam and Eve. The Jewish respondent rejects the Christian interpretation and, by extension, the severity of the blame it places on Adam and Eve for, he continues, they were not condemned to eternal punishment but rather forgiven by a merciful creator.[20] Such polemics refer to human mortality as "Adam's curse." Yet despite this powerful image, medieval Jewish writings seldom speak of death as "Adam's curse," whereas Eve is regularly portrayed as having imposed death on humanity.[21]

Discussion of Eve's faults were often framed by the broad tale of Eve's creation. Various midrashim explain why God used one of Adam's ribs (from Adam, *meAdam*) rather than other parts of his body to form Eve. Such texts provide a head-to-toe inventory of alleged female faults, which suggest both divine wisdom and women's collective shortcomings, and ultimately justify Eve's punishment:

> R. Joshua of Sakhnin said in the name of R. Levi: It says: "And he fashioned" [*vaYiven*] [Gen. 2:18]. God contemplated [the anatomical options] from which he might create woman. He said: "We shall not create her from his head, lest she be haughty; nor from his eye, lest she be wanton; nor from his ear, lest she be an eavesdropper; nor from his mouth, lest she be a chatterbox; nor from his heart, lest she be envious; nor from his hand, lest she be unable to keep her hands off others; nor from his foot, lest she be a gadabout. Rather, she will be created from a hidden place within man so that, even when a man stands naked, that spot remains covered." And for each limb that God created for the woman, he said: "Modest woman, [be a] modest woman" and, despite this, "You spurned all my advice" [Prov. 1:25]. [God said:] "I didn't create her from his head, yet she is haughty and 'walks with head thrown back' [Isa. 3:16]; nor from the eye, yet [she has] 'wanton eyes' [ibid.]; nor from the ear, yet she eavesdrops, 'And Sarah heard in the tent door' [Gen. 18:10]; nor from the heart, yet she is envious 'Rachel envied her sister' [Gen. 30:1]; nor from the foot, so she wouldn't be gadabout, [but] 'Now Dinah went out' [Gen. 34:1]."[22]

Medieval commentators repeated portions of this midrash quite often, elaborating on select details.

For example, R. Asher b. Yehiel (d. 1327) wrote: "'*VaYiven*' [and he fashioned]: I heard from R. Moshe the Preacher [*haDarshan*] that this [use of the root *y.v.n.*] means 'understanding' [*havanah*],[23] that God understood the mindset of women: so he built her from a hidden place in the man; but not from his feet, so she would not be a gadabout; and not from his hands so she would not be a thief. . . . God said, 'This is what I hoped for [*kivanti*] but it did not work!' A gadabout—Dinah; a thief—Rachel; a chatterbox—Miriam; etc."[24] Furthermore, women were considered less refined than men because they were created from flesh rather than earth.[25] In contrast to this understanding, most Christian commentators presented the creation of woman as superior to that of man. Adam was created from earth, whereas according to Christian traditions, Eve was created in Paradise.[26] Peter Abelard (d. 1142) and other theologians even suggested woman was created from Adam's side to promote the idea of equality.[27]

These medieval commentaries were hardly restricted to exegesis. The commentators read the story of the creation as foreshadowing the future behaviors of women, and through these narratives they articulated the social order they wished to promote. A review of biblical commentaries from medieval Ashkenaz attests to the pervasive attention to this narrative. Rare is the commentary on Genesis 1–3 that does not include a statement about women through exegesis or the explanation of a current practice. For example, one popular tradition posits that women exhaust men.[28] Yet another widely circulated teaching describes an aspect of medieval dress codes that resulted from creation: " 'And this shall be called woman' [*lazot yikare ishah*] [Gen. 3:23]. A midrash: Why does a man go out with his head uncovered but a woman goes out with her head covered? This is like a man who sinned and is embarrassed. She advised Adam [lit., the first man] to eat from the Tree of Knowledge; thus, her head is covered from shame."[29] Such allusions to daily life, while vague, detail normative practice. It is well documented that medieval Jewish women would cover their heads when they were outside their homes, whereas their male counterparts did not.[30] Since the subject of head coverings is hardly discussed in the sources that have reached us, we cannot know if Eve was regularly mentioned in this context, but it is significant that this is noted in the few discussions of this topic.

In another discussion of differences in men's and women's praxis, these distinctions are also traced to biblical origins. Thus one commentator explained that men are obligated by positive time-bound commandments whereas women are not, because Eve was created at a different time from Adam, so she does not have the same time-related obligations.[31] Another example of a practice attributed to Eve's deeds is related to funeral processions.

Already in late antiquity commentators explained the custom of women leading funeral processionals (to or from the cemetery)[32] as recalling Eve, who led man to his death.[33] This custom persisted in medieval Ashkenaz and was explained by some in the same way—for example, in the commentary on the *Semak* by R. Moses of Zurich (fourteenth century).[34] The custom of women heading the funeral procession as mourners returned home after a burial seems to have continued in various locales[35] and had a parallel in medieval European Christian practice. John Beleth (d. 1182) reports that women should not walk in front of the body on the way to burial.[36]

This last custom is but one example of a wide range of practices ascribed to Eve. Her relation to birth and death is undoubtedly the most pervasive in medieval Jewish culture, further underscoring her transgression and punishment. Her actions and God's retribution were widely considered catalysts of her "fate" (*goral*), which in turn had implications for practical aspects of women's lives. For example, the phrase "your sorrow" (Gen. 3:16) was interpreted by some as menstrual blood, a biological reality for all healthy women.[37] As numerous commentaries state: "If she says, 'I will give birth in health,' she will give birth in sorrow; and, if she says, 'I will save myself from having relations with my husband,' the Bible says, 'And your urge will be to him.' (Gen. 3:16)."[38] Eve's lot (*pitkah shel hava*)[39] is an expression used for those who experience suffering at birth. This understanding has a parallel in contemporaneous Christian culture, which referred to women who gave birth without pain as sharing Mary's lot, contrasting Eve to Mary.[40]

One of the earliest traditions that connects Eve with practical aspects of Jewish women's lives is perhaps the most central and well known: The Mishnah discusses three routine activities performed by Jewish women, that became known as the women's commandments or as *mitzvot hannah* (the commandments of hannah). Here hannah is an acronym, rather than a reference to the biblical character Hannah, that stands for: *hallah* (separating a portion of dough, Num. 15:20); *niddah* (Jewish menstrual regulations, Lev. 15:25), and *hadlakat haner* (candle-lighting on the eve of the Sabbath and other holy days). Neglect of these three responsibilities was associated with women's deaths during childbirth and with the biblical Eve. The Mishnah recounts: "For three transgressions, women die in childbirth: because they do not carefully maintain separateness at proper periods, separate the first cake of the dough, or light the lamp [for the Sabbath]."[41]

Over time, within the broad context of religious praxis, these three commandments became elevated as paradigmatic observances of Jewish women, especially in the writing of men.[42] An early medieval midrash associates these three commandments with Eve, ascribing violations of each one to her in Eden. The midrash begins by quoting the Mishnah cited above:

> These three commandments come from the Bible. From where [in the Bible] do we learn the commandment concerning *niddah*? For it says: "When a woman has a discharge of blood" [Lev. 15:25]. And *hallah*, from where [is it derived]? For it says: "The first yield of your baking" [Num. 15:20]. And sabbath candles, from where? For it says: "If you call the Sabbath 'delight'" [Isa. 58:13]. And why were women given [lit., commanded with] these commandments? Our sages said that God's creation began with Adam; then Eve came and shed his blood because he listened to her, for it says: "For dust you are and to dust you shall return" [Gen. 3:19]. Thus, God said that she should be given the commandment of *niddah* so she could atone for the blood that she spilled. Why *hallah*? Because Adam was the bread of the earth [*halato shel olam*], and Eve came and contaminated him [*timatehu*], so God said: "Give her the commandment of *hallah* so she can atone for the bread of the world, which she defiled."[43] . . . And the commandment of lighting candles: from where [do we learn it]? Because Adam was God's candle, for it says, "The candle of God is man's soul" [Prov. 20:27], then Eve came and extinguished it. God said: "She shall be given the commandment of candle-lighting to atone for the candle that she extinguished; this is why women are commanded to light Sabbath candles."[44]

This midrash explicitly binds Eve to every Jewish woman and her actions.

This understanding of this triad of commandments was popular in medieval and early modern Jewish culture, as evidenced by its frequent citation in medieval commentaries and halakhic tractates that addressed women's legal obligations.[45] No less important, the Mishnah quoted earlier, which states that death in childbirth is an outcome of neglecting these three precepts, regularly appears in medieval Ashkenazic liturgy. Every Friday night Jews would recite these words in synagogue.[46] This midrash about Eve and these three commandments is included in commentaries on the siddur.[47] This teaching was also incorporated into popular liturgy, as one of the *piyutim* recited on the Sabbath states: "If women light their candles, abide by the laws of *niddah*, and make their bread, then God will protect them. If the time of their birth comes near and they had neither observed them nor were chosen, their death is near."[48] These liturgical examples illustrate how liturgical practice amplifies specific teachings.[49]

Let us now examine how each of these three activities was incorporated into daily life and related to Eve.

Hallah

The biblical commandment to separate a portion of the *hallah* dough for the priests in the Temple was not specifically assigned to women (Num. 15:20). Moreover, after the destruction of the Temple, this practice should have ceased. However, as the Mishnah quoted earlier demonstrates, it continued and became the role of women when the Temple no longer existed, ostensibly because of their responsibilities for cooking.[50] Rashi defines *hallah* as what was called *torteille* in Old French, meaning "a small cake."[51] Yet this word serves for both "cake" and "bread" in modern terms. Bread-baking practices in medieval northern Europe are difficult to document. Halakhic writings frequently discuss bread in relation to restrictions on consuming bread produced by non-Jews. Medieval Ashkenazic Jews were permitted to eat bread if a Jew had a role in the baking process; often, this action took the

Figure 1.1
Women and men preparing matzah. Note the women's white clothing.
Southern Germany, circa 1300. Jerusalem, Israel Museum, 180/057.
Photo © The Israel Museum by Moshe Caine.

symbolic form of lighting the fire or casting a match into the oven. Thus Jews sometimes produced their own bread and at other times participated more symbolically in its preparation.[52] Whatever the case, it was a precept and a task assigned to Jewish women. The standards of bread preparation are reviewed in many compendia.[53] Some sources suggest that women would combine their batches of dough, whereas others speak of the actions of individual women when making dough.[54]

Portioning off a section of the dough is also commonly discussed with regard to preparing matzah for Passover, another form of baking entrusted solely to Jews. In this case, men also recited these blessings; therefore women's deeds or misdeeds per se were not a central concern.[55] It is noteworthy that medieval illuminations of matzah-baking depict both male and female participants. One striking feature in discussions of women who make matzah are occasional, seemingly incidental, mentions of their ritual purity. As a result, preparing dough becomes at least tangentially, connected to menstrual purity. Various texts on preparations for the festival of Shavuot and the initiation rite held for boys on this holiday in medieval Germany also make note of the ritual purity of the women who make dough for the special cake prepared for children; at least one text specifies that the woman who prepares that cake should be "a pure virgin."[56] Allusions to ritual purity may also be evident in depictions of Passover preparations from medieval illuminated *haggadot*. For example, in the Birds' Head Haggadah, the women portrayed making matzah are wearing white clothing that may signify their purity. Given that white pigment was particularly difficult to produce, the care used to illustrate these women—the only figures dressed in white in the entire manuscript—was perhaps deliberate.[57]

Isaac b. Moses (d. 1270), author of *Sefer Or Zaru'a*, notes the association between Eve and the commandment of *hallah* in his Laws of Hallah; he presents the midrash attributing responsibility for these three commandments to women by combining the versions from *Midrash Shoher Tov* on Psalms, in reference to "My God, my God, why have you forsaken me?" (Psalm 22:2) and from *Tanhuma* (quoted earlier). In the *Or Zaru'a* version, Esther draws on this psalm to ask God why he has forsaken her. In the verse, the speaker calls to God twice, but the midrash creates a trio, "My God, my God, my Lord" (*eli, eli, elohai*). With this formulation, the midrash states that Esther was asserting that she had observed all three commandments (*hallah*, *niddah*, and candle-lighting); therefore, she was asking how God could abandon her.[58]

This attribution that Esther—who, according to rabbinic tradition, was not married—observed these commandments is fascinating on its own and as a representation of the phenomenon studied here. Nevertheless, R. Isaac b. Moses is an exception in this regard. In stark contrast to biblical commentaries, which repeat this midrash and ascribe this commandment to Eve, her actions, and their consequences,[59] halakhic discussions of *hallah* rarely mention her at all.

Candle-lighting

The second practice related to Eve and her sin is candle-lighting. Following the verse in Proverbs 20:27, "the spirit of man is the candle of the Lord," candles are treated as symbolic of the soul in rabbinic literature. In medieval Ashkenaz, several practices related to candles were explicitly assigned to women, while others were not gender specific. Jewish daily life made use of candles in the synagogue and within various frequent rituals (such as weddings, circumcision ceremonies, and holidays such as Yom Kippur). It is noteworthy that, due to the natural resources available in northern Europe, candles made of wax or tallow were used far more than olive oil, in contrast to the reality depicted in the Mishnah, which was composed in the Land of Israel, where olive oil is abundant. Thus in medieval Europe, candles became ever more important.

Candles were made by women, and candle-making was recognized as a mark of female practice and, at times, piety: Dulcia of Worms is reputed to have produced candles for Yom Kippur; and descriptions of preparations for circumcision rituals report that women would make twelve candles for these ceremonies.[60] Wedding processionals also included candle-bearing.[61] In a world without electricity, candles were a practical necessity. This was especially true on the Sabbath, when the need for candles and adaptations of this basic requirement in accordance with the laws of Sabbath were themselves aspects of lighting Sabbath candles.[62]

This ritual took on greater symbolism as medieval Jews would each ceremonially light a candle in synagogue before Yom Kippur. On this occasion, each candle represented the soul of the person who kindled it and its destiny in the new year. According to this belief, if a candle burned bright throughout the holiday, it signaled success, but if it dimmed or blew out, ominous events were anticipated—even death. In the context of lighting individual candles on Yom Kippur, some argued against women participating in this ritual.[63]

In contrast to the citations regarding Yom Kippur candles, all sources concur that lighting Sabbath candles was a women's obligation and was to be fulfilled by men only if they were away from their wives.[64] Interestingly, there is no biblical precedent for lighting Sabbath candles.[65] Moreover, although this ritual coincided with the beginning of the Sabbath, it did not in fact create it. Whether or not candles were lit, the Sabbath would arrive. During the Middle Ages in Ashkenaz, certain aspects of this practice were consolidated, including the custom of lighting two Sabbath candles and the codification of the blessing.[66] In this instance the rabbis credited their practical knowledge of this commandment to women. Famously, Rabbenu Tam (d. 1171) referred to the way his sister, the Rabbanit Hannah, lit Sabbath candles; he stated that her observance should serve as a model, for if "she isn't a prophetess, she is the daughter of prophets."[67]

I would suggest that candle-lighting was especially important because it was imbued with both religious and hierarchical significance.[68] This is evident in the only illustration of candle-lighting that has reached us (Figure 1.2), where lighting the candles is highlighted as the prime feature of the Sabbath activities. Such lamps appear in other manuscripts as symbols of the Sabbath as well. That two such lamps appear over the family's table indicates their use in the Shabbat ritual.

Medieval commentators discussed the various materials from which candles could be made and the merits of women who lit purer candles, quoting late antique texts that emphasized the peacefulness that entered the house once the candles were kindled.[69] From a hierarchic perspective, lighting Sabbath candles had been designated as a female domestic responsibility long before the medi-

Figure 1.2

Siddur (book of prayers). Note the Sabbath candles that illuminate
the table around which the family has gathered. Southern
Germany, circa 1300. MS JTS 8972, fol. 119b. Image provided with
permission by the Library of the Jewish Theological Seminary.

eval period. The same mishnaic chapter that enumerates the three commandments incumbent on women assigns a related trio for men: "At dusk on the eve
of Sabbath, a man must make three statements: 'Have you separated the tithe?'
'Have you prepared the *Eruv*?'[70] 'Light the lamps!' "[71] In this passage men are
featured as guiding their wives on the correct time to light candles, even dis-
patching their children home from synagogue to convey this message.[72] These
instructions for men are cited in numerous medieval texts, giving men responsibility for certain aspects of order and the household schedule.

Most custom books provide detailed instructions for lighting Sabbath and holiday candles. *Mahzor Vitry* affirms this ritual as an obligation and reviews talmudic discussions about its requirements.[73] In his *Sefer Rokeah*, R. Eleazar of Worms details the blessing and preferred materials for this practice.[74] *Sefer Tashbetz*, written by R. Samson b. Tzadok in the late thirteenth century, provides instructions for this ritual for men who are away from their families on the Sabbath.[75] Isaac b. Moses, in his *Sefer Or Zaru'a*, quotes the midrash that we saw earlier, which associates Eve and her sin with this responsibility, and he offers further details on its observance.[76] The story of Eve and Adam accompanied this practice, as evidenced by medieval texts that quote the midrash and by the many early modern sources that pair Eve with candle-lighting. For example, in the early modern Yiddish work *Tsene uRena*, traditions are cited to demonstrate how elements from the creation and expulsion from Eden narratives continue to shape womanhood, and by extension manhood. The extensive passage that details this concludes by explaining that Eve extinguished the "candle of Adam" (man); as a result, women must light Sabbath candles.[77] Thus the connection between Eve and this mundane practice was preserved throughout the Middle Ages. It was employed to reinforce gender hierarchies and domestic order, citing the biblical narrative as an anchor.

Niddah

The laws of menstruation, known as *niddah*, and the process of childbirth were intimately connected to such a degree that authors treated them as two parts of a single topic. I would argue that the entire midrash quoted earlier from the *Tanhuma*, which links Eve's sin and the so-called women's commandments, gained its credence from the interwoven relationships among Eve, menstruation, and birth. Of the three activities related to Eve and among the explanations given for their attribution to her, *niddah* was undoubtedly the most significant. When discussing the laws of menstruation and the practicalities of childbirth, medieval exegetes regularly referred to this midrash. The high death rate during childbirth, an omnipresent part of medieval life, deepened this bond.[78] The link between blood and ritual impurity heightened the punitive aspects of birth and menstruation. During this era the intimate areas of a woman's body and their biological functions were generally regarded as unclean and unpleasant. Expressions such as "tomb" to refer to the womb or "filth" for childbirth appear in Hebrew medical treatises as well as in polemic literature.[79] Alexandra Cuffel has demonstrated how such pejorative terminology featured in religious disputes.[80] For example, *Sefer Nizzahon Vetus*, in challenging the belief in the divinity of Jesus, insisted that Jesus was born from a place of filth, like all other men.[81] Can these texts inform our understanding of medieval women's own views of *niddah* and its incumbent obligations? Or the way their attitudes toward the biblical Eve figured in their lives?

Many Jewish women, from ancient times, followed biblical directives and immersed in a ritual bath (*mikveh*) after their monthly bleeding ceased. This included bathing immediately when they stopped bleeding and then immersing after seven days had passed during which they did not bleed. Over time, specific customs related to bathing and preparing for the ritual immersion were elaborated, first in late antique literature and then by later generations. These customs included separation between husband and wife and specific practices related to eating and sleeping together. The observation of these customs is what was known as *niddah* in medieval texts. As a number of scholars have demonstrated, Ashkenazic observance of *niddah* was significantly transformed during the High Middle Ages.[82] Jewish women, and thus couples and families, became far more stringent in their performance of the laws of *niddah*, particularly the requirements for separation during the days immediately preceding immersion in a ritual bath (*mikveh*) and the immersion itself.[83] Over the course of the thirteenth century, it became customary in many German communities that menstruants would refrain from attending synagogue services. The medieval rabbis who documented these practices attributed these rigors (at least in part) to the women themselves, in an attempt to ensure their purity and advance their expressions of piety. Indeed, medieval Ashkenazic Jewry and their Christian neighbors were characterized by growing concerns with purity.[84] This tendency was also evident in the construction of Jewish ritual baths as part of the institutionalization of the Jewish community in many places, as exemplified by the monumental baths that were built in Cologne, Worms, Speyer, Strasbourg, and Friedberg, among other cities.[85]

As Shaye Cohen and others have outlined, this concern with purity was not simply an attempt to avoid defilement and impurity.[86] Rather, intensified adherence to the laws of purity, especially women's observance of the laws of *niddah*, was a source of pride in medieval Ashkenaz. R. Joseph Bekhor Shor of Orleans (twelfth century) declared that attention to the laws of *niddah* was of equal importance with the act of circumcision. Eleazar b. Judah of

Worms lauded those who followed these laws by suggesting a special blessing to be recited by scrupulously observant communities: "Blessed are you . . . who has sanctified us with his commandments . . . separating us from impurity and cautioning us to beware of menstruants and their discharges."[87] Surely some of the pride taken in these practices was shared by women as well. *Mahzor Vitry* tells of Marat Belette, the sister of Isaac b. Menahem (twelfth century), who instructed the women of her city regarding how to immerse properly.[88] More than two centuries later, R. Jacob Moellin (known as Maharil, d. 1427) discusses women who were experts in the laws of immersion.[89] How did these women speak of this practice among themselves?

This question must remain unanswered, for it reveals the limitations of the sources. However, given the significance attributed to the laws of menstruation among Ashkenazic Jews during the High Middle Ages, these practices effectively became symbols of identity for medieval Jewish women. Alongside the underlying tropes of sin and blame, medieval women and men took pride in these practices and their explication. An interesting testimony that may display one woman's affinity for the laws of immersion appears in a late fourteenth-century manuscript from the Rosenthaliana Library (Amsterdam) (Figure 1.3).[90] This copy of *Sefer Mitzvot Katan* (*Semak*) was elegantly transcribed and selectively illustrated by Hannah b. Menahem Tzioni, author of the *Sefer Tzioni* (fourteenth century). Colette Sirat has suggested that Hannah decorated the laws of immersion as a display of her empathy and identification with them.[91] This interpretation is suggestive, although not conclusive, as the decorations adorn the laws of immersion of vessels rather than the laws of *niddah*.

Another manuscript of the *Semak* also displays reverence for this commandment via a gracefully rendered pair of illuminations (Figure 1.4). In this case, the illustrations undoubtedly are concerned with ritual immersion for *niddah*, featuring the preparations for immersion (in a tub) and immersion in an abstract depiction of waters.

The commandment to immerse in a *mikveh* as a means of purification from *niddah* was further elaborated on and praised in additional illuminations and treatises. For example, a fourteenth-century Hamburg manuscript that contains a prayer book includes another such illustration accompanying a poem for Hanukkah, "*Odekha hashem ki anafta*." In this poem, after the Romans banned ritual immersion, *mikvaot* miraculously appeared in homes so Jewish women could immerse (Figure 1.5). Here the husband awaits his wife at home while she immerses in a *mikveh*.

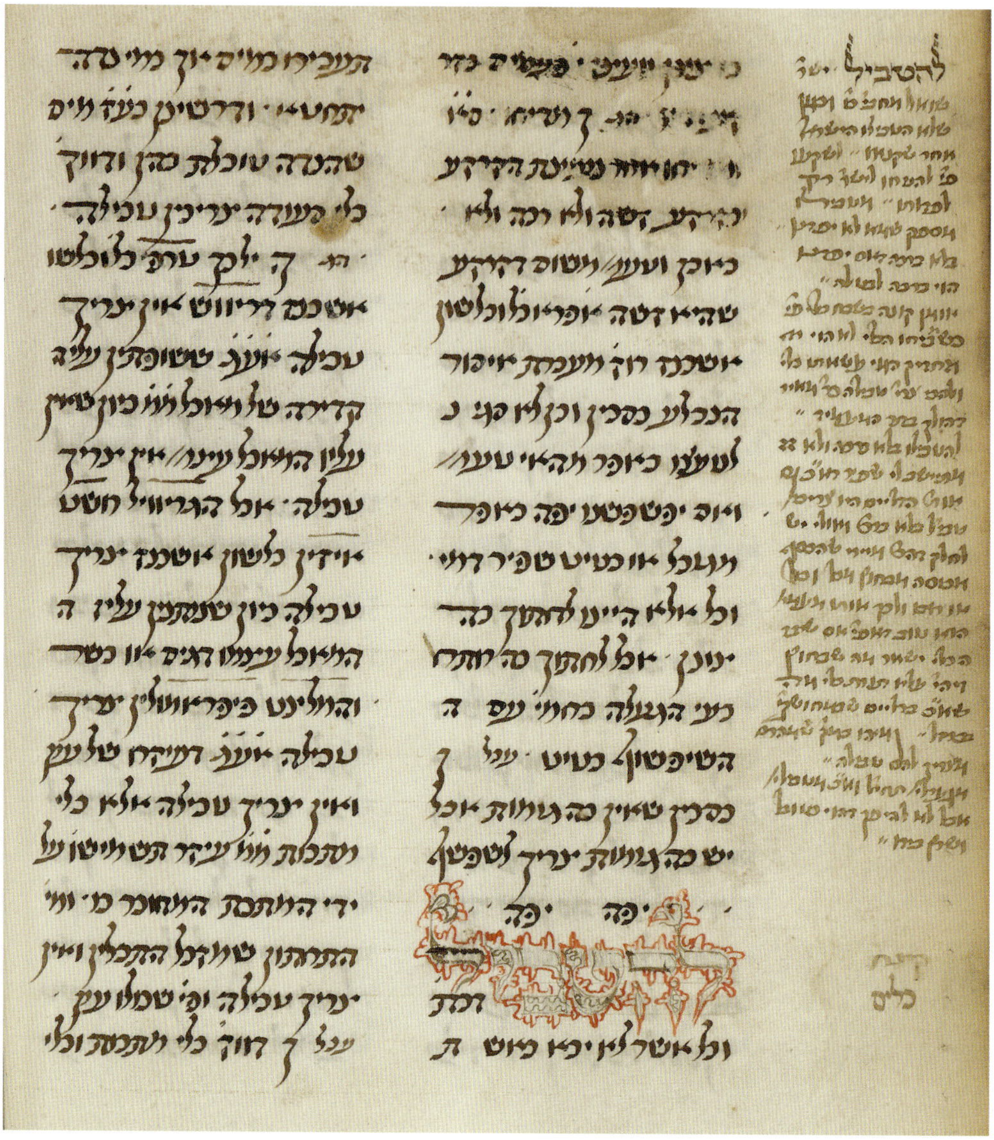

Figure 1.3

Illuminated decoration in a *Semak* manuscript copied by a woman, Hannah
b. Menahem Tzioni, with a decorated heading for the laws of immersion.
MS Amsterdam, University Library, Ros. 558, fol. 152v. Image provided with
permission by the Bibliotheca Rosenthaliana, University of Amsterdam.

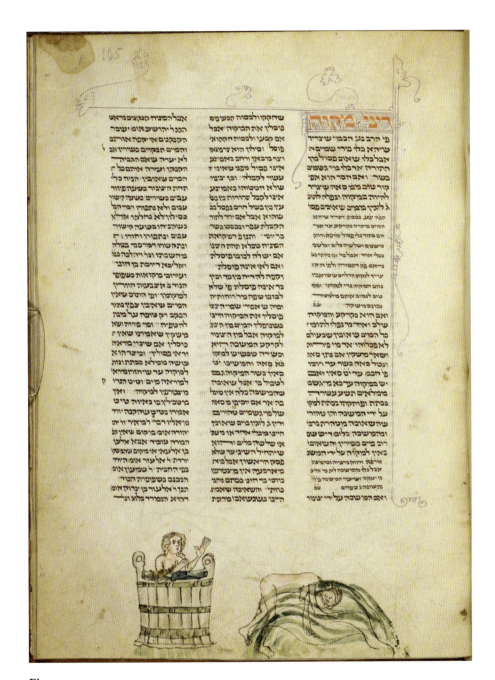

Figure 1.4

Illuminated decoration in an Ashkenazic *Semak* manuscript of the laws of
immersion from 1346, featuring a woman washing herself in a bathtub in
preparation for immersion. John Rylands Library, Manchester, Heb. 31, fol.
105r. Image provided with permission by John Rylands Library, Manchester.

Figure 1.5
Illuminated prayer-book. An illustration for the poem "*Odkha hashem ki anafta*" features a woman immersing in the ritual bath while her husband awaits her at home. Germany, 1434. © Hamburg State and University Library, Heb. Cod. 37, fol. 79v.

These beautiful illustrations offer a glimpse of the fulfillment that may have been experienced by women who immersed monthly and considered adherence to these commandments a central component of their lives.[92] Thus one can see how a practice that was explained as originating from a sin also became central to defining religious identity.

Here it is instructive to note that Christian commentators also believed that Eve's sins informed the lot of contemporary women. Rupert of Deutz, a twelfth-century Christian exegete, explained—much like the popular midrash quoted earlier—that Eve committed three sins, but he did not link them to specific observances.[93] Although neither *hallah* nor *niddah* was practiced by Christian women, menstrual purity was a subject of debate among early medieval Christians. Scholars suggest that this debate had been resolved by the thirteenth century, when these biblical restrictions were categorically abandoned.

By contrast, women in Christian culture were associated with a practice that is somewhat akin to lighting Sabbath candles, the sole nonbiblical practice that Jewish traditions attributed to Eve. Lighting candles in medieval churches and the use of candles in religious devotion were features of women's piety. Lighting candles as part of religious practice was also justified through citations in the New Testament, which depicts the purification of the Virgin Mary in the Temple and the comparison between Jesus and a light.[94] The contrasting relationships between lighting candles and sanctified time in Judaism and Christianity, and their differing biblical examples, may have made sharing this practice less ideologically fraught. Moreover, as we have seen, in Jewish sources candle-lighting is presented in relation to Eve's sin, whereas Christians associated candles with Marian purity. Nevertheless, in both religions candles were linked to Eve or Mary.[95] Likewise, although the practices that echoed Eve's sin were not shared by medieval Jews and Christians, this association was a common motif from late antiquity well into the Middle Ages.[96]

Eve and a Tradition of Select Rights for Women

We have just seen that Eve was notably a symbol of sin, subservience, and culpability. She connected birth, death, and sin with practices performed by all Jewish women that underlined these ideas. Yet she also became pivotal in the explanation of, and to some extent justification for, certain rights for women. Immediately after God delivers his punishment to Adam and Eve, the Bible recounts: "The man named his wife Eve because she was the mother of all the living" (Gen. 3:20). This verse was often mentioned in legal discussions of both financial and psychological aspects of marriage. The Talmud cited this verse to explain that when spouses came from different social classes—specifically if the wife was used to greater luxury than her husband—in certain spheres the man must uphold the customs his wife was familiar with prior to marriage. For example, if she came from a family in which mothers were unaccustomed to breast-feeding, he must hire a wet nurse for their children.[97] At the time of her death, he must ensure that her burial follows the standard that her family would have provided. Citing Genesis 3:20, the Talmud states: "She was given for life, not for sorrow" (*lehayim nitnah velo letza'ar*), meaning that she should live with dignity rather than suffer with her husband.[98]

During the thirteenth century, on the basis of this verse and the talmudic passage that followed the same logic, a precedent was founded by rabbinic authorities. At issue was an effort by rabbis in Germany and northern France to ban men from beating their wives, a phenomenon that had compelled these leaders to concerted action.[99] As Avraham Grossman has shown, whereas wife battery was not as strongly condemned in other locales, in medieval northern Europe such actions drew focused attention in the twelfth through fourteenth centuries.[100] The most prominent of these rabbis, R. Meir of Rothenburg (known as the Maharam, d. 1293), cites both Genesis 3:20 and the talmudic precedent that was founded on this biblical verse. When ruling on the case of a woman who was being tormented by her husband's family, R. Meir instructed that the couple move into private living quarters, stating: "Eve was called Eve 'since she was the mother of all the living'; therefore, she [this woman too] should be allowed to live without suffering."[101] This mention of Eve by name is indicative of the resonance that her story held. If Eve were merely a symbol of sin and punishment, invoking her name would not have been rhetorically effective.[102]

Admittedly, this is a singular example, and I could not locate any additional cases in which Eve is cited for the betterment of women's treatment.[103] Yet a fascinating parallel of sorts is found in the converse circumstance, that of a wife hitting her husband, a situation that is rarely discussed. R. Haim Barukh, the teacher of the anonymous author of the thirteenth-century northern French *Sefer haNiyar*, discussed this possibility and stated: "A woman who angered her husband should fast for three days. And regarding a woman who hit her husband: cut off her hand [Deut. 25:11][104] or instruct her to fast for forty days over the course of one year. And a woman needs to be bent before her husband, with words and labor and anything he desires, for it says 'And your desire will be to him etc.'"[105] This interpretation lends further credence to R. Meir's use of the verse about motherhood as Eve's defining trait and, once again, reinforces the identification of all men with Adam and, especially, all women with Eve.

This use of Genesis 3:20 also has parallels in medieval Christian texts that cite this verse to justify valuing rather than despising women. In her study on what lay readers in Carolingian times deduced from the Bible, Janet Nelson quotes this verse as it appears in a response to a query regarding why women should not condemned, indicating the centrality of the Bible in formulating social categories.[106] Gemma Louise Wain demonstrated that Hugh of St. Victor uses these verses in his *de sacramentis* to argue that women are equal to men as marriage partners and deserve to be treated in these terms.[107]

Adam and Eve: Love and Companionship

As the wedding poem that opens this chapter suggests, an examination of wedding imagery in liturgical wedding poetry and other texts reveals that Adam and Eve held another, far more affirming, role in the collective imagination. This impression is confirmed in various additional sources and interpretations of the wedding liturgy. Adam and Eve's marriage was considered the ultimate ceremony, for they were envisioned standing under a divinely designed canopy. Midrashic texts recount that God prepared multiple canopies—ten, thirteen, or twenty-four, depending on the source—for this first couple, reflecting the scale of their love for one another.[108] The fabled grandeur of Adam and Eve's wedding is evident in the seven traditional benedictions that were composed in antiquity and continued to be recited by medieval Jews. The third blessing praises God who created humans, and the sixth references Eden by wishing the happiness that Adam and Eve enjoyed for the new couple: "Grant perfect joy to these loving companions, as you did for your creations in the Garden of Eden. Blessed are You, LORD, who grants joy to groom and bride."[109] Heaven and the Garden of Eden also appear in the medieval liturgy of northern Europe, which depicts the (human) bridegroom in heaven, delighting in eternal bliss. Thus whether by explicit mention or by allusion, Adam and Eve are constant features of this liturgy.[110] In his commentary on the wedding benedictions, Eleazar of Worms highlights this theme as he explains all seven benedictions in relation to Adam and Eve, and all that God created for them.[111]

Another commentator, R. Solomon b. Samson of Worms (thirteenth century), remarks on the third blessing:

"Blessed is God who created [hu]man" . . . it is fitting to recite this prayer to God, who created the first man; thus, it is not the couple being blessed. "Who created man" and created from him [*hitkin lo mimeno*]: this is Eve, who was taken from his rib and was created to be a helper; she was designed like a building, for it says "And he built the rib" wide at the top and narrow at the bottom, in order to support a fetus. And this form is eternal, just as the bond between husband and wife is eternal. [Thus,] "Blessed is God who created man" is a blessing for the creation of Eve, his wife.[112]

As a result of the link between Eve and Adam and all marriages, multiple commentaries explain aspects of the wedding ritual using the story of creation.[113] The custom of braiding the bride's hair was meant to mirror the way God adorned Eve, specifically by braiding her hair for presentation to Adam;[114] the custom of eating a fish meal after the wedding derived from the fish's symbolic resonance as a food with roots in creation.[115] A central element of the marriage ritual that was associated with Eve, although it was not technically her responsibility, was procreation. The medieval rabbis interpreted the biblical commandment to procreate as a requirement for men, but Eve or women were essential for its implementation.

A comparison with Christian discussions of the marriage ritual reveals a similar emphasis on Eve. As marriage became a sacrament of the Christian church in the High Middle Ages,[116] theologians called upon Eve as a model of uxorial companionship.[117] Adam and Eve are featured as exemplars of marriage, whose union began in the Garden of Eden and before the Fall.[118] Each Christian wedding ceremony include a prayer that the couple would procreate and multiply as Adam and Eve had.[119] Among Jews the wedding benedictions also recounted this narrative, albeit without a blessing for fertility per se, although this hope is articulated in numerous wedding poems as well as commentaries on the wedding blessings and Genesis 1–3. These commentaries include discussions of the physiology of fertility, the sexual positions that could or should be engaged, and the social expectations held by men and women. In this way, as a model couple, Adam and Eve as served as both justification and exemplar. Thus despite her sin, Eve becomes a symbol of a good and pious wife and Adam and Eve an ideal loving couple. In this light, perhaps we can better understand a formula that appears on some medieval tombstones, which wishes the deceased a place with Adam and Eve in heaven.[120]

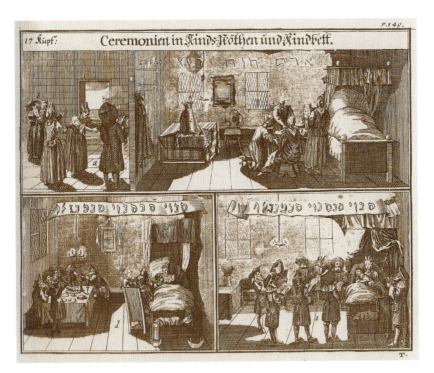

Figure 1.6

The picture depicts the activities in the birthing chamber. The amulet against Eve is displayed at the top of the picture. Paul Christian Kirchner, *Jüdisches Ceremoniel oder dererjenigen Gebräuche, den dieser neuen Auflage mit accuraten Kupfern von Sebastian Jacob Jungendres* (Nürnberg, 1724), 149. Photo courtesy of National Library, Jerusalem.

The celebratory wedding thus led Eve to be associated with birth and motherhood not only through sin and punishment, as we saw earlier, but also through creation and procreation as positive ideals. Ultimately she became the most trusted protector of women during childbirth. In the thirteenth century this role is articulated in some texts and in inscriptions on amulets. By the early modern period, such amulets had evolved into a common form that invoked Adam and Eve to protect the parturient and her baby from Lilith (*Adam veHava, hutz Lilit*), and were posted at the entrance of birthing chambers.[121] These are evident in an eighteenth-century illustration that accompanied the description of the birth rituals written by a Christian Hebraist, Paul Christian Kirchner (Figure 1.6), and in additional texts describing the ceremony.[122]

These Jewish amulets have parallels in Christian amulets and girdles. Lea T. Olsan and Peter Murray Jones have documented a fourteenth-century practice of writing verses on paper or new parchment that was wrapped around a woman's thigh during labor. The Christian amulet includes two lines that make a typological comparison of Eve and the serpent versus the Virgin, who conceives via her ear (*"vipera vim perdit sine vi pariente recedit / dum sacra virgo dominum aure concepit"*).[123] Don Skemer also documents the ubiquity of birth amulets.[124] Hebrew writings offer further evidence of their usage: For example, the thirteenth-century circumcisor Gershom of Worms mentions a woman in Cologne who makes such girdles for Jewish women.[125] These wedding poems and songs, as well as birthing amulets, all illustrate everyday references to the Bible that can be added to the scholarly literature that has most often been studied to date. These widely used amulets indicate the centrality of the biblical narrative in everyday practice.

▪ Eve: Between Jews and Christians

Up until this point we have discussed a range of common activities and rituals that are thematically related to Adam and Eve as biblical figures and as interpreted in rabbinic literature; these are used as part of daily and weekly routines and life-cycle rituals. We have examined a defense of women's rights that cited Eve as well as the wedding ritual where hopes for marital compatibility evoked Adam and Eve as forebears. I would suggest that, by investigating these references, we are homing in on medieval (and early modern) mentalités, where biblical figures had an important role in identity formation as role models or figures to be emulated and where they were used as a mode of explanation.

Let us probe this notion further by situating these coexistent, though not necessarily compatible, Jewish understandings that linked Adam and Eve as a couple, and especially Eve as a persona, to the everyday actions of medieval Jewish men and women within the majority culture in which they dwelled. While scholars have primarily considered the exchanges between learned Jews and their educated Christian peers—for example, monks from the Abbey of St. Victor in Paris who studied the Hebrew Bible with local Jews in the twelfth and thirteenth centuries, or Peter Comestor (d. ca. 1178), who engaged in conversations with Jews in his hometown of Troyes—these encounters extended well beyond discrete scholarly pursuits.[126] As noted in the Introduction, medieval Jews and Christians shared neighborhoods as well as ideas. Even when recounting a shared narrative, Jews and Christians would have treated it as their own, with each group appropriating elements and adapting them into their religious culture.

The story of Adam and Eve and its interpretations provide an example of this mechanism. The Old Testament was sacred for medieval Christians, and this Genesis narrative was frequently dramatized, depicted in art, and referenced in sermons. Moreover, these figures had additional resonances within Christian culture.[127] As noted earlier, Eve was often seen as negative, with the Virgin Mary serving as a second, more positive role model.[128] So, too, the sin in the Garden of Eden held a separate set of theological implications among Christians. As Jeremy Cohen has outlined, in the early Middle Ages, Gregory the Great proclaimed that neither marriage nor procreation had taken place in Eden.[129] This assertion cohered with a system that valued celibacy and virginity over marriage. Despite this basic dissonance, medieval marriage rites gradually incorporated references to a pre-Fall commandment to procreate, especially after marriage became a sacrament; nevertheless, Adam and Eve remained sinners.[130] The serpent that lured them to transgress was ascribed with a feminine quality, as evident in medieval art where the serpent assumed a female head (see Figure 1.8).[131]

Yet at the same time, Adam and Eve were symbols of love and companionship in Christian culture, as they were in Jewish culture. Following the interpretation suggested by Augustine, their marriage would have been ideal, had they not sinned.[132] The benediction at every wedding ceremony recalled them although by the thirteenth century, they were joined in some rites by Mary and Joseph.[133] In this way, the nuptial ceremonies in these two religious cultures, which constituted mutually exclusive rites that were distinct for each religion, shared this common foundation.[134]

With the notable exception of weddings and births, and to some extent the lighting of candles, none of the ritual activities that Jews relate to Adam and Eve were common to both cultures. Jewish women lit candles for the Sabbath, observed menstrual laws, and removed a portion of the dough when baking bread, whereas Christian women did not, although they lit candles in honor of the Virgin Mary. Birth was associated with Eve in both religions, but in Christianity, Eve was superseded by Mary, who was the guardian par excellence of women in labor, and who lacked the traces of sin that tinged Eve. In Christianity, Eve also often symbolized women's work, with the image of Eve at a spindle found in sculpture, on stained-glass windows in

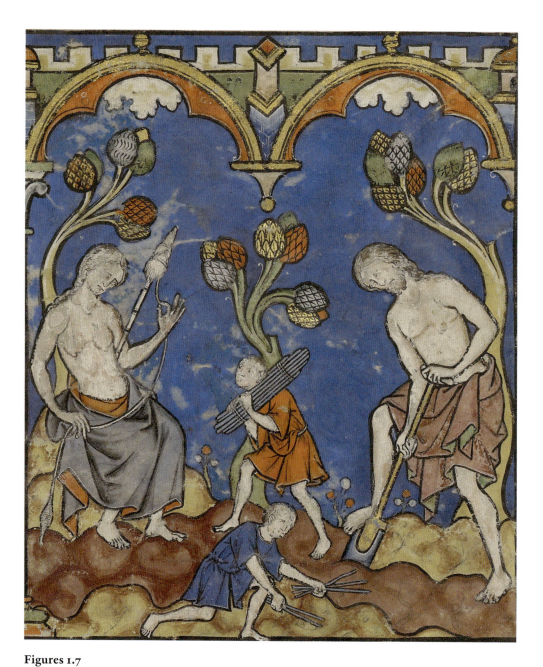

Figures 1.7

Old Testament Miniatures. This illumination depicts Eve with
the spindle, working alongside Adam, an image rarely portrayed
or discussed by medieval Jews. Paris, circa 1250. Morgan Library
M638, fol. 2r (detail). Courtesy of the Morgan Library and
Museum, New York.

churches, and in illuminated manuscripts as in Figure 1.7.[135] Adam, too, was featured working. This image or understanding—where Adam was the only one who toiled and Eve was not depicted with a spindle—was not common among medieval Jews. This is not because Jewish women worked less than Christian women in everyday life.[136] Instead, it has to do with the ways these figures were articulated in images.

Jews were keenly aware of Christian perceptions of Eve, as medieval Hebrew book illuminations demonstrate, but they chose selectively. Christians, for example, often portrayed the snake with the head of a woman (Figure 1.8). Medieval Jewry adopted some signature Christian traits, as the depiction of Adam and Eve in a late thirteenth-century manuscript from Paris (circa 1280) shows:[137] Here the snake, whose head resembles a woman's, is turning toward Eve, much as in contemporaneous Christian renderings (Figure 1.9).[138] Perhaps the existence of a competing interpretation, in which Eve was replaced by Mary, paradoxically allowed for a more positive, albeit still ambiguous, portrait of Eve among Jews.

Late medieval and early modern Jewish writings underline this complexity. While the foundational myths of Eve as a symbol of women and their faults continued, as evidenced by the texts already discussed, more positive conceptions developed concurrently. For example, the Provençal R. Yeruham b. Meshulam (fourteenth century) titled his book on daily ritual *Sefer Toldot Adam veHava* (*The Book of the History of Adam and Eve*). He explains his title by stating: "I have divided my book into two parts: 'Adam' and 'Eve.' The 'Adam' section is [about the time] when [a man] is born until he marries, and the 'Eve' section is from marriage until death. And this is why I called [this volume] *Sefer Toldot Adam veHava*." Yeruham then enumerates the instructions included in the Adam section and concludes: "Here you are: Up to this point was the 'Adam' section, because all of these [instructions] should be known before one marries. From here on 'Eve,' in other words, a man and his wife."[139]

Early modern Jewish moral literature reinforced positive interpretations of Eve. On the one hand, Eve's sin and her responsibility for women's destiny continued as a motif in early modern literature for women (and men). This theme recurs in the form of ethical teachings in didactic compilations from that era, such as *Brantspiegel* and *Tsena uRena*, and *Meneket Rivkah* (a volume written by Rivkah Tiktiner), as well as in halakhic compilations. Some of these texts display a level of resistance to connecting Eve with sin and death whereas others follow traditional explanations. For example, Rabbi Benjamin Slonik, who—like his colleague, Rabbi Moses Hanokh Althschul-Jeruschalmi

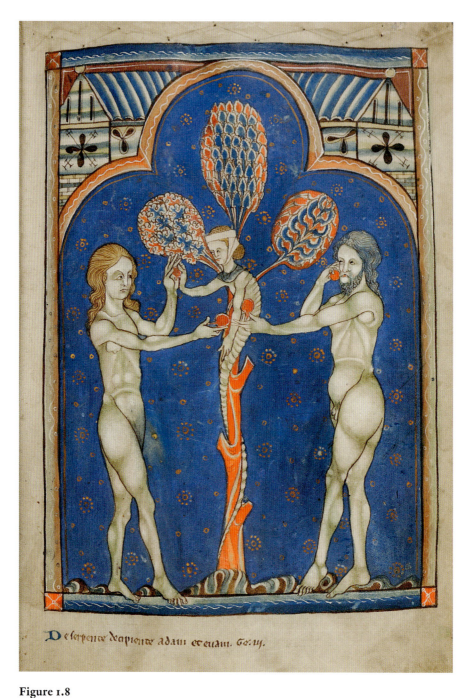

De serpente decipiente adam et euam. Ge. iij.

Figure 1.8
Adam, Eve, and the serpent. The serpent has a woman's head.
Psalter, fourteenth century. St. John's College MS k. 26 f. 231.
By permission of the Master and Fellows of St. John's College,
Cambridge.

זה יהודה וחוה ערומים ועץ הדעת והנחש

Figure 1.9
Adam, Eve, and the serpent with a female head portrayed very much like contemporary Christian depictions. *North French Miscellany*, produced in Paris, late thirteenth century. BL MS Add. 11639, fol. 520v. © The British Library Board.

of Prague, author of the *Brantspiegel*—wrote a popular sixteenth-century handbook on the three female commandments, reiterates woman's responsibility for sin in the Garden of Eden while he also commends Eve.[140] As Ted Fram remarks in his recent edition and translation of Slonik's ouevre, the reason for his praise of Eve has to do with the importance of biblical women as role models: "Biblical women appear as historical paradigms for the female petitioners of the late sixteenth century. God had heard the prayers of Eve, who prayed for her husband Adam. He had heard the prayers of Sarah … surely he would answer them as well."[141] In contrast to some of the male authors who still critique Eve, Rivkah Tiktiner, the sole female among these writers, offers a wholly positive representation of Eve by omitting any discussion of punishment or sin and by focusing on women's capacity to cultivate righteousness in their husbands and children. She does not mention *hallah*, *niddah,* or candle lighting at all. She says:

> This is how the Gemara explains the words that our dear Lord God said to Eve when she ate the apple: "I will make most severe your pangs." This means, "I will increase your pain." This refers to the raising of children, because raising children is essential and much depends on it, as I will write here. "Your pregnancy" … refers to the arduousness of pregnancy. … I could also explain the verse as follows: "Your pangs," which means "your pain" in Yiddish. This means her menses cause her distress before she can [once again] dress herself in white and immerse herself. This is the greatest distress, because some women would rather become pregnant and have children, if it were God's will. But we do not want to talk of this. One does not question God's judgments, we cannot understand it [anyway].[142]

In Tiktiner's narrative, the pain imposed on women is the anguish of those who are unable to conceive rather than pregnancy or childbirth. Tiktiner continues: "The verse here is referring to the fact that the distress of raising children is contained in 'your pangs.' And it alludes to it again because the distress of raising children is greater than all others. … So why did the Holy One, blessed be He, write here 'I will increase your pangs'? He meant it rather as follows: the more distress you have raising your children, the more reward I will give you. The Gemara also explains that our Patriarch Jacob had more merit than Abraham and Isaac because he had distress in raising his children."[143] She concludes with advice on lactation, bathing, and general care of infants: "Now I would like to begin writing how a woman should educate her children in two paths. The first related to the body and the other to the soul."[144] As Frauke von Rohden remarks, for Rivkah Tiktiner, female pain led to merit; never does she present it as a form of punishment.[145]

Similarly, the sixteenth-century *Tsena uRena* explains that all women were condemned to suffer the travails of pregnancy and childbirth, along with what the author calls "the curse of Eve," but then a social corrective is also provided: "Whether rich or poor, it doesn't matter, for Eve knowingly ate from the Tree of Knowledge. But the punishment [lit., curse] meted out to the first man is not the same for all types of people. Sometimes one sees that the wives of rich men have a harder time in labor than the wives of poor men because rich women don't suffer from the curse of 'by the sweat of your brow you shall eat bread'; this is why they are given greater sorrow during childbirth and [why] God, in his mercy, grants them [poor women] easy births."[146] This author implies that poor women and their families endure enough hardship; therefore they are spared sorrow during delivery. This reflection presents a compelling echo of the medieval biblical commentary (discussed earlier)[147] concerning the uneven application of Adam's punishment to men of differing social strata. In this case, poor wives suffer less from the experiences shared by all women, whereas their wealthy counterparts had enjoyed easier daily circumstances.

Tsena uRena also presents Eve as a heroine of sorts, calling her "good Eve" in contrast to "foolish Adam."[148] These reversed characterizations of Adam and Eve do not abrogate the accusatory material discussed earlier. To the contrary, they merge with the other traditions and tease out ideas that had previously been articulated, as we have seen, in medieval discussions. When discussing the first chapters of Genesis, *Tsene uRena* also recounts a practice that may have been customary in the Middle Ages but was definitely well known by the sixteenth century. Each year, at the end of the Feast of Tabernacles, pregnant women would take an etrog, the citron that serves as a ritual object during that holiday, and bite off its style and stigma. This portion of the etrog was considered a fertility aid, and it was believed that this gesture would assure an easy and safe delivery.

This act is detailed here:

Some say that the tree [the Tree of Life in the Garden of Eden] was an etrog tree, which is why the custom has spread among pregnant women to bite off its stem on Hoshana Rabbah [the final day of Tabernacles] and to give charity to the poor, for charity saves from death. Thus, they will have an easy birth, just as a hen lays an egg without pain because, if Eve had not eaten from the tree, all women would give birth easily and without pain. When she bites the etrog, she should say the following prayer: "Master of the Universe, although Eve ate from the Tree of Life and, therefore, we today share her fate, suffer for her sin, and even sometimes die, I promise you that, if I had been there [in Eden], I would not have enjoyed the fruit."[149]

This prayer goes on to explain the how carefully the pregnant woman handled the citron during that holiday week, much as she would have exercised caution in Eden.

So, too, a *tekhinah* written by Sarah Rebecca Rachel Leah Horowitz (also known as Leah Horowitz, 1680–1755) considers Eve among the matriarchs (with Sarah, Rebecca, Rachel, and Leah).[150] Horowitz suggests, as does *Tsena uRena*, that although Eve sinned, contemporary women would not have erred in this way. In a poem composed for women to recite when immersing in the *mikveh* prior to restoring sexual relations, the *tekhinah* has each woman distinguishing herself from Eve.[151] It is difficult to determine the significance that female authorship has for this poem. However, by contrast, texts written by early modern men follow the midrash from the *Tanhuma* closely. For example, a *tekhinah* from the eighteenth century written for a woman about to give birth states: "May the merit of the three *mitsves* which You have commanded every woman to keep– *nide, khale* and *hadlokos neyres*—protect me that I may not—*kholile*– be punished for *khave*'s sin, and may I not—*kholile*—suffer any great pain."[152] The importance of these three commandments is also evident as the topic of moral compilations written for women[153] and as an attribute on tombstones. For example, the tombstone of Breindel b. Hirsch from Wallerstein (d. 1754) described her as giving charity to the poor and carefully observing these commandments.[154]

As discussed earlier, *hallah, niddah,* and candle lighting were part of internal Jewish discourse. They had no status in Christian culture or observance. From this perspective, it is hard to compare Jewish and Christian attitudes and practices; perhaps this is one factor that prompted these rituals to become central to Jewish female identity. However, there is evidence that the story of Eve and her connection to women and their societal position—which were explained by Jews via specific commandments—were equally vital for Christian teachings, where she was a universal symbol of womanhood.

Interestingly, much like the early modern Yiddish writings discussed earlier, Christine de Pisan (1364–1430) declared:

I say she never did play Adam's false
In innocence she too the enemy's
Assertion, which he gave her to believe,
Accepting it as true, sincerely said,
She went to tell her mate what she had heard.
No fraudulence was there, no planned deceit,
For guilelessness which has no hidden spite,
Must not be labelled as deceptiveness.
For none deceives without intending to.[155]

Christine continues by asserting that women were further redeemed by Mary, whose contribution to humanity exceeded the damage caused by Eve.

These texts from the fourteenth century and onward, which distance contemporaneous women from the biblical Eve, have no parallel in high medieval culture, although there were exampla that touched on similar themes from a different perspective, usually arguing that, like Adam, medieval people would have sinned.[156] Yet Eve's presence on birth amulets and in poems suggests that some of these ideas may have been current.

Artwork and material culture from the early modern period present elaborate depictions of all three commandments, as Shalom Sabar has shown. Although he has argued these were meant to project male perspectives, the elaborate drawings and expensive artifacts indicate that the attitude toward these precepts was not purely condemnatory; rather, they are foreshadowed by the illuminated manuscripts that feature the commandment of *niddah* noted earlier.[157] Most famous among these is the Italian jewelry casket from 1470 that depicts all three commandments on its side (Figure 1.10).

Illustrations of all three commandments also appear on cover pages of prayer books, in books written by Christian Hebraists, and in special books made for women that included "their" commandments.[158] Such books were gifts to the bride and included all the blessings she was meant to recite. Sabar has also documented late eighteenth-century German amulets for mothers giving birth that included the three commandments as if to imply that the woman giving birth had observed these three commandments and so should not be harmed.[159] Thus works from this period convey a mixed rather than a wholly condemnatory depiction.[160]

Figure 1.10
The three "women's" commandments are depicted on the sides of this cask, which likely had been a wedding gift. Northern Italy, 1470, silver and gilt. Jerusalem, Israel Museum, 131/030. Photo © Israel Museum, Jerusalem, by Yoram Lehmann.

The representations of Eve analyzed here, which accompanied and framed everyday activities while justifying and consolidating gender roles, offer one demonstration of the extent to which the Bible and biblical interpretation can provide a significant key to the quotidian lives of medieval Jewry.[161] Eve was modeled at birth, marriage, and death, undoubtedly the three most crucial events for any person, and the life-cycle rituals that shaped womanhood. Eve had unparalleled explanatory power. Some of the evidence assembled affirms that multiple activities and references, such as amulets and prayers, linked Eve to everyday life, despite their rare mention in most medieval sources that have reached us. As mother and wife, Eve was typically portrayed as an individual or as accompanying Adam. Rarely was she grouped with the women in Genesis who are often clustered together as "the matriarchs": Sarah, Rebecca, Rachel, and Leah. Epitomizing the "ideal mother," those four matriarchs were frequently evoked in public rituals. In the next chapter, we will investigate their stories and the roles and practices attributed to them.

Personal and Communal Liturgy

Prayers to the Matriarchs

May the One who blessed [*mi sheberakh*] Sarah, Rebecca, Leah, and Hannah bless and cure Mistress So-and-so, daughter of R. So-and-so [*Plonit b. R. Ploni*], who is in difficult labor [lit., having difficulty: *hamakshah*], for R. So-and-so, son of R. So-and-so [*R. Ploni b. R. Ploni*], vows to give charity on her behalf. May the One who cured Hezekiah, King of Judah, and Benjamin the Righteous [*haTzaddik*] and Miriam the Prophetess ensure [lit.. send] her a speedy recovery, for her entire body and flesh, and save her from the travails of labor [*hevlei ledah*] with all daughters of Israel who give birth. And let us say: "Amen."

—Fourteenth-century prayer book

This prayer from a fourteenth-century prayer book appears among a collection of blessings that are said for those being called up to the Torah. As a group they are typically known by their shared opening phrase, *mi sheberakh* ("may the One who blessed . . ."). The blessing quoted here was recited when a husband whose wife was in labor was called to the Torah, asking God to watch over her as he had protected the matriarchs of Israel before her. The husband's contribution to charity was intended to ensure the divine protection of the woman in labor (*hamakshah*), seeking to assure her survival despite the dangers of childbirth (Figure 2.1).

A close look at the formula reveals a telling choice. Rather than listing the four matriarchs from Genesis—Sarah, Rebecca, Rachel, and Leah—this blessing substitutes Hannah, mother of Samuel, for Rachel. The obvious reason for this omission is that Rachel died in childbirth, while delivering Benjamin;[1] therefore, it was not fitting to evoke her when praying for a woman who was giving birth. Rather Hannah, who prayed for a child and whose prayer was answered, was a more suitable model.[2]

Such prayers were not reserved for women in labor. They were also recited for the sick and, in a variant form, for the dead. When said for women, the matriarchs were invoked (including Rachel and omitting Hannah); and

Figure 2.1

Prayer book. *Mi sheberakh* blessings for women. Ashkenaz, fourteenth century. Jerusalem, National Library, Ms. Heb. 4°681, fol. 7b–8a. Image provided with permission and photo courtesy of National Library, Jerusalem.

for men, the patriarchs (Abraham, Isaac, and Jacob) were named, often with additional biblical figures, such as Joseph, Moses, Aaron, David, and Solomon. Unlike the patriarchs, who are central in the standard prayers, the matriarchs do not appear in the formal liturgy.[3] With its simple formula, the *mi sheberakh* blessing did not require great expertise, and therefore it could be readily understood and adapted to various situations and to the gender of its subject.

The four matriarchs and their role in Jewish collective memory, as reflected in liturgy and daily practice, are the focus of this chapter.[4] I consider the *mi sheberakh* blessing and argue that, as an innovation of this time and place, its formula offers insight into the medieval Ashkenazic mindset and daily practice. By tracing the recitation and formalization of these blessings and the incorporation of the matriarchs in them, I strive to identify a distant voice that is not conveyed in the majority of the prayer-book manuscripts that have reached us; and I will argue that this voice, which utilized biblical models as part of routine activities, though restricted over time in some communal frameworks, persisted within everyday culture.

The first section of this chapter outlines the development of *mi sheberakh* blessings and associated religious practices, with special attention to women's participation. I then compare the appearance of the matriarchs and patriarchs in liturgy, distinguishing between standardized communal compositions and more personal prayers, such as the *mi sheberakh*. In the next section, I contextualize changes in practices related to the *mi sheberakh* vis-à-vis other shifts in women's involvement in synagogue rituals. I then turn to examine mentions of the matriarchs in other contexts: on tombstones, in the wedding liturgy, and in conduct books, and then in artistic renderings and early modern ethical literature and *tekhines*.[5] Throughout the chapter I compare my findings concerning the inclusion of the matriarchs in personal liturgy and communal memory in medieval Ashkenazic writings and material culture with evidence from medieval Christian art and liturgy. I argue that these traces of the matriarchs lead us to a layer of Jewish culture that initially seems to be absent from medieval sources but, in fact, was central to everyday life.

■ *Mi Sheberakh* Formulas in Medieval Ashkenazic Culture

In 1959, Avraham Ya'ari presented a panoramic view of the *mi sheberakh* blessing, mapping the wide-ranging circumstances when these prayers were recited, as well as their sweeping geographic spread.[6] Ya'ari and those who continued his work were primarily interested in the breadth of this phenomenon and paid little attention to chronology. As Ya'ari noted, *mi sheberakh*s were said to mark a wide range of circumstances, including for the sick; for those who contributed charity to the community or to memorialize the dead; for recipients of honors at significant times in the festival cycle, such as the holiday of Simhat Torah; as well as for personal and communal observances.

The origins of these prayers can be traced to two distinct yet connected sources.[7] The first is the responsive litany for fast days that was first recorded in the Mishnah. Here the Mishnah presents the benedictions that supplemented each of the prayers recited during fasts:

Upon the first blessing, he shall say [in conclusion], "May the One who answered Abraham on Mount Moriah answer you and hear your cry on this day. Blessed are you, O Lord, Redeemer of Israel!" Upon the second, he shall say, "May the One who answered our ancestors at the Red Sea answer you and hear your cry on this day. Blessed are you, O Lord, Lord, who remembers the [things that have been] forgotten [by humans]!" Upon the third, he shall say, "May the One who answered Joshua at Gilgal answer you and hear your cry on this day. Blessed are you, O Lord, who hears the sound of the shofar!" Upon the fourth, he shall say, "May the One who answered Samuel in Mitzpah answer you and hear your cry on this day. Blessed are you, O Lord, who hearkens to [the human] cry!" Upon the fifth, he shall say, "May the One who answered Elijah on Mount Carmel answer you and hear your cry on this day. Blessed are you, O Lord, who hearkens to prayer!" Upon the sixth, he shall say, "May the One who answered Jonah in the entrails of the fish answer you and hear your cry on this day. Blessed are you, O Lord, who answers in times of distress!" Upon the seventh, he shall say, "May the One who answered David and his son Solomon in Jerusalem answer you and hear your cry on this day. Blessed are you, O Lord, who has compassion upon the earth!"[8]

This series of supplications linking biblical narratives to those who are in the midst of prayer during a fast, emphasized God's obligation to help them in that process. This litany remained a liturgical standard for fast days and the High Holidays.[9] It was also echoed in specific *piyutim* that adapted this format.[10]

The second and more closely related antecedent of the *mi sheberakh* prayer is the general *mi sheberakh* for the entire community.[11] This blessing was recited during the time after the Torah reading and before the scroll was returned to its place, a moment that served as a liturgical position for the insertion of various benedictions, such as a blessing for the upcoming new moon. It begins by calling on the patriarchs and blesses the entire community (*kol hakahal*). This prayer is first found in medieval Ashkenazic manuscripts.[12]

The communal blessing is closely related to a blessing that appears in *Seder R. Amram Gaon*, the earliest extant book of liturgy book, penned by Amram Gaon (a ninth-century rabbi). It was recited after the Torah reading on Monday and Thursday mornings: "May the One who blessed Abraham, Isaac, and Jacob bless all of our brothers and sisters who come to synagogue for prayer and for charity. May God [lit., the Holy One, blessed be He] hear the sound of their prayer [*kol tefilatam*] and satisfy their wishes and fulfill their requests for good. And let us say: 'Amen.' "[13] This prayer in *Seder R. Amram* sought a blessing for each individual in attendance at the synagogue, in contrast to the prayer for the community in the medieval siddurim, which sought a blessing for the entire community. This prayer was most probably the basis for the blessing for the entire community that appears first in medieval Ashkenazic prayer books. Thus the text in R. Amram's composition is a precursor of the communal prayer known from Ashkenaz.

Ya'ari and others suggested that this personal blessing encouraged participation in services.[14] Notably, it evokes both men and women coming to the synagogue. Moreover, in contrast to the other communal and personal blessings from the Gaonic period, which were composed in Aramaic, this prayer is in Hebrew.[15] It would seem that in Gaonic times and in the early Ashkenazic prayer books, this blessing served as one for the community and the individuals in it. The personal prayers that were developed in medieval Ashkenaz and which form the heart of this chapter were an offshoot of this tradition.[16]

It is challenging to track the development of the personal prayers in medieval Ashkenaz, given that they appear as addenda to the liturgy and are not included in most medieval mahzorim or siddurim. Even the blessing for the entire community appears infrequently. However, these blessings can be documented more extensively from the late thirteenth century onward. Israel Ta-Shma suggested that they could be found as early as the twelfth century and attributed them especially to *Hasidei Ashkenaz*.[17] I have found the personal *mi sheberakhs* in both German and northern French manuscripts.

Perhaps the most distinct example of these blessings is the *Nürnberg memorbuch*, written in the late thirteenth century. This composition has attracted scholarly interest for its detailed record of the victims of attacks on the Rhenish Jewish communities in 1096 and 1298, and during the Black Death, and for its extensive lists of charitable donations given by community members.[18] This manuscript includes three folia that present prayers that were inserted after Torah reading in synagogue.[19] These prayers include a blessing for those who fasted on Mondays and Thursdays and one for those who gave charity, known as *matnat yad*, on festivals.[20] Both of these prayers bless the congregation (*hakahal*) rather than individuals, without specific reference to men or women.[21]

The *Nürnberg memorbuch* also preserves two memorial formulas that resemble the *mi sheberakh* formulas with which this chapter began. These commemorative prayers call on the patriarchs in petition for the souls of community members who died sanctifying the name of God and who led attempts to thwart the plans of enemies who sought to harm the community, respectively.[22] The *Nürnberg memorbuch* does not include any individual *yizkor* formulas. However, the blessings for the community presented therein affirm the pattern that Ya'ari outlined. These supplementary prayers were inserted in the morning service, after the Torah reading, and in this context the community honored particular individuals or groups. This position in the liturgy is fitting, for at this juncture, most of those attending the synagogue service would have been present, making this an ideal time for special announcements.[23] At the same time, being a less formal part of the liturgy, it often was not detailed. It was supposed to be self-evident for those leading the prayers, as stated in some prayer books as part of the instructions: "And he commemorates the souls and blesses the community and starts with "*Ashrei yoshvei beitekha*" [a prayer said before the Musaf services, Psalm 84]."[24]

The inclusion of these blessings in this *memorbuch* may explain why few examples of these compositions have reached us. They were necrologies and for this reason were not included in standard prayerbooks. The *Nürnberg memorbuch* is the sole known medieval manuscript from this genre, although many early modern examples exist.[25] Nevertheless, there are several references to the *yizkor* ritual in custom books (but no actual records of the prayer, with the exception of the Nürnberg one). Mahzorim often note that charity was given to honor community members, whether living or deceased, but without detailing the liturgies used.[26] *Sefer Hasidim* also discusses the personalized commemorations, which specifically involved men or women, but without providing a formula.[27]

Several variations of personal *mi sheberakh* blessings, such as the one cited at the beginning of this chapter for women in labor, can be found in select fourteenth-century manuscripts. Most prayers for women list Sarah, Rebecca, Rachel, and Leah as the figures to call on. For instance, a different manuscript reports that Sarah, Rebecca, Rachel, and Leah should be called on for a woman who is sick, but for a woman in labor, Sarah, Rebecca, Rachel, and other righteous female forbears (*Sarah, Rivka, Rahel, vetzadkani-yot rishonot*) should be mentioned instead.[28] These same names were noted in prayers for women who were infirm or dying (rather than giving birth) and for the commemoration of female relatives.[29] For example, a different blessing from the fourteenth-century manuscript with which this chapter opened reads: "May God remember the soul of my mother, daughter of R. Ploni, who passed away [*halkhah le'olama*], for [*ba'avur*] I hereby pledge charity for her soul and in honor of this festival (*haRegel*). In return for this [donation] [*bisekhar zeh*], may her soul be bound up in the bond of [ever-lasting] life with Sarah, Rebecca, Rachel, and Leah, and all the other righteous women [*tzadkaniyot*] in the Garden of Eden."[30] This same manuscript, as well as a few others, include blessings for men as well.[31]

These blessings for the sick, whether male or female, open with an identical formula calling on God to heal the sick as Miriam the prophetess and Benjamin the *tzaddik* (or in other versions, Na'aman or Hezekiah) were cured.[32] Similarly, in prayers for the dead (*yizkor* formulas), those praying for women would ask God to remember them together with the matriarchs.[33] Analogously, other *mi sheberakh* formulas call upon the patriarchs—Abraham, Isaac, and Jacob (or Israel)[34]—in similar circumstances: when praying for sick men, praising those who give charity, or in memorial formulas for individual men.[35]

Additional examples of the personal *mi sheberakh* can be found in some late thirteenth- and early fourteenth-century manuscripts as part of the liturgy that celebrates the bridegroom on the Sabbath after a wedding. Much like the commemoration formulas, or those for the sick or women in labor, the groom was blessed when called up to the Torah. As he ascended the podium (*bimah*) he was given a special invitation and benediction (*reshut*), and after he made the blessing, he was blessed.[36] A number of different versions of the blessing exist, but the opening line called on Abraham, Isaac, Jacob, Moses, Aaron, David, and Solomon and blessed the groom for giving a large donation (*matanah merubah*).[37]

A final example is the *mi sheberakh* said for the individuals called up to make the blessing when the Torah reading cycle was concluded and restarted on the holiday of Simhat Torah in the fall. Like a groom after marriage, this man was summoned by a lengthy prayer (*reshut*), and after he made his blessings, a *mi sheberakh* was recited for him.[38] Here the blessing followed that for the groom, calling on Abraham, Isaac, Jacob, Moses, Aaron, David, and Solomon and praising this individual for his donation.[39] These blessings demonstrate some variety in their formula and also can first be found in late thirteenth-century manuscripts.[40]

As I have already noted, this custom is not discussed in great detail in the ritual books (*sifrei minhagim*) of the time. Only a few custom books, such as *Mahzor Vitry*, and responsa literature mention the custom in passing, and primarily then in the context of the commemoration of the dead.[41] One exception I have found appears in *Sefer Or Zaru'a*, where R. Isaac b. Moses comments on "*Yekum purkan*," the Aramaic prayer preceding the *mi sheberakh* blessings, and questions the recitation of these blessings. He states: "It is customary for the prayer leader [*sheliah tzibbur*], when he reads from the Torah on the Sabbath, to sometimes bless the person reading the Torah and say: 'May the One who blessed Abraham, Isaac, and Jacob bless Ploni, who vows to give [charity] in honor of the Torah.'" Isaac b. Moses continues by explaining that his father "was perplexed by this custom."[42] In the subsequent discussion, Isaac ponders the necessity of pledging money on the Sabbath, when money cannot be handled. From this comment it seems that on regular Sabbaths, and not just on special occasions, those called up to the Torah were blessed individually.

In the context of this study, I am not aiming to present a comprehensive analysis of the development of the *mi sheberakh* custom. Undoubtedly the personal *mi sheberakh* was modeled on the communal one. What is important for our purposes is that this was a nascent phenomenon, and the composition and recitation of these blessings for a broad range of personal purposes were expanding during the High Middle Ages. This coincides with the *reshut* for the groom, the first of which was composed by an eleventh-century Ashkenazic poet, Shimon b. Isaac.[43] This is further illustrated by the variable wording that appears in these blessings, such as the substitution of Hannah for Rachel, in the prayer that opens this chapter and the range of biblical figures who were noted as cured in variants in other manuscripts. Some formulas invoke men and women, whereas others praise those who gave charity or those who were silent in synagogue. Still other formulas were recited for the sake of those who had been arrested (*tefusim*), for brides and grooms, or for other communal occasions, including the payment of taxes.[44]

In addition, the biblical figures mentioned in these thirteenth- and fourteenth-century formulas vary greatly. Some blessings for men and women mention all patriarchs and matriarchs, while others mention the matriarchs or patriarchs in accordance with the gender of the individual being acknowledged or memorialized. In some cases, the patriarchs are mentioned for commemorations of men and women alike. For example, in another addendum to a thirteenth-century mahzor from Germany, the memorial formula following burial reads: "May God remember the soul of Ploni because Ploni has given charity for him and on behalf of his soul. In return, may God remember him and grant him a place in the Garden of Eden to preserve him. And may his soul be bound in the bond of [everlasting] life with Abraham, Isaac, Jacob, Sarah, Rebecca, Rachel, and Leah and with all the righteous men and women [*tzadikim vetzadkaniyot*] in the Garden of Eden. And let us say: 'Amen.'"[45] In other cases, not only the patriarchs but also, as we saw earlier, Moses, Aaron, David, and Solomon were called on.

The *mi sheberakh* was more than a private prayer that was uttered in a whisper. This blessing was bestowed on one person by another, such as one who said this prayer for a sick or deceased relative. This liturgical ritual drew communal attention to the state of an individual. I would suggest that the significance of awarding such public and social recognition to the subject of a *mi sheberakh* should not be underestimated. A Jewish man or woman who made a donation could be certain that their contribution would be publicly acknowledged, and that they or their beloved would receive a blessing. As one fourteenth-century German writer explained: "It is customary, on the final days of [each of] the three pilgrimage festivals [*regalim*], while the prayer leader [*hazan*] is on the tower, with the Torah scroll is in his arms, preceding *Ashrei*, that the most prominent member of the community [*gadol sheba'ir*] would take an object and a book in his hand and go from one person to another and bless the entire community one by one on account of their pledge to honor God and the festival. And in places where it is the custom, they [also] remember the dead and recite *Av haRahamim*."[46] This public mention of a variety of individuals effectively incorporated numerous community members in the liturgy and likely encouraged charitable contributions that would ensure such recognition.

From the fifteenth century onward, a change can be found in these personal blessings as they become focused on the family rather than a single individual: "May the One who blessed Abraham, Isaac, and Jacob bless Ploni b. Ploni—himself, his wife, and his children [lit., sons] and his progeny and all that he has—for he will give charity to honor the Torah and *matnat yad* to honor the festival. On this account [lit., for this], may God protect him and save him . . . etc."[47] That is the form the *mi sheberakh* formulas took on in modern times in communal public settings. Other versions continued to have currency (for the sick, the deceased, and women giving birth, among others).[48]

Personal Prayers and Communal Identity: Matriarchs and Patriarchs

As detailed earlier, medieval Ashkenazic Jews modeled these *mi sheberakhs* on ancient prayers. Yet these were prayers that were intended for blessing individuals, much like other personal prayers that were composed at this time: prayers for literal or metaphorical journeys, such as travelers and people fasting, for good health, and for other personal requests (*bakashot*).[49] These innovations represent creative channels through which medieval Ashkenazic Jews expressed their concerns and desires by articulating a personal link between the men and women of medieval Ashkenaz and biblical figures.

To better understand this positioning of the matriarchs, we can briefly compare how the patriarchs were incorporated into Jewish prayer. The patriarchs have been part of the daily liturgy since its earliest stages, namely, in the opening blessings of the Amidah (*shmoneh esreh*), a sequence of benedictions that have a central place in the morning, afternoon, and evening prayers on all days of the year. Inclusion of the patriarchs also takes various forms in Sabbath, festival, and, especially, High Holiday liturgies, as evidenced by formal communal prayers as well as songs and poems that were components of specific communities and their distinct customs.[50] While each medieval Ashkenazic community would choose to develop a repertoire of particular sung poems, many shared themes. Notably, on Simhat Torah, the patriarchs were evoked in the prayers for rain[51] since late antiquity. In Ashkenaz, the poem "*Zakhor Av*" (written by Eleazar Kallir; ca. 570–640, Palestine) evokes the blessing of rain, and an account of water in the life of each of the patriarchs, was recited.[52]

Alongside these formal sections of the prayers, the patriarchs were also the subject of numerous poems that congregations performed as a litany. Some were complex, but others were simple and accessible to all. For example, on Simhat Torah:

> I will rejoice and be happy on Simhat Torah
> The Redeemer [*tzemah*] will come on Simhat Torah . . .
> Abraham was happy on Simhat Torah
> Isaac was happy on Simhat Torah
> Jacob was happy on Simhat Torah

The poem continues with Moses, Aaron, David, Solomon, and others rejoicing on Simhat Torah.[53] Within the genre of liturgical poems, it is remarkably simple and unlike most poems belonging to genres that are much more complex.[54] The medieval manuscripts include a range of figures that are called on: Some name Pinhas (Phineas the High Priest); others include Solomon; whereas others omit both Pinhas and Solomon and invoke only Abraham, Isaac, Jacob, Moses, Aaron, and David. While these choices reveal little about the individuals who sang these songs, the names or presentation occasionally offer insight on the scribe or owner of a manuscript. For example, in *Mahzor Leipzig*, the name "Isaac" is decorated, and scholars assume that this illumination signals the name of its scribe.[55] An even more explicit identification in this song ap-

Figure 2.2
Prayer book. Prayer for Simhat Torah that includes the owner/copyist
of the book among the patriarchs. Ashkenaz, fourteenth century.
Vatican MS ebr. 326, fol. 85r. © 2020 Biblioteca Apostolica Vaticana.

pears in a fourteenth-century manuscript in the Vatican collection (Figure 2.2).
The owner/scribe of the manuscript added his name, Joslin, after the names of
all the biblical figures and wrote "Joslin rejoiced on Simhat Torah."[56]

Patriarchs were also appealed to in other personal prayers; for example, in
a prayer written when finishing copying a manuscript[57] and in a prayer composed for recitation at the grave of a righteous person:

> May it be pleasing before Your will, O King of Kings, to bestow
> mercy upon Israel and upon me by granting me a good life, avoidance
> keeping me from sin in this world, and providing me a good place
> [lit. part] in the Garden of Eden on the merit of the one [*tzadik*]
> who is buried here and enabling me to rejoice when the Messiah ar-
> rives and the dead are revived. On the merit of [the] citizen [*ezrah* =
> Abraham], [the one who was] sacrificed [*ne'ekad* = Isaac], and [the]
> innocent [*tam* = Jacob], save me from all sorrow; on the merit of
> Moses, David, R. Akiba, and his fellows, don't turn me away empty;
> and on the merit of all dead and holy ones, hear my prayers at this
> grave—as you heard the prayers of our ancestors at the Red Sea—
> with mercy. Blessed are you, God, who hears prayer.[58]

I have located this prayer in only one manuscript, and it is not the standard
prayer people were instructed to recite when visiting a cemetery.[59] Its author
seems to have incorporated a variety of traditional motifs, including some

that have already been discussed in this chapter. For our purposes, this prayer is striking for its similarity to the prayer in Tractate Ta'anit that calls on God, who saved the Jewish people at the Red Sea, and offers appeals to the patriarchs and other biblical figures, and which was discussed earlier as a precursor of the *mi sheberakh*. Although we know little about this type of prayer, we do know that Jews offered prayers at the graves of the righteous and relatives. Interestingly, many rabbis discouraged this custom. R. Haim b. Isaac (thirteenth-century Germany) dismisses this as a practice of "women and men who are not knowledgeable" (*nashim ubnei adam she'enam yodi'im*).

The Matriarchs: Jewish and Christian Ritual Uses

The variants on the *mi sheberakh* prayer—whether said to aid a woman giving birth, to honor a donor, on behalf of a sick person, as a memorial for the deceased, or at the graveside of a righteous figure—all belong to a wider genre that extends beyond the scope of this study. Although they are not often found in the manuscripts that have reached us, I would argue that such prayers were a standard feature of everyday life, and one possible indication of this is their further development in early modern Jewish culture, especially in Yiddish. Medical and magical manuscripts indicate that medieval Jews recited scriptural verses and various liturgical formulas as part of their daily routines, when embarking on travel, in sickness, and at other critical junctures.[60] Few of these compositions have survived, for they were not transcribed, much like the *mi sheberakh* that we know was recited but appears in few manuscripts. These prayers often contained adjurations and magical elements, underlining the close connection between magic, medicine, and religious ritual. These formulas were predominantly in Hebrew or Aramaic, although some included medieval French or German vocabulary.[61]

These prayers had parallels in the surrounding Christian culture, specifically the commemorative formulas and prayers for sickness, childbirth, and travel. In some cases, Christian and Jewish chants resemble one another. For example, an eleventh-century Christian prayer for the dead petitions God to liberate the soul of the deceased:

> As you freed Enoch and Elias from the world's common death,
> . . . as you freed Lot from Sodom and the flames of fire . . .
> As you freed Moses from the hand of Pharoah, king of Egypt,

. . . as you freed Isaac from sacrifice . . .
As you freed Peter and Paul from being imprisoned.[62]

In other cases there was a noted distinction between the Jewish and Christian prayers, as Christians regularly called on saints[63] whereas there was no parallel to saints in Jewish culture. This form of Christian prayer has survived abundantly from the later Middle Ages in Latin and in the vernacular.[64]

The Christian prayers said during childbirth provide another interesting comparison to the *mi sheberakh* prayers calling on the matriarchs. Some ask God to bless the pregnant woman as he blessed Mary when she gave birth to Jesus.[65] The most common formula for women in labor, which some scholars call "the peperit charm,"[66] was recited in church and at bedside. This prayer recounts the succession of births in the New Testament: Anna delivered Samuel, Elizabeth gave birth to John, Anna gave birth to Mary, and Mary gave birth to Christ ("*Anna peperit Samuelem, Elisabet genuit Johannem, Anna genuit Mariam, Maria genuit Christum*"). It continues with hopes that the baby, whether male or female, be delivered safely ("*infans, sive masculus sive femina exi foras*"), and, as Mary had been protected from suffering in childbirth, may this mother give birth without pain ("*Sancta Maria peperit salvatorem, peperit sine dolor*").[67]

As Marianne Elsakkers observes in her study on this prayer, Hannah (Anna), the mother of Samuel, is the sole figure from the Hebrew Bible who appears with New Testament women and, in some cases, more contemporaneous mothers.[68] She also notes that these were oral prayers, and each recitation of them was distinctive. She has documented more than sixty versions of this text. In addition to being read in church and in the presence of the parturient in labor, this text was written on bread, amulets, and belts.[69]

Jewish conversance with prayers in the vernacular and, perhaps, in Latin is evident in a number of manuscripts. In some cases, Jews changed elements; in others the prayers were adapted. Scholars of medieval magic have demonstrated this in love charms as well as in formulas meant for protecting from evil and catching thieves.[70] As discussed in Chapter 1, Jews, too, employed amulets during childbirth. They also embroidered biblical verses on girdles for pregnant women.[71] Where Christians turned to saints and various biblical figures, especially from the New Testament, Jews turned to the patriarchs and matriarchs.

As we saw earlier, invoking the patriarchs in prayer has been normative since the earliest Jewish liturgical formulas, however the matriarchs rarely appear in this genre.[72] No parallels to the Simhat Torah poem cited earlier are sung to celebrate the matriarchs. Thus their appearance in the medieval *mi sheberakh* blessing is a novelty. However, the parallels with Christian prayers may indicate that such formulas were far more common than scholars have acknowledged to date. By searching for the matriarchs in additional medieval genres, we find support for this assertion. In what follows, I will consider three sources: tombstones, wedding imagery, and art.

Tombstones

In addition to the liturgical references to the matriarchs in *mi sheberakhs* detailed earlier, the matriarchs were also mentioned on epitaphs. The medieval Jewish cemetery in Worms offers two surviving examples. One tombstone is that of Sarah, described as "an elder Mistress." Sarah died on Adar 20 (March), 1165, and was lauded as having been "happy and praiseworthy" (Figure 2.3).

Figure 2.3
Tombstone of Sarah of Worms (1165) that states she is "to be remembered with the matriarchs in heaven." http://www.steinheim-institut.de/cgi-bin /epidat?id=wrm-151&lang=en. © Bert Sommer-Photos.

This inscription hopes that she will join the matriarchs in the Garden of Eden ("*im ha'imahot beGan Eden tehe mehuberet*").[73]

Similarly, the epitaph of Sarah b. Joseph haLevi, who died on 20 Kislev (December) of 1175, depicts her sitting with the matriarchs and righteous women in the Garden of Eden (*imahot vetzadkaniyot*).[74] While I have not found tombstones that memorialize particular men to be dwelling in Eden among the patriarchs, one known formula for tombstones hoped that the deceased would be held in the bosom of Abraham in heaven.[75] This imagery was also common in the Christian world, where the funeral liturgy expressed the hope that the deceased would be blessed by Abraham, Isaac, and Jacob, and merit to be held in the bosom of Abraham.[76] Here again a generalized connection to the matriarchs and patriarchs can be seen. Over the thirteenth and fourteenth centuries, these formulas became less common on the Jewish epitaphs, and are replaced with hopes that the deceased is in heaven with the righteous men or women, without references to the patriarchs or matriarchs.[77] This may have resulted from the introduction of a new formula that ended with "Amen, Amen Sela," rather than mentioning the matriarchs, who continued to appear on select stones.[78]

Wedding Imagery

The matriarchs and patriarchs are also mentioned in discussions of ideal marriage and in the songs and customs practiced as part of this ritual. In halakhic literature and biblical exegesis, the four matriarchs primarily appear in contexts that relate to their roles as wives. Some of these images have roots in late antiquity, and they were repeated by medieval Ashkenazic authors who stressed some of their practical implications.[79] For example, from the angels' words to Sarah when they inform her that she will become pregnant (Gen. 16:2), a discussion ensues over how men should communicate with another man's wife. The rabbis advised that a man may ask a companion about the welfare of his wife but he may not convey his regards to her directly. Even though Moses of Coucy (thirteenth century) characterizes this as proper etiquette, his commentary suggests that this was not actual practice.[80] From Rebecca, the sages learn that a man may marry a woman only with her consent.[81] This requirement is stated time and again throughout Jewish sources, citing this matriarch. Interestingly, canon law also derives this reference and practical lesson from Rebecca.[82] The process of choosing wives for Isaac and Jacob is presented as a guide for both arranging marriages and conducting wedding rituals.[83] The biblical stories are also used to prescribe women's behavior, highlighting submission and obedience as desired qualities.[84]

Textual references to the matriarchs lack the focus on birth that is omnipresent in discussions of Eve. Why stress the matriarchs as wives rather than as mothers? This question sounds almost tautological, given that maternal qualities are inherent in the term "matriarch." One possible solution is to assume that all wives were expected to be mothers by definition. Alternatively, by emphasizing the matriarchs' dependence on their husbands, the Jewish commentators may have been acknowledging a tension that had been present in Jewish law and life since late antiquity. According to Jewish law, the commandment to procreate is incumbent on men but not women. From this perspective, underlining the matriarchs' place as wives rather than mothers reinforced this distinction.[85] A third option is that perhaps Jewish understandings were similar to Christian teachings that stressed the primacy of women's marital responsibilities above motherhood.[86] All three of these explanations may have had currency in tandem.

Beyond exegetical commentaries, the matriarchs were featured in the marriage liturgy. For example, in the popular liturgical poem "May God Bless the Groom and the Bride," which was sung by the community on the Sabbath after the wedding:

> May God bless them with everything, free from lack, as He blessed
>   Abraham and Sarah.
> May he bless them with enduring faith as He blessed Isaac and
>   Rebecca,
> May he bless them with full fruit of the womb as He blessed Jacob,
>   Rachel, and Leah . . .[87]

These blessings recall the blessing addressed to Ruth and Boaz in the Book of Ruth: "May the LORD make the woman who is coming into your house like Rachel and Leah, both of whom built up the House of Israel."[88] This verse was interpreted by medieval Jews as a reference to the custom of welcoming the bride, whether for her first wedding or to a remarriage, as stated in *Sefer haNiyar*: "From where in the Torah do we learn about wedding blessings? From Rebecca, for it is written 'And they blessed Rebecca' (Gen. 24:60). And from where in the Torah do we also learn the blessing for widows [who are remarrying]? For it is written: 'And he took ten men of the elders of the city' (Ruth 4:2), and it is written: 'And all the people that were in the gate' (Ruth 4:11), and it is written: 'May the LORD make the woman who is coming into your house like Rachel and Leah.'"[89]

The poem "May God Bless" appears in multiple variations in medieval manuscripts. Every version begins with Adam and Eve and the matriarch-patriarch couples, but some mention Moses and Tzipporah, while others include Mordekhai and Esther, and Joseph and Asenath.[90] This lack of uniformity offers evidence of the "social life" of this poem, which varied according to local custom. In this way, these poems are analogous to the Simhat Torah example mentioned earlier. Similar formulations that invoke the biblical matriarchs and patriarchs as couples are found in other contemporaneous Ashkenazic wedding poems. For example, in *Mahzor Vitry*, "May God Bless" is immediately preceded by "God the Lord Redeems" (*Elohim HaShem haEl goel*), a poem that concludes with these words:

> May your love be strong, bound in boughs;
> May God make your love strong and never lacking;
> Eternal and never departing from you,
> And bless you like Abraham and Sarah.
> May your love and desire be great,
> With the pious and encircled bride;
> May God grant you permanence and bless you like Isaac and Rebecca.
> May God give you this named woman,
> Who is committed [lit., acquired] for your house to come,
> Entering under the wedding canopy, to be married to you,
> Like the matriarchs, Rachel and Leah.[91]

These poems present the matriarchs as models for wifehood, modeling their interpretation on traditional biblical exegesis, such as Rashi's and others.[92]

A similar formulation concerning complete and enduring love appears in *Sefer haMa'asim*, a thirteenth-century collection of Hebrew stories. In one tale, in a scene recalling the story of Tristan and Isolde, a young couple in love is discovered in a shared bed by the woman's father. As an expression of his approval, he blesses them: "May it be the will of the God of Israel that your bed be complete and that no fault be found with you."[93] Here the prayer mentions "a complete bed" rather than "complete love," but the idea is similar.[94]

Wedding benedictions that include the matriarchs were also part of the standard medieval Christian liturgy. The couple being wed was blessed: "May she be as dear to her husband as Rachel, as wise as Rebecca, as long-lasting and loyal as Sarah [*Sit amabilis ut Rachel viro suo, sapiens ut Rebecca, longuiva et fidelis ut Sarra*]."[95] The matriarchs were also mentioned in some variants of the Christian marriage celebrations. Early medieval formulas invoked six biblical mothers to bless the couple: Sarah, Rebecca, Rachel, Anna, Elizabeth, and Mary.[96] These blessings were chanted in public, perhaps on the street or in the church, much as the poem "May God Bless" was sung in the synagogue as a component of the Jewish marriage ritual.[97]

Additional blessings and their variations further emphasize the significance of the matriarchs and patriarchs in this Christian ritual. A fourteenth-century missal from England blesses the couple: "May God bless your bodies and souls and grant you his benediction, as he blessed Abraham, Isaac, and Jacob. Amen."[98] A number of wedding blessings quote or refer to the passages from Genesis that bless Adam and Eve, then Noah and his offspring with fertility, bidding this couple also to be fertile and multiply. These blessings often express hope for pure hearts, bodies, and spirits.[99] A tenth-century manuscript includes a blessing for the newly married couple to be like Adam and Eve, and like Tobias and Sarah (from the Book of Tobit).[100] Whereas I have found references to Adam and Eve to be less common, those to Tobias and Sarah from the Book of Tobit, are quite standard.[101] The couple is blessed: "All powerful and eternal God, who created our first parents, Adam and Eve, by your virtue and sanctified them with your blessing and connected them to each other, so too may you sanctify and bless our hearts and bodies. . . . You who sent the angel Raphael to prepare the nuptials of Tobias and Sarah, so too may you dispatch your angel."[102]

An eleventh-century formula from Spain expands the standard prayer for wedding couples as a formula for blessing the bride: "O God, who cast a pallor over Rebecca when she beheld Isaac, may your spirit guide your student, and may you lead this woman to be enveloped in a veil by the angels. . . . As you cared for Abraham their father and Sarah their mother, and similarly for the mother of our holy bridegroom, may the faithful procreation of your children be preserved. [Amen]."[103]

The portrayal of the matriarchs as models for wifehood is also common in medieval Christian genres beyond the marriage liturgy. For example, in the composition known as *Le Ménagier de Paris* (fourteenth century, Paris), whose anonymous writer sought to instruct his young bride on how to be a good wife, the section on the proper treatment of her husband includes a detailed summary of Genesis, paraphrasing Peter Lombard and the popular *Bible historiale*.[104] The author notes that Sarah was deeply "loving, trusted, and obedient to her husband," while Leah and Rachel "simultaneously and in the same house served Jacob their husband in peace and love"; therefore, he concludes: "So much should women, with their God-given sense and reason have perfect and solemn love for their husbands."[105]

The notion that biblical figures provided exemplars for teaching women how to comport themselves is explicitly state in a composition from the second half of the thirteenth century (1300 CE at latest) known as the *Miroir des bonnes femmes* (*Mirror of Good Women*),[106] often appended to the so-called *Somme le roi*, a popular moral text that included a lot of biblical material.[107] Its author claims to have written this work at the king's request. In this essay this author explains to his (female) readers: "Beautiful girls, when you see the good and understand the bad, you can then adopt good habits [*Belles filles, Qui le bien voit et le mal prent a bon drois puis s'en repent*]."[108] The *Miroir* recounts thirty-five tales of "bad women" (*les males fames*) and thirty stories of "good women" (*les bones fames*), all drawn from the Bible, both the Old and New Testaments. The author was an anonymous Franciscan monk who refers to his religious order several times in this work. Given that Franciscans actively preached to "the laity," the topic of this book and its message seem to be aligned with their calling. It offers exhortations against keeping up with French fashion trends alongside interpretations of biblical passages and tales that read as moral exempla.[109] The intended audience for the *Miroir*, as for *Somme le roi*, were aristocratic women, but as recent research has suggested, the book was widely used.[110]

Such use of biblical figures as personal models appeared in additional examples of medieval conduct literature of the thirteenth century, as illustrated in *L'enseignment des princes* and *Du chastoiement des dames*, by Robert de Blois. Little is known of Robert, who lived during the first half of the thirteenth century, but he is assumed to have had a close relationship to Thibaut of Champagne.[111] Subsequent writings that were similar to the *Miroir des bonnes femmes* include *Le livre du chevalier de la Tour Landry* by Geoffrey de la Tour-Landry[112] and *Le livre de la vertu du sacrement de marriage* by Philippe de Mézières, both from the second half of the fourteenth century.[113] All of these books present biblical examples, but none with the intensity of the *Miroir des bonnes femmes*.[114]

Each chapter of the *Miroir* focuses on one biblical episode, followed by an exemplum that relates to a specific vice or virtue.[115] This composition may have been intended not only for aristocratic women but also as a manual for preachers. The *Miroir* provides examples from nonbiblical material as well.

Figure 2.4

Old Testament Miniatures. Rebecca is seen here behind Jacob when Jacob, disguised as Esau, receives the blessings from Isaac, Paris, circa 1250. Morgan Library M638, fol. 4r. Courtesy of the Morgan Library and Museum, New York.

The four matriarchs all appear in the *Miroir*. With the exception of Rebecca, the matriarchs are lauded for qualities that lack robust parallels in Jewish exegesis. Sarah is praised for remaining chaste while being held by Abimelekh. She is also compared to Deborah. Leah is praised for her humility, a quality that this Franciscan author highlights, by emphasizing that her children were divine gifts rather than speaking of her own fertility or other virtues. Rachel is the sole matriarch who appears on the lists of both "good women" and "bad women": by contrast with Leah, Rachel is condemned for having begged Jacob for children rather than understanding that God alone directs such matters. However, she is praised as a model wife who always tried to please her husband.[116] Rebecca receives the lengthiest treatment and is praised for three reasons: her saintly humility; her preference for Jacob, the son who revered God most; and her strong conviction that her sons should not marry into families that did not recognize the Lord's law.[117] Of the four matriarchs, Rebecca is portrayed in art most frequently, and various episodes from her life are often illustrated in medieval Bibles and psalters. Most prominently, she is depicted in the scene when Isaac blesses Jacob. The illuminations often position her directly behind Jacob, a position she does not hold in the biblical narrative (Figure 2.4). Christian mentions of the matriarchs as a medium for moral advice were accompanied by theological interpretations that were far more theoretical than practical. For example, Rebecca's marriage to Isaac was often seen as a prefiguration of the unification of the church and Jesus.[118]

In closing this survey of the matriarchs in wedding imagery, I want to emphasize the significance of female biblical figures in Christian conduct literature. This genre is a transmission of principally oral teachings that were used in sermons and in daily advice. Although the Bible and its male and female heroes were prominent in all ethical literature, their centrality in women's literature is far greater than in writings for men.[119] This leads me to speculate that a similar phenomenon was current in medieval Jewish society, a notion supported by early modern practice.

The Matriarchs in Jewish Art

Christian manuscripts that include illuminations of the biblical story lead us back to medieval Jewish culture. The Christian retellings of the Genesis narratives, much like Christian wedding benedictions, praise Rebecca as an exemplar. Within Jewish commentaries and halakhic discussions as well (though not in the liturgy), Rebecca is singled out as a model bride. As noted earlier, among other lessons, the rabbis identify the importance of bridal consent in marriage from her story.[120] Medieval Jewish illuminated Bibles are far less abundant than their Christian equivalents. Yet the matriarchs are portrayed in a number of manuscripts, some of which are Bibles but others of which are *haggadot*, the text recited at the Passover seder.

As Katrin Kogman-Appel has demonstrated in her study of the Second Nürnberg and Yehudah *haggadot*, fifteenth-century manuscripts that were illuminated by a single scribe, the matriarchs frequently decorate the margins of the traditional text.[121] Their depictions are quite surprising, given that they are not mentioned in this text and thus do not complement its content. Rather, the designers of these *haggadot* elected to tell a story that that differs from the *haggadah* itself. Kogman-Appel has suggested that this choice may be aimed toward the female audience that used these books.[122] Women participated in the Passover ritual and would have enjoyed these illuminations as the ritual unfolded.

The matriarchs, especially Rebecca, appear prominently in these *haggadot*. Rebecca is portrayed in multiple scenes: entering Sarah's tent when she marries Isaac and, thereby, bringing light back into this tent; praying with Isaac when she failed to conceive (following Rashi's commentary on Gen. 25:21); consulting with a sage when the twins were wrestling with one another in her womb (Gen. 25:22); and accompanying Jacob to receive his blessing (Gen. 15–31) (Figures 2.5–2.9). All these scenes elaborate on the biblical text and follow Rashi's commentary, an indication of how well known his interpretations were. This is also evident when reading later popular commentaries, such as *Tsena uRena*, where these same interpretations are conveyed.[123]

As Kogman-Appel has noted, not only are these scenes entirely unrelated to the narrative of the *haggadah*, they also present Rebecca in a far more central a role than any other single text. Although many of these stories appear in exegetical writings, it is difficult to gauge their prominence or popularity. Within mainstream liturgy, as we have seen, Isaac, not Rebecca, is called upon. Following Kogman-Appel, it would seem that the artistic plan of these *haggadot* anticipates a specific audience, namely women, children, and less-educated men who participated in the Passover ritual and were likely to engage with such illustrations.[124]

I have found one echo of Rebecca's prominence in the siddur commentary by Eleazar b. Judah (Rokeah). Eleazar states that *Nishmat Kol Hai*, a prayer that was included in the Sabbath liturgy and recited by especially pious Jews every day, refers to Isaac and Rebecca in its praise of the righteous ("*befi yesharim . . . ubedivrei tzadikim*"). He explains: "For the merit and honor of Isaac and Rebecca, the prayer leader says these words alone, that on their merit God will grant us good [lives]. . . . And those who don't say these

Figure 2.5

Second Nürnberg Haggadah. Rebecca sees Isaac from afar and falls
off her camel. Nürnberg, circa 1470. Second Nürnberg Haggadah,
fol. 31v. © Collection of David Sofer.

Figure 2.6

Second Nürnberg Haggadah. Rebecca entering Sarah's tent.
Nürnberg, circa 1470. Second Nürnberg Haggadah, fol. 32r.
© Collection of David Sofer.

Figure 2.7

Second Nürnberg Haggadah. Rebecca and Isaac praying for offspring. The depiction is drawn according to Rashi's commentary on the topic. On the bottom of this folio Rebecca inquires about the meaning of her pregnancy. Nürnberg, circa 1470. Second Nürnberg Haggadah, fol. 32v. © Collection of David Sofer.

Figure 2.8

Second Nürnberg Haggadah. Rebecca giving birth; Rebecca
with her sons. Nürnberg, circa 1470. Second Nürnberg
Haggadah, fol. 33r. © Collection of David Sofer.

Figure 2.9
Second Nürnberg Haggadah. Isaac
blesses Jacob as Rebecca stands
behind him. Nürnberg, circa 1470.
Second Nürnberg Haggadah, fol.
34r. © Collection of David Sofer.

words for Isaac and Rebecca say them in honor of the righteous and the pious
[*hasidim*]."[125] Here Eleazar alludes both to a tradition of calling on Rebecca
during prayer and to a debate among medieval Jews regarding the appropri-
ateness of this custom.

A Prism for Everyday Practice

What is the significance of finding the matriarchs within so many elements
of medieval Jewish daily life? I would contend that, beyond opening opportunities to investigate previously unstudied aspects of medieval Jewish life,
this evidence invites a new assessment of women's ritual praxis. If viewed
through a gendered prism that considers the presence or absence of women
and men, this offers a case study. On the one hand, the changes in the *mi
sheberakh* present a custom in which we have seen the modification of the
prayer from an individual blessing for men or women to a benediction for a
male head of household. Recent research situates this shift within a broader
dynamic related to gender and gendered visibility that has been documented
and debated by social historians (myself included) over the past two decades.[126] This shift coincides with other ritual changes that curtailed many

Personal and Communal Liturgy: Prayers to the Matriarchs

ritual activities that women had previously performed in public communal space, most significantly in the synagogue. Scholars agree that a slow shift occurred during the High Middle Ages. While the late thirteenth century seems to have marked a turning point, this change was gradual, and it was expressed in different ways over time and across the literary genres that can be studied to assess its contours. On the other hand, examining the representation of the biblical matriarchs, as in this chapter, can provide an interesting test case for understanding the implications of this change. As such, the analysis that follows can be seen as a corrective of sorts to historiographical narratives that present all-or-nothing arguments and can provide an additional perspective on the limitations of the literary genres available for such scholarly inquiries into social processes.

Historians and scholars of halakhah to date have assessed what they define as a late thirteenth-century marginalization of women. Some of the unique features of medieval Ashkenazic life are the roles that women took upon themselves, de facto and under the watchful eye of legal decisors, during the High Middle Ages within the public communal sphere. The sources that have reached us contain scant information about the Jewish communities of medieval Germany and northern France prior to the First Crusade. However, rabbinic sources, especially those from the twelfth and thirteenth centuries, suggest that Ashkenazic women were engaged in arenas of communal praxis in ways that were exceptional by comparison with other Jewish communities, such as those of Spain and North Africa.[127] Among other activities they attended synagogue regularly and elected to follow practices that were not traditionally performed by women. These included the observance of commandments connected to festivals (for example, those involving the lulav, succah, and shofar) and personal obligations (such as wearing *tzitzit* or *tefillin*) that had been considered male obligations from which women were exempt. These activities were approved, although grudgingly in some cases, by local rabbinic authorities.[128] These Ashkenazic women also actively participated in circumcision ceremonies (as *ba'alot brit*), gave donations to charity, went on communal visitations to the cemetery, and were present at communal celebrations. As Ephraim Kanarfogel has recently argued, throughout this period, even as these activities were approved by some decisors, there were dissenters to this norm.[129] By the late thirteenth century, responsa and custom books present a growing number of passages indicating that some of these practices were no longer seen favorably and that legal authorities were seeking to restrict women from performing certain rituals, among them the donning of *tefillin* and participating in circumcision ceremonies. Additional stringencies were being proposed in the realm of ritual purity or marital law.[130]

This process was neither swift nor unidirectional as there were many competing issues involved. When viewed as a process that took place over time and, especially, was embedded within the context of medieval Christian society, this transition can be documented in relation to broader trends among Christian women and their religious observances.[131] For example, scholars have argued that financial autonomy among married women was also curtailed over the course of the thirteenth century.[132] However, prescriptive rabbinic literature provides but one prism for assessing this change. Other genres that describe actual practice rather than articulating religious guidelines, supply additional perspectives and demonstrate that these transitions often had slower pacing than rabbinic leaders may have hoped.[133] One example involves women's participation in the circumcision ceremony, a topic I have explored at length elsewhere.[134] Despite a fierce objection by R. Meir b. Barukh to a woman holding the baby on her lap during this ceremony, it is evident that his instructions were initially disregarded in the thirteenth century, and women continued to participate in the synagogue ritual. Not until the late fourteenth- and early fifteenth centuries do sources clearly indicate that the norm had shifted, and this rabbinic opinion had been translated into normative practice, excluding women from the ceremony.[135] Contemporary art reflects the implementation of this ruling as well, indicating the tensions at play within the community.[136]

The subject of circumcision brings us back to the Bible, for the biblical precedent of Tzipporah as a circumcisor underwent interesting shifts in medieval texts. As Shlomo Spiegel has shown, in some twelfth- and thirteenth-century texts, Tzipporah was cited to demonstrate that women could circumcise. In his close analysis of progressive versions of *Sefer Mitzvot Gadol*, Spiegel demonstrates how Tzipporah as an exemplar was gradually excised from this text in the late thirteenth and early fourteenth century.[137] Yet Tzipporah appears as a circumcisor in fifteenth-century illuminated *haggadot*.

While the rabbis may have recommended one course of action, these illustrations indicate that other community members, among them women, may have followed another. These voices are hidden from our historical tapestry because they did not leave written testimony; but investigating the use of symbols, such as the matriarchs as depicted in customs, art, and other less canonical genres, reveals the complexity of changing customs, as well as their gradual rather than abrupt transformation. The personal prayers that were said during childbirth or beside a gravesite discussed earlier have hardly survived. Yet based on the evidence presented here, I suggest that these prayers were far more present in daily observance, particularly in the lives of women and less-educated men, than has been taken into consideration until now.

If we consider printed evidence from the early modern period, the reliance on the matriarchs as models for wifehood and as benefactors in prayer is striking.[138] In many ways these texts continue the trends seen in the medieval *mi sheberakh* prayers examined earlier as well as in the various other genres this chapter has addressed. While new Protestant ideas that underlined the Bible may also have been contributing factors, given the centrality of female biblical figures in medieval Christian conduct books, I would suggest that there was continuity as well. Moreover, following an argument made by other gender scholars, I would posit that gender hierarchies, expectations, and models changed gradually.

For example, the composition *Meineket Rivkah*, by Rivkah Tiktiner (d. 1605), can serve as an example that presents the matriarchs as models when teaching conduct, much as in *Miroir des bonnes femmes*. Tiktiner views the Bible as the key for instructing young women how to be good wives.[139] Early modern *tekhines* literature calls on the matriarchs as benefactors and models, especially the *tekhines* that were composed by women, as Chava Weissler demonstrated more than two decades ago. The *Tekhine of the Three Gates* (circa 1735), by Sore bas Toyvim, systematically mentions the patriarchs and matriarchs and many other biblical figures, invoking each of their merits.[140] After appealing to Abraham, Isaac, Jacob, Sarah, Rebecca, Rachel, and Leah, she calls on Moses, Aaron, David, and Solomon, who also appeared in some of the *mi sheberakhs*, as well as on women she locates in heaven, including Deborah, Miriam, Batya (the daughter of Pharaoh), Hannah, and Esther. She repeatedly petitions God to listen to her prayer because of "the merit of our matriarchs" (*bizkhus unsere mutters*), and she also calls on the merit of her own mother.[141] This provides insight into the personal connection envisioned between those who say prayers and the figures invoked within them.[142]

Sore bas Toyvim details specific biblical events in her prayers, and her prayers correspond with practice. For example, there is evidence that Jewish women gathered at their local cemetery annually, on the day that preceded the onset of Yom Kippur, to prepare wicks for the candles that would be used in synagogue throughout the year.[143] Candle-making and religious activities related to candles were also a responsibility associated with women in medieval and early modern Christian and Jewish communities.[144] Sore bas Toyvim's *tekhine* for this occasion describes these women preparing each wick in honor of a particular biblical figure. The first wick is dedicated to Adam and Eve, the second to Noah, and so on. The fourth wick commemorates Sarah: "And through the merit which I gain by preparing the wick for the sake of our mother Sore, may God [*haShem yisborekh*]—praised be He—remember us for the merit of her pain when her beloved son Isaac [*Yitzhok*] was led to the binding. May she defend us before God—praised be He—that we should not—God forbid [*hos vesholom*]—be left widows this year and that our children should not—God forbid [*hos vesholom*]—be taken away from this world in our lifetime."[145] Rebecca's merit is attributed to her role as the one "who caused the blessings of our father Jacob [*Yankev avinu*] to be bestowed upon us."[146] This explanation, which is rarely found in traditional commentaries, credits Rebecca with the scheme that led Jacob rather than Esau to receive their father's blessing. This is the spirit behind the illuminations in the *haggadah* we saw earlier and also in line with what was accepted in Christian retellings of the Bible.

The early modern evidence I have just considered briefly has been treated at length by experts on the period. Chava Weissler has argued: "Unlike Hebrew prayers, *tkhines* contained many references to the matriarchs—Sarah, Rebecca, Rachel, and Leah—and other women of the Bible; these women are figures with whom the female reader can identify."[147] Weissler has used *tekhine* literature to differentiate between gendered spheres. Women offered individual prayers: in Yiddish, at home, as preparation for domestic rituals. Men prayed the communal liturgy in Hebrew, in the synagogue at set times.[148] The circumstances and contexts of Jewish life in the early modern period were undoubtedly influenced by the advent of print and other cultural currents that fostered new genres and forms of writing. Yet, some strands of continuity also endured. Based on the evidence in this chapter, I would modify a portion of Weissler's conclusion in light of what we have learned by following the matriarchs. By the sixteenth and seventeenth centuries, separate liturgical spheres for men and women and their associated forms, settings, and contexts for prayer may have been firmly established. Yet calling on the matriarchs and patriarchs does not represent an early modern innovation. Rather, this practice began in the medieval synagogue, on behalf of women and men, and it was based on more ancient precedents. Certain components of this medieval custom, such as *yizkor* formulas, remained current throughout the medieval and early modern periods, whereas others did not. Beyond the synagogue, invoking these biblical ancestors was part of the personal prayers that accompanied daily activities. These were said by Jewish men and women, much in the way their Christian contemporaries prayed to saints as part of their routines.

The matriarchs may have "experienced" a certain loss of presence in the communal liturgy, a change that is congruent with similar shifts in Ashkenazic Jewish ritual, but seeking out the matriarchs in other genres and media, as in illuminated *haggadot*, demonstrates that here, too, this marginalization was not conclusive, for the matriarchs continued to hold a key role. Similarly, early modern liturgy, albeit private prayers, underlines the importance of the matriarchs and patriarchs in collective memory and religious practice. This is why the matriarchs can help provide a key to the daily practice of those who were not learned rabbis. As we have seen, the rabbis sometimes objected to these very practices, attributing them to women and to men "who don't know," yet they evolved and persisted over time.

At Her Husband's Behest
Deborah and Jael

A righteous woman fulfills her husband's desires
[*ishah tovah ʻosah retzon baʻalah*]

—*Tanna deVei Eliyahu*

A woman of valor and modest
as Deborah, woman, torch
Her name is known in the gates.

—Epitaph, thirteenth-century Worms

The midrashic composition *Tanna deVei Eliyahu* (or Seder Eliyahu, thought to be a ninth-century compilation, location undetermined) concludes its description of two of the most outstanding women in the Bible—Deborah, the prophet and judge, and Jael, her accomplice—by stating: "A righteous woman fulfills her husband's desires [*ishah tovah ʻosah retzon baʻalah*]." Following this depiction, medieval and early modern sources consistently portray these biblical figures as modest, obedient, and submissive; by illustration, in early modern Germany, "modest as Deborah" became a widespread formula on the grave markers of Jewish women.[1] Yet even a cursory reading of the biblical portrayals of these women (Judges 4–5) affirms that neither Deborah nor Jael is presented in those terms. How were these figures transformed from the biblical narrative to the medieval representations, and what were the implications, practical and ideological, of these alterations?

Judges 4–5 recounts a time when Israel was threatened by the Canaanite army commanded by Sisera. God called on Deborah to lead the people of Israel to victory. She is joined by Barak, who heads the Israelite army. After defeat in battle, Sisera escapes and seeks refuge in the tent of Jael, wife of Heber the Kenite. She permits him to enter and plies him with milk; he falls asleep, and she decapitates him. This results in the Israelites' decisive victory, made possible by two women. The narrative is followed by a poem, sung by Deborah, of her triumph and Jael's part therein. Deborah is the only female judge in the entire book of Judges. Traditionally these scriptural chapters were read in synagogue on the same Sabbath when the Song of the Sea, celebrating the crossing of the Red Sea (Ex. 15), was chanted.

In this chapter, I examine the divergence between the biblical story of Deborah and Jael and its interpretations in medieval Ashkenaz by comparing Jewish and Christian approaches, examining the social norms that characterized their authors' milieux, and considering the implications of these renderings, as reflected in Jewish daily life. The portrayals of these two figures serve as a vehicle for exploring women's public presence in medieval Ashkenazic society and the mechanisms for challenging and upholding patriarchal hierarchies among male and female community members, as well as their literacy and leadership. I will argue that the nuances and contradictions between various interpretations offer a glimpse of some of the daily tensions in this community's life.

This discussion is informed by the book *Deborah's Daughters: Gender Politics and Biblical Interpretation*, Joy A. Schroeder's comprehensive study of Christian interpretations of the story of Deborah, from the early church fathers through the present, with a brief comparison to Jewish exegesis.[2] Part of the research presented here offers a mirror image of her work, albeit within a tighter temporal frame, as I focus on medieval and, to a limited extent, early modern Jewish writings on Deborah, while drawing on various Christian texts as points of comparison.

This chapter also analyzes the figure of Jael, who plays a crucial role in this biblical narrative and, like Deborah, is depicted in the midrash as an exemplary wife who follows her husband's instructions. In hierarchal and patriarchal cultures, where the positions of judge, military leader, and combatant were typically associated with men, how were these ancient stories and their anomalous heroines received? How did these figures relate to the responsibilities that Jewish women held and power struggles within medieval Jewish communities? Furthermore, what can Jewish and Christian reworkings of these biblical accounts teach us about quotidian religious similarities and differences?

As in the preceding chapters, we will consider these biblical women in Jewish religious literature and artistry, in tandem with the practical realities of life for medieval Jews, and in relation to select Christian comparisons. First, this chapter traces the retellings of the story, from the biblical origins through rabbinic, medieval, and early modern Ashkenazic exegesis, followed by a comparison of Jewish and Christian traditions. I then examine female leadership in medieval Ashkenazic society and the place Deborah and, to a lesser extent, Jael occupy in discussions of these leaders, and the evidence that has reached us regarding their positions. Female teachers are central in this discussion. The final section of this chapter looks at a sample of early modern Yiddish discussions of Deborah and Jael, and reflects on genres in which they appear and the information this material conveys, as well as the mentions of Deborah and Jael on tombstones.

■ Deborah in the Bible and Late Antiquity

Deborah is introduced in Judges 4 as the savior of the people of Israel who ended twenty years of oppression by Jabin, king of Canaan, and his captain, Sisera. Having become a judge after the death of her predecessor, Ehud ben Gera, Deborah is described as "a prophet [*ishah nevi'ah*], the wife of Lapidoth, she judged Israel at that time. And she sat under the palm tree of Deborah, between Ramah and Beth-El in the hill country of Ephraim; and the children of Israel came up to her for judgment" (Jud. 4:4–5). According to this passage, Deborah was a recognized authority prior to this biblical episode, for she served as a judge in Israel for at least part of the period of subjugation by Sisera. Her role is carefully outlined in Judges 4: She adjudicated for those who sought legal decisions and advised the leaders of the Israelite military. Described as the wife of Lapidoth, she summoned Barak ben Abinoam of Kedesh Naftali to lead the troops to war. Barak predicated his service on her guidance, saying: "If you go with me then I will go, but if you do not go with me, I will not go!" (Jud. 4:8). The biblical text is explicit regarding Deborah's leadership in battle and emphasizes her place in the victory over Sisera's forces, who were "given over into the hand of a woman" (Jud. 4:8). However, it is unclear whether Deborah participated directly in the fighting or whether she dispatched instructions from the mountaintop, since Barak alone is described as descending from Mount Tabor to engage in combat.

The account of Deborah is fascinating, not only for her service as prophet, judge, and general but because of the other two women who are prominently mentioned in this narrative. The ultimate defeat of Sisera is exacted by Jael (Jud. 4:17–22; 5:24–27), and in the poem that Deborah recites to celebrate the Israelite conquest, Sisera's mother is portrayed awaiting her son's return from battle and then recognizing that devastating news would arrive instead (Jud. 5:28–30). The prose and poetry of Judges 4–5 are exceptional for their multiplicity of principal female figures as well as for the stability achieved by this battle: "And the land had rest forty years" (Jud. 5:31).

From the Rabbinic Period to the Early Middle Ages

Neither Deborah nor Jael is mentioned in tannaitic literature, though Deborah's leadership is outlined by Josephus and Pseudo-Philo. On the whole Josephus is loyal to the biblical narrative.[3] The story of Deborah is significantly expanded and altered in *Biblical Antiquities* (*Liber antiquitatum biblicarum*).[4] Here the story of her tenure as judge occupies three full chapters and includes many details unknown in other texts. These innovations leave almost no trace in medieval Ashkenazic culture, although *Biblical Antiquities* was known to medieval Jews,[5] an indication of the deliberate choice the medieval authors had when culling from the sources at their disposal.

Medieval Ashkenazic Jews stayed closer to talmudic traditions. Deborah is discussed in various places in the Talmud, most centrally in the Babylonian Talmud, Tractate Megillah, where a retelling of this narrative is presented as interlinear explanations of verses from Judges 4, starting with Deborah's identity: "What is meant by 'a woman of flames' [*eshet Lapidoth*]? For she used to make wicks for the Temple."[6] Here the Talmud ascribes a traditional female role to Deborah: prior to the invention of electricity, women were typically responsible for making wicks.[7] This passage continues: "'And she sat under a palm tree' [v. 5]. Why under a palm tree? R. Shimon b. Avishalom said: [to avoid] seclusion."[8] This explanation of Deborah's physical placement follows the norms for interactions between men and women: By literally holding court in an outdoor venue, she eliminated the possibility of meeting with a man alone.

The section continues by enumerating all women referred to as prophets in the Bible and then returns to Deborah with a quotation from R. Nahman: "R. Nahman said: Pride does not befit women. There were two proud women, and their names are odious. The name of one was 'bee' [*ziborta*], and the name of the other was 'weasel.'"[9] R. Nahman explains that Deborah's name signifies arrogance (*yehirut*), referring to her as "bee" in Aramaic rather than the Hebrew *devorah*: "It was written [in Scripture] about [this] bee: 'And she sent and called for Barak' [Jud. 4:6], but she did not go to him.[10] The implication is that Deborah was haughty because she demanded that Barak come to her rather than approaching him. This reading is reinforced by her use of the pronoun "I" (superfluous in Hebrew grammar, so considered an emphatic insertion) in her song: "Until I arose" (Jud. 5:7). A different discussion in Tractate Pesahim explains that this haughtiness led to the loss of her prophetic powers.[11]

The talmudic passage also reassesses the actions of Jael. Although Deborah praises her—"Above women in the tent shall she be blessed" (Jud 5:17)—the rabbis of late antiquity did not cast her in such a positive light.[12] The Talmud presents her as promiscuous, claiming that she engaged in incessant sexual relations with Sisera before killing him. Her "blessed" status thus poses a conflict for the scholars, who resolve this difficulty as follows:

> R. Nahman b. Isaac said: A transgression performed with good intention is better than a precept performed with evil intention. But has not R. Judah, citing Rav, said: A man should always occupy himself with the Torah and [its] precepts, even though it be for some ulterior motive, for the result will be that he will eventually do them without ulterior motive?—Read then: [A transgression performed with good intention is] as good as a precept performed for an ulterior motive, as it is written, "Blessed above women shall Jael be, the wife of Heber the Kenite. Above women in the tent shall she be blessed," and by "women in the tent," Sarah, Rebecca, Rachel, and Leah are meant. R. Johanan said: That wicked wretch [Sisera] had intercourse seven times [with Jael] at that time, as it says, "At her feet he sunk, he fell, he lay;" etc.[13]

Thus Jael's interactions with Sisera are considered an example of a transgression performed with good intentions rather than an unambiguously positive or heroic deed.[14] In contrast, *Leviticus Rabbah*, also composed in late antiquity but in the Land of Israel, presents Jael as escaping from sin with Sisera.[15] These sharp critiques, of Deborah as arrogant and Jael as promiscuous, reflect the undertow of impropriety being read into their roles, which Schroeder labels the "disruptive potential" of this text.[16]

Tanna deVei Eliyahu: A New Model

Other late antique texts use different means toward a similar goal. Rather than recasting these the two women as negative models, they focus on additional aspects of their characters to alleviate any discomfort that the biblical narrative may have prompted. Thus the authors of late antique and early medieval midrashim, such as *Tanna deVei Eliyahu*, stand out for their extensive discussion of Deborah and Jael, and the understanding they put forward is then repeated, especially in the popular Ashkenazic *Yalkut Shimoni*.[17] These midrashim can be broadly described as attempts to tame Deborah and Jael. Thus *Tanna deVei Eliyahu* subjugates women to their husbands, establishing Deborah as the exception that proves the rule and Jael as the epitome of the rule, by linking the actions of these women to halakhic precedents. This midrash is quite lengthy, but I consider it worthy of a close reading. This text reads:

> They said, Deborah's husband was a boor [*am ha'aretz*]. His wife said to him: Come, let us make wicks and go to the temple in Shiloh so that your portion [in life; or destiny] may be with the righteous [*ksherim*] and you will merit the world to come. He made thick wicks so their light would be abundant, which is why his name was Lapidoth. They said he had three names: Barak, Lapidoth, and Michael. Barak because his face shone [was like lightning]; Lapidoth because he made wicks and went to the temple in Shilo; and Michael, named for [the angel] Michael.[18]

This passage already presents a departure from the talmudic interpretation, which read "the wife of Lapidoth" as a description of Deborah as one who makes wicks. By contrast the midrash assigns her husband as the maker of wicks and names him "Lapidoth," combining Barak and Lapidoth into one person,[19] thus rendering Lapidoth an active man and Deborah a passive woman. This transformation is even more dramatic as Lapidoth is depicted as a boor. This midrash employs a complicated strategy. Since wick-making was a woman's task, this couple's roles are being reversed. Although Deborah is credited for both her deeds and her husband's, he is the agent who crafts wicks and goes to the Temple. The midrash continues: "God, [who] examines the heart and searches the mind,[20] said to her: Deborah, [since] you intentionally made thick wicks so their light would be abundant, I will multiply you in Israel, in Judah and, indeed, throughout the twelve tribes of Israel. And who caused Lapidoth to merit being among those who ascend to heaven? They said: His wife Deborah. About her and all those like her, it is said: 'The wise woman builds her house']Prov. 14:1]."[21] The maxim that ends this section credits women for their husbands' good behavior but, no less important, holds them accountable for men's errant ways. It appears elsewhere in medieval compositions.[22] This adage develops the message of Proverbs 14:1: "Every wise woman builds her house; but the foolish plucks it down with her hands." Commentators on this verse explain that Deborah, Miriam, and the wife of On ben Pelet (Num. 16) personified wise women,[23] whereas Korah's wife and Zeresh were examples of evil.[24]

This passage from *Tanna deVei Eliyahu* continues by examining the adverse scenario, women who were wicked and caused their husbands to sin, illustrated by Jezebel, who persuaded her husband and his peers to practice idolatry, demonstrating that women are also responsible for the evil deeds of the men they marry.[25] The midrash then returns to Deborah and summarizes the topic of women's merits and influences on their husbands:

> Blessed is the Holy One, who compensates people according to their deeds and each individual according to their actions, enacting that which is said: "In the measure that a person measures, so it is measured out to him" [Mishnah Sotah 1:7]. Therefore, it is said: "Now Deborah, a prophet . . . and she sat under the palm tree of Deborah between Ramah and Beth-El" [Jud. 4:4–5]. They said: Just as Samuel judged in Ramah, so Deborah judged in Ramah; that is why it says: "And she sat under the palm-tree" [Jud. 4:4–5]. They said: Israel lacked scholars except for half of a palm tree [meaning that few scholars were capable of leading]; that is why it says: "She sat under a palm tree" [Jud. 4:4–5]. Another one: Since it is not woman's way [i.e., inappropriate conduct for women] to be alone with men inside a house, Deborah went and sat beneath a palm tree and taught Torah in public; that is why it says: "She sat between Ramah and Bet-El" [Jud. 4:5].[26]

This conclusion underlines that the midrash is not seeking to interpret the Bible literally. Teaching Torah and administering judgments are not synonymous. This midrash also ascribes the need for Deborah's leadership to a paucity of male Torah scholars, implying that, in the presence of capable male leadership, women need not assume such responsibilities. The author further clarifies that Deborah was careful to maintain propriety at all times.

Our midrash concludes with three additional passages that each relate to Deborah or aspects of her story. The first relates directly to Deborah and explains why she had to summon Barak (her husband?). This section asserts that Barak had been an aide to the elders when Israel was led by Joshua, and after Joshua's death, he continued to help them; therefore, he was uniquely qualified to assist Deborah. In fact, this narrative seems to suggest that Barak's confidence in Deborah enabled her to succeed:

> There are people who rise early and stay late at the synagogue or the house of study to busy themselves with Torah at all times. How were Zebulun and Naphtali [the tribes that, led by Deborah, turned the war in Israel's favor] different from all the other tribes so God chose to bring victory through them? They say that Naphtali served our father Jacob and he found he was comforted by him, and Zebulun served Issachhar by providing a home for him. It is evident that Barak trusted the God of Israel and believed Deborah's prophecy, for it says: "Then sang Deborah and Barak son of Abinoam" [Jud. 5:1] and he said to her: "If you will go with me then I will go, but if you will not go with me, I will not go. [Jud. 4:8]."[27]

In sum, the anxiety prompted by the biblical depiction of Deborah and the rabbinic attempts to reshape the scriptural story are intended to offset its perceived threat to gender roles. In this new narrative Deborah was divinely appointed as a judge due to the absence of qualified men. She was committed to fulfilling her role without compromising the bounds of propriety. Barak recognized this balance and supported her success. The references to Zebulun and Issachar further emphasize the desired social hierarchies and divisions of labor.[28]

The midrash offers a similar frame for the depiction of Jael. Whereas Deborah praises Jael as a "tent dweller" and "as most blessed of women" in the Bible, as we have seen, the Talmud presents her as a woman who sinned to achieve a positive outcome (*mitzvah haba'ah beaveirah*). By contrast, the midrash avoids this talmudic interpretation and offers an alternative: "And how did Jael, the wife of the Kenite, differ from all [other] women who brought redemption to Israel? They said: She was a righteous [*k'sherah*][29] woman who fulfilled her husband's desires; this is why it is said: 'A righteous woman is at her husband's behest.'"[30] Thus, without attributing any specific act to Jael, she is transformed into a model of subordinacy and limited to her home. Lest any ambiguity remain, this passage closes with a saying that defines ideal conduct for wives: "A righteous woman is at her husband's behest." This aphorism is applied to both Deborah and Jael.

This lengthy midrash concludes with a vignette about a supposed event in Jerusalem which seeks to explain why God gave wives to men by stating that, much as wheat and barley are of negligible value until they are ground into flour, so too women are valuable because of their ability to enable men to realize their potential. On all levels this midrash seeks to establish the desired hierarchy between men and women: Women are created to support men.

Medieval Ashkenazic Interpretations

Tanna deVei Eliyahu was highly influential in medieval Ashkenaz.[31] Already in the eleventh century, this compilation is quoted by the Italian rabbi Nathan b. Yehiel, the author of *Sefer heArukh*.[32] This midrash then journeyed to Ashkenaz, where the *Arukh* was cited frequently. Medieval Ashkenazic exegetes continued to present Deborah and Jael as exemplars of submissive wives, although they soften a number of misogynistic tropes. The medieval northern French sages of the eleventh and twelfth centuries portray Deborah as a wealthy owner of fertile lands. Rashi reads each location mentioned in the Bible as one of her properties: "Under the palm tree: She had palm trees in Jericho, vineyards in Ramah, olive trees in the Beth-El Valley, and light earth [*afar hiver*] at Mount Ephraim."[33] He further suggests that she became a judge due to her wealth: "And Deborah would sit in the place where palms grew, for she was rich and so had the ability to judge."[34] At the same time, Rashi follows the Talmud (BT Pesahim 66b) and posits that she lost her power of prophecy after the events described in the Book of Judges.[35] These commentaries make little mention of arrogance, as in the talmudic tradition, and the association between Deborah and a bee is also not underlined.[36] Similarly, although these medieval sages were certainly familiar with amoraic remarks about Jael and her sexual promiscuity, they distance themselves from this subject as well. The verses that describe Sisera's death are interpreted quite literally, with vernacular (*la'az*) translations of the various implements used and without reference to the woman who wielded them.[37] Rashi explains "blessed from women in the tent" (Jud. 5:24): "Sarah, of whom it is said [in Scripture]: 'In the tent' [Gen. 18:9]; Rebecca, of whom it was said [in Scripture]: 'And Isaac brought her into the tent' [Gen. 24:67]; Rachel and Leah, of whom it is said [in Scripture]: 'And he went out of Leah's tent' [Gen. 31:33]." He continues by clarifying why Jael was more blessed than the matriarchs: "Why Jael? They [the matriarchs] gave birth and raised [their children], but

At Her Husband's Behest: Deborah and Jael

if not for Jael, that evil man [Sisera] would have come and destroyed [their children], this is as it says in *Genesis Rabbah*. Another interpretation: Jael also sat in her tent; and that is why she is mentioned as 'blessed in the tent' [Jud. 5:24]."[38] Rashi's explanation is far from satisfactory, and his provision of two reasons for this accolade signals his acknowledgment that neither answer is sufficient.

R. Joseph Kara (d. c. 1135) further expands on this matter: "This statement is one of the unexplained verses.... It says: 'Most blessed of women be Jael,' but it is not specified why she is blessed; and it is then said: 'Most blessed of women in tents' without explaining why she is more blessed than the other women in the tents. Here is the reason that she is most blessed of all other women: he 'asked for water, she gave him milk' (Jud. 5:25) to induce drowsiness so he would fall asleep and she could drive the tent peg into his temple. And why is she more blessed than [other] women in the tent? For no [other] women who dwelled in the tent caused a [military] victory as she did."[39] The most frequently quoted commentary concerning Jael relates to the tent peg with which she killed Sisera. This midrash details that the hammer[40] and tent peg were her weapons of choice, rather than a sword or more conventional weapon. Emphasizing that Jael's place was in the home (her tent), she chose instruments that were available in her surroundings. This gesture attests to her modesty and obedience for the Bible states categorically that women should not use male armaments (*kli gever*).[41]

As R. Haim Paltiel (thirteenth century) explains: "'*Lo yehiyeh kli gever*' (Deut. 22:5)—That she will go frivolously among the men, for this is the manner of those who commit adultery. According to the simple meaning, she would not go to war with a sword, as a man does; therefore, Jael took a hammer but not a sword."[42] Another variation on this interpretation is transmitted in *Sefer haZikhronot*, compiled during the fourteenth century, which ascribes a prayer to Jael: "Sisera escaped on foot to the tent of Jael because she came out to greet him and served a beverage to him, covered him, then he fell asleep. And Jael prayed to God, saying: 'Please strengthen the arm of your maidservant.[43] In this way I know that he shall be given to me: If I lower him to position him on the ground and he doesn't wake.' And she did so and then took a peg from the tent and a hammer in her hand, and she struck the peg into his head, as in the prophecy of Deborah."[44] This prayer is based on *Biblical Antiquities*, the source that *Sefer haZikhronot* often used as its foundation.[45] This description is also free of the negative insinuations presented in the Talmud. In addition, the description of Deborah in *Sefer haZikhronot* focuses on her military prowess and ignores almost all the other aspects that were underlined in talmudic discussions: "And after him [Shamgar], Deborah and Barak battled with Sisera as God struck every chariot and all his troops [Jud. 4:15] with strong winds, hail and steady rain, thunder and lightning as they shielded their faces, were unable to remain standing, and were struck down."[46] The author of *Sefer haZikhronot* (Yassif dates this specific passage to the mid-fourteenth century) does not dwell on Deborah but swiftly turns to Gideon, without devoting special attention to the heroines in this story.

Christian Comparisons

A brief comparison between the Jewish interpretations presented earlier and Christian exegesis in late antiquity and the Middle Ages reveals both similarities and pronounced differences. Late antique *onomastica*, such as those by Origen and Jerome (third and fourth century respectively), commented on the semantic link among Deborah's name, the Hebrew noun "bee" [as earlier], and the Hebrew root *d-b-r*, "speech." In his interpretation of her name, Jerome declared: "Deborah means the bee whose prophecy is the sweetest honey,"[47] associating Deborah with bee or speech (*apis vel loquax*) and suggesting that her speech should be interpreted as a sweet prophecy.[48] This interpretation was supported by verses in the Old and New Testaments that refer to prophecy as delectable food and characterized by sweetness (Ezek. 3:3; Rev. 10:9; Luke 24:42–44).

This metaphor was recurrent in medieval literature: It appeared in the *Glossa ordinaria* and in many exegetical collections. The honey of Deborah's prophecy was also applied to law: "How sweet are your words to my lips, sweeter than honey to my mouth" (Ps. 118:103). In late antiquity Ambrose had already remarked that Deborah was the sole woman to become both a prophet and a judge, a paired status that was rare among men.[49] Much like Jewish sources, Christian lists of female prophets included Deborah alongside Miriam, Huldah, Sarah, Rebecca, Rachel, and Leah, as well as New Testament figures Anna, Elizabeth, and Mary.[50] Like their Jewish counterparts, Christian exegetes were interested in the identity of Deborah's husband and sought to clarify the relationship between Deborah and Barak, with some suggesting that he was her husband.[51] Other interpreters portray Deborah as a widow, an idea that is found in early modern Jewish exegesis as well.[52]

Medieval Christian scholars also expounded on Deborah's involvement with the battle she waged. Peter Comestor emphasized her position during combat, comparing the mission she led with Barak to Moses's confrontation with the Amalekites.[53] This attention to Deborah as a warrior is also evident in select medieval biblical illustrations, as can be seen in illustrations of Old Testament scenes in psalters and picture Bibles. For example, both the thirteenth-century Parisian Bible and the St. Louis Psalter from the same place and time feature Deborah at war (Figures 3.1 and 3.2).[54]

As Schroeder has demonstrated, medieval Christian authorities were concerned that Deborah would become a precedent for women as leaders. Some commentators in medieval Germany, Rupert of Deutz (d. 1129) among them, elevated Barak as the hero of the story, effectively overshadowing Deborah.[55] The *Glossa ordinaria* explained that she taught through preaching and exhortations, a line of argument that echoes medieval Jewish interpreta-

Figures 3.1 (*below*) **and 3.2** (*opposite*)
Deborah leading her troops into battle. These pictures correspond with the emphasis on her role in the battle in some Christian and Jewish texts. *Figure 3.1*: Old Testament Miniatures (Paris, circa 1250), Morgan Library M638, fol. 12r. Courtesy of the Morgan Library and Museum, New York, NY. *Figure 3.2*: Bible of Saint Louis (Paris; circa 1250), Paris BN Lat. 10525, fol. 47r. © Bibliothèque nationale de France.

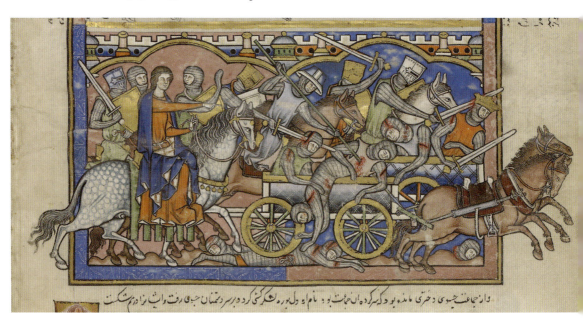

tion.⁵⁶ The status of a preacher has distinct significance in each religious culture. The subject of women's eligibility as preachers was fraught in Christian society throughout the Middle Ages, given the importance of this practice among mendicants and the prohibition against women in this role based on understandings that were derived from the New Testament. This is not to suggest that Jewish authorities would have taken a different position toward women delivering sermons. However, as we will see, Jewish exegetes and legal decisors focused on women as judging and teaching rather than on preaching, for the latter does not seem to have arisen as a major factor in medieval Jewish discourse.

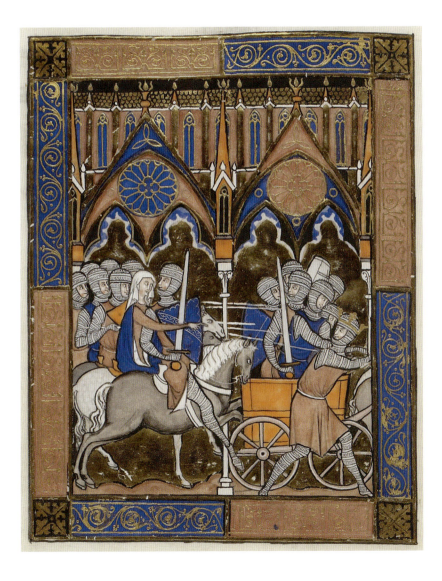

At Her Husband's Behest: Deborah and Jael

Among Christians, Deborah also becomes a model for women who took vows of celibacy. For example, Peter Abelard presented Deborah as the personification of the cloistered woman.[57] He also ascribed her presence to the dearth of male leadership, much as medieval Jewish commentators suggested. The hymn he composed for the nuns of Paraclete is illustrative:

> When the strength of men dried up
> This courage rushed into many women
> Such as judge Deborah
> And the widow who killed Holofornes
> And the famous mother of seven brothers[58]
> Who merited a solemn mass.[59]

Schroeder notes that, following the death of Abelard, Peter the Venerable (d. 1156) compared Heloise (d. 1163 or 1164) to Deborah, praising her erudition and leadership.[60] Like her Jewish counterparts, Heloise served as a teacher but not a judge.

The men who celebrated Hildegard of Bingen (d. 1179) also compared her to Deborah, though she never spoke of herself in such terms.[61] Similarly, Elisabeth of Schonau (d. 1164), a medieval mystic and Benedictine nun, was likened to Huldah, Deborah, Judith, and Jael.[62] Schroeder lists many other mystics who were described in this way; she ascribes this pattern to Deborah's inclusion in "lists of holy women as a standard convention."[63] This is visible in medieval Christian art as well, where Deborah appears as part of the *Speculum virginum*, featuring the models for nuns, as in Figure 3.3. Hagiographers sometimes contended that medieval Christian women were holier than biblical figures since, as nuns, they had consecrated themselves to God alone.

Some Christian exegetes explicitly suggested that Deborah should be admired but not imitated.[64] Gratian (died before 1159) states that her position was recognized in the time of the Old Testament but changed with the coming of Christ and those who followed in his footsteps.[65] In this vein the author of the thirteenth-century *Miroir des bonnes femmes* presents Deborah as a prophet because she was so pure that God granted her the ability to perceive the future.[66]

The association between Deborah and Jael was also deepened by Christian interpreters. Albert the Great (d. 1280) praised both as exemplars who overcame lust.[67] Most Christian exegetes stress the importance of Jael's role to a degree that is unparalleled in the Jewish sources. Jael is featured prominently in medieval art for, following the late antique and medieval exegetes, illuminated Bibles and moral compilations depict her as a prefiguration of

Figure 3.3

Deborah featured with other biblical figures who serve as role models for nuns. Germany, first half of the thirteenth century. *Speculum virginum*, Walters Art Museum, Baltimore, W72, fol. 61r. © Walters Art Museum, Baltimore.

the church.[68] These illuminations often focus on the hammer and the peg that Christian exegetes interpreted as symbols of the cross and nails.[69] Sisera appears as a contemporary knight, with shield and armor, whereas Jael is depicted either in simple garb that signals her piety or as a matron in the high medieval fashion. Numerous *Speculum humanae salvationis*, popular in the fourteenth century, volumes include elaborate illustrations of Jael, comparing her deeds to the killing of Cyrus by Tomyris.[70] By tracking these depictions over time, we can chart the fashion currents among matrons and knights, as demonstrated in the accompanying images (Figures 3.4–3.7). In all the images the peg and hammer stand out as instruments as well.

Figures 3.4–3.7
Jael killing Sisera in her tent. The changes in her representation, especially in her clothing, and the representation of Sisera reflect changing styles. *Figure 3.4*: Old Testament Picture Book, Paris, circa 1250. Morgan Library, M638, fol. 12v. Courtesy of the Morgan Library and Museum, New York, NY. *Figure 3.5*: Bible of Saint Louis (Paris; circa 1250), Paris BN Lat. 10525, fol. 47v. © Bibliothèque nationale de France. *Figure 3.6*: *Speculum humanae salvationis*, Cologne, Germany, circa 1360. Darmstadt Landesbibliothek ms 2505, fol. 57r. © Darmstadt Landesbibliothek. *Figure 3.7*: *Speculum humanae salvationis*, Flanders, fourteenth century. Morgan Library, M385, fol. 33r. Courtesy of the Morgan Library and Museum, New York, NY.

Figure 3.4

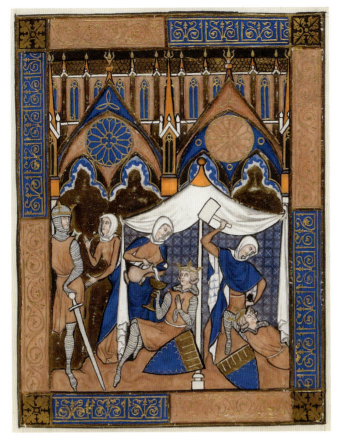

Figure 3.5

Figure 3.6

Figure 3.7

Figure 3.8

Weltchronik, Rudolf v. Ems. In this depiction of Jael killing Sisera, the men are wearing "Jewish" hats. Germany, 1360. Hochschul- und Landesbibliothek Fulda, Sign. Aa 88, fol. 172r. © Hochschul- und Landesbibliothek Fulda.

One rendering of Jael that is distinct from all others is preserved in a beautifully illustrated fourteenth-century biblical chronicle that contains the *Weltchronik* by Rudolf von Ems (circa 1250).[71] Without exception, the men depicted in the biblical scenes of this manuscript are portrayed as medieval Jews, as signaled by their "Jewish" hats. In this illustration, Jael is driving a tent peg into the clothed Sisera in her tent. In contrast to Sisera, Jael is fully dressed in the garb of a respectable matron.

The appearance of Deborah and Jael in illustrated Bibles, world chronicles, and multiple copies of the *Speculum* are indicative of a wide audience of readers that include educated laity and broad knowledge of the story of Deborah in the context of general biblical literacy.[72] In this context it is worthwhile asking to what extent Jewish and Christian exegetes were aware of each other's interpretations. The Jewish interpretations are much more focused on taming Deborah and Jael. Were they aware of the theological importance for

Christians of the hammer and the peg and did this lead to an underscoring of these same tools as symbols of domesticity and subservience? Did Christians pick up the tradition that Deborah was the wife of Barak from Jewish interpretation as some have suggested?[73] And did the popularity of Deborah and Jael in Christian culture resonate with Jewish audiences although their tone was different? These are questions that cannot be answered conclusively, but the proliferation of depictions at least hints to possible familiarity with Christian interpretations and thus heightened sensitivity.

From Exegesis to Practice: Women as Teachers, Not Judges

Let us now shift our focus from exegesis to practice by situating these interpretations of Deborah, and to a lesser extent Jael, in medieval discourse on women's public roles. Among Christians we saw how Deborah was lauded as a model for nuns. In cases like those of Heloise and Hildegard of Bingen, medieval women were compared to her, as teachers not as judges. Deborah was envisioned by Christians in the cloister. However, the cloister was irrelevant for medieval Jewish society, where this institution did not exist. So what did Jewish writers do with her?

With respect to Deborah, although medieval Ashkenazic scholars seem to accept her unusual position more readily than their late antique and early medieval forbears, this affirmation was contingent on more constricted roles: Deborah became a teacher rather than a judge. For example, the twelfth- and thirteenth-century Tosafists cite Deborah in their argument for women exercising authority, in their commentary on the tannaitic rule that "whoever is allowed to judge is allowed to testify." When pondering how this statement applies to women, who are broadly disqualified from giving testimony, they ask: "Would you say that a woman is capable of judging?" As it says in Scripture: "And Deborah she was the judge of Israel at that time" (Jud. 4:4). They then explain: "Deborah judged through speech [al pi hadibbur]; thus, she did not judge, rather she taught."[74] Similarly, when considering acceptable witnesses for a conversion and, specifically, the ability to attest to its immersion ritual, the Tosafists offer a near-verbatim repetition of this quotation: "Deborah spoke [dibra] but did not judge."[75]

It is also important to note that Deborah's role as judge (or teacher) is also mentioned with regard to concrete scenarios. For example, in the thirteenth century one query to R. Meir b. Barukh of Rothenburg asks whether two litigants in a dispute may receive judgment at night.[76] This situation required consideration from a decisor because, according to Jewish law, legal decisions must be rendered during the day.[77] Meir of Rothenburg states that, if both parties agree, this can be done concerning financial issues, much as testimony from women and others who are considered unqualified as witnesses can be presented in monetary cases if all parties agree to their participation. He explains: "Any matter of monetary law that they agree to is permitted . . . as with Deborah who judged Israel, for they accepted her as an authority over them."[78] In this responsum Deborah is referenced as a judge, following the medieval norm that women could testify about fiscal issues.[79] Yet this ruling by Meir of Rothenburg represents an exception rather than the rule. Other medieval German rabbis promulgate the position discussed earlier, that Deborah taught rather than judged. For example, the thirteenth-century commentary by Mordekhai b. Hillel Cohen (d. 1298) states: "And even though it says that Deborah judged, 'She judged Israel' [Jud. 4:4], she didn't actually judge; rather, she taught [*melamedet*]."[80] These rabbinic discussions of Deborah present a fascinating tension. On the one hand, the rabbis appear eager to tame Deborah and align her role with normative practice. On the other hand, at minimum, the learned men who composed these texts were keenly aware of her status a leader and a judge in the Bible; given that this narrative was widely known, they had to respond to its content.

This idea is reflected in medieval exegesis on Tractate Avot as well. For example, the commentary in the manuscripts of *Mahzor Vitry* enumerates the authorities who received tradition from Moses (Avot 1:1). In their list of judges, Barak appears rather than Deborah, erasing her from the record.[81] This omission resonated in the passages discussed earlier, where Rashi and other exegetes highlight Deborah's wealth, biblical verses which the Talmud does not address. Rashi explains "And the princes of Issachar were with Deborah" (Jud. 5:15) by clarifying that Deborah led with men rather than alone: " 'The leaders of Issachar are the Sanhedrin that toiled with the Torah, they knew wisdom of all times [*binah leitim*]' [1 Chron. 11:32]. They were always with Deborah, who taught Israel law and justice [*hok umishpat*]."[82] Here, too, Deborah is not a judge but a teacher, and rather than acting autonomously, she is accompanied by the Sanhedrin. Thus these medieval scholars too were trying to curtail her authority, albeit in gentler terms than their predecessors.

Within medieval Ashkenazic life, some rabbis even scrutinized the propriety of Deborah serving as a teacher, as demonstrated by two passages in *Sefer Hasidim* that discuss the permissibility of instructing women in Torah, following a talmudic anecdote in BT Yoma:[83] "A matron asked R. Eliezer: Why were those who committed one sin by worshipping the golden calf given three deaths?[84] He replied: A woman's wisdom only resides in her loom, as it says [Ex. 35:25]: 'And all the skilled women spun with their own hands.'"[85] This response silenced the matron. According to the original talmudic narrative, R. Eliezer was then rebuked by his son Hyrkanos: "His son Hyrkanos said to him: By refusing to offer her [the matron] even one lesson from the Torah, you made me lose 300 *kur* in annual tithes. He [R. Eliezer] replied: The words of the Torah should be burned rather than entrusted to women. When she departed, his students said to him: You refuted her with a weak answer [lit.. a reed, a flimsy stalk]. How would you reply to us?" This exchange between the matron and R. Eliezer appears in the Talmud (PT Sotah, 3:4) and presents one of the harshest rabbinic positions regarding women and Torah study.[86] By contrast the passage in *Sefer Hasidim* does not adopt the Talmud's misogynistic tone or embrace R. Eliezer's uncompromising rejection of teaching Torah to women. Rather, it weaves together additional talmudic traditions and evokes Deborah as an exemplar:

> And why shouldn't Torah be taught to women? For it says [in Scripture]: "And teach your sons" [Deut. 6:7], your sons but not your daughters. Anyone who teaches Torah to women, it is as if he taught her *tiflut* [licentiousness][87] but it is a mitzvah to teach her [a daughter or any woman] prayers, commandments, and the laws of *issur veheter* [what is permitted and forbidden]. However, do not teach them the reasons for these commandments. If they don't know the words of the Torah, how could they [men] instruct women and how did Deborah, who judged Israel, [come to] know [this]? For it says [in Scripture] "and she judged Israel" [Jud. 4:4]. Rather, they [women] should be taught Torah so they will know what to do, for one [a woman] who jokes could be checked as a suspected adulteress [*sotah*] and a woman who "is glad at calamity shall not be unpunished" [Prov. 17:5].[88]

Here Deborah serves as an example of a woman who has been educated in Torah and is a model for teaching women Torah. This passage defines knowledge of Torah as conversance in Jewish law (halakhah), particularly the laws of what is permitted and forbidden (*issur veheter*) that all Jewish women were expected to know to run a household. Although it is difficult to determine how the author of *Sefer Hasidim* envisioned Deborah's exact role, he does not picture her as a judge. Rather, this text implies that all women, like Deborah, must be sufficiently schooled to adhere to the law and instruct others in turn, for it states: "If they don't know the words of the Torah, how will they instruct [other] women?" It seems plausible that *Sefer Hasidim* refers to women teaching girls or younger women, rather than considering a woman who was a judge, guide, or teacher.

This idea is affirmed by the immediately preceding passage in the Parma manuscript of *Sefer Hasidim*, where the author notes that girls must learn the basis of Jewish practice but "should not learn the rationale for the commandments [*ta'amei hamitzvot*]," using the same argumentation: "Although it says [in Scripture]: "And you shall teach your sons" [Deut. 6:7], your sons but not your daughters, a man should teach his daughters so they will know how to pray, and also the commandments, but he should not teach them the commandments in depth. Nor should he not allow his daughters who have grown up [matured] to study with young men [*bahurim*], lest they sin with them; rather, he should teach them [on their own]."[89] These comments about Deborah and the limits (and scope) of what girls were taught are informative, for they indicate that medieval Ashkenazic rabbinic authorities concurred that Jewish women should be knowledgeable about the details of everyday practice.[90] Moreover, the recommendation that concludes this passage is quite far from a blanket statement that women should not study Torah. To the contrary, it instructs readers of *Sefer Hasidim*, who were male by definition, to take upon themselves to educate their daughters, lest they study with young men and be led to sin with their tutors or study partners. This scenario is more reminiscent of education among elite Christian woman, like the case of Heloise, who was infamously seduced by her tutor (so perhaps this was not an entirely uncommon occurrence), than a milieu in which women remained uneducated.[91]

In fact, I would suggest that the case of Heloise and the advice in *Sefer Hasidim* suggest that Jewish and Christian women studied and taught as part of their daily lives, and that these commentaries reflect an attempt to monitor and control these activities rather than to mirror this reality. Various scholars have been quick to assert that we have scant evidence of the process of educating Jewish girls and women. Consequently, they have also downplayed women's knowledge[92] by reading this passage as the apex of their education; however, perhaps this source should be read as the limit of knowledge that certain rabbis wanted to impose. This possibility is corroborated by one of the most famous sources about a Jewish woman from medieval Germany. Eleazar b. Judah of Worms, the disciple of Judah b. Samuel who is credited with the composition or editing of sections of *Sefer Hasidim*, eulogized his wife Dulcia of Worms in a poem after her violent death in 1196.[93] He describes her as knowledgeable in the laws of what was permitted and forbidden (*issur veheter*) and also of prayer. The poem suggests that she taught prayers to other women.[94]

In this poem, Eleazar also describes the couple's daughters, who were killed in the same attack, stating that Bellette (age 13) and Hannah (age 6) knew their prayers. Moreover, Bellette studied with him (*lishmoʾa torah mipi*).[95] This tangible description of actual practice reflects the guidance on educating daughters in *Sefer Hasidim*, but its tone is notably altered: Eleazar seems to be proud of this learning and knowledge. Furthermore, the introduction of *Sefer Mitzvot Katan* (*Semak*), penned by a student of R. Isaac of Corbeil (d. 1280), suggests that the compilation was written for women as well as men, assuming they (the women) could read it. The writer explains: "He also wrote further to tell the women [*lomar lanashim*] the commandments that apply to them, [both] positive and negative commandments. And that reading [*kriah*], attention to detail [*dikduk*] and study [*talmud*] of them [the commandments] will benefit them, just as preoccupation in [the study of] Talmud [*eisek haTalmud*] benefits men." This source implies that women could read and study. These sources aptly illustrate how prescriptive texts can differ from descriptions of practice. The gap between these descriptions and the recommendation made in *Sefer Hasidim* is remarkable. Which one more accurately reflects practice?

While I cannot answer this question conclusively, a source that features female teachers affirms the example provided by Dulcia and her daughters over the theoretical guidelines prescribed in *Sefer Hasidim*: namely, tax lists from late thirteenth-century Paris, which detail some professions.[96] In his analysis of these lists and related records that span the fourteenth century, William Courtenay has demonstrated the activity of female educators in medieval Paris, focusing particularly on teachers of young children. He has identified two female teachers in city records from 1286 and 1288, respectively. In 1292, twelve male and one female teacher appear on the tax rolls.[97] As Courtenay notes, additional teachers would not have been recorded, as they did not earn sufficient income to pay taxes. His article affirms that, although their numbers were modest by comparison to their male counterparts, it was commonplace for women to be professional teachers.[98]

Courtenay's findings confirm a growing consensus concerning girls' education, namely that medieval Christian women, especially those in urban settings, like their male counterparts, learned how to read as children.[99] This education was often provided, at least initially, in the home by women. Rebecca Jacobs-Pollez has analyzed Vincent de Beauvais' treatise *De eruditione filiorum nobilium*, completed in the mid-thirteenth century, and noted that it is clear Vincent expected noblewomen and many other women to know how to read.[100]

Assuming this level of literacy was characteristic, a reassessment of literacy, and by extension, of female teachers (like Deborah), is called for. Scholars have always assumed a high level of literacy for Jewish men and questioned women's literacy.[101] However, in light of Courtenay's findings in Paris and a comparison with information about Jews in that same city, I would argue that Jewish women, like Christian men and women and like Jewish men, were literate and taught to read. Jews are included in these tax lists from medieval Paris. The record from 1292 includes one male Jewish teacher, Abraham *le mestre*, who paid a tax of twelve sous. With this designation, he is differentiated from other learned men, such as rabbis, who are identified as *le prestre*. Two Jewish teachers appear in the list from 1296: Barul, who paid thirty-six sous in taxes; and Sarah *la mestresse*, who paid eight sous.[102] Taking the small Jewish population relative to the Christian majority into account, these figures suggest that Jews, much like their Christian neighbors, employed female teachers for their children; thus, the portrayal of Deborah as a teacher becomes far more realistic than previous scholarship has suggested. If *melamdot* (female teachers of children) were a communal norm, rabbinic admonitions that fathers should teach their daughters rather than entrust their education to others takes on new meanings.

In addition to the evidence from medieval Paris concerning female teachers, in documents of practice we find a comparative abundance of female leaders: some learned, others wealthy. Admittedly, it is hard to gauge how common such women were. Some likely achieved their stature through their association with learned or powerful men—their husbands or fathers. Others may have been independent.[103] A discrete number of women are remembered for their teaching and halakhic acumen in various communities. In spite of its brevity and frequent mention in contemporary scholarship, this list merits repetition here.[104] Its French members include women who instructed the women of their communities in halakhah, like Bellette, the sister of Isaac b. Menahem (of Joigny?), and Hannah, the sister of Rabbenu Tam (twelfth century), among other women from Rashi's family, and the wife of R. Judah Sirleon (d. 1224) of Paris.[105] From Germany, Dulcia of Worms, wife of Eleazar (discussed earlier), is reported to have instructed the women in "all the communities."[106] She, like a number of others, also led other women in prayer (*mitpallelet hanashim*). Orgia, daughter of R. Abraham the cantor, was a prayer leader from Worms (d. 1275).[107] A few decades later Guta b. Nathan from Esslingen is commemorated as a prayer leader after her death in Worms (d. 1308).[108] Other such women are noted on the list of the dead from Nuremberg.[109]

Some of these women are listed in association with a male relative, be he a brother, father, or husband. In cases where they are noted as authorities, they are recorded as having taught their own customs or those of the men in their families, particularly on gender-specific observances: the laws of food preparation, candle-lighting, and immersion in the *mikveh*.[110] These examples indicate that, despite the reticence conveyed in prescriptive sources detailed earlier, Ashkenazic writings confirm the existence of women leaders and teachers whose knowledge is presented in positive terms.

Wealthy women are also mentioned in multiple sources. For example, the Crusade chronicles feature Marat Mina of Worms, who was approached by Christians in her city during the attack on the Jewish community in May 1096. According to the chronicle she was told: " 'See, you are a valiant woman [*eshet hayil*], and you know and see that God has no desire to save you, for they [Jews] are lying naked in the streets and there is no one to bury them. Baptize yourself [lit., defile yourself]'. And they fell before her and did not want to kill her for her name preceded her, for all the great men of her city and the lords of the land frequented her."[111] Despite this appeal, Marat Mina refused to convert and was slain. So too, Pucellina of Blois, who featured in the Blois Affair of 1171, is portrayed as a woman who conducted business with the local count, Thibaut.[112]

Other wealthy women are recorded as having made sizable donations to their communities, independently or with their husbands, and engaging in business as well.[113] For example, certain epitaphs, by including the term mistress (*gevirah*), suggest that there were women who held high standing in the community. This title is characteristically found on the tombstones of daughters of prominent men, such as Bat Sheva, daughter of Rabana Moshe (d. 1141, Mainz), or on those of older women (*hazekenah*), like Eve b. Avraham haLevi (d. 1246, Worms), who was a midwife, or Magtin b. Samuel (d. 1300, Worms).[114]

Women are also prominently named as benefactors alongside their husbands in dedications. For example, couples who had donated *mikvaot*, cemeteries, and other communal institutions. These formulas do not present the women or their contributions as less noteworthy than their husbands or their husbands' gifts. For example, the synagogue in Worms founded in 1034 was dedicated by Jacob b. Judah and his wife, Rachel. Jacob is described as an "insightful [or wise] man [*ba'al tevunot*]" and Rachel as "important [*hashuvah*] among the happy ones." When the woman's synagogue in that same city was dedicated in the thirteenth century, a couple was also honored as patrons: R. Meir b. Joel the priest (*kohen*) and his wife, Judith. Similarly, in Mainz (shortly after 1283), a synagogue dedication inscription identifies Isaac and his wife, Sarah, as benefactors; in Strasbourg (twelfth century), the men's synagogue was donated by Menahem b. Samuel and his wife, Marat Rachel b. Jonathan. Rachel is mentioned with reference to her father, a detail that is absent from the other inscriptions. This may signal that she belonged to a particularly wealthy or respected family.[115] These acknowledgments signal that women's philanthropy was accorded significance and that women, too, reaped the social capital associated with wealth and patronage. Interestingly, none of these men or women are known from halakhic literature or other writings. This impression is reinforced by a blessing in the *Nürnberg memorbuch*, included by its compiler, R. Isaac of Meiningen, for recitation every Sabbath:

> These are the souls remembered on all Sabbaths of the year:
> Mar Shlomo and Marat Rachel, who toiled for the communities and rescinded the decrees [*bitlu hagezerot*] [and purchased the land for the cemetery in Mainz]; Rabbenu Shimon the Great [*hagadol*], who toiled for the communities and rescinded the decrees; Rabbenu Gershom, who illuminated the eyes of the Exile with his Torah [his statutes (*takkanot*)]; Rabbenu Shlomo (Rashi), who enlightened the eyes of the Diaspora with his exegesis; Rabbenu Yaakov (Rabbenu Tam) and his brother Rabbenu Shmuel (Rashbam), who taught Torah; all the [other] rabbis who taught Israel Torah; Mar Isaac and Marat Beila, who annulled the taxes in Koblenz; Rabbenu Meir b. Barukh of Rothenburg, who taught Israel Torah.[116]

Here, as in the memorial formulas discussed earlier, two couples who merited perpetual acknowledgment are included. While this formula clearly privileges rabbis who were great teachers of Torah, it does not distinguish between their prestige and the couples' status. To the contrary, one rabbi is described in similar terms to those describing the couples. Indeed, with respect to social standing, these two couples are arguably on a par with learned rabbis. Such parity is rare in the writings that have reached us from medieval Jewish communities, at least in part because these works were penned by the rabbinic elite. However, this formula, like those referenced earlier, may suggest that the prominent women, like wealthy men, whose actions are featured in various documents, wielded significant power.

Recent research on finance and trade also indicates more regular women's engagement than was previously estimated. We have already seen one example from the Paris tax lists. In addition, these lists include approximately 120 Jews on its rolls; a third are women, many of whom appear independently. Archival records, mainly from the fourteenth century, attest to women as key financial actors and negotiators in trade throughout Germany. In some cases, women are also featured as independent actors.[117] Thus documents of practice reveal a female involvement in trade that is far broader that we would assume based on rabbinic dictates assessed to date. Indeed, I would suggest that even the large number of women mentioned in the responsa literature signal the degree of female involvement in everyday financial and communal affairs. Admittedly, financial agents were not all teachers or judges; yet the presence of women in the public sphere, together with evidence of female teachers, indicates that the medieval norm of leadership was less male dominated (despite being squarely patriarchal) than scholars have assumed to date. In conclusion, it seems that the interpretations of Deborah should be placed in a context where women were active players rather than submissive and focused on domestic matters.

Jael is far less commonly featured in writings by rabbinic scholars and exegetes. However, she does appear on a "document of practice": tombstones. The inscriptions on many medieval tombstones convey hopes that the deceased would ascend to heaven. One formula, albeit quite rare, refers to dwelling in the "tent of the women"—in other words, with the matriarchs and Jael, who was "blessed more than all women in tents." This phrase, for example, is included on the tombstone of Hannah b. Judah from Mainz, who died in 1292.[118] Mentions of Deborah appear on tombstones as well. Only one epitaph from medieval Ashkenaz that cites Deborah still stands: Leah b. Asher—the wife of Anshel Oppenheim—who was buried in Worms in

1320, is described as a "woman of valor and *hasidah*; like Deborah the wife of Lapidah [*sic*], her names were known at the gates."[119] These two grave markers can be seen as evidence for the persistence of Deborah and Jael in cultural memory, which also provides a glimpse beyond exegetical compositions.

Adding this evidence "from the ground" to the comparison between Jewish and Christian exegesis and practice raises two additional points that are worthy of consideration. First, we have seen parallel interpretations from exegetes of both religions, alongside some differences. Perhaps the most striking distinction is the realm of practice in which each religious culture associated with Deborah. By relegating her to the sequestered world of nuns, Christian teachings may have contained her "disruptive potential." Nevertheless, within this cloistered environment, and like her Jewish counterparts, Heloise was a teacher rather than a judge.

A second important insight that emerges from this comparison of Jewish and Christian exegesis is the high level of familiarity with the biblical story of Deborah and Jael. Medieval Christian texts that were intended for educated laity assumed knowledge of these figures; basic knowledge of these narratives was part of general Christian biblical literacy.[120] I would suggest that Jewish sources examined here reflect a parallel circumstance, as the discussions of teaching women Torah in *Sefer Hasidim* illustrate. *Sefer Hasidim* prescribes the halakhic material that one could teach women without discussing their degree of biblical literacy. Ephraim Kanarfogel has detailed the curriculum for Jewish males, positing that Scripture was taught from childhood onward.[121] Given the warnings against teaching young women in the presence of young men (*bahurim*), whether as tutors or peers, we might infer that young girls and boys were introduced to the Bible in similar ways.[122] Therefore I would argue that Jewish girls, like Jewish boys, were taught these stories. Jewish and Christian exegetes and legal decisors were thus challenged to derive acceptable roles and conduct from the biblical Deborah and Jael due to their familiarity. These authors were sensitive to the potential influence of these personae, and as a result, they were vigilant in their assertion of the boundaries of societal norms. Despite this insistence on these guidelines, a comparison between these teachings and documents of practice suggests that these biblical role models were far more appealing and applicable to medieval daily life than anticipated, and in fact women teachers and leaders were not rare. As such the rhetorical energy expended in curbing Deborah's power may reflect a desideratum more than actual norms.

Early Modern Deborah and Jael

I have argued thus far that medieval Jewish men and women were familiar with the story of Deborah, but the medieval texts themselves suggest this implicitly rather than explicitly. With the appearance of early modern Yiddish literary genres, we can discern less-educated Jews' knowledge and views of Deborah with greater confidence.[123] Sixteenth-century Yiddish poetry conveys various biblical narratives, replete with details.[124] Oren Roman's recent work studies the how biblical precedents and contemporary sixteenth-century German biblical translations informed Yiddish interpretations of this story.[125] Here, too, Deborah is a rich woman, the wife of Barak, who prepares wicks for the temple. She is consistently referred to as a prophet.[126] Some versions explicitly mention her as a judge.[127] These Yiddish retellings incorporate various rabbinic commentaries while strongly adhering to the biblical text.

Morality literature that is comprised of biblical anecdotes reveals further details. One of the earliest extant Yiddish works of this type has been titled *Many Pious Women* by its editors and translators.[128] This volume, found in manuscript and dated to the seventeenth century, presents descriptions of many biblical women accompanied by teachings that are applicable to its entire readership, with a focus on how pious women can further heighten their religious observance. Its author dedicates a full section each to Deborah and Jael, stating:

> We shall move on from Ruth as well and say how very pious and prudent was Barak's wife, Lady Deborah. She was a prophetess, pious and renowned. She made all the wicks to be burned in the Holy Temple. But that pious deed was nothing alone, all of Israel came to her for judgment. She did not want to sit alone in the house, alone with men, so she shrewdly thought [of a plan] in order that no one should have bad thoughts about her. Under a date palm she judged, on her bench, there she sat, in public. At the same time, she also waged battle against Sisera. This would have been enough for King David, that worthy man![129]

> Now when she had won that battle so that King Jabin had been properly cast down, completely, Deborah and Barak certainly sang on that day. Two times, on that battlefield, they sang "I" as had been

done on Mount Sinai. And besides they recited other praises as well. If I were to write them down it would be too hard for me, there are too many of them, so I do not want to recount them. For forty years she kept the land tranquil. Because of the song that Deborah sang with her troops, Israel's sins were completely forgiven, all of Israel enjoy her merit.[130]

This passage is exceptional for its reliance on prior exegesis and its insistence on countering some of the interpretations we saw earlier. Contrary to the Talmud, this author does not consider Deborah as arrogant for using the term "I" (Jud. 5:7, "Until I arose O Deborah"); rather, he compares her poem, which he posits that she and Barak recited in unison, to Moses's Song of the Sea (*Shirat hayam*; Ex. 15). Moreover, Deborah is presented as a great warrior, as mighty as King David. At the same time these early modern texts fully embraced the longstanding emphasis on Deborah's modesty. In these texts her wisdom enabled her to avoid gaining a bad reputation, and her modesty does not interfere with her responsibilities as a judge. Thus the overall image of Deborah as a pious and modest woman is upheld alongside her authority as a judge.

This approach is also displayed by this anonymous author's account of Jael, which begins: "Lady Jael was also very pious, beyond measure. Sisera on foot, fled into her tent."[131] This opening statement makes clear that Jael is not considered a seductress. He continues:

She went toward him, courageously she betrayed him. She said: "Be secure in my house without any worries." Under a blanket she hid him. He was tired; it was hot and sweaty for him. He asked her for water, she gave him milk so that his [eyelids] would get heavy and he would fall asleep from it. [He said,] stand in the doorway gentle maiden. If anyone asks you about me, then answer in sense like a brave man, "nobody is inside." When he had fallen asleep in the chamber, she took a nail and a hammer; she stuck the nail through his temple, so that he would have to be buried in the churchyard [*ti-fla hof*]. Barak was chasing after Sisera. [Jael] said, Come, I shall tell you a new tale through which I honor you. I shall show you the man I desire. He went with her. There Sisera lay with all four limbs stretched out. The nail was stuck in his temple.[132]

This description of Jael is especially striking, not only for its emphasis on her piety but for its suggestion of a counter narrative to Christian interpretations of this figure as well as its familiarity with Christian burial customs. In this version, Sisera would be buried in a churchyard (identifying him as Christian?) and adapts a view that states Sisera was crucified. This section concludes by reinforcing Jael with classic descriptions as modest: "That pious woman was worthy of all honor for not preferring to take a sword instead; out of piety she left it aside. She had come across the verse 'a woman shall not bear the arm of a man.' Otherwise she would have struck him down with a sword or with a halberd; however she didn't want to act against the holy Torah. She was recompensed for her piety; she was blessed more than all women in tents—more than Sarah, Rebecca, Rachel, and Leah."[133] Here this author follows the medieval midrashim discussed earlier.

These accounts of Deborah and Jael in *Many Pious Women* are echoed in Yiddish translations of the Bible and in *Tsena uRena*. For example, the latter discusses Deborah as part of the readings for Parashat Beshalah (Ex. 13–17). Each year, when the story of God splitting the Red Sea during the last stage in the Israelites' Exodus from Egypt (Beshalah; Ex.13–17) was read in synagogue, Judges 4–5 was also recited. The interpretation of these chapters from Judges in *Tsena uRena* quotes R. Behayei (Bahya b. Asher, d. 1340), who explains that it is no wonder that Scripture included a "woman who was such a prophet, for Sarah was also greater in prophecy than Abraham, for it says 'Whatever Sarah tells you, do as she says' [Gen. 21:12]," and the list of women prophets from Tractate Megillah that we saw earlier is recited.[134]

Tsena uRena further explicates that "Deborah was as important as Moses [when] she sat in a field under a palm tree. One should learn from this that a woman should take care to avoid walking without a chaperone in the house of a stranger, lest she become suspect. Even though she was modest, Deborah would not trust that her modesty [would be unquestioned] despite being a prophet, so Deborah was careful so she would not be doubted."[135] This text then discusses Deborah's admonition that Barak's military leadership would be underestimated if he led a victory that was achieved "at the hand of a woman" (Jud. 4:9). After describing the defeat of Sisera's army, this description continues: "And Sisera fled on foot until he reached the tent of Jael, the wife of Heber the Kenite, because there was peace between him, the King of Hatzor, and the house of Heber the Kenite. And Jael invited him in: 'Come in my lord, come in here, do not be afraid' [Jud. 4:18]. So he entered her tent and she covered him with a blanket. And he asked her: 'Please let me have some water; I am thirsty' (Jud. 4:19). And she opened a jug of milk before him and offered him milk to drink."[136] Next Rashi's explanation that milk induces sleep is quoted.[137] The text counters a key element of the talmudic and midrashic interpretations: "Some sages say that Sisera did not touch Jael and this is why it says 'with a blanket' [Jud. 4:18] meaning God attests that Jael is a righteous woman and did not sleep with him. From here, one should learn that a woman must beware of entering a home [host unspecified] on her own, so they will not suspect her. They wouldn't be inclined to believe that she is pure for we see that, even though Sisera escaped and Jael killed him, the suspicion that Sisera slept with her remained and God himself had to bear witness to her purity."[138] *Tsena uRena* then offers a report on the death of Sisera, followed by the Song of Deborah. For this seventeenth-century author, ancient Israelite soldiers in battle are analogous to Jewish men who dedicate themselves to the study of Torah. This passage in *Tsene uRena* ends with the hope that the enemies of Israel will be obliterated like Sisera, and all who revere God will be like "the rising sun" on land that "rested for forty years" (Jud. 5:31).[139]

A fascinating aspect of this commentary is its dual aim of offering advice to its female audience (as listeners or readers) and its transformation of Jael's gesture into the moral to be gleaned from this story. Furthermore, this interpretation contradicts the Talmud and follows medieval Jewish and Christian perspectives of Jael as a pious, virtuous matron. The comparison between Moses and Deborah is also noteworthy, as it echoes ancient traditions underlined by the reading of Deborah's song on the Sabbath when the story of the Crossing of the Sea was read as part of the weekly Torah portion. Yet *Tsena uRena* makes this comparison emphatically, stating: "Deborah was as important as Moses," a sentiment not frequently echoed by the medieval writers who were interested in practice.[140]

Rivkah Tiktiner, whose work has been encountered in previous chapters, is another early modern author who wrote about Deborah (albeit without mention of Jael). Rivkah boldly affirms the wisdom and prophecy attributed to Deborah and emphasizes that her acumen surpassed her male peers' abilities, subversively contradicting the traditional commentary. She quotes *Reshit Hokhmah*, a sixteenth-century volume on morality that was popular in Eastern Europe: "But *Reshit Hokhmah* writes that 'The wisdom of women' refers to Deborah the Prophetess which is a great surprise for our sages. They are surprised because Phineas the Priest lived in those times, and God, blessed be He, loved him greatly, but let his prophecy rest upon a woman and not on Phineas."[141] In a subsequent quotation of Rivkah's from *Reshit Hokhmah*, *Tanna deVei Eliyahu* is quoted, stating that God bestows prophecy on any deserving person, irrespective of gender or religion. This source then refers to Bityah, daughter of Pharoah, as a daughter of God who, despite being a gentile, merited entry to the Garden of Eden. Rivkah concludes her remarks about Deborah by saying: "There is more similar material that I do not want to write about here because it all belongs in its own place."[142]

Rivkah then surveys what we know about Deborah and the lessons we should learn from her example:

> Now I would like to write more about how our sages explain why Deborah was called "The wife of Lapidoth." Who was Lapidoth? Our sages, may their memory be a blessing, say that Lapidoth was Barak. Why was he called Lapidoth? Because Deborah made wicks [*lapidot*] in the temple and gave them to her husband who lit them. And she made sure he studied Torah day and night. It was given in thunder and lightning. Now the question must be posed: if he was her husband, why did she send for him to campaign against Sisera? It sounds as if he were not her husband. But since prophecy was granted to her, she separated herself from him, which is why she had to send for him. This is also why he said, "If you want to go with me, then I too want to go, but if you do not want to, then I also do not want to go." How could he have said that he wanted to go with another woman? Rather, she was his wife and only separated herself [11a] from him because he knew she was a righteous woman. [He said to himself] "Perhaps I will enjoy her merit."[143]

This passage incorporates segments from the many midrashim that we have already seen. It also conveys the importance of proper behavior and thereby emphasizes that modesty is central in rabbinic interpretations of this story. When Rivkah arrives at the specific message this narrative conveys, she promotes women's agency in the service of their husbands. She states: "Every pious woman can learn from all the issues that I have written here, that she should bring her husband to good deeds, and discourage him from bad things. She should not tell him everything that goes wrong in the house—

she should excuse him from involvement."[144] Rivkah then outlines how women should coax their husbands toward piety and good deeds. She closes with this instruction: "Every pious woman should remember this, and should make sure that her husband is involved only in very good deeds."[145] Notwithstanding the intellectual and spiritual qualities Rivkah ascribes to Deborah, her modesty is elevated as her essential characteristic.

In another passage Rivkah discusses Deborah as a teacher, and explains that respectable women "should associate only with pious people and should accustom herself to read Yiddish books. If she cannot read then she should listen to others read or listen to sermons, as we find with Deborah the prophetess, who said: 'My heart is with Israel's leaders.' This means my heart is attached to the scholars of Israel. She was privileged that the salvation of Israel occurred through her, because she favored scholars."[146]

In this early modern literature, we see a bricolage of previous interpretations with new emphases, some subversive and others that reinforce earlier explanations. Deborah is a prophet, and doubts that women may be imbued with this capacity are not raised in this literature. She is a judge, but a notably modest one. Deborah is a prophet of equal caliber to Moses, perhaps on account of their deep modesty. She also models how to support Torah scholars. Drawing on these varied abilities, Deborah is viewed as a woman who exercised agency while becoming an idealized wife and community member. It is also crucial to note what this portrait of Deborah omits: Here she is neither a community leader, nor great scholar, nor judge; thus the rabbis ultimately succeeded in their attempts to tame her.

Deborah and Jael are also commemorated in another register in early modern Germany, specifically on tombstones. In this case they are included in a variety of formulaic epitaphs. By the eighteenth century, Deborah was most frequently mentioned in a series of biblical women to whom the deceased was compared: "Her wares were fine; she was modest as Deborah" (*ta'amah ki tov sahra, tsnua haita keDevorah*).[147] This laudatory couplet succinctly conveys the joining of modesty and engagement in the public sphere. Here, Deborah is envisioned as an unassuming merchant rather than a teacher. This is a further evolution, following the transition that we saw in medieval sources, where she was depicted as a teacher rather than a judge. The equivalence among rabbis, community leaders, and benefactors that was articulated in select medieval texts may have been a catalyst for this further transformation.

However, this is just one of a number of formulas. On tombstones that have survived from early modern Frankfurt am Main, women are described as having scrupulously observed the commandments, as Rebecca and Deborah[148] or Hannah and Deborah did.[149] A gravestone from early eighteenth-century Schmalkalden memorializes a woman (whose name is not legible) as having observed the so-called women's commandments (see Chapter 1) as Deborah did.[150] A grave marker from Worms (1683) describes Nuha b. Judah as resembling Eve, Sarah, Rebecca, and Deborah in her admirable traits.[151] Various tombstones from eighteenth-century Hamburg Altona compare the deceased to Deborah, specifying yet other qualities: One woman is portrayed as having been modest and fine;[152] another as knowledgeable, educated, and articulate;[153] one more as sitting home and preparing wicks;[154] and three others with the formula noted earlier, "Her wares were fine; she was modest as Deborah."[155]

Jael is also mentioned, albeit on fewer stones: Giodkhen, daughter of Abraham Joseph and wife of Yishai Landau, from Frankfurt (d. 1605), is remembered as a "decent woman, like Jael the wife of Heber the Kenite";[156] Beila b. Naftali of Hamburg-Altona (d. 1700) is described as being like the wife of Heber, the pride of her husband and their home. She is even likened to a peg that anchored her house.[157] The "wife of Heber" refers to Godlen b. Yehiel (Frankfurt am Main, d. 1622), who went to synagogue daily, morning and evening;[158] as well as Schonlein b. Shlomo (Frankfurt am Main, d. 1628)[159] and Malka b. Zanvil (Frankfurt am Main, d. 1741).[160]

If we view these early modern exemplars as an outcome of the development of the interpretations of Deborah and Jael during the medieval period, we can see how these biblical personae continued to serve as models for women who were religious models and leaders despite the efforts to "tame" them. The changes in emphases expand our understanding of the adaptation of each figure in different times and places. When examining exegesis, comparisons with Christian interpretations reveal shared perspectives alongside inter-religious polemics over time. When we look at women's daily praxis, a spectrum of portraits arises. In some cases they were depicted as pious, God-fearing women who observed commandments associated specifically with women or with all Jews. In many sources the figure of Deborah was identified with public female roles, including those of nuns, teachers, and merchants, but not judges. Thus, each religion reinterpreted the positions of judge and prophet according to its cultural standards in medieval northern Europe.[161] I understand the position of the Bible and biblical models to be of cardinal importance for explaining this reshaping of societal norms. Rabbis who sought to modify contemporary practice retold this narrative from the Book of Judges to redirect their conventional thought. At the same time, other men and women cited the figure of Deborah, and to a lesser extent Jael, to define current observance. Despite all efforts to domesticate or diminish her public persona, Deborah persisted as a judge.

Women as Fiscal Agents

Charitable like Abigail

4

Here a woman of valor [Prov. 31:10] is buried.
Charitable like Abigail,
She saw her business thrive.
She was modest like Deborah,
All her deeds were pleasant.
All glorious is the King's daughter within the palace [Ps. 45:14].
All her days she walked on the path of righteousness,
She observed the commandments day and night.
She went to synagogue and prayed earnestly.

—Epitaph, seventeenth-century Worms

These lines constitute one of a number of common formulas that appeared on the tombstones of Jewish women in early modern and modern Germany.[1] Using phrases from the "woman of valor" (*eshet hayil*; Prov. 31), among other biblical references, the deceased and her pious actions are praised.[2] The previous chapter discussed the paths by which Deborah became lauded as "modest." This chapter considers the figure of Abigail, who is praised here as "charitable" (*tzedaka 'asta keAvigail*). How did Abigail become identified with charity? As in the other chapters of this book, I will trace her figure, beginning with the Bible through medieval and early modern Ashkenaz. This tombstone is admittedly late relative to the period that is the focus of this study. However, as I will demonstrate, this formula is explicitly referenced in medieval texts and as a result provides a prism through which the practice of charity by women in medieval times may be understood.

As a prelude to this discussion of Abigail, a comment on research into medieval charity and women's engagement in this religious practice is necessary. Charitable giving among medieval Jews has recently garnered attention from a number of scholars. In his study of charity, as featured in documents from the Cairo Geniza, Mark Cohen has noted the difficulty of locating any mention of women. He acknowledges that this challenge is compounded by the social norm in Muslim culture which refrained from recording women's names as a sign of respect for their modesty.[3] The sources from medieval Ashkenaz that discuss charity are relatively scarce, and those that mention women are truly rare.[4] As such, this chapter provides an example of how by following a biblical figure, a practice can be better understood.

▪ Biblical Abigail

Abigail is the only woman described explicitly in the Bible as both beautiful and intelligent.[5] She is introduced in 1 Samuel 25 as part of the narrative concerning David's rise to kingship at the point when David, having been anointed by Samuel, is on the run from Saul. David demands a "protection fee" of sorts from Abigail's husband, Nabal, in return for guarding his herd, but Nabal, who is described as "a hard man and an evil doer," refuses. After being informed of this exchange by a servant, Abigail gathers a vast store of food, which she covertly delivers to David. During their encounter, Abigail begs David to spare her husband's life, predicts David's future success, and asks him to remember her once his reign is secured. Nabal subsequently dies a sudden (but natural) death, and the chapter ends with David summoning Abigail to become his wife.[6] The biblical text makes no mention of Abigail after this sequence of events, and her son, Chileab, is spoken of unremarkably as one of David's offspring.[7]

As numerous biblical scholars have remarked, Abigail is depicted in positive if not effusive terms. For our purposes the Bible does not present Abigail as performing acts of charity; rather, she acceded to David's demands, supplying him with an immense quantity of food. Retellings from late antiquity cast a more ambiguous light on Abigail's character.[8] As in the case of Deborah, the most significant mention of Abigail in rabbinic sources from late antiquity appears in Tractate Megillah (Babylonian Talmud), where she is listed as one of the seven female prophets.[9] Her prophetic nature is demonstrated by her foresight: She predicted both her husband's death and David's reign as king.[10] This explanation corresponds with early Christian exegesis on Abigail, where her very name is interpreted as "one whose father rejoiced in her" due to her prophetic acumen.[11]

Along with this positive assessment of her prophetic ability, the Talmud also presents Abigail in an ambiguous light. A fresh interpretation of the biblical verse, "And so it was, as she rode her ass and came down by the covert [*seter*] of the mountain" (1 Sam. 25:20), focuses on Abigail's journey from her husband's house to deliver food to David's camp: "It should say 'from the mountain.' Rabbah b. Samuel said: This means that she came in reference to the blood that came from her hidden parts [*setarim*]. She brought blood and showed it to him."[12] The Talmud depicts Abigail as engaged in a battle of wits with David after having defied her husband's orders. She presents David with menstrual blood, asking for his ruling on whether it renders her ritually impure (*niddah*). "He said to her: 'Should blood be shown at night?' She replied: 'Are capital cases tried at night?' He said to her: 'He [Nabal] is a rebel against the king and no trial is required for him.' She replied: 'Saul is still alive, and your fame has not yet spread through the world.'" This exchange is meant to exhibit Abigail's wisdom. She raises the fraught topic of menstrual blood in her conversation with David, one that may be considered inappropriate for a married woman to discuss with a stranger, although King David is reputed as an authority on menstrual purity elsewhere in the Talmud.[13] This interaction leads David to recognize that he cannot kill Nabal without having blood on his hands.[14] In this way the Talmud fills in the lines between the biblical verses, providing the background for David's pronouncement: "Then he said to her, 'Blessed be thy discretion and blessed be thou, thou hast kept me this day from blood guilt [*damim*]'" (1 Sam. 25:33).

The talmudic interpretation continues: "The term *damim* [blood guilt] is in the plural form, to indicate two types of blood. This passage teaches that she bared her thigh, and he traveled three parasangs by its light [out of desire for her]." The Talmud expands the biblical story to explain the remainder of David and Abigail's conversation as it appears in the Bible. The sight of Abigail with her thigh bared tempted David to such an extent that he traveled by the power of that sexual attraction:[15] "'Listen to me.' She replied: 'Let *this* not be a stumbling block for you.' [1 Sam. 25: 31] The word 'this' implies that something else would be, and so it was eventually. Meaning what? The incident with Bathsheba that came to pass."[16] The Talmud suggests that Abigail resisted David's sexual overtures and warned him against making the mistake with her that he would commit in the future, for as a prophet she predicted his sin with Bathsheba.[17] Thus she counseled him to avoid adultery and overcome his attraction to her.

Although the passage includes a nod to Abigail's wisdom, it is less than complimentary: As a married woman who tries to entice David and discusses discreet matters related to menstrual blood with him, albeit for a just end, she falls short of her untarnished depiction in the Bible. Moreover, the talmudic conclusion of this David-Abigail encounter is undeniably pejorative: "Upon leaving, she said to him: 'And when the Lord has prospered, my lord, remember your maid' [1 Sam. 25:31]. R. Nahman said: 'This bears out the popular saying, "While a woman talks, she spins." Some adduce the adage: 'The goose stoops as it walks along, but its eyes see far and wide.'"[18] Here Abigail's request that David remember her when he becomes successful is interpreted as a negative comment on women who look out for their own interests, scheming for a future spouse while still married, much as geese gaze sideways while walking in a straight line.[19] Overall, this is not an especially positive portrayal of Abigail, despite the credit she receives for being wise and prophetic.

Abigail: Charitable Against Her Husband's Will

Like Deborah, Abigail, too, evolves within medieval commentaries. Early medieval midrashim material present Abigail as morally sound, at least with regard to her union with David. One midrash emphasizes that she conceived her son three months after Nabal's death (following the Jewish law restrictions for widows, who are not permitted to remarry within the first three months of a husband's death) and suggests that her son's name Chileab (*ke-le-av*), meaning "he resembles his father," supports this view, indicating this son resembled his father, David.[20]

The Gaonic midrash on the biblical prophetic books, *Midrash Shmuel*, cites the Talmud verbatim and explains the two alternate spellings of Abigail's name that appear in the Bible, where once her name is given as Abigail (1 Sam. 25:1) and once as Abigal (1 Sam. 25:32). The midrash explains that her name was shortened because she set her sights on David while she was still married to Nabal.[21] A more positive view of Abigail is presented in *Midrash Tadshe*, dated to circa 1000, a collection that was well known in medieval Europe. In this midrash, Abigail is consistently referred to as a righteous foremother and prophet.[22] *Midrash Shoher Tov*, a midrashic collection on Psalms that has been dated to the Gaonic period (at the earliest) but which was copied in medieval Ashkenaz, so parts of it may actually reflect that later period, also discusses Abigail.[23] In this source she is praised as an exemplar of a good wife who increases her husband's spiritual well-being. David's redemption from sin stemmed from her advice, as an explanation of the word *mahalat* (in Ps. 53) states: "Abigail was better for David than any sacrifice in the world [could have been], for if he had behaved toward Nabal as he had intended, all the sacrifices in the world could not have atoned for his deed; rather she came and redeemed him."[24] This exegete is playing with the Hebrew root *m-h-l* (meaning "to forgive" or "to condone") to explain that Abigail's deeds helped David to avoid sin. This favorable assessment of Abigail's character can be seen as a foreshadowing of how her image would be assessed by Ashkenazic scholars—exegetes and halakhic authorities alike.

As we turn to medieval Ashkenaz, Abigail is seldom mentioned in biblical commentaries. Those biblical and talmudic commentaries that discuss her express a novel view of her character that diverges from the Talmud. Joseph Kara (ca. 1100) stated that Abigail was intelligent enough to mitigate the evil that Nabal carried out: "Because this woman was wise and clever in all areas, she knew how to repair whatever he ruined."[25] The Tosafist commentary on Tractate Megillah,[26] written in the thirteenth century, responds to the talmudic assertion that Abigail played the seductress with David: "It is difficult to grasp how this righteous woman [*tzadikit* or *tzadeket*] might have acted thus."[27] How then is she connected to charitable practice?

Charity and Consent

Halakhic deliberations on married women's agency with respect to charitable contributions, a topic often appended to broader discussions of married women's financial independence, are closely related to how medieval commentators portrayed Abigail.[28] In Tractate Bava Kama, the Babylonian Talmud permits women to unilaterally sell a "small amount" (*davar mu'at*) in business transactions. By extension, this logic was applied to charity collections from women: "Charity collectors may accept small items from them [women, minors, and slaves], but not large items." The Talmud continues with a story: "Ravina once came to the city of Mahuza, and the housewives of Mahuza came before him casting their chains and bracelets, which he accepted. Rabbah Tosfa'ah said to Ravina: 'Is it not taught: "Charity collectors may accept small items from them [women, minors, and slaves], but not large items"?' He, however, said to him: 'These objects are considered small amounts among the people of Mahuza.' "[29] This talmudic vignette confirms the principle that married women had license to contribute only small amounts while also raising the issue of relative value.

Hebrew texts from medieval Ashkenaz (primarily halakhic responsa, but also narrative and exempla) suggest that women were intensely involved in family finances.[30] Women were active participants in the monetary exchange system and often made autonomous decisions.[31] Twelfth-century sources from Germany and northern France discuss women who engaged in business, both with family members and independently. Women are also mentioned as having engaged in trade as fully authorized proxies when their husbands were on the road and as having traveled beyond the bounds of their home cities for their own economic pursuits.[32]

Some medieval scholars explicitly detailed the range of women's commerce, starting with Eliezer b. Nathan (Ra'avan; first half of twelfth century), who wrote that women "in our times (*haidna*) give and take, lend and borrow, pay and are paid, deposit and receive money."[33] His statement has been read as evidence of the extraordinary agency women had within the realm of medieval commerce. Most relevant for our inquiry, Ra'avan built on this reality and asserted that, just as they took part in business without restraint, married women could freely give charity: "From women (as opposed to minors and slaves), they (charity collectors) take even large sums, for they act as their husbands' agents."[34] Ra'avan's words articulated the norms of his era. He acknowledged that the current practices "in our time" (*haidna*) differed from previous generations, for women acted as partners in their husbands' businesses and they were authorized in commercial and charitable matters. While it seems that everything they did was assumed to have been with the consent of their husbands, the sources indicate that some women had a remarkable degree of economic agency.[35]

In contrast to Ra'avan, numerous thirteenth-century rabbinic authorities stipulated that women could not conduct business or donate charity without their husbands' consent, and this became the prevailing opinion over time. Despite their knowledge of Ra'avan's teaching, those later rabbis did not quote his position. Rather than emphasize the distance in time and perspective between their era and late antiquity, those medieval authorities applied talmudic principles to their communities.[36] By way of illustration, in his *Sefer Or Zaru'a*, Isaac b. Moses repeated the talmudic instructions for receiving charity from married women verbatim, without acknowledging the more lenient practices of his own generation as represented by Ra'avan.[37] This approach is also articulated by Isaac of Corbeil in his *Sefer Mitzvot Katan*, and from commentators on the *Semak*, including Peretz and Moses of Zurich, none of whom mention alternate positions or practices.[38]

Meir b. Barukh of Rothenburg and some of his followers also restricted the scope of women's fiscal activities. Meir curbed the reach of Ra'avan's stance by ruling that a woman's independent financial conduct was limited to the monies and properties she had owned prior to marriage. In *Sefer Tashbetz*, which is based on the teachings of Meir, Samson b. Tzadok (late thirteenth century) also reformulated the talmudic principle, stating: "It is permissible to accept small amounts from a woman, but only if her husband is not strict with her. But if he [the charity collector] knows that her husband is strict with her, he may not collect at all."[39] Asher b. Yehiel (Rosh), one of Meir's pupils, asserted that he was ruling according to Meir when teaching that women could be business partners with their husbands, but if they hired tutors for their sons or gave charity without their husbands' consent, neither their promises nor their obligations need be upheld.[40]

These attempts to limit the agency of Jewish women can be placed in the broader framework of women's economic roles in medieval Europe, a topic that has recently been subject to considerable scholarly attention.[41] As the late medieval economy shifted from a family-based model to increasing reliance on the authority and prestige of the men in a given household, the activities assumed by and expected of women were altered. As Martha Howell recently asserted with regard to the period prior to the late thirteenth century: "Hence, this was 'no golden age' of women's work if that is understood to mean that their work made women the approximate equals of men. Rather it was a moment in European history when the imperatives of the emergent market coincided, however unstably, with the imperatives of the patriarchal household."[42] The halakhic rhetoric from the late thirteenth century, which can also be explained by internal Jewish factors (such as a return to more stringent adherence to talmudic principles or a reevaluation of the difference between talmudic and medieval life),[43] reflects the transformations that were taking place in European urban economies in which Jews were participants.

Abigail and Charity

This is the social and halakhic context in which discussions of the biblical Abigail were introduced, where women's fiscal responsibilities were debated and ultimately restructured. Abigail is first mentioned in the context of married women's charity in *Sefer Hasidim* (a work of the late twelfth or early thirteenth century).[44] *Sefer Hasidim*, whose authorship is attributed to Judah b. Samuel, his father, and his disciple, Eleazar b. Judah of Worms, discusses money that is declared part of a *herem* (a compulsory collection within the

Jewish community) and rules that such money could be received from women, even if their husbands had forbidden such donations and had threatened physical abuse as a consequence:

> [In the case of] a man who is strict [*kapdan*] and tells his wife: "Know that if you give any charity, I will hit you or harass you." If the charity collector knows this and goes against the husband's wish, he should not accept even a small gift from her. However, if the community has declared that a certain amount must be given to charity and her husband ignores this ban, she should give and be blessed. [. . .] As with David who took from Abigail even though it went against Nabal's will for her to give [anything to] David, since he [Nabal] was an evil doer who did evil through his actions and his words. This corresponds to the spoils of enemies. And further, David did many favors for Nabal, which is why the lads told Abigail, so it was as if she owed him.[45]

The rhetorical strategy of this exemplum is quite complex. The first part refers to the talmudic ruling in BT Bava Kama (mentioned earlier), which confirms that charity collectors should not take money from a woman against her husband's will. In contrast, the conclusion overrides the talmudic instructions, even at the price of risking abuse from her husband. Most interestingly, the story of Abigail, Nabal, and David is presented as the proof text for this position. Just as David went against Nabal's decision by accepting food from Abigail, so too charity collectors can go against a husband's will, since a recalcitrant husband owes that money to communal charity. The discussion implies that charity of this sort was compulsory rather than voluntary,[46] analogous to Abigail and Nabal being indebted to David for his many favors to them. The Bologna edition of *Sefer Hasidim* substitutes for the longer explanation a simpler statement: "And David accepted from Abigail, etc.," evidence of a form of shorthand. The Bologna edition likely abbreviated the passage quoted earlier.

Moreover, this abridged version suggests that Abigail and David served as a code for an idea being conveyed in *Sefer Hasidim*. An additional passage affirms this interpretation:

> [In the case of] a son who knows that his father is so stingy that he refuses charity to the poor and [moreover] realizes that if he asked his father to contribute charity that he would not do so, [this son]

may petition his father for a large sum of money [with the intention of] giving to the poor [himself]. If the father is wealthy and does not want to act justly, he will be convinced that he [his son] is taking it all for himself and contributing as if it came from his own funds. So too in the case of a wife vis-à-vis her husband: [*Sefer Hasidim* Bologna, no. 315] if her husband is miserly but grants her an allowance to use at her own discretion, she should take what he gives her and give to charity. This is what Abigail did. She gave [a portion of Nabal's bounty] to David [1 Sam. 25:27, 35].[47]

Here a parallel is drawn between the strategies recommended for sons and wives, two categories of dependents that were featured in talmudic discussions of financial autonomy. In this case, *Sefer Hasidim* suggests a maneuver that enables women to circumvent their husbands' prohibition. Abigail is presented as an adept strategizer who devised a way to donate provisions to David despite her husband's refusal of his earlier request. In addition, she is once again referred to in shorthand, without retelling the entire biblical story, the assumption being that readers/listeners would know the story.

If we connect the content of these passages in *Sefer Hasidim* with the changing medieval views of women's agency in charitable giving, it is significant that this compilation was composed in the late twelfth or early thirteenth centuries. At that time its authors and other rabbinic authorities were advocating a return to talmudic directives, as part of a more general phenomenon that extended beyond discussions of charity or gender.[48] Situated in the environment outlined earlier, in which legal authorities were making it increasingly difficult for married women to contribute money independently, invoking Abigail as a model enabled women to give charity, with or without their husbands' permission. Thus calling on a biblical figure justified the promotion of a practice that was subject to scrutiny in other contexts.

A responsum by Jacob b. Moses Moellin from late medieval Germany supports this analysis of mentioning Abigail as a bulwark counter to other contemporaneous norms. Maharil was asked to rule on a case where the wife of a rich man gave money to charity; subsequently it was claimed that those same funds represented an outstanding debt owed to creditors. In their accusation the creditors argued that the money in question should never have been donated to charity since the woman's husband had not consented to her contribution.

In his deliberation, Maharil considers this case from several angles. He first raises the scenario of an elderly husband without sons, whose wife was tacitly operating as his deputy. However, Maharil concedes that in this particular case the wife gave money to charity in the absence of her husband's consent or despite his possible opposition to her actions. To reiterate his stance that women should seek their husbands' permission before dispensing funds, Maharil repeats the talmudic principle that women must secure their husbands' authorization before making charitable donations and notes that he routinely reminds women of this duty. Nevertheless, the overarching message indicates that Maharil opposes the return of these funds that had been given for charity. He justifies the contribution from the woman in question as follows: "Even if, God forbid, this all transpired because he [the husband] has a heart like Nabal the Carmelite and she behaved like Abigail, she should be blessed."[49] Here we see Maharil returning to the justification in *Sefer Hasidim* for married women who autonomously give charity, supported by the same biblical model. In this ruling, Maharil does not raise the possibility that the money in question might have been saved from the allowance she received from her husband, effectively making them her funds. Rather, he constructs an argument that favored a woman's decision to give money against the express wishes of her husband, in the hope that he would eventually change his stance and approve of her decision.[50]

Maharil's fifteenth-century decision articulates a biblical interpretation closely aligned with twelfth- and thirteenth- century rabbis and expresses halakhic reasoning that echoes *Sefer Hasidim*. He also seems to imply that women are inherently more charitable than men, a notion that circulated in a number of medieval sources, as in this exemplum from *Sefer Hasidim*:

> A certain righteous woman had a stingy husband who did not want to buy books or to contribute to charity. When her time to visit the ritual bath came, she had no interest in going. He said to her: "Why are you not immersing [so we can resume sexual intercourse]?" She said: "I will not immerse until you buy books and give charity." He did not want to do either. And so, she [continued to] refuse to immerse unless he conceded to buy books and give to charity. He complained to a Sage, who told him: "She will be rewarded for compelling you to do a religious commandment, and she doesn't know another way to [persuade you]." The Sage then said to the wife: "If you can find other ways to make him act righteously, you will have acted properly. But do not do it by using sex [for leverage]; this will only frustrate him, and he may start to contemplate sinning with other women.

Chapter 4

And by preventing yourself from getting pregnant, you will only incite him. "[51]

In this instance, the Sage offers different counsel to husband and wife, an indication that a conflict of interests between upholding the husband's authority without refusing the woman's charity is at play here. The Sage suggests that the wife is sending an appropriate message via the wrong tactic.[52] As in the cases that invoke Abigail, these passages stress that women should make contributions to charity only after having secured their husbands' permission while they urge husbands to allow such donations.

How did Abigail evolve into such an effective model for women's charity? And why did her identity as a married woman who gave charity without her husband's consent come to be cited as an exemplar at this particular juncture during the High Middle Ages? A variety of medieval texts demonstrate that medieval Jewish women gave charity to the community on a regular basis. They donated on the holidays, as part of pro anima practices and as part of last wills and testaments.[53] These texts do not indicate whether women received permission from their husbands for these donations, but in light of Ra'avan's assertions it is not unlikely that, during the twelfth and thirteenth centuries, Jewish women donated to charity according to their means and financial independence, often without explicit spousal acquiescence.

Following the halakhic texts quoted earlier, we have seen that the rabbis wished to change these practices, and over the course of the thirteenth century there is a growing group of voices stressing that women should not donate money to charity without their husbands' permission. However, this was just one set of opinions. The *mi sheberakh* blessing we saw in Chapter 2 that was specifically for individual women giving charity was first recorded while this change was under way. These halakhic directives in and of themselves are evidence of conflicting approaches. This is why some rabbis were trying to reinforce them, whereas others did not. In this case, it is also likely that thirteenth-century community leaders and charity collectors were reluctant to surrender charitable revenue from women, and so they sought a means to circumvent the talmudic injunction. Abigail was an ideal role model since she, too, went against her husband's instructions when she gave food to David.

This biblical precedent became an effective mechanism for countering the Talmud's more restrictive ruling, and more important, this tactic highlights the competing modes of argumentation at play. Whereas halakhic sources typically adhere to legal precedents, and their rhetoric suggests a diminution of the agency afforded to women giving charity, moral exempla (such as those in *Sefer Hasidim*) reveal another voice within this discussion. Given that the same authors often composed these two genres, exempla seem to have provided a register that made it possible for a different mode of reasoning to be voiced. Does this type of recourse to biblical models occur frequently enough to merit future research? Was this strategy particularly useful in discussions of women's practice? I return to this broader topic in Chapter 6.

Abigail in Medieval Christian Sources

Medieval Christian sources lend additional insight and parallels. Among Christian interpretations, Bede's understanding of Abigail dominated most subsequent medieval Christian exegesis. Bede (known as Venerable Bede [*Beda venerabilis*]; d. 735, England) presented Abigail as a significant counter-image to Nabal, particularly in relation to David, who is seen to prefigure Jesus. In this reading Abigail is portrayed as the "true synagogue" (*synagoga fidelis*), parallel to Jews who believed in Jesus rather than spurning him. While Bede and his followers did not develop the link between Abigail and charity, Bede made note of her righteousness, as did earlier Jewish and Christian commentators who explained that her father rejoiced in her deeds.[54]

Abigail was also praised by Peter Abelard as a model for a laywoman. When explaining the mercifulness of God, Abelard states:

> It is written that mercy is exalted above judgement and that judgement is without mercy to him that has not done mercy [Jas. 2:13]. So taking this to heart, the psalmist David granted the appeal of Abigail, Nabal's wife, and though he had sworn in justice to destroy the man along with his entire house, he showed her mercy and broke the oath that he had sworn. In this way he set prayer above justice and what the husband had done wrong the wife wiped clean.
>
> There is an example in this for you, my sister. . . . For surely God our father loves his children more than David loved this woman who entreated him and while David was known as merciful and pious, God is mercy and piety itself. Besides, this woman Abigail was only secular and lay, not joined to God by a religious calling.[55]

Although Abigail was not central in medieval Christian teachings, she appeared regularly in illustrated Bibles, where she is typically portrayed as an urban wife approaching King David, occasionally bearing gifts. Her clothing is not monastic; rather it is fashionable clothing worn by matrons.[56]

Abigail was also portrayed as a precursor to the Virgin Mary in the popular German composition *Speculum humanae salvationis*, which in many cases is accompanied by illustrations.[57] Her depiction as a stately matron (rather than a nun or other pious figure) lends authority to the Jewish interpretations of Abigail's charitable actions as those befitting a righteous urban woman, although this attribute is not overtly communicated in the drawings or the texts that accompany them.[58] In all three illuminations featured here (Figures 4.1, 4.2, and 4.3), Abigail is dressed in red, a color that is associated with respectability. These Christian portrayals, especially the image from the *Speculum*, all emphasize Abigail rather than David. This depiction may also hint at the importance of the female figures in popular culture. Additionally, in a manner that especially pertains to the Jewish commentaries discussed here, Abigail appears in the *Miroir des bonnes femmes*. She is described in this way: "Abigail appeased David; she showed how a wife should endeavor to protect her husband even though he is wrong."[59] This model corresponds with the image of Abigail presented in *Sefer Hasidim* and other Hebrew sources which depict her as the epitome of the woman who does what is proper, such as giving charity, even against her husband's will.

In the early modern period, Abigail gained tremendous popularity among Protestants and especially in Puritan circles, where she was viewed as a wise and industrious wife.[60] In his famous poem about twelve meritorious biblical women, *Der ehren-spiegel der zwolf durchleuchtigen frawen dess alten testaments*, written in 1530, Hans Sachs depicted Abigail as having good sense (*die vernufftig*) (Figure 4.4), a quality reflected in other contemporaneous works, including artistic images.[61]

These Christian perspectives on Abigail resonate with two features that were crucial in the Jewish reinterpretation of her character in the High Middle Ages: namely presenting Abigail as central in urban activities related to business and showcasing her as a woman who was sensible and knew how to do the right thing, even her husband did not. The Christian texts do not underline charitable giving, but the connection between women acting righteously despite their husbands and charity can be found in other Christian texts. This is a thirteenth-century Christian phenomenon that Sharon Farmer has called "persuasive voices," a reference to Christian preachers and

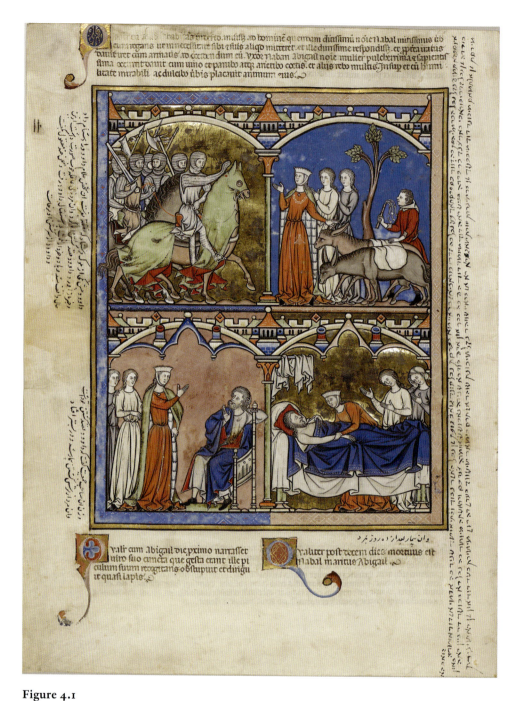

Figure 4.1

Old Testament Miniatures. Abigail beseeching David. She is portrayed as a rich woman accompanied by her servants. The color of her clothing reflects her wealth and social standing. Paris, circa 1250, Morgan Library M638, fol. 33v. Courtesy of the Morgan Library and Museum, New York, NY.

Figures 4.2 (*left*) **and 4.3** (*below*)
In both these depictions Abigail is
presented as a wealthy housewife, dressed
in the style of her time. *Figure 4.2*:
Speculum humanae salvationis, Germany,
late fourteenth century, Morgan Library
M140, fol. 39v. Courtesy of the Morgan
Library and Museum, New York, NY.
Figure 4.3: *Speculum humanae salvationis*,
Augsburg, 1450. Morgan Library, M 782,
fol. 68v. Courtesy of the Morgan Library
and Museum, New York, NY.

Figure 4.4

Abigail, among other women of the Old Testament, is portrayed as sensible.
Nürnberg, 1530. Hans Sachs, *Der ehren-spiegel der zwolf durchleuchtigen
frawen dess alten testaments*. © Trustees of the British Museum.

priests who strategically encouraged women to give charity, thus redeeming
their husbands' souls.[62] As the Parisian authority, Thomas of Chobham (c.
1160–1236) argued in his manual for confessors: "If he is avaricious she
should arouse generosity in him, she should secretly give alms from their
common property, supplying the alms that he omits. For it is permissible for
a woman to expend much of her husband's property, without his knowing in
ways beneficial to him and for pious causes."[63] Thomas concludes by stating:
"Therefore this ought to be the first and foremost concern of the priest, that
he instruct the wife in this way." Caesarius of Heisterbach (1180–1240) expressed a similar idea regarding women's willingness to give charity in an exemplum: "Priests are often accustomed to grant permission to wives to take
money from miserly and uncharitable husbands and give it to the poor."[64] We
saw a similar idea expressed in the *Miroir* referenced earlier. As with rabbis,
Christian confessors and leaders counseled the need for wifely obedience to
their husbands' authority, but they also observed that women contributed

more readily; thus they were willing to accept wives' donations in the hope that their husbands would change their minds. As did *Sefer Hasidim* and Jacob Moellin (Maharil), Christian clergy upheld patriarchal authority while providing a way to circumvent it, at least in the realm of charitable contributions. Medieval Jews and Christians also shared the conviction that women should be obedient and behave decorously (and charitably), when pulled between competing values and authorities. It seems significant that, in the mentions of Abigail in *Sefer Hasidim* and Maharil's responsum, the rabbis are advocating for charity that will be directed to the community, much as a Christian preacher or confessor would have advocated for his parish or church.[65]

From the Middle Ages to Early Modern Germany

Following Abigail from fifteenth-century Germany to the tombstone with which we began requires a chronological leap, as little evidence is extant for the period between Maharil and the seventeenth century. While early modern halakhic authorities endorsed the talmudic principle that married women should limit themselves to modest donations,[66] the figure of Abigail as a symbol of all women who give charity (not only those who acted against or without their husbands' permission) began to appear on memorial inscriptions.[67] An examination of the database wherein hundreds of medieval and modern tombstones from Germany were assembled by Michael Brocke of the Steinheim Institute[68] reveals increasingly frequent mention of the biblical "woman of valor" (*eshet hayil*) on women's tombstones during this period.[69] A variety of formulas including references to Abigail can be found on dozens of tombstones until the mid-nineteenth century, when the reference to Abigail stops.[70]

The tombstone of Dobrash, wife of Shlomo Oppenheim, from the early eighteenth century (1736), exemplifies this pattern: "The important old woman, Dobrash, wife of Shlomo Oppenheim. Here 'a woman of valor' is buried. She gave charity like Abigail, 'she perceives that her merchandise is profitable' [Prov. 31], she was modest like Deborah, 'her deeds were pleasant.'"[71] The epitaph continues, emphasizing that Dobrash[72] walked the righteous path and was modest as well as virtuous. It also notes that she was the daughter of an important rabbi, Yair Bachrach (d. 1702). The four-syllable

Figure 4.5
Tombstone of Dobrash Oppenheim, daughter of Yair Bachrach, d. 1736 in Worms. Dobrash is remembered as "charitable like Abigail." http://www.steinheim-institut.de /cgi-bin/epidat?sel=wrm&function=Ins& projekt=&lang=de&jahrv=1736-01-17. © Bert Sommer-Photos.

Hebrew pronunciation of Abigail (*A-vi-ga-il*) was advantageous for composing an epitaph that rhymes, since it matches *eshet hayil*. However, this is not the only way this name was used.[73]

This evidence demonstrates the extent to which biblical women were cited as role models when charitable activities (and other actions) of female community members were memorialized. Another case in point is Rivkah Tiktiner (d. 1605), author of a manual for young wives, *Meneket Rivkah*, who was praised with a comparison to Abigail on her tombstone: "'Many women have done well, but you surpass them all' [Prov. 31:29]: 'Our heart trusted her' [Prov. 31:11], like Abigail whose merit protected her throughout her life."[74] Tiktiner's book *Meneket Rivkah* provides an outstanding example of how biblical women were elevated to guide the behavior of female readership, as we have seen in other chapters.[75] Similarly, Moses Henochs Altschul Jeruschalmi's *Brantspigel* (Krakow, 1596) interweaves many biblical women into his moral teachings. Abigail features most significantly as the model of a

צרת בעל הבית וישתו שובתים מלוכה · כמרדכי היהודי ויסתר בת יביחיל
והיו שותה לבד והיו תובעת כוס של ברכה · כי לו היו נבל והיו עטתו עביגל ·

Figure 4.6
Abigail and Nabal are portrayed sitting at the Sabbath table, Prague,
1514. *Birkat haMazon veZemirot*, fol. 27r. Photo courtesy of Hebrew
National Library, Jerusalem.

good wife in the chapter on the reality of a righteous man (*tzaddik*) married
to an evil wife or an evil man married to a pious wife. He notes: "Like the
hated Nabal who had Abigail and she was truly modest in all her deeds."[76] He
goes on to explain this as the catalyst for David's words: "And blessed be your
prudence" (1 Sam. 25:32).[77] Thus her image grew from the prototype for
women who were so intent on giving charity that they would do so even if it
required defying their husbands' directives to the symbol of a virtuous matron, worthy of emulation in her charitable (and other) activities, even when
her husband wasn't as highly regarded.

This development is evident in an illustration in a booklet of Sabbath
prayers and songs published in Prague in 1514 (Figure 4.6). The page that
precedes the Friday night prayer for wine is illuminated with a depiction of
two couples sitting at a Sabbath table. The caption reads:

Women as Fiscal Agents: Charitable like Abigail

This is a picture of a householder [*ba'al habayit*] and his wife resting from labor [i.e., on the Sabbath]: Like Mordechai the Jew and Esther daughter of Avihail,

And he is drinking alone but she insists [that he share] the cup and blessing

As if he were Nabal and she were his wife Abigail.[78]

Once again we see a reference to Abigail and Esther as pious women.[79]

This view of Abigail is echoed, and her popularity underscored, in the early sixteenth-century composition *Many Pious Women*, whose author states: "There are still many pious womenfolk whom I have not mentioned such as Sarah, Rebekah, Rachel, Hannah the prophetess and Abigail [may her name be remembered for good]. I have left out these good women because their piety is known to children in their cradles. If I were to speak about their piety too, I would make a book that would be a load for a donkey to carry."[80] In the case of Abigail, by contrast with Deborah, who we saw mentioned in legal treatises, Abigail is more typically named in exempla; though, like other biblical women, she is invoked in epitaphs and popular literature. Our final quote refers to her as "known to children in their cradles," again implying familiarity with the Bible that extended far beyond the readership of formalistic rabbinic writings. This association of Abigail with a central communal practice further underlines the usefulness of making such links in everyday life. While we lack the documentation to construct an uninterrupted narrative of how Abigail was used as part of the rhetoric related to charity, the evidence assembled here offers a glimpse of a circulated image and the changes in depiction and practice over time.

A Woman of Every Season
Jephthah's Daughter

Everyday practices that were linked to biblical women were associated, as we have seen, with particular areas and times of life. Eve and the matriarchs became prototypes for ideal wives and mothers over the centuries, and the activities related to them were connected to the life cycle of birth, marriage, and death. Deborah, Jael, and Abigail were transformed to match aspects of women's roles in the public and communal spheres and were positioned within medieval social hierarchies. This chapter will consider how a connection was developed between Jephthah's daughter and the calendrical cycle, which provides an annual and seasonal frame for quotidian concerns. The discussion will focus on Jewish understandings of the solar equinoxes and solstices—phenomena referred to as *tekufot*, literally "circles" or "periods" in Hebrew (sing. *tekufah*)—which demarcated the four seasons.[1] The marking of these moments and the adoption of specific customs during their occurrence indicate medieval Jews' attributions of significance to astrology and astronomy.[2] In medieval Ashkenaz each *tekufah* was considered an ominous time, and as a result, Jews refrained from drinking water during the hours of the solstices and equinoxes. This chapter examines this custom and its relationship to the story of Jephthah's daughter.

Let us first consider this biblical narrative and various interpretations of its details. For reasons pertaining to the transmission of parabiblical texts, I will present Christian and Jewish interpretations simultaneously, and in the case of medieval exegesis from Ashkenaz, I will introduce Christian commentaries before their Jewish counterparts. After a survey of these exegetical traditions, I will discuss the custom of refraining from drinking water that was linked to Jephthah's daughter.

▨ Jephthah and His Daughter: Biblical Narrative and Exegetical Traditions

The story of Jephthah's daughter, who was sacrificed by her father after his return from war, has long been the subject of inquiries from a variety of scholarly prisms: hagiographic, sacrificial, literary, religious and, most recently, feminist perspectives.[3] The lacunae in this biblical narrative (Jud. 11–12), have invited generations of readers to reinterpret this story, by adding and subtracting details and shifting emphases according to contemporaneous needs and beliefs. The Jews of medieval Ashkenaz were no exception.

This biblical narrative centers on Jephthah, not his daughter. Subsequently, he was remembered as a father and military leader in the Jewish liturgy. When the rabbis in late antiquity determined the haftarah readings, they elected to incorporate this tale but, for unspecified reasons, they omitted its conclusion, which elaborates on the fate of his daughter and the ritual preservation of her memory.[4] Nonetheless, medieval Ashkenazic Jews, following other late antique precedents, were familiar with an augmented version of this tale, in which the daughter was no less, and arguably more, significant than her father.

The Bible first mentions Jephthah in the Land of Tob, far from his tribe, after being scorned and banished by his siblings. His kin then beg Jephthah to return and lead their fight against their enemy, Ammon. He agrees on the condition that his leadership be accepted by all. The Bible then describes the oath Jephthah swore before departing for battle: "And Jephthah vowed a vow to the Lord and said: If you will deliver the children of Ammon into my hand, then it shall be that whatever comes out of the door of my house to meet me on my safe return from the Ammonites shall be the Lord's and shall be offered by me as a burnt-offering" (Jud. 11:29–30). On his return after his military victory, Jephthah's homecoming is heralded by the unnamed daughter who comes out to meet him "with timbrels and dance" (Jud. 11:34). Jephthah is struck with sorrow, having been entrapped by his own vow. Before "his only child; he had no other son or daughter" (Jud. 11:35),[5] he declares that he does not know how to retract this oath: "For I have uttered a vow to the LORD, and I cannot retract" (Jud. 11:35). She acknowledges his obligation: "Father, you have uttered a vow to the Lord; do to me as you have vowed, seeing that the Lord has vindicated you against your enemies the Ammonites" (Jud. 11:36). However, she also makes one request: "'Let this be done for me: Let me be for two months, that I will go with my companions and lament upon [lit., down upon] the hills and there bewail my maidenhood.' 'Go,' he replied. He let her go for two months, and she and her companions went and bewailed her maidenhood upon the hills" (Jud. 11:37–38). Exegetes have been bewildered by some details of her plea. For example, how is it possible to "go down upon the hills?" Yet the closing verses of this narrative have posed the greatest puzzle. Upon returning from two months in the mountains, the Bible reports: "After two months' time, she returned to her father, and he did to her as he had vowed. She had never known a man. So it became a custom in Israel, for the maidens of Israel to go every year, for four days in the year, and chant dirges for the daughter of Jephthah the Gileadite" (Jud. 11:39–40). The biblical text does not specify Jephthah's action toward his daughter. While the implication that he offered her as a sacrifice is clear, it is not explicitly stated. Furthermore, no other source reports on this custom among "the maidens of Israel," an ellipsis that troubled future generations. Dismay at this human sacrifice and queries why Jephthah could not annul his vow provided additional topics for exegesis.[6]

One of the earliest and most influential reworkings of this narrative appears in *Biblical Antiquities*, which is attributed to Pseudo-Philo, a Jewish author in first-century Palestine. This text composed in Hebrew was translated into Greek and then Latin; only the Latin version has reached us.[7] This reinterpretation of the Bible was adopted and incorporated by both Jewish and Christian authors throughout the Middle Ages.

Pseudo-Philo devotes an entire chapter to Jephthah and another to Seila, the name provided for Jephthah's daughter.[8] By conferring a name on this young woman, this text acknowledges the significance of her role. Pseudo-Philo also expands the conversation between father and daughter. After Jephthah exclaims that he cannot revoke this vow, Seila recalls the sacrifice of Isaac and requests that he similarly make her an offering to God.[9] This interpolation is followed by the major innovation in the form of a dramatic monologue in which Seila laments her death as a virgin and the fact that she will never marry. She implores the trees to bewail her youth and her maidenhood, describing the bridal chamber and the garments she will never wear. In this source the underworld becomes her bridal chamber.[10] Pseudo-Philo also felt compelled to explain why Jephthah's vow was not rescinded. He claimed that when God recognized that Seila's wisdom surpassed all men and women and acknowledged her willingness to die, he accepted her desire and did not permit any sages of her time to annul her father's vow.[11] This justification highlights Seila and her character, rather than her father's agency.

The amoraic traditions in the Talmud and the Midrash also refer to the story of Jephthah and his daughter. The midrashic texts focus on two main questions: Why wasn't Jephthah's vow rendered invalid? And does a leader such as Jephthah, who was clearly inferior to other biblical leaders, merit respect? While the rabbis supported Jephthah's leadership and declared him qualified for his generation and, therefore, worthy of respect (they compare Jephthah in his generation to Samuel for his),[12] these commentators had more difficulty addressing the subject of Jephthah's vow. They declared his oath unfit, and they also state that Phineas the high priest should have annulled it; however, due to excessive pride, neither man approached the other to save Seila's life.[13]

Notably, the rabbis avoid the comparison between Jephthah's daughter and the sacrifice of Isaac. They address it only briefly in the Talmud.[14] Although both were offered up by their fathers, the precipitating conditions and outcomes of these paternal actions were quite different. Pseudo-Philo, too, recognizes this parallel and incorporates it into Seila's exchange with her father. She states: "Have you forgotten what happened in the days of our fathers when the father placed the son as a burnt offering and he did not dispute him but gladly gave consent to him, and the one being offered was ready and the one who was offered rejoiced?"[15] She objects to the sacrifice and declares: "But let my life not be taken in vain. May my words go forth to the heavens and my tears be written before the firmament, in order that a father not venture to sacrifice a daughter whom he has vowed, and a ruler not let his only daughter be promised for sacrifice."[16] Perhaps the rabbinic decision to minimize attention to this topic reflects an effort to distance themselves from the Christian interpretation that emerged during the early centuries of the Common Era and after the lifetime of Pseudo-Philo. Christians routinely made the analogy between Isaac and Jephthah's daughter.[17] Following Augustine, they depicted Jephthah as prefiguring Christ himself, for both figures were rejected by their brethren. Similarly, Christian commentaries presented Seila as the flesh of Christ.[18]

From Late Antiquity to the European Middle Ages

More than forty years ago, Margaret Alexiou and Peter Dronke identified the contemporaneous material reflected in Pseudo-Philo's recasting of this biblical episode and the textual traditions that this account of Seila influenced in turn. Their groundbreaking study traced these sources within the late antique Greek and medieval Christian frameworks through the thirteenth century.[19] Alexiou and Dronke first examined depictions of Seila in Byzantine versions of this story and compared them to contemporary portrayals of Epigone, Antigone, and Persephone, thereby considering the monologue in *Biblical Antiquities* within its literary context.[20]

Alexiou and Dronke devoted the remainder of their study to mapping familiarity with Pseudo-Philo's version of Seila in Latin Western Europe. A more recent examination of medieval acquaintance with traditions from *Biblical Antiquities* has demonstrated that this source was known in Western Europe by the ninth century, and passages from it appear in the writings of Rabanus Maurus (780–856). Both Maurus and Rupert of Deutz (1075/80–1129) refer to this later account of Jephthah's daughter.[21] Peter Abelard was among the first medieval Christian commentators to display in-depth knowledge of the story of Jephthah in *Biblical Antiquities*: This account is the subject of *Planctus virginum Israel super filia Jephte*. In this lament Abelard followed the account by Pseudo-Philo, despite taking certain liberties with this tradition. He too called Jephthah's daughter Seila and establishes her, rather than her father, as the protagonist. However, in contrast to *Biblical Antiquities*, where Seila and Jephthah each have a chapter, Abelard focused only on Jephthah's daughter, with little attention to her father. Like Pseudo-Philo, he concentrated on the wedding scene that would never take place and details the wedding garments that would not be worn. He extended the account by embellishing Seila's words to her father and augmenting the role of her virgin friends (from the Bible and *Biblical Antiquities*).[22] These maidens declare, "Girl more to be marveled at than mourned—how rare to find a man as brave as she!"[23] As in Pseudo-Philo, here too Seila compares herself with Isaac. As we saw earlier, in *Biblical Antiquities*, Seila states that her death will be in vain unless it becomes a lesson against such sacrifices for other fathers. Abelard's

Seila asserted that her death will have greater meaning than Isaac's, since God did not accept him but will accept her. Rather than decrying her death, Abelard praises it as a model to be emulated.[24]

Abelard expanded on these ideas not only in this *planctus* but also in his correspondence with Heloise. In his letter "The Origins of Nuns," he explained that Seila was a symbol of holy virginity who consecrated herself to God:

> Who would not consider that daughter of Jephthah to be a vine to be gathered in the praise of virgins? Who lest her father be held to account for his vow, albeit a rash vow, and lest the benefit of divine grace be cheated of the promised victim, urged her victorious father against her own throat. . . . Sent away by her father for two months in freedom at the end of that time she returns to her father to be slain. Freely, she betakes herself to death and provokes rather than fears it. Her father's foolish vow is punished and she redeems her father's promise, a great lover of the truth. . . . How great is this fervor of the virgin towards her carnal as well as towards her heavenly father. Wherefore deservedly this fortitude of a girl's courage by a special privilege was entitled to obtain this, that the daughters of Israel yearly assemble together to celebrate the obsequies of this virgin with solemn hymns and compassionately deplore her suffering with pious tears.[25]

Throughout his writing, Abelard emphasized that Seila—not Jephthah—should be lauded. Yet Abelard went beyond the shift in emphasis from Jephthah to his daughter. He altered the traditional approach, which counted Jephthah among the saints, and labeled him insane. He also innovated the image of Jephthah's daughter. She is presented not just as a virgin who died to fulfill a paternal vow but as a model for monastic women who devote their lives to God, a sacrifice analogous to death.

With this transformation of Seila, Abelard expands a theme first seen in the ninth century, when the story of Jephthah's daughter was discussed in conjunction with the dedication of Samuel to the Temple by his mother, Hannah.[26] The sacrifice of Seila is portrayed as proof of her father's authority and, consequently, the permissibility for parents to consecrate their offspring to religious orders without their children's consent.[27] The inclusion of Seila in discussions of oblation anticipates the direction Abelard adopted by presenting Seila as having devoted her life to celibacy and worship of God. This understanding of her fate is also evident in the two hymns he composed for the nuns of Paraclete, the lament quoted earlier and a hymn for the Night Office and Vespers that we saw in Chapter 3 concerning Deborah, which reads:

> The strength wells up in many women
> When the courage of men runs dry,
> Deborah the Judge is witness,
> The widow who laid low Holofernes
> The woman worthy of solemn Mass,
> The mother renowned of seven sons.[28]
> The daughter of victorious Jephthah
> Livened his hand to her own throat,
> Choosing death so that her father
> Would not defraud himself of grace.[29]

During the following years, greater familiarity with this image of Jephthah's daughter is apparent in texts from Germany, northern France, and (with a slight twist) Spain. Jephthah's daughter become a symbol for child oblation and, particularly, for women who devoted themselves to the church and called on Seila as a model.[30] Abelard's critical approach to Jephthah is evident in other commentaries as well as pictorial renderings. In medieval art, as in Abelard's writings and in other northern European texts, Seila is the protagonist, portrayed as a nun who dies by sword at the hands of her father.[31] Echoing the same tradition, the contemporaneous *Glossa ordinaria* depicted Jephthah's daughter as prefiguring the church, and identified the four days when she is memorialized annually in the Bible as symbolic of the four corners of the world and the church.[32]

Illustrations from the High Middle Ages reflect these varying interpretations of Jephthah's daughter. As Lois Drewer argued, portrayals of Jephthah's daughter as a slain nun were especially common during the High Middle Ages in northern Europe.[33] Images from France, Germany, and England all emphasize her death by sword and the spilling of her blood (Figs. 5.1–5.3). Drewer states, "Even when the sacrifice is represented violently, it can . . . be interpreted symbolically to signify a dedicated life."[34] These illustrations incorporate further allusions to the *Biblical Antiquities* tradition and Abelard's *Planctus*. Thus, for example, in a picture from northern France, circa 1250 (Fig. 5.1), flowers are shown bewailing the sacrificed virginity. These renderings also accentuate the killing of Jephthah's daughter by sword, and in some

Figures 5.1–5.2

Jephthah's daughter bemoaning her virginity with her friends on the mountains, and being beheaded by her warrior father. In the second picture one can see the sword dripping blood. *Figure 5.1*: Bible of Saint Louis (Paris, circa 1250). Paris BN Lat. 10525, fol. 54r. ©Bibliothèque nationale de France. *Figure 5.2*: Huntingfield Psalter (Oxford, 1210–20). Morgan Library, New York, NY, M43, fol. 14v. Courtesy of the Morgan Library and Museum, New York, NY.

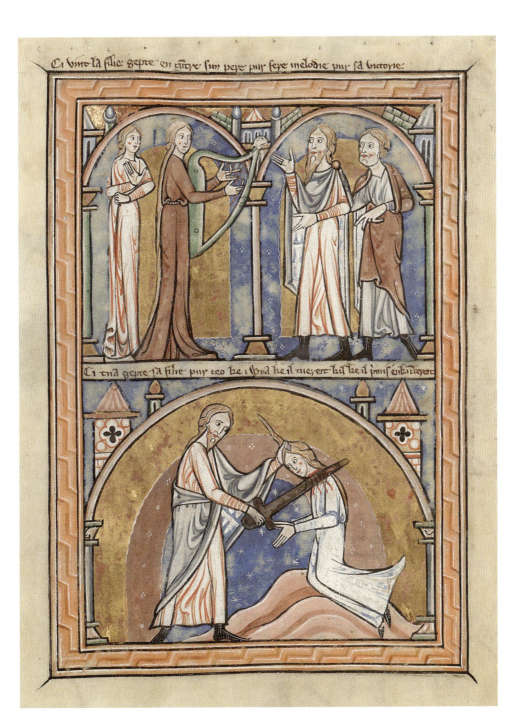

Ci tnd gepre sa filie pur teo he: kud he il eueye hil he il puis enkeraeyer

Figure 5.3

Speculum humanae salvationis. Jephthah slaughtering his daughter.
As is evident in the text below the depiction, she is compared to
Maria, mother of Christ. Germany 1380. Morgan M 140 fol. 8r.
Courtesy of the Morgan Library and Museum, New York, NY.

cases (see Figs. 5.1–5.3) with blood dripping from the weapon. It is impossible to determine whether Abelard's writings influenced this artwork or whether both stem from a common source.

In other texts, Jephthah's daughter incorporates visual motifs of the Virgin Mary, and her death is consonant with the purification of the Virgin. This is the case in in copies of the *Speculum humanae salvationis* (Fig. 5.3), a popular early fourteenth-century compilation, where the sacrifice of Jephthah's daughter is featured alongside the Virgin's presentation in the Temple;[35] the latter event was commemorated each February in medieval Europe, especially from the twelfth century and onward.[36] We already saw how central the *Speculum* was in our discussions of Deborah and Abigail, once again reinforcing the importance of the Bible and of biblical figures in lay education.[37] Following earlier picture bibles, the *Speculum* added texts and commentary.[38] This parallel furthers the association of Jephthah's daughter with cloistered life, since Mary, too, was elevated as a prototype for medieval nuns. Other medieval texts compare Jephthah's daughter to the Temple in Jerusalem.[39]

Medieval Jewish Retellings of the Story

Within medieval Jewish textual traditions, the story of Jephthah and his daughter receives brief treatment in the East as one among many points of contention between Karaites and Rabbanites. In contrast to the interpretations considered thus far which assumed Jephthah killed his daughter, the Karaites posited that Jephthah's daughter was not slain as a sacrifice; rather she was consecrated to God.[40] Among the Jews of medieval Europe, both options can be found, with the Ashkenazim assuming she was slaughtered and the Sephardim following the Karaite argument.

As noted earlier, in the West the earliest version of the story of Jephthah's daughter following the narrative as told in *Biblical Antiquities* dates to the eleventh century. The first Jewish text that shows links to this tradition is *Divrei haYamim leYerahmiel*, which has survived in *Sefer haZikhronot*, a compilation by R. Eleazar b. Asher haLevi (fourteenth century, Rhineland). As Eli Yassif has shown, the materials from the Book of Judges in this source are all based on Pseudo-Philo's *Biblical Antiquities* and were copied from a manuscript that included a book written by Yerahmiel.[41] Yassif dates this work by Yerahmiel to the late eleventh or early twelfth century,[42] when it traveled north from Italy and became known to various Ashkenazic scholars, such as Eleazar b. Asher haLevi.[43]

Yerahmiel, like Abelard, condenses the two chapters from *Biblical Antiquities* into a single chapter that focuses on Seila, with little reference to her father. Albeit in a truncated form, this version of Seila's speech provides a description of her dedication to God. As in Abelard's version, Seila announces that her sacrifice should not be in vain. Yerahmiel presents Seila asking the trees and stones to mourn for her and for her unrealized marriage but, as in Abelard's *Planctus*, rather than bemoaning her fate, she embraces it. Unlike in *Biblical Antiquities*, where Seila explains that she must surrender her life on account of her father's vow, which has ensnared them both, but expresses the hope there will be no future sacrifices, Yerahmiel portrays Seila as fearing that she is not sufficiently worthy and lacking any sadness regarding her imminent death. He quotes her statement from *Biblical Antiquities*: "I am not worried about death. . . . I am only fearful that the sacrifice of my soul will not be accepted and thus my death will be in vain."[44] But he does not include her hope that after her death no further sacrifices will be offered. Yerahmiel's Seila also compares herself to Isaac, and her father to Abraham: "Remember our ancestors and the father who offered the son as a sacrifice; for the offerer and the one whom he offered were accepted. Do thus to me, my father, as you have declared."[45] *Sefer haZikhronot* includes Seila's request for two months in the mountains and her soliloquy while surrounded by weeping flora and fauna.[46] Yassif observed that Yerahmiel diverges from the content of *Biblical Antiquities*, noting the addition of Seila's readiness for death.[47] The spirit of these modifications corresponds with the tradition conveyed by Peter Abelard.

The commonalities shared by Abelard's version and its Hebrew counterpart suggest a lost tradition, textual or oral, that was available to both Jews and Christians.[48] Indeed, Peter Dronke has suggested the influence of an unrecorded source on Abelard's writing.[49] Lack of evidence prevents us from tracing these strands from *Biblical Antiquities* through Byzantium to Medieval Europe; however, Yerahmiel's inclusion of these stories in his work supports the scholarly hypotheses concerning their transmission.[50] These texts affirm a renewed medieval interest in the Jephthah's daughter that stems from *Biblical Antiquities* while introducing new elements.

Another composition in which traces of Jephthah's daughter's story can be found are the Crusade Chronicles, written in Hebrew in mid-twelfth century. Jeremy Cohen and Avital Davidovich-Eshed have recently identified references to Jephthah's daughter as a cultural symbol in the chronicles.[51] Davidovich-Eshed analyzes the account about Sarit of Cologne, who was killed in Ellen by her father-in-law, R. Judah b. Avraham, in June 1096, lest she be baptized by the advancing Crusaders.[52] Like Jephthah's daughter, Sarit is described as a virgin bride, and Davidovich-Eshed draws parallels between these two women and the paternal figures who take their lives. She observes not only the significance of these slaughters by sword, but the decapitation of their bodies.[53] In sum, medieval Ashkenazic tradition portrays Jephthah's daughter as a virgin bride who was killed by her father as a result of a rash and immoral vow.[54] Like their Christian counterparts, medieval Ashkenazic Jews saw this death as worthy and idealized it.

In contrast to the interpretation found in northern Europe, Jewish commentators in medieval Spain, like the Karaites, explained that Jephthah's daughter was not slaughtered; rather, she was consecrated to God, like a nun. Modern scholars, too, have considered this possibility. David Marcus has argued for this approach, based on comparisons of the Jephthah narrative with other biblical and Near Eastern sources.[55] More recently Joshua Berman has traced this reading from early Karaites to medieval Christian Spain.[56] Berman has shown that medieval Jewish Spanish exegetes, including prominent figures such as David Kimhi, Abraham ibn Ezra, Nahmanides, and Abarbanel, transformed Jephthah's daughter into an anchorite nun. His work documents the influence of contemporaneous medieval female monasticism on Jewish Spanish commentaries regarding Jephthah's daughter.

A fascinating illumination based on R. David Kimhi's interpretation illustrates this understanding of Jephthah's daughter as an anchorite nun and conveys the complexity of the shared Jewish and Christian understandings of the story. In 1430 a Christian Bible in medieval Castilian was created at the behest of Don Luis de Guzmán. It contained a translation of the Hebrew Bible into Castilian, executed by R. Moses Arragel, as well as many traditional Jewish commentaries in translation, including that of Kimhi. In it, Jephthah's daughter is portrayed as an anchorite nun with women flocking to her cell four times a year. Similarly, Abarbanel summarizes the generations of commentators that preceded him:

> Since she was to be secluded [*perushah*] in a single house, without departing from that house for the rest of her life, she petitioned to go wherever she wished for two months, to fulfill her soul's desire for wandering and walking, since she would not walk or wander for the

Figure 5.4

Duke of Alba Bible. Jephthah's daughter portrayed as an anchorite nun looking out the window . This bible was based on Jewish interpretations, and this follows the Sephardic commentaries of the period. Spain, 1430. Duke of Alba Bible, fol. 187v. Photo courtesy of National Library of Israel.

rest of her days. This is why [she says]: "And I will bewail my virginity," for she would not marry and she also wished to choose her place of seclusion. And my meaning is that Christians [lit., the nations of Edom] have learned from this to create houses of seclusion: cloisters for women who enter them and do not come out for the rest of their days, and they never see another man in their lifetimes. And it does not mean that this custom was observed throughout the generations but, in her days, as long as she was in the house of seclusion, the daughters of Israel would go to chant dirges for the daughter of Jephthah, i.e., to talk to her and to chant dirges for her virginity. It seems that even those women did not see her, but they would go there and hear her words, and lament with her about her seclusion, or they would console her and talk with her for four days each year.[57]

In this fascinating comment, Abarbanel seems to suggest that this passage from the Hebrew Bible provides the provenance for Christian monasticism. Unfortunately, he does not engage with this attribution at length or on its implications.

Now let us turn to the medieval custom of *tekufah*, noted at the outset of this chapter. Following that discussion, we will return to the distinctions between Sephardic and Ashkenazic interpretations of the fate of Jephthah's daughter.

Tekufah: A Medieval Jewish Custom

The term *tekufah* refers to the solstices and equinoxes that were marked in all medieval calendric materials.[58] It is hard to exaggerate the importance of these solar occurrences in the medieval period, as the majority of ritual books include general instructions regarding the calendar and specific guidance regarding the *tekufot* (Fig. 5.5).[59] Many siddurim as well as specific calendric manuals include tables or lists of the *tekufot*. The prevalence of these lists in manuscripts points to their necessity. They were important for astrology, a central interest of medieval Jews for determining horoscopes and predicting futures, but also had implications for daily practice. A widespread custom among medieval Ashkenazic Jews was to refrain from imbibing water during the hours of the *tekufah*; therefore it was especially important to know its precise timing.

The water-related observances of the *tekufah* by medieval northern European Jews were hardly an innovation. The practice was already said to have been discussed by R. Hai Gaon (d. 1038).[60] Traditions state that he attributed this custom to the need to start each season with something flavorful; thus the season should begin with the taste of something sweet, rather than with a sip of water. R. Hai reportedly stated that he was unaware of the origins of this prac-

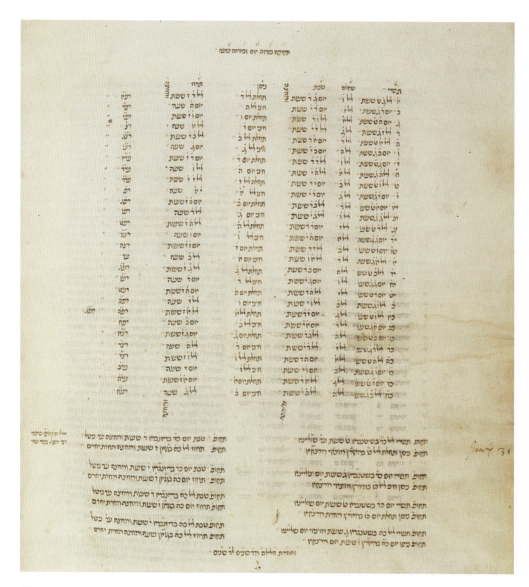

Figure 5.5

'Evronot. A Hebrew calendar noting the *tekufot* with the association
of each *tekufah* and its Christian date. France, 1418, detail). MS Paris
BN héb. 407, fol. 235v. ©Bibliothèque nationale de France.

tice, which he described as a tradition that was handed down by "the elders" (*zekenim*).[61] Other sources that discuss this custom suggest that "each of the four *tekufot* [pl.] has an angel assigned to it and, when one angel is replaced by the next, a person could be harmed."[62] This rationale was also applied to a related custom, namely, abstaining from drinking water on Saturday evenings before *Havdalah* (the ceremony performed to mark the end of the Sabbath) because a changing of the angelic guard was believed to be in process.[63]

While the *tekufah* is also mentioned in Spanish sources,[64] this custom was particularly popular in medieval Germany and northern France.[65] This practice is often featured in sources that discuss the spring equinox, which usually falls during the month of Nisan, since water was essential to the preparation of matzah for Passover during that season.[66] Consequently, the potential dangers of using water during this *tekufah* were often discussed.[67] Medieval Ashkenazic writers provide a novel explanation for the perils that would result from drinking water during the *tekufot*: During these four periods, due to the vulnerability resulting from the angels changing guards, water temporarily turned to blood.[68]

This transition in angelic oversight was only one component of the medieval Ashkenazic explanation for refraining from water during this time. It was also framed by biblical events in which water turned to blood, and among these Jephthah's daughter featured prominently. The interpretation of the different biblical events was a medieval novelty. In his twelfth-century composition *Sefer haKavod*,[69] R. Judah heHasid (the Pious) explains:

> Where do we learn about the four *tekufot* of the year? From the Torah. For we find:
>
> The *tekufah* of Nisan, how so? Because God decreed that the water of the Nile River in Egypt, that is, all of the water in the Nile, would turn into blood. Therefore, we observe the *tekufah* of Nisan.
>
> The *tekufah* of Tammuz, how so? Because when our ancestors were in the desert and water was brought forth, God said to Moses and Aaron: "Speak to the rock." What did Moses do? He hit the rock and water flowed. It does not say "water came out" [*vayetse*]; rather, it says "was discharged" [*vayazovu*] and the word "discharge" is only used with respect to blood, as it is written: "When a woman has a discharge of blood" [Lev. 15:25].[70] And the waters of the world were all turned into blood at that time. Therefore, we observe the *tekufah* of Tammuz.

The *tekufah* of Tishrei, how so? Because Isaac was sacrificed on the altar. And when Abraham reached out his hand and took the sword to slay him, the sword dripped with blood. Therefore, we observe the *tekufah* of Tishrei.

The *tekufah* of Tevet, how so? Because during this *tekufah* Jephthah made his vow concerning his daughter, and for four days during this same *tekufah*, the daughters of Israel mourned her. When Jephthah slaughtered his daughter, all the waters turned to blood, as it is written: "Every year for four days in the year" [Jud. 11:40]. Therefore, we observe all four *tekufot*. "And the Lord protects the simple" [Ps. 116:6].[71]

R. Judah's explanation for observing the *tekufah* was preceded, albeit in a shorter form, in the early twelfth century by the interpretation of one of Rashi's students, R. Jacob b. Samson.[72] Versions of it appeared in various medieval and early modern sources from Germany and northern France, becoming the standard among books and treatises concerned with time and calendars, as well as in custom books (*sifrei minhagim*) (Figure 5.4).[73] The fourth *tekufah*, that of Tevet, was linked to the story of Jephthah's daughter, and each *tekufah* was presented as one of the four days when she was commemorated.[74]

The thirteenth-century author of the addenda to *Mahzor Vitry*,[75] who quoted this rationale for the custom, expanded on this interpretation: "The *tekufot* of Nisan and Tammuz, when blood came forth from the water, are not dangerous. The *tekufot* of Tishrei and Tevet [the sacrifices of Isaac and Jephthah's daughter], when blood came forth from humans, are dangerous for the nations of the world. But Israel is safe, for it says: 'The Lord is your guardian, the Lord is your protection at your right hand'" (Ps. 121:5).[76] According to this author, Nisan and Tammuz are less dangerous because the normal source of water was transformed into blood, meaning that no person was harmed, in contrast with the other two instances. Other medieval Ashkenazic authorities assert that, if water was used for a good purpose, there was no need for fear, even during the *tekufah*.[77] However, the numerous texts that consider the *tekufah*, including those by scholars who rebuke their communities for unnecessary fearfulness, leave no doubt that many medieval Jews refrained from using water during the *tekufah*.[78]

It is apparent that, according to the accepted and popular explanation in Ashkenaz, Jephthah's daughter's story had a central role in the medieval understanding of this custom. The directive to remember Jephthah's daughter four

Figure 5.6

North French Miscellany. Illumination of the water in the Nile turning to blood in the month of Nisan. Paris, late thirteenth century. BL Add. 11639, fol. 309r. © The British Library Board.

days each year (Jud. 11:40) became part of the explanation for this practice; it entailed avoiding the intake of water during certain hours of the *tekufah*, which took place four times each year.[79] As Ernst Roth observed more than fifty years ago, this is a case of a common practice whose significance was augmented through this biblical interpretation.[80] But why was Jephthah's daughter selected?

This medieval Ashkenazic explanation for the *tekufah* is especially interesting given the textual traditions about Jephthah's daughter discussed earlier, where explicit parallels are drawn between Abraham and his son, Isaac, and Jephthah and his daughter in Christian exegesis, but less prominently in Jewish commentaries.[81] These two explanations for *tekufot* are suggested without any distinction in their significance. In addition, as noted in the introduction to this volume, the tradition regarding the binding of Isaac, which suggests that Abraham actually drew blood before being commanded to cease, was a well-known example of medieval innovation among Jewish commentators following the First Crusade.[82] This idea seems to have resonated with medieval Ashkenazic Jews, so that one can say that the textual basis for observing the *tekufah* reflects contemporaneous biblical exegesis and popular thought.

Just as the interpolation of the sacrifice of Isaac into medieval Ashkenazic writings during the years after the First Crusade can be understood contextually, so too can the popularity of this tradition about Jephthah's daughter. Certainly, the Ashkenazic Jews who idealized "sanctifying God's name" (*Kiddush haShem*) would have reason to recount and commemorate a father who slaughtered his daughter to fulfill his obligation to God. At a time when parents were lauded for killing their children to protect them from conversion to Christianity, this role model would have been particularly attractive.[83] Indeed, certain elements in the Ashkenazic explanation for avoiding water during the *tekufah* further support this medieval tradition. The Hebrew text concerning the *tekufah* stresses Abraham's sword, which dripped with blood and bloody water, a consistent symbol in illustrations of Jephthah's daughter.

However, as noted earlier, there is a key distinction between the depiction of Jephthah's daughter among medieval Jews in Germany and northern France and her portrayal among their Christians counterparts. According to Abelard and his followers, Seila was martyred as a virgin nun. Her virginity was central in Abelard's writings, and as such, he positioned her as a role model for women who, too, would devote themselves to God. This emphasis resonated in other medieval commentaries, which elevated her virginity and viewed her death as a symbol of ecclesiastical and Marian devotion.[84]

The Jewish sources that discuss Jephthah's daughter incorporate two distinct attitudes toward her virginity and her death. While the custom of abstaining from water and the explanations for this practice were popular,[85] with the exception of Yerahmiel's story and the allusion to her in the Crusade chronicle, Jephthah's daughter is not recounted as a prominent example of *Kiddush haShem*. Perhaps the qualities that enabled Seila to be envisioned as virgin who became consecrated as a nun and martyr also prompted a certain reticence toward her from the rabbinic elite. It is understandable that Jewish commentators—who, even if they were unversed in these specific interpretations, were well aware of the interpretations ascribed to virgin women such as Jephthah's daughter within medieval Christianity—would have been uneasy with this portrait of this biblical figure. The belief in Mary's virginity and, even more so, the call for celibate life among Christians were major subjects of fierce debate between medieval Jews and Christians. In fact, medieval Jewish commentators expressed deep scorn toward Christian understandings of and admiration for virginity,[86] and exhibited strong suspicions toward Jewish women whose actions were reminiscent of Christian nuns.[87] In the event Jewish women found religiously motivated chastity worthy of imitation, the leaders of the time did their utmost to suppress that inclination. Thus, admiration for Jephthah's daughter could potentially have undermined the distance rabbis sought to place between the beliefs and values embraced by Jews and those of Christians. Despite this dissonance, the death of Jephthah's daughter seems to have been sufficiently engaging on a popular level to sustain her association with the custom of the *tekufah* and its practical implications.

A brief comparison of the story of Jephthah's daughter and another popular medieval account of *Kiddush haShem*—"The Mother and Her Seven Sons," based on the story in Maccabees 2 of the mother whose seven sons were killed because they refused to obey the emperor, and then her own death after following suit—supports this suggestion.[88] Like the expansions of Jephthah's daughter, this tale reached Germany and northern France via Byzantine and then Italian channels.[89] Like Jephthah's daughter, who makes the analogy between herself and Isaac, this mother compares herself to Abraham.[90] This equation appears already in late antique texts, and the medieval versions of the story continue this tradition with the mother declaring: "My sons, tell Abraham not to be too proud. He sacrificed but one son, I sacrificed seven."[91] This narrative appeared in the Hebrew Crusade Chronicles, collections of stories, and in *piyutim*.[92] However, the tale of this martyred mother was far less controversial than the account of Jephthah's virgin daughter, for this mother represented the protective ideal of every Jewish woman.[93] Even so, the figure of Jephthah's daughter continued to resonate in medieval Ashkenaz, despite the discomfort it aroused.

One text that follows the standard explanation of the *tekufah*, while offering some expansions, seems to imply this unease. A Hebrew manuscript from early fourteenth-century Germany provides this explanation for the *tekufah* of Tevet: "The *tekufah* of Tevet. When Jephthah went to war and swore a vow to the God of Israel, he said, 'If God will make me victorious, I will sacrifice the first that comes out of the door of my house' [Jud. 11:31]. As he was accustomed to a certain deer coming toward him. God granted him victory, but when he returned from the war, his daughter came out to greet him. Since his promise was unjust, when he slew her, all the waters of the world turned into blood due to her sorrow, for she was bewailing her virginity. Therefore, we observe the *tekufah* of Tevet."[94] While this passage does not offer a new explanation for the observance of this *tekufah*, it emphasizes the source of this young woman's lament. Not only is she mourning her impending death, as described by Christian exegesis; she is also bewailing her eternal virginity. A Christian woman who elected to become a nun would rejoice at that pious status. The emphasis on mourning virginity, beyond echoing the biblical motif, also reinforces a dissonance between Jewish and Christian values. This medieval Jewish text accepts the preoccupation with Jephthah's daughter but distances itself from reverence for virginity.

As discussed earlier, Spanish Jewish commentators rejected the notion that Jephthah's daughter was killed, and they modified the Christian interpretation that depicted her as either an anchorite or a cloistered nun. The divergence between these views of the fate of Jephthah's daughter echoes a well-known distinction between the Sephardic and Ashkenazic Jewish cultures. As scholars have noted, Sephardic and Ashkenazic attitudes toward martyrdom differed throughout the Middle Ages.[95] Whereas medieval Ashkenazic culture promoted the exercise of agency in the face of threat, the Sephardic approach was more passive.[96] In my opinion, the Spanish scholars' dismissal of this Ashkenazic position is particularly interesting. In *Sefer haIbbur*, his composition on the calendar, Abraham ibn Ezra displays both his conversance with the Ashkenazic reading of this narrative as well as his vigorous objection to it: "I have already explained that neither Isaac nor Jephthah's daughter were slaughtered; rather, Jephthah separated her from the others, to sit in solitude and devote herself to God, like those who are secluded in their homes."[97]

Ibn Ezra also referred to this subject in his *Sabbath Epistle* (*Iggeret haShabbat*), a composition on the calendar and time which he wrote during his time in northern Europe. One of his goals was to better equip his fellow Jews when confronting adversarial Christians, lest they be considered a "laughing stock" by them.[98] Here, too, he derides the custom of refraining from drinking water during the *tekufah* and states: "And those who know the truth do not say that [water] will harm those who eat or drink it and the matter of swelling [as a result of drinking water during the *tekufah*] is the chatter of old women [*sihat hazekenot*]."[99] Ibn Ezra knew that the narrative of Jephthah's daughter was associated with the practice of avoiding any intake of water during the *tekufah*, and he scorned this custom. He decries its observers as adherents of the "chatter of old women."[100] Those "old women" allegedly claimed that drinking water during the *tekufah* would cause swelling (*nipuah*). Indeed, this notion appears in medieval Ashkenazic literature, including halakhic materials, without ascription to women or other specific sources but as a commonly held belief. For example, *Sefer Asufot*, a thirteenth-century miscellany from Germany, notes: "Anyone who drinks water during this time is harmed and their stomachs swell."[101]

The scorn for this Ashkenazic idea is echoed by R. David Abudraham (d. 1340), who wrote extensively on synagogue liturgy in fourteenth-century Seville: Paraphrasing Ibn Ezra, Abudraham describes this practice during the *tekufah*, which he attributes to Jews in the "West." He explains: "I have found written that one should be cautious when drinking water during the four *tekufot* because of danger, so one will not be harmed and swell up."[102] Abudraham then recounts the four biblical events (presented earlier) that purportedly caused water to turn to blood. He concludes by quoting Ibn Ezra and credits these ideas to "old women's chatter."[103]

As Ibn Ezra implied in *The Sabbath Epistle*, Sephardic scholars were not alone in their mockery of this Ashkenazic ritual; contemporary Christians also ridiculed this belief and practice regarding water during the *tekufah*. In his recent publication of various medieval Christian texts on the Jewish calendar, C. Philipp Nothaft demonstrates that many Christian authors were well versed in the computation of *tekufot*, sometimes referred to as *circuli*.[104] For example, John of Pulchro Rivo, a thirteenth-century German Franciscan monk, reports: "On these four 'cupha' [i.e., *tekufot*)] they [the Jews] are wont to observe certain customs, which are perhaps taken from their Talmud. He who wants to know about these [customs] should ask the Jews themselves, but few will admit them, because they are ridiculous."[105] In a different composition on the calendar, John further details:

> And they also find the exact hour of these "cuphas" at which they observe certain erroneous customs. For it is worth knowing that the Jews claim that any given thing has its guardian or angel . . . and during this change of guards there will be a short moment without a guardian. And because of this, they pour out all the water they have left in their houses at this particular hour. For they say that if anybody drank from it, he would become dropsical or die. And they conclude that it is for this reason that many Christians are dropsical but few or no Jews become dropsical. But they do not pour away wine or beer even though it would seem the same reasoning applies here.[106]

John is familiar with these "erroneous customs" but, interestingly, does not reference the biblical proof texts cited in the Hebrew texts.

■ Religious Praxis: Lay and Elite, Jewish and Christian

What can we learn from the connection between stories and practice, and especially about the people who heard these stories and observed these customs? In Ashkenaz, according to the rabbinic texts, both the rabbinic elite and the community at large adhered to the custom of not drinking water during the hours of the *tekufah* and based this practice on the four biblical events recounted earlier. However, as John of Pulchro's text suggests and some rabbinic texts hint, the rabbinic elite did not uniformly approve of this custom and, furthermore, some rabbis objected to the excessive observance practiced by both men and women.[107]

A comprehensive understanding of this custom and its explanations requires consideration of everyday life and practice. It is crucial to stress that water was not highly regarded as a beverage in medieval Europe, although it was in constant use.[108] As a beverage, water was used to dilute wine or beer. At the same time, water was also essential for the preparation of cooked foods. With respect to its sources, standing water was thought to be especially dangerous.[109]

Medieval Christians also believed that midsummer and midwinter (the solstices) posed great danger for water sources. Trachtenberg and Frazer discussed the bonfires and celebrations that accompanied these times which were intended to fend off the noxious dragons that purportedly inhabited wells and springs.[110] As one medieval Hebrew French source commenting on Christians notes, they (the Christians) believe that the demons that rule the water are at liberty to harm it during the *tekufah*.[111] *Mahzor Vitry* and R. Judah heHasid both infer that, since they fear God, Jews have no basis for fearing the *tekufah*, whereas non-Jews do have reason for concern.[112] Germanic folklore features practices such as covering wells and refraining from drinking their waters during the solstices; by contrast, on certain days, such as the summer solstice, water was thought to be blessed.[113] However, none of these traditions makes associations with the biblical events that Jewish sources cite to explain the *tekufah*.

In addition to shared Jewish and Christian beliefs concerning the safety (or danger) of water, Jews frequently made reference to Christian events and holy days when calculating the *tekufah* and ascertaining when it would fall.[114] Whereas many Jewish calendric computations described the occurrences of the *tekufah* using Jewish dates, some lists from medieval France do so noting Christian saints' days (Figure 5.4).[115] This is yet another indication of the pervasive observance of the custom and its importance for daily life.

One gesture Jews used to shield themselves from harm during the *tekufah* was placing an iron object into the water. As reported in *Sefer Maharil*: "One should take a new iron rod [in some versions, a nail] and hang it from a string into water during the *tekufah*, as is the custom throughout the world."[116]

Since antiquity, iron was reputed to have protective qualities, which could purportedly save lives and repel demons.[117] Medieval Jews offered a two-fold explanation of these powers. The first relates to the first plague on the Nile and, thus, to the explanation for the *tekufah* of Nisan. Since the Bible states that "there shall be blood throughout the land of Egypt, even in the vessels of wood and stone" (Ex. 7:19) but not in the vessels of iron, the latter was considered a protective substance.[118] The second explanation relates to the prophylactic folk uses of iron implements. For example, an iron knife was often placed under the pillow of a woman in childbirth, and postpartum women would hold such a knife to ward off evil spirits as they walked in their homes. They explained that the iron (*barzel*) would safeguard women during and immediately after childbirth because this four-letter Hebrew word formed an acronym for the four wives of Jacob: Bilha, Rachel, Zilpa, and Leah.[119] Such preventative usage of iron was widespread in medieval European society but was especially common among women, who incorporated such measures into their daily lives.

As mentioned earlier, Ibn Ezra and Abudraham both refer disdainfully to the observance of the *tekufah*, dismissing it as rooted in an old wives' conversation.[120] Perhaps the attribution of the *tekufah* of Tevet to Jephthah's daughter and her commemoration as the structural frame for this practice indeed stem from an oral tradition communicated among women.[121] This possibility would help us to reconstruct the actual lives of medieval Jews and, especially, women who commemorated Jephthah's daughter four days each year.

Approaching the *tekufah* as a female practice is congruent with another water-related practice. During the High Middle Ages, it was customary to avoid drinking water as the Sabbath was ending, for fear of "robbing" the dead of their water. However, immediately after the Sabbath ended, women would rush to draw water from the well. According to medieval accounts of this custom (which are in many of the same sources that discuss the traditions associated with Jephthah's daughter), these women acted in the hope that Miriam's well, which accompanied the Israelites throughout their years in the desert, would also cure their maladies. The same verse that explains the distinct qualities of iron (Ex. 7:19) is associated with this weekly custom. Israel Ta-Shma and Ephraim Shoham-Steiner have each discussed this observance in relation to leprosy. Ta-Shma has suggested an affinity between this belief in the healing powers of water and Christian associations between Mary and water.[122] Shoham-Steiner elaborates on another medieval observance that involves water in relation to mortality: After someone died, all water that had been stored in that home was discarded.[123] Most recently, Inbar Gabay-Zada has examined the traditions that discuss Miriam's well and demonstrated their affinity to medieval Christian customs associated with the Virgin Mary.[124]

Beyond these studies, I would emphasize that the figures who are keenly aware of the power of water and actively preserve these traditions—namely, the women—were responsible for water. Drawing water from wells was generally a gender-specific task.[125] Furthermore, folklorists have shown that many medieval female rituals incorporated water.[126]

The contrast between the Sephardic exegetes' approaches to the *tekufah* and the story of Jephthah's daughter and related Ashkenazic beliefs and practices allows a more nuanced comparison of the positions promulgated by learned rabbis and the realities of less erudite community members. Since Spanish sources suggest that Ashkenazic Jews were superstitious, their comments might also be read as indications that the *tekufah* was not practiced in medieval Spain. For this reason, it is particularly noteworthy that, when the Inquisition interrogated women who were suspected of Jewish practice, these accusations sometimes included observance of the *tekufah*. Such evidence suggests a stratification within medieval Spanish Jewry, a society that included members who shared this belief and practice, although perhaps without a textual connection to Jephthah's daughter. In both cases it was the women who carried this memory.

Early Modern Traditions

The story of Jephthah's daughter and the *tekufah* provides an interesting example of change over time. The *tefukah* continued to be practiced in early modern Europe (sixteenth to eighteenth centuries), and this custom appears in *Sifre Tekufot* (books concerning the calendar), often accompanied by a poem that summarizes the medieval reasons for this custom.[127] This is evident in pictures as well.[128] These illuminations vividly present the motif of the sword dripping blood, as in the example in Figure 5.7.

Elisheva Carlebach has outlined the early modern references to this custom and analyzed the connection between women and this observance. Some references to this custom underscore the significance of Jephthah's daughter, whereas others discuss the four *tekufot* as a group, without mention of biblical references. The changing attitudes toward martyrdom may have led to the diminished role of Jephthah's daughter in connection with the custom, which continued to be observed. Irrespective of its causes, by the early modern period, Jephthah's daughter became less central.[129]

In conclusion, this examination of medieval interpretations of Jephthah's daughter has enabled us to map her story according to the times and places where it was recounted. In medieval Europe, her life takes dramatically different turns. In Ashkenaz, Jephthah's daughter is believed to have been slaughtered by her father: Ashkenazic Jews focused on her death by sword and her sorrow over having been a virgin who never married; whereas Christians celebrated her martyrdom, which was equated with becoming a consecrated nun. By comparison, the Jews of Sepharad believed that she remained alive but as a virginal recluse. No less important, the exegetical contrasts be-

עברזנות

תקופה טבת מפני שחיטת יפתח את כתו שלאותו פרק נהפכו כל המים לדם

ה ניסן לפי שכל מימי מצרים נהפכו לדם ולקו כל מימות שבעולם

Figure 5.7
Sefer Evronot. Illustration of *tekufat Tevet* and *Tishrei* The top part of
the picture features Jephthah's daughter. The sword is dripping blood.
The bottom part features the sacrifice of Isaac. Germany, 1689. MS.
Oct. 3150, Fol. 19b. Courtesy of Staatsbibliothek zu Berlin, Preussischer
Kulturbesitz—Orientabteilung.

tween these religious cultures reveal the attribution of traditions to the "the
old women" who conveyed her story. It seems that the practices observed
during the *tekufah* were widespread, and its Ashkenazic adherents sought
textual justification. Here the choice of Jephthah's daughter is a telling example of the Bible's role in the daily lives of medieval Jews and Christians.

From Medieval Life to the Bible . . . and Back

6

I n late November 1196, a Jewish family was attacked by two "marked men" (*shnaim mesumanim*) who entered their home: The mother and her two daughters were killed, but her husband and son survived the attack.[1] The woman, Dulcia, was the wife of R. Eleazar b. Judah of Worms (known as Rokeah, for he authored a volume entitled *Sefer Rokeah*); their daughters were Bellette (age thirteen) and Hannah (age six). As a tribute to his wife and daughters, Eleazar composed a poem that is modeled on the "woman of valor" (*eshet hayil*) in Proverbs (31:10–31). Many lines of this portrait of his wife begin with opening phrases from those poetic verses. He then departs from that biblical framework and describes his daughters, outlining their everyday routines, including the recitation of prayers.[2]

This elegy to Dulcia was published by Abraham Habermann in his 1946 collection of narratives written in response to medieval Ashkenazic persecutions.[3] This composition received little attention until 1986, when Ivan Marcus translated and analyzed this work as an unparalleled homage to a medieval woman, calling his article "Mothers, Martyrs and Moneymakers." Since that time, this work has received frequent attention. Marcus's essay highlights three of Dulcia's central qualities as described in Eleazar's poem, for she was mother to three children, killed by Christians, and the primary earner for her family.[4] Judith Baskin furthered the study of this poem with her examination of Dulcia's religious practice and devotion to God.[5] Eleazar was renowned as the student of Judah b. Samuel heHasid (author of *Sefer Hasidim*) and as a key figure among medieval Jews who sought to raise the level of piety in their lives. Baskin presents Dulcia as the wife of this pious man, and as a devout and singular presence on her own merits.[6]

This commemoration of Dulcia incorporates several notable features that are useful for summing up a number of underlying themes throughout this study. Eleazar chose to memorialize his wife by comparing her to a biblical ideal, a woman of valor (*eshet hayil*). While this would become a common form of remembrance on tombstones in future centuries, it was not yet common in twelfth-century Ashkenaz.[7] Moreover, as Esperanza Alfonso has demonstrated in her analysis of commentaries on Proverbs 31, despite modern readings of this poem as praise for an exemplary woman, medieval commentators made great efforts to interpret the woman of valor as a metaphor for the people of Israel or the Torah rather than as honoring a specific woman. Some commentators disparagingly detail why this description could not portray an actual woman.[8] Eleazar's biblical comparison seems intuitive to modern readers, yet it is fair to query whether his choice was considered so in his time.

The answer to this question is complex. On the one hand, earlier medieval poetry about the "woman of valor" affirms this impression. As Yehoshua Granat has discussed, two known poems from the early Middle Ages are based on this biblical passage:[9] both speak of Jewish women in the abstract, focusing on their attention to ritual purity, the sexual pleasure that they experience with their husbands, particularly on the Sabbath, and their domestic responsibilities.[10] By contrast, Eleazar wrote about Dulcia as a distinctive figure, presenting her actions in vivid detail, but without any mention of ritual purity or sexuality. His "woman of valor" is highly personalized, unlike the prototypical tropes in earlier poetry. At the same time, in his use of the designation "woman of valor" for characterizing Dulcia, he follows multiple exegetic passages and midrashim. So, as scholars of the past, how might we understand his poem? In many ways this poem is both an innovation and a continuation of tradition.

Eleazar's poetic elegy is the product of tragedy rather than a standard tribute. If Dulcia had not been viciously murdered, it would never have been written. He eulogized his beloved wife as a multi-dimensional woman even as he situated her deeds within a biblical framework, effectively weaving this scriptural model into the lives of medieval Jews. Dulcia was neither fiction nor fantasy, but a real person who lived and died in twelfth-century Worms.[11] She was married to a leading rabbinic figure of her generation, a prolific writer of numerous compositions and commentaries. His poem depicts her as a vital Jewish leader who worked in Worms and in other cities. Yet, had her life not ended in violence, we could not expect to have any record of her life, unlike that of her well-published husband. Such anonymity characterizes the lives and deaths of most medieval Jews (and human lives at large). As the story of Jephthah's daughter teaches, it is especially difficult to commemorate someone whose name is unrecorded. Given that this book has endeavored to provide some access to those who are in many ways inaccessible, the case of Dulcia offers an instructive exception to the rule. In contrast to other medieval Jewish women and men who left little or no evidence of their lives, Dulcia can be contextualized and identified as a historical figure, thereby providing invaluable evidence of daily activities and communal frameworks.

Dulcia is described performing multiple domestic functions. As her husband's helpmate, she and her activities made it possible for him to devote himself to study Torah. He reports that she cooked for her family and for his students. She also clothed the poor, dressed brides, and prepared the deceased for burial. She attended synagogue daily, taught women to pray, and recited psalms as well as parts of the liturgy that were often ascribed to men alone. She bought and sold the parchment that was necessary for the ritual objects she also made: handwritten scrolls of the Torah and other biblical books, *tzitzit*, and *tefillin*.[12] Dulcia was killed together with her two daughters. Memorializing his daughters, Eleazar details their proficiency in domestic crafts (sewing, embroidery, weaving) and specific prayers. He also emphasized their piety and devotion to God.[13] Thus when we are introduced to Dulcia and her family through her husband's memorial poem, we also encounter values from her lifetime. These include spiritual emphases, such as the importance that Eleazar, and presumably their whole family, placed on "worshiping their Creator joyfully," alongside the daily activities through which they expressed these beliefs.[14]

Since the "discovery" of Dulcia, scholars have demonstrated the degree to which nearly all her regular activities have been corroborated in other medieval Jewish contexts, many localized in Ashkenaz. In some cases women were deterred from engaging in certain practices. For example, Dulcia's eagerness to perform commandments is illustrated by her seeking white wool so she can make *tzitzit*.[15] Halakhic authorities often state that women were forbidden from making *tzitzit*: Rabbenu Tam famously ruled that *tzitzit* which had been tied by a woman should be disqualified.[16] Dulcia is also described lighting candles in synagogue on Yom Kippur, a detail that spurred scholars to trace women's roles in producing and lighting candles in Jewish communal spaces.[17] However, when we try to generalize from the knowledge we have of Dulcia to other women, the overarching question is: To what extent she was exceptional? Throughout this study, I have suggested that the women who are reflected by these biblical models are more widespread than scholars have previously assumed. That is to say, much in the way select rabbis objected to women studying Torah despite the reality of female teachers, the paucity of "Dulcias" in prescriptive sources does not disprove their existence in real life. One genre that has featured in many chapters throughout this study and which requires further attention is tombstone inscriptions, for they depict women and men in a wide variety of roles.[18] This unique source provides evidence of actual people, and the ways they are commemorated reflect a far broader part of the community than select rabbinic writings, even if these epitaphs were crafted by those who had greater literacy. The variety of formulas on tombstones indicates a repertoire that goes beyond a handful of scholars.

Eleazar could have recounted Dulcia's personal qualities in other literary forms, and it was not obvious that, having selected poetry, he would follow the format of a biblical chapter. However, his decision to use a biblical woman, albeit a metaphorical one, as a standard—much as Abelard presented the idealized life of nuns to Heloise, and as the authors of medieval Christian moral literature and early modern Jewish writings for women portrayed biblical women as models for their lives—suggests a mutually held literary convention.[19] Throughout this volume I have contended that the Bible served not only as a theoretical ideal but also as a religious trove that was readily available when teaching women and, by extension, children and lesser-educated men as well as educated men, whether formally or casually. Given its qualities of familiarity and authority, the Bible offered potent messages that were central in medieval Jewish life in a way that has not been taken into consideration by scholarship.

The Bible and Everyday Life

The present study has also noted the numerous contexts where medieval Jews, men and women alike, encountered the biblical narratives. The synagogue was a central locus where biblical figures were featured throughout scriptural readings and frequently referenced in the liturgy.[20] Biblical narratives were frequently included in story collections.[21] One of the challenges of studying everyday life is probing beyond the written words that have reached us to the lived experience behind them. This obstacle is debated by social historians, who have applied various strategies in response, and the chapters of this book have attempted to present new vistas within Jewish studies for dealing with these difficulties. Nonetheless, written texts held significant roles in everyday life. Thus I have argued throughout this volume that the Bible provides an unparalleled tool for circumventing the limits that textual sources impose, as a written text that had a multivalent oral life as well. Once the Bible was read, silently or aloud, it could be contemplated, discussed, and repeated among less-educated interlocutors.[22]

As Beryl Smalley declared: "How deeply the interpretation [of the Bible] will penetrate language, thought, politics, and finally everyday life. The types are so real and so familiar that they may be used as arguments from authority, as well as for illustration."[23] The ubiquity of the Bible as a point of reference may be attributed to its pertinence in personal, domestic, and communal rhythms. As we have seen, family and social roles, life-cycle events, and the annual liturgical cycle were elucidated via biblical sources. The Bible was also crucial in relationships between Jews and their Christian neighbors, serving as a common denominator while simultaneously constituting a dividing factor. Referring back to the Bible as a proof text of sorts was part of a traditional method of explication, as we saw in the calendrical passages about *tekufot* (see Chapter 5): "Where do we learn of the four seasons [*tekufot*] of the year? From the Torah." This pattern appears commonly in rabbinic discussions.[24] But this was also a common way of explaining practical activities. For example, Eleazar b. Judah employed this technique to explicate numerous rituals as enacted by medieval Ashkenazic Jews, including the ceremony that marks a boy's school initiation and the wedding rites. In these instances he cites the giving of the Torah on Sinai as the precedent for these observances.[25] Such attributions are hardly medieval innovations; to the contrary, in the form presented by Eleazar of Worms, they represent a specific mode of explanation that originated in late antiquity.[26] However, medieval halakhic authorities favored proof texts from the Talmud and later halakhic compositions,[27] and referenced the Bible for rhetorical emphasis or to buttress their arguments when legal proofs were not available.

As the discussions in this book make evident, biblical models were also employed frequently in art and non-halakhic genres, namely exempla, liturgy, and exegesis; to some extent they appeared more in these models than in halakhic discourse, such as responsa and custom literature. Throughout this study I have aimed to illustrate the extent to which these narratives, all based on biblical models, are located in diverse sources, relating to specific customs and beliefs, thus providing wide-ranging evidence for their application to praxis. The inclusion of multiple genres in discussions of social and cultural practice allows a broader understanding of medieval Jewish life as we extend our focus beyond the longstanding reliance on halakhic literature.

I have proposed that, as opposed to the complex intricacies of medieval halakhah, the Bible remained the default for most medieval Jews, even if those with more formal education could counter biblical allusions with other authoritative sources. I am not suggesting that a quote from the Bible provided irrefutable evidence. As the case of Abigail illustrates, a biblical passage or figure was occasionally offered as validation in the absence of stronger evidence or to reinforce prevalent practices and beliefs. In some instances, the need for a narrative explanation diminished, and the biblical reference was gradually abandoned. This is a tension I have endeavored to balance throughout the book: the constancy of the biblical text and the dynamism of changing interpretations. Alongside the attempts to recast stories afresh, aspects of the biblical original remained or, in some cases, resurfaced over time. Deborah may have been tamed, but that tendency did not deter subsequent interpreters from restoring her status as a judge rather than maintaining her medieval status as a teacher. Jephthah's daughter received little attention in rabbinic literature, but the power of her story drew medieval interest, which effectively revived this narrative and its female protagonist.

Providing Meaning

I have argued that, beyond serving as a source for proof texts, the Bible provided social models for daily conduct. Decades ago, scholars noted the importance of biblical history in medieval chronicles; thus the medieval Jews who were attacked in 1096 attributed these assaults to their biblical transgressions, establishing a theological connection between themselves and their biblical ancestors.[28] This study has not investigated theological ties but rather analyzed how the social and cultural-historical roles of the Bible can be utilized to consider medieval Ashkenazic mentalités. Stories lent meaning to the social order, daily routines, as well as annual and life-cycle observances, and provided a framework for articulating beliefs and resolving tensions that inevitably arose. Robert Cover has emphasized the place of storytelling in legal sources, stressing how narratives give meaning to law.[29] Following Cover, Jane Kanarek has explained that "sacred stories undergird, shape and give authority to law,"[30] and I have sought to demonstrate that this same approach is applicable to social practice. As in modernity, those who lived in the medieval period sought ways to explain their beliefs and actions to themselves, and tracing the stories they called upon allows us to better understand their mentalités and the way they perceived the world in which they lived.[31] Although these tales could convey contradictory messages or highlight different lessons, as a corpus they were a means for developing self-definition and explaining actions and tensions.[32]

Modern readers have often had an anachronistic view of medieval Jewry, with respect to their social norms and their daily challenges. Despite the corrective that recent decades of research have achieved in countering the view of a steep hierarchy that was steered by rabbinic leadership, modern scholars' reliance on the sources written by those medieval rabbis represents a structural impediment to accessing other perspectives from their era. It is my hope that each chapter in this volume has allowed a glimpse of a more nuanced society, tracing a landscape that is more multifaceted than that which has often been envisioned on the basis of writings by medieval rabbis. I have endeavored to expose the numerous registers in which texts were interpreted and stories were told.

I have suggested throughout the book that stories went beyond setting examples that embodied the societal status quo. For those who seek to understand the world of medieval Jewry, they also provide a template for an opportunity to tune in to the soundscapes outside the study halls of the erudite. In Chapters 1 and 2 we saw multiple liturgical passages that feature Eve and the matriarchs. These songs and blessings were heard by all who attended the synagogue, and as I have argued, they were easily comprehended. A similar level of communal access and experience can easily be imagined with respect to stories being told, particularly by applying the advice that *Sefer Hasidim* offers to teachers: Belief should be imparted with biblical stories. This principle sheds light on the value attributed to teaching through narratives, an instructional method among Jews and Christians, especially for educating women.[33] This technique appears in a commentary in *Sefer Hasidim* on the verse, "The beginning of wisdom is [to] acquire wisdom: With all your acquisitions, acquire discernment" (Prov. 4:7):

"With all your acquisitions, acquire discernment"—For he [a child] should have a teacher [rabbi] who is knowing. And even if he only teaches him Hebrew, he [the child] has to understand what he is learning. And when he teaches him Bible, he has to arrive at the essence of how to fear God, such as honoring the Torah and learning that the Creator is in the heavens and it is He who gives and provides. And he [the teacher] should show him that God is in heaven and, when he grows up, he should teach him of the existence of Hell [*gehenom*] and Paradise [Garden of Eden], for the hearts of children resemble dreaming adults, they believe that everything is true. In this way, children believe that all of your words are true.[34]

While this is but one approach to storytelling, it underlines the importance of narratives as a component of education and a means for reinforcing the social order. Scholars of medieval Judaism have rarely taken these features of the past into account when trying to assess belief and practice, and have focused mainly on religious ideology rather than daily life. It is my hope that the examples discussed in this volume demonstrate the promise of this methodology.

This book has made the case that the Bible infused meaning into quotidian activities and also that daily experiences contributed to a more complex reading of medieval biblical commentaries. The latter point was illustrated in Chapter 5, where we saw three distinct interpretations for the martyrdom of Jephthah's daughter, according to different times and places. In medieval northern Europe, Jews and Christians alike believed that her father killed her by sword, but their analyses differed: Christians viewed her death as a model for women entering the convent, whereas Ashkenazic Jews idealized her as a Jewish martyr, a bride who died for her faith. By comparison, learned Jews in Spain explained that she became a cloistered nun but was not killed by her father, as a reflection of their different understanding of martyrdom; however, it seems that less-educated Spanish Jews, about whom we have evidence only of practice rather than interpretation, shared an understanding of this event with their Ashkenazic companions and also observed *tekufah* practices. Interest in this story lessened over time, as martyrdom diminished from the experience of early modern Jews.

No less important is the practical context in which these messages were conveyed. Daily activities of drawing water at four specific times of the year allowed a reinforcement of the biblical connection. Another such example that is worthy of further study in this context is the association of the biblical

Miriam with the drawing of water on Saturday nights, at the end of the Sabbath.[35] In both these cases a routine activity that would have taken place regardless of any biblical connections becomes a practice infused with religious significance on multiple levels within the Jewish community and in communication with the surrounding Christian society.

We have also seen that Jewish awareness of a competing Christian tradition of biblical interpretation could at times prompt polemical debates and at other times serve as a common denominator that led to the mutual sharing of ideas and insights.[36] It is hard to determine why one or the other of these two options was followed at specific moments and when medieval people preferred polemics over appropriation. In many cases, as we have seen, medieval Jews both appropriated and argued with parallel traditions. It is likely that seemingly shared interpretations were joined by subtleties that remain undetected by modern readers and also that polemic positions included some degree of shared interpretation. The presence of these resources—that were jointly held, as with many motifs related to Deborah and Jephthah's daughter, or strongly contrasted, as in portrayals of Eve—heightens the potency of day-to-day medieval connections with the Bible.

Women as a Prism for Medieval Society

The texts analyzed throughout this study, like the living exemplar with whom this chapter opened, all focus on female figures. Many of the practices discussed here were traditionally performed by women. As I set forth in the Introduction, this choice stems from the reality that women are a discrete social cohort: Being separate from the small, influential circle of learned men, women's lives provide windows onto other strata of Jewish society and their widely held beliefs. Moreover, gender roles in medieval European society were such that the men who left written records often distanced themselves from their female peers. In the texts that have reached us, this delineation is expressed in sharper terms than class divisions and, at times, religious differences between Jews and Christians. Without a doubt medieval life incorporated situations in which gender bore less consequence and others where it was a critical factor; however, the style and content in the corpus of extant writings most readily signal this distinction.

Yet in Chapter 2 we also saw an example related to the custom of praying beside gravesites. Rabbinic authorities distanced themselves from this practice, which they attributed to women and "men who don't know." The prayer that was recited in this setting relied almost exclusively on biblical figures: Abraham, Isaac, Jacob, Moses, David, and R. Akiba were invoked for the welfare of that petitioner's soul. According to this rabbinic critique, when "men who don't know" prayed, they prayed like women, a categorization that has parallels in early modern culture, when popular books were written for women and "men who are like women."[37]

The reference to women and "men who don't know" in this rabbinic responsum resonates with the Sephardic rabbinic belittlement of the custom of *tefukah* (discussed in Chapter 5). Despite having been widely observed by medieval Jews—men, women, and rabbis—this practice is labeled the "chatter of old women." Thus it seems that Jews who were not part of the rabbinic elite were more reliant on the Bible, and specifically biblical stories, than their educated authorities were. The chapters in this study also elucidate this relationship to the Bible. Women were often educated with didactic tales, and in turn they were also storytellers, as a range of the texts examined in this study have suggested. Women also participated in community rituals, and they heard and chanted the liturgy. Moreover, as I suggest in Chapter 3, they had a higher level of literacy and therefore had more direct access to the Bible than has been assumed to date. As we have seen, women who worked as teachers were not unusual. Thus when we focus our attention on women, their agency becomes more apparent, even though scant direct evidence of this social capital has been transmitted in written records. Following studies of medieval Christian women, we might also posit that Jewish women functioned as the repositories of familial and communal memory.[38] We saw an example of this in the *mi sheberakh* formula using the figure of the matriarchs.

By highlighting women's voices as a significant force in medieval Jewish life and as a portal to additional, lesser-known voices, I have sought to expand the range of lived experience that we can detect from the past. This is particularly significant as the discrete cohort that authored our textual records surely did not represent all Jews within a given community. If stories were shared by all members of society, we may logically assume that their telling varied according to the individuals or groups involved as presenters and listeners. Indeed, one of the most frustrating aspects of this project has been the awareness that medieval Jews were telling the stories that I longed to hear, coupled with the disappointment that their activities had not been recorded. This dissonance was the catalyst for a commitment to documenting what we do know, and to try to the best of my ability to "eavesdrop" on this lost world of stories to recreate aspects of these worlds that are hidden from us.[39] These voices remind us that the medieval halakhic texts and records that have been so central in modern research on medieval Ashkenaz represent just a small part of the medieval community.

The Jews of Medieval Ashkenaz

Locale is a vital factor for any historical study.[40] However, this study examines a considerable geographic and cultural span. While it would be of great value to examine how stories were told at a local level, as scholars of fourteenth-century England have when studying the plays performed in different towns,[41] no such details are available for the communities of medieval Germany and northern France.[42] Only in the early modern period can this be done more extensively.[43] Moreover, given that engagement with the Bible long preceded the Middle Ages and was ubiquitous in all regions discussed here, northern Europe has provided the backdrop for this study. By emphasizing Ashkenazic custom and belief—whether in practice, such as the expansion of *mi sheber-akh* blessings that were an Ashkenazic innovation, or in Ashkenazic economic and communal activities, as related to the figures of Abigail and Deborah—I have made every effort to detail the known contours of medieval Ashkenazic Jewry. Liturgy is a genre that I consider worthy of further exploration, for it records practice and words that were recited, even if the people saying them did not necessarily understand the contents fully, and offers a way to access the praxis of a large proportion of medieval Jews.[44]

As I have emphasized throughout this book, biblical stories were not only read and heard; their protagonists also proved indispensable in the educational discourse. In that light I conclude with this image from an illuminated mahzor from southern Germany, produced in the early fourteenth century (Figure 6.1). This illustration adorns *Adon Imnani*, a *piyut* by Shimon b. Isaac, the famous poet from medieval Mainz (d. ca. 1020).[45] The poem is complemented by a depiction of the people of Israel receiving the Torah on Mount Sinai.

Moses is featured displaying the Ten Commandments, whereas Aaron and a group of Jewish men are positioned at the foot of the mountain. Sarit Shalev-Eyni and others, most recently Zsofia Buda, have described this scene in great detail.[46] The men all have vividly rendered faces, and, with the exception of Aaron, whose hat resembles a bishop's miter, each wears a "Jewish hat." These scholars have remarked on the extent to which the clothing depicted

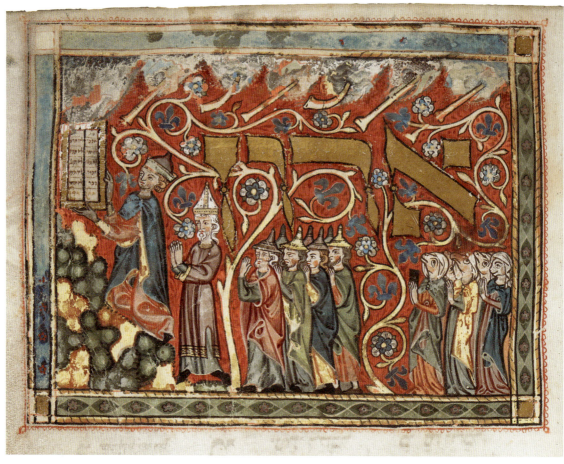

Figure 6.1

Tripartite Mahzor. Illumination of the Jews receiving the Torah. The men stand in front of the women. The first woman holds a tablet in her hands. Germany, circa 1325, Germany. MS BL Add. 22413, fol. 3r. © The British Library Board.

here reflects that period. Farthest from the mountain stand the women. The first woman is holding a tablet (or, perhaps, a book), and three others are behind their leader. By contrast to the men, these women have zoophilic rather than human faces. Three resemble birds, and one has mammalian features.

Shalev-Eyni and Buda join a long tradition of scholarship that sought to interpret this depiction of women as animals. Shalev-Eyni suggests that this reiterates their responsibility for the "original sin" initiated by Eve in Eden, and their animalesque portrayal has misogynic connotations when compared to that of the men in this scene. She further claims that this rendering alludes to a midrashic tradition which teaches that receiving the Torah eliminated lust from the Jewish people, nullifying the sin Eve brought to the world. Shalev-Eyni interprets the tablet held by the first woman as a corrective (*tikkun*). Rather than a red apple, the accepted medieval symbol of Eve's sin, and despite their subordinate position to the men, these women hold a tablet, a symbol of law.[47] In many ways Shalev-Eyni's interpretation locates this image within the sphere of the educated male elite, which would have been capable of interpreting this image based on their sophisticated knowledge of complex midrashim. Buda develops this interpretation by expanding her focus to the widespread phenomenon of zoophilic figures in medieval Jewish and Christian illuminated manuscripts. She contends that this imagery need not be considered derogatory but, rather, as a sign of differentiation, to distinguish groups from one another, in this case men from women.[48]

I propose that we approach this image from a social perspective, following the insight of Marc Michael Epstein. He suggested that the first woman is holding a prayer book rather than a tablet.[49] He posits that, if this is accurate, she is a leader of women's prayers (*mitpalelet hanashim*), a role Dulcia and others fulfilled in their communities.[50] Such a woman may also have been designated to convey stories from the Bible and other sources to her counterparts. This image of Jews receiving the Torah at Mount Sinai with its distinctly medieval features provides a fitting conclusion for this study. As typifies medieval art, the biblical figures appear in medieval garb. The bishop's hat worn by Aaron prompts consideration of Jewish-Christian differences and similarities, whereas the visual contrasts between men and women stress their positions within medieval society and invite reflection on their consequences. When viewed receiving the Torah as a group, these men and women are dressed so similarly that it is tempting to argue for the inconsequentiality of gender; however, the persistent social distinctions are subtly indicated by the visibility of the men's faces and shoes, as opposed to the women's animal visages and draped legs.

This book has endeavored to elucidate shared and contrasting aspects of medieval life—among women and men, Jews and Christians—and to offer a glimpse of the significance that medieval communities brought to biblical stories and their related quotidian practices. It has also sought to illuminate those very practices and the ways they were understood by medieval people, underscoring the opportunities and agency medieval Jewish women and men had to construct and interpret the traditions with which they shaped their lives.

Notes

Introduction

1. Perry and Voß, "Approaching Shared Heroes," 1–13, explore the roles of heroes in medieval and early modern culture, some of whom are biblical. See also the work of Raspe, *Jüdische Hagiographie*.
2. See my *Practicing Piety*, 215, 222.
3. For a survey of this topic, see Chazan, *Jews of Medieval Western Christendom*. For some of the differences and similarities related to customs, see Ta-Shma, *Early Franco-German Ritual*, 14–16, 22–27 (in Hebrew). Although Grossman distinguishes between the areas in his books on the Sages' lives, he treats them as one area when examining women: *Early Sages of Germany*; Grossman, *Early Sages of France*; Grossman, *Pious and Rebellious*. Others have argued for greater differentiation: Zimmer, *Society and Its Customs*, as well as the review of this book: Soloveitchik, "Review Essay *of Olam Ke-Minhago Noheg*," 223–25; Soloveitchik, "Piety, Pietism and German Pietism," 455–93; See also Kanarfogel, *Intellectual and Rabbinic Culture*.
4. For surveys of Jews in medieval Byzantium, see Bonfil, *History and Folklore*; Toch, *Economic History*, 9–36; Holo, *Byzantine Jewry*.
5. Soloveitchik, "The 'Third Yeshiva of Bavel,'" 150–201, describes the circumstances of these communities prior to 1000 CE; Grossman, *Early Sages of Germany*, discusses the leading rabbinic figures of these Rhineland cities.

6. Jordan, *French Monarchy*; Grossman, *Early Sages of France*. About the fairs, see Chapin, *Les villes de foires*, as well as Fourquin, *Les campagnes*, esp. part 1. For medieval German trade and Jews' place within it, see some comments by Soloveitchik, *Principles and Pressures,* 62–85. Yet we are still lacking a social history of Jewish trade that will allow a better understanding of its geography and dimensions.

7. Finkelstein, *Jewish Self-Government.*

8. Grossman, Early *Sages of Germany,* 27–28.

9. Ta-Shma, *Early Franco-German Ritual,* 14–16; 22–27.

10. These demographic and geographic patterns are clearly demonstrated in the maps compiled by Alfred Haverkamp and his team; see Haverkamp, ed., *Geschichte der Juden.*

11. For a summary of these processes, see Chazan, *Jews of Medieval Western Christendom, 1000–1500.*

12. See Marcus, "Jewish-Christian Symbiosis," as well as my earlier work: Baumgarten, *Mothers and Children*; Baumgarten, *Practicing Piety*; Baumgarten, Karras, and Mesler, "Introduction," 1–20.

13. For the purposes of this study, "the Bible" refers to the Hebrew Bible or Old Testament, rather than the Christian definition of the term, which includes Old and New Testaments.

14. See in the notes that follow.

15. J. Cohen, *Living Letters*; J. Cohen, *Be Fertile and Increase.*

16. This issue has long been recognized in biblical studies and in the field of Jewish-Christian polemics. See Van Liere, *Introduction to the Medieval Bible*, 100–101, for a recent summary, and also see Smalley, *Study of the Bible in the Middle Ages*; McAuliffe et al., *With Reverence for the Word*; Berger, ed., *Jewish-Christian Debate in the High Middle Ages*; J. Cohen, *Be Fertile and Increase*; Lourdaux et al., eds., *Bible and Medieval Culture.*

17. Funkenstein, *Perceptions of Jewish History*, 172–200; Funkenstein, "Changes in the Patterns," 125–44.

18. See n. 23. See also the work of Touitou, *Exegesis in Perpetual Motion*; Signer, "God's Love," 123–49; Klepper, *Insight of Unbelievers*; de Visscher, *Reading the Rabbis*; Goodwin, *Take Hold of the Robe*; Curiá, *In Hebreo.*

19. Soloveitchik, *Use of Responsa*, 100–106. As Soloveitchik notes, the use of the Bible for legal rulings was prevalent especially until the late eleventh century in northern France and in cases in which there was no talmudic precedent. See also his "Authority of the Babylonian Talmud," 2:75.

20. Kanarfogel, *Intellectual and Rabbinic Culture.* Kanarfogel operates on the premise that, in addition to their expertise as halakhists, medieval rabbis were also conversant in other genres and fields. His desire to demonstrate their versatility is at the heart of this volume's uniqueness. Kanarfogel's work exemplifies the widely accepted method of tracing the history of halakhah, with minimal emphasis on the role of the Bible, despite his lengthy chapters concerning the biblical oeuvre of these scholars.

21. Ibid.

22. See n. 17 and see also the discussion of this matter in Berger, ed., *Jewish-Christian Debate*.

23. See n. 18. See also Smith, "Continuity and Change," 17–30; Smith, *Ten Commandments*; Smith, *Glossa Ordinaria*; Signer, *Glossa Ordinaria*; Reiner, "Bible and Politics," 59–72.

24. One partial exception is scholars of art, as many of the illuminated Hebrew manuscripts include biblical scenes. Yet, these scholars are often reticent to connect between everyday medieval realities and the illuminations. See Shalev-Eyni, *Jews among Christians*; Kogman-Appel, *Mahzor from Worms*. I agree with this approach as art does not reflect reality. However, I am suggesting that the art is tied to everyday life and that it can be mined with caution.

25. Langer, "Biblical Texts," 63–90; Reif, "Use of the Bible," 71–92. Among Christians, see Danielou, *Bible and the Liturgy*; Zieman, *Singing the New Song*; Boynton, "Bible and the Liturgy," 10–33.

26. Elbogen, *Jewish Liturgy*. See also Vitz, "Liturgy as Education," 20–34, for a broad discussion of the place of liturgy in education in medieval Christian society.

27. See n. 7. Also see *Sefer Hasidim Parma*, no.835, no.1502. For parallels see *Sefer Hasidim Bologna*, no. 313; MS JTS Boesky 45, no. 335–337; MS Bod. Opp. Add. 34, no. 116.

28. See n. 33. Van Liere, *Introduction to the Medieval Bible*; Dyer, "Bible in the Medieval Liturgy," 659–79; Poleg, "'A Ladder,'" 205–27.

29. See Sa'ar, *Jewish Love Magic*, 173–87; Olsan, "Charms and Prayers," 357–64.

30. See the chapters that describe this process in various locations in Marsden and Matter, eds., *New Cambridge History of the Bible*.

31. The abundance of scholarship on these works nearly defies summary. Some studies focus on specific Bibles, while others broadly examine this phenomenon. Psalters represent another form of books that were often illuminated as well. See Williams, ed., *Imaging the Early Medieval Bible*; Sed-Rajna, *Hebrew Bible*; McKendrick and Doyle, eds., *Art of the Bible*; Bogaert et al., eds., *Bibles en Français*.

32. Muir, *Biblical Drama*.

33. Ibid.

34. *The New Cambridge History of the Bible* (noted earlier) includes an article on each of these modes of presentation of the biblical text, with a survey of research on that subject.

35. Baumgarten, "Shared and Contested Time," 253–76.

36. Buc, "Pouvoir royal," 691–713.

37. Tanner and Watson, "Least of the Laity," 395–423; Hamilton, *Church and People*.

38. Van Liere, *Introduction to the Medieval Bible*, 14.

39. The work of Hamilton, *Church and People*, has been especially important for my own inquiry. See also Arnold, *Belief and Unbelief*.

40. For a recent analysis of *piyutim* that emphasizes a variety of biblical models, see Novick, *Piyyuṭ and Midrash*.

41. Einbinder, *Beautiful Death*, 9.

42. Ibid. See also her other discussions of this subject, especially when analyzing poems that existed in both Hebrew and Old French: Einbinder, "Troyes Laments," 201–30; see also Fudeman, *Vernacular Voices*.

43. Kanarfogel, *Jewish Education*; Olszowy-Schlanger, "Learning to Read," 47–69.

44. For an overview of such retellings in rabbinic literature, see Yassif, *Hebrew Folktale*; Kushelevsky, *Tales in Context*.

45. Assaf, "Lovely Women and Sweet Men," 231–50.

46. Müller et al., eds., *Die Grabsteine*.

47. *Hebräische Berichte*, ed. Haverkamp; Chazan, *In the Year 1096*.

48. Spiegel, *Last Trial*.

49. G. Cohen, "Hannah and Her Seven Sons," 51–54.

50. J. Cohen, *Sanctifying the Name*.

51. See n. 79.

52. Lehnertz, "Erfurt *Judeneid*," 12–13.

53. This field has been especially rich in the late antique period, as the biblical text was the basis for tannaitic and amoraic interpretation. I have found Kanarek, *Biblical Narrative and the Formation of Rabbinic Law*, especially helpful. See her introduction and especially 1–21. See also Rubenstein, *Stories of the Babylonian Talmud*; Fishbane, *Biblical Myth*; Wimpfheimer, *Narrating the Law*; Simon-Shoshan, *Stories of the Law*. Yet all these books share a feature that differs from this study. They are not interested in practice or in non-elites. Their focus is on the rabbis and their deduction process. A book whose focus is more similar to my general intent though not identical is Ulrich, *Good Wives*. Ulrich combines images and reality and uses the biblical models as symbols of different functions. As study of gender has evolved since this book was written thirty-five years ago, this is just a rough comparison. Thompson, *Writing the Wrongs*, follows the commentary in ways similar to my own work, as does Schroeder, *Deborah's Daughters*. Yet neither of these more recent studies makes the direct connection between biblical interpretation and daily practice that I investigate in this volume. These studies are among the many works that have inspired this project.

54. See Malkiel, *Reconstructing Ashkenaz*, who defines this as deviance, 148–99. See Soloveitchik on this matter: "On Deviance," 283–93.

55. Woolf, *Fabric of Religious Life*; Yuval, "Heilige Städte, Heilige Gemeinden," 91–101.

56. Over the past years (2016–2022), I have led a research group entitled *Beyond the Elite: Jewish Daily Life in Medieval Europe*, funded by the European Research Council. I see this monograph as part of this larger project. For more information about the project as a whole, see https://beyond-the-elite.huji.ac.il.

57. The classic study in this field remains Joan Wallach Scott, *Gender and the Politics of History*. Her work was followed by vast amounts of scholarship on gender. For a recent summary of this literature in medieval contexts, see Bennett and Karras, eds., *Oxford Handbook of Women and Gender*.

58. Grossman, *Pious and Rebellious*, 162–70; Baskin, "Some Parallels," 41–51.

59. The elegy for Dulcia as it appears in *Sefer Gezerot Ashkenaz veTzarfat*, ed. Habermann, 168–70, and published by Marcus, "Mothers, Martyrs and Moneymakers," 34–45; Baskin, "Dolce of Worms: Women Saints in Judaism," 39–70; Baskin, "Dolce of Worms: The Lives and Deaths," 429–37. I would argue most women were literate on the level of decoding the alphabet and that they could probably sound out the Bible. I cannot determine if they could understand what they read. See also Turniansky, "Women and Books," 7–10. Most recently, see Epstein, "Standing at Sinai."

60. Dronzek, "Gendered Theories," 143–44.

61. Arnold, *Belief and Unbelief*; Biller, "Intellectuals and the Masses," 323–39; Smoller, "'Popular' Religious Culture(s)," 340–56.

62. In my reflections on these concepts, I have found the following writings particularly thought-provoking: Ehrenschwendtner, "Literacy and the Bible," 704–21; Joselit, *Set in Stone*; Edwards, ed., *Rethinking Biblical Literacy*.

63. Goody, *Power of the Written Tradition*, 20.

64. Doležalová and Visi, eds., *Retelling the Bible*; Zacher, *Rewriting the Old Testament*; Poleg and Light, eds., *Form and Function*. On the social consequences of literacy, see Britnell, ed., *Pragmatic Literacy*; Nedkvitne, *Social Consequences of Literacy*.

65. Koopmans, *Wonderful to Relate*; Cubitt, "Folklore and Historiography," 189–223; Vansina, *Oral Tradition*.

66. Koopmans, *Wonderful to Relate*, 15–18.

67. My thanks to Micha Perry, who introduced me to Hopkin's work.

68. Hopkin, *Voices of the People*; Hopkin, "Ecotype, Or a Modest Proposal," 31–54.

69. Hasan-Rokem, "Ecotypes."

70. Gubrium and Holstein, *Analyzing Narrative Reality*, 225–28.

71. Cubitt, "Folklore and Historiography," 220.

72. Ibid., 210.

73. As quoted by Koopmans, *Wonderful to Relate*, 11, and see Southern, *Saint Anselm*, 278. Southern scorns this topic, an indication of how research interests have shifted.

74. Hopkin, *Voices of the People*, 13.

75. For narrative theory as a means of analysis, see the school founded by Ruthellen Josselson and Amia Lieblich and their series, *The Narrative Study of Lives*.

76. See n. 88.

77. See the excellent discussion in Kanarek, *Biblical Narrative and the Formation of Rabbinic Law*, 12–28. She distinguished between "story" and "narrative" but also noted they are often used interchangeably, as I have done here; ibid., 3–4.

78. Ibid., 12–13.

79. See Chapter 4 for a discussion of this matter.

80. See, for example, Boureau, *Lord's First Night*; Bynum, *Metamorphosis*; Kleinberg, *Flesh Made Word*; Koopmans, *Wonderful to Relate*.

81. Yassif, "Hebrew Story," 3–8; Reiner, "From Joshua to Jesus," 281; Raspe, "When King Dagobert," 146–58.

82. For a survey of documented sermons, see Saperstein, *"Your Voice like a Ram's Horn"*; Eleazar ben Judah, *Derashah leFesaḥ*. For the types of social content conveyed via sermons in Christian society and the role of the Bible within them, see Muessig, "Sermon, Preacher and Society," 73–91.

83. Sharon Koren has outlined the extent to which the kabbalistic discussions of biblical figures are not related to everyday life. See her "Immaculate Sarah." As for magic, I discuss this matter briefly in Chapter 1. This is a topic for future exploration as magical formulas often refer to biblical figures.

84. Most recently, see Raspe, "On Men and Women Reading Yiddish," 199–202.

85. Similar work has been done on male figures, although without the emphasis on practice. See n. 48. For David, see the recent book by Karras, *Thou Art*.

86. See, for example, the work of Schäfer, *Mirror of His Beauty*. For a thorough study of biblical female figures within Kabbalah, see Koren, "Immaculate Sarah," 183–201; we await her book on the topic. For studies not related to Kabbalah, see Ta-Shma, "Be'era shel Miriam"; Shoham-Steiner, "Virgin Mary, Miriam, and Jewish Reactions to Marian Devotion," 75–91; and most recently the work of my student Inbar Gabay-Zada, "Ritual of Miriam's Well."

Chapter 1

Epigraphs: MS Munich Cod. Hebr. 69, fol. 23r on the margins. This is a fourteenth-century mahzor of the Eastern Ashkenazic rite.

The poem "Elohim Hashem haEl Goel," in Simha b. Samuel, *Mahzor Vitry*, ed. Horowitz, 598. We await the Frankel-Wasserstein compendium of medieval marriage poems.

1. This will be evident throughout this chapter. This is also true in Christian culture and in the Bible at large before Jewish and Christian traditions developed, as commented by Ricœur: "Adam is not an important figure in the Old Testament" (*Symbolism of Evil*, 237).

2. Fries, "Evolution of Eve," 2–3.

3. Duby, *Women of the Twelfth Century*, vol. 3. The entire third volume is subtitled "Eve and the Church." For opposition to this position, see Wain, "Nec Ancilla Nec Domina: Representations of Eve in the Twelfth Century."

4. It is also noteworthy that Christians considered Adam as a prefiguration of Christ, a perspective that could also have challenged Jewish exegetes. The Eve-Mary dichotomy is discussed at length in what follows.

5. For Lilith, see Trachtenberg, *Jewish Magic*, 36–37; Bohak, *Ancient Jewish Magic*, 299–300; Baumgarten, *Mothers and Children*, 98–99, 117–18.

6. See, for example, the thesis by Wain, "Nec Ancilla Nec Domina." Wain argues that in the twelfth century central scholars were intent on "improving" Eve's image. Yet the contrast between Eve and Mary remains constant throughout the period, as can

be seen in the choices made by the compilers of the *Glossa ordinaria*, ed. Rausch, Gen. 3, p. 103, Procopius, "Mariae typus Eva fuit." This comment ends by proclaiming Mary praiseworthy and Eve at fault.

7. See, for example, Flood, *Representations of Eve in Antiquity*. On p. 6, Flood states that "Eve is useful neither as a shorthand for women nor for the oppression of women; her history is too rich and varied."

8. Modeled on the Talmud, BT Bava Batra 65a, and on midrashic passages. See, for example, *Genesis Rabbah*, 1–29 as one of the earliest midrashim.

9. *Sefer Tosafot haShalem*, Gen. 3:16, nos. 1, 3, 7. See also R. Joseph Bekhor Shor, Gen. 3:16.

10. See n. 18.

11. A comprehensive study of Adam as a figure and subject of commentaries goes beyond the scope of this study but is a worthy subject for future research. See, for example: Benarroch, "Mystery."

12. Flood, *Representations of Eve*, 68–70.

13. See the summary of these matters in ibid., 11–14.

14. For a summary of Augustine's position, see Brundage, *Law, Sex, and Christian Society*, 84.

15. Ibid., 426.

16. *Sefer Tosafot haShalem*, 8: Ex. 19:3, no. 5. It is notable that this explanation is a direct contrast to other interpretations that explain the mention of the women before the men as the result of women's piety and their leadership. See ibid., nos. 4 and 5.

17. Ibid., 1: Gen. 3:19, no. 2.

18. Ibid., Gen. 1:1, no. 73.

19. Ibid., Gen. 2: 18, nos. 8, 11, 14.

20. Berger, *Jewish-Christian Debate*, no. 189.

21. As in the discussion that follows.

22. *Genesis rabbah*, ed Theodore and Albeck, 2: 24, 18, no. 2, and see its medieval version as it appears in *Sefer Tosafot HaShalem*, Gen. 2:22, no. 1. For a detailed discussion of these passages, see Fisher, "'His Yetzer.'" This is also evident from Christian etymologies of Eve in Jerome's *Liber interpretationis* and throughout the medieval period. For example, Isidore of Seville, who identifies the name "Eve" as an anagram of "woe" (comparing their Hebrew and Latin equivalents), sees her as responsible for the inception of death through deceit, calamity (from *cadere*, the verb "to fall"), and life (*vita*). See Poleg, "Interpretation of Hebrew Names," 219.

23. This commentator reads the word *vayiven* in relation to "understanding" rather than "building" or "creating."

24. *Sefer Tosafot haShalem*, Gen. 2:22. no. 1.

25. *Sefer Tosafot haShalem*, p. 116, no. 23. He follows the tradition of *Avot deRabbi Nathan*.

26. Flood, *Representations of Eve*, 25.

27. Wain, "Nec Ancilla Nec Domina," surveys the attitudes of Abelard and others. See also Nelson, "Lay Readers of the Bible," 45.

28. *Sefer Tosafot haShalem*, p. 115, no. 11.

29. Ibid., p. 117, no. 27.

30. Zimmer, *Society and Its Customs*, 17–43; Baumgarten, *Practicing Piety*, 181–82.

31. See *Sefer Tosafot haShalem*, 105, no. 7. See also Baumgarten, *Practicing Piety*, 138–71.

32. My student Elah Langer-Ravitsky wrote a short paper, "Mipnei shehaSatan meraked lifneihen," on the topic of women's place in medieval funeral processions in 2014. Her interest was in traditions concerning Satan rather than Eve. I thank her for all that I learned from her. See also Tubul, "Excluding Women," *47–52; Golinkin, *Status of Women*, 212–29, esp. 213.

33. See PT Sanhedrin, ch. 2, no. 4.

34. MS JTS MS 8219, Moses of Zurich, *Semak Zurich*, 62a margins.

35. I do not delve further into this practice here because medieval traditions do not refer to Eve frequently. Rather, following the Talmud, BT Berakhot 51a, they explain that women lead the processional to the cemetery since Satan dances among them. Most medieval compositions follow this tradition and explain the custom as passed on by R. Joshua b. Levi. See, for example, *Mahzor Vitry*, ed. Goldschmidt, no. 32; Shimshon b. Tzadok, *Sefer Tashbetz*, no. 449. Other passages explain the reason for this custom as pertaining to modesty, an idea some Tosafists protest. See BT Sanhedrin 20a and Mordechai b. Hillel, *Sefer Mordechai*, Sanhedrin, no. 664.

36. Jean Beleth, *Summa de ecclesiasticis officiis*, CCCM 41a, ch. 161, p. 318, lines 125–29.

37. Ibid., 138, nos. 3, 6.

38. Ibid., no. 3.

39. *Midrash Sekhel Tov*, ex. 1: "And the midwives said to Pharoah: 'The Hebrew women are not like the Egyptian women': For Hebrew women are not subject to Eve's lot, as it says [in Scripture], 'In sorrow you will bear children,' for they are righteous and therefore don't need them [the midwives]."

40. Baumgarten, *Mothers and Children*, 41; Rublack, "Pregnancy," 90–93.

41. Mishnah, Shabbat 2:6.

42. Moshe Rosman made this point beautifully in a series of lectures in Fall 2020 at Fordham University, and we await his book on early modern Jewish women. As he remarked, when Jewish women write about their religious lives in the early modern period, they do not single out these commandments. In contrast, men call these ritual acts "the women's commandments."

43. This midrash provides a systematic explanation for comparing Adam to bread, starting with the creation narrative.

44. *Genesis Rabbah*, 17:8; *Midrash Tanhuma*, 1: Genesis, Parashat Noah, nos. 1, 27–28. See, for example, in liturgical verse, *Liturgical Poems of Rabbi Yannai*, ed. Rabinovitz, 1:437.

45. See, for example, Jewish laws that discuss the women's commandments and those practiced on Sabbath eve: R. Eliezer b. Nathan, *Sefer Ra'avan*, no. 340; R. Eliezer b. Joel haLevi, *Sefer Ra'aviah*, 1: Shabbat, no. 199; Isaac b. Moses, *Sefer Or Zaru'a*, 1: Laws of Hallah, no. 225: 2: Laws of Sabbath Eve. See also Eleazar b. Judah,

Perushey siddur hatefilah laRokeah, no. 87, 2: 488–97, who expands on these three *mitzvot*; *Sefer Tosafot haShalem*, Rashi, BT Shabbat, 32b, s.v. "hareni notel nishmoteikhem"; *Orhot Haim*, part 1, Perush "bameh madlikin"; *Sefer Kolbo*, no. 36.

46. This tradition already appears in Amram Gaon, *Seder Rav Amram Ga'on*, 65, and in medieval discussions of Friday night liturgy as well; see *Mahzor Vitry*, ed. Goldschmidt, Kiddush veSe'udah, no. 5, 1: 175. Eleazar b. Judah of Worms, *Perushey siddur hatefilah laRokeah*, interprets the entire chapter in his commentary on the liturgy; and see especially 2:493–95, where he retells this very midrash.

47. Eleazar b. Judah of Worms, *Perushey Siddur*, 2:493.

48. This appears in a fourteenth-century manuscript, MS Leipzig, B.H. Duod. 43, fol. 33r. I learned of this text from my student Ariella Lehmann, and I thank her for this reference. See also MS Parma Palatina 1912, fol. 24a. See Lehmann's broader discussion of this text: "Between Domestic and Urban Spaces."

49. For a discussion of visual depictions of this trio, see Sabar, "Mitzvot Hannah," 386–413.

50. Medieval Jews followed some tithing practices, and it is necessary to investigate the place of hallah in this system. Yet this question extends beyond the scope of this chapter. See Galinsky, "Custom, Ordinance or Commandment?" 203–32.

51. Rashi, Numbers 15:20, "hallah."

52. Strauss, "Pat 'Akum in Medieval France and Germany."

53. See, for example, Isaac b. Shlomo (Rashi) and H. L. Ehrenreich, *Sefer HaPardes*, Hilkhot Pesach; Eleazar b. Judah, *Sefer Rokeah*; Moses b. Jacob of Coucy, *Sefer Mitzvot Gadol (Semag)*; Isaac b. Joseph of Corbeil, *Sefer Amudei Golah HaNikra Sefer Mitzvot Katan*; Barukh b. Isaac, *Sefer haTerumah*. See also the recent edition of *Sefer haTerumah* based on MS London 518.

54. See, for example, Eleazar b. Judah, *Sefer Rokeah*, nos. 357–59; Barukh b. Isaac, *Sefer haTerumah*, no. 83 (Friedman ed.); Jacob b. Moses Moellin, *Sefer Maharil*, 84–86. Interestingly, most of the medieval compilations refer to the baking of bread as a male activity, and references to women are often quotations from late antique sources. See, for example, *Mahzor Vitry*, ed. Horowitz, hilkhot pesah, no. 38.

55. See, for example, Isaac b. Moses, who details this procedure and makes explicit that women knead this dough: *Sefer Or Zaru'a*, 2: no. 240; R. Jacob Moellin is reported to have done this himself: *Sefer Maharil*, Minhagim, Hilkhot afiyat matzot, nos. 14–16, 71.

56. For an overview of this ritual, see Marcus, *Rituals of Childhood*. For the importance of a virgin in the ritual, see the text published by Roth, "Educating Jewish Children on Shavuot," 9–12, attributed to R. Abraham of Bonn.

57. For a recent discussion of the garments depicted in this *haggadah*, see Epstein, *Medieval Haggadah*, 64–75.

58. See n. 54.

59. See, for example, *Sefer Tosafot haShalem*, Gen. 2:7, no. 29, p. 98.

60. For Dulcia, see Habermann, *Gezerot Ashkenaz veTzarfat*, 165. For the circumcision ceremony, see Jacob and Gershom the Circumcisors, *Sefer Zikhron Brit*, 59–61.

61. Eleazar b. Judah, *Sefer Rokeah*, no. 353.

62. Candles and wax were donated to the synagogue as part of regular practice. The donation of wax becomes part of the formula of the *mi sheberakh* blessing. See Chapter 2.

63. The practice is attested to throughout the Middle Ages. It appears already as part of communal ordinances attributed to R. Gershom Me'or haGolah (d. ca. 960); see Finkelstein, *Jewish Self-Government*, 123. Dulcia of Worms (d. 1196) is reported as preparing these candles; see *Sefer Gezerot Ashkenaz VeTzarfat*, ed. Habermann, 166. A discussion about whether women should light these candles can be found in Jacob b. Moses Moellin, *Sefer Maharil: Minhagim*, Hilkhot erev Yom Kippur, no. 13 (322).

64. Samson b. Tzadok, *Sefer Tashbetz*, no. 12.

65. See Fraiman, "Sabbath Lamp," 24 and also BT Shabbat 25b; *Mishneh Torah*, Laws of Sabbath, 5:6. In a comment on this same matter, Isaac of Corbeil, author of *Semak*, notes the varying opinions held by different authorities. See *Semak*, no. 278.

66. For a summary of this topic, see Ta-Shma, "Ner shel Kavod," 37–128; Baumgarten, "Tale of a Christian Matron," 83–99.

67. Jacob b. Meir (Rabbenu Tam), *Sefer HaYashar: Hiddushim*, no. 44, section 7, p. 100.

68. See the work of Ariella Lehmann, who discussed the practicalities of preparing for the Sabbath in medieval Ashkenaz and devotes an entire section to the lighting of Sabbath candles, "Between Domestic and Urban Spaces."

69. See *Semak* of Zurich, who comments on this as well (Moses of Zurich, Har Shoshanim edition), mitzvah 275, no. 223.

70. An *eruv* was a divider that separated the area where carrying was permitted on the Sabbath and where it was not.

71. Mishnah Shabbat 2:7, *Sefer Tashbetz*, no. 2, quotes the Mishnah on what a man must say to his wife.

72. Admittedly, this was not far. In the close quarters of Jewish neighborhoods, synagogue and home were in close proximity.

73. *Mahzor Vitry*, ed. Goldschmidt, 1: Hilkhot shabbat 170, no. 2.

74. Eleazar b. Judah, *Sefer Rokeah*, nos. 44, 46.

75. Ibid., n. 63.

76. Isaac b. Moses, *Sefer Or Zaru'a* (Farbstein ed.), 1: Hilkhot Hallah, no. 225.

77. See *Tsene uRena*, Gen. 2:24. Another interesting tradition related to Havdalah notes that God did not invent fire until the end of the Sabbath (*Tsene uRena*, Gen. 2:4).

78. Scholars have estimated that 1 in 6 or 1 in 8 women died in childbirth during medieval times. This means that a woman's death during childbirth was a common phenomenon. Moreover, since women often had more than one child, chances of death were greater than these numbers suggest. See the recent summary of this topic: Johnson, "Praying for Deliverance," 200–201.

79. See, for example, n. 79.

80. Cuffel, *Gendering Disgust*. For comparison to Islamic conventions, see Spellberg, "Writing the Unwritten Life," 305–24; Ahuvia and Gribetz, "Daughters of Israel," 1–27.

81. See Berger, ed., *Jewish-Christian Debate*, 178, 195.

82. For a survey of this literature, see Baumgarten, *Practicing Piety*, 24–34.

83. See Zimmer, *Society and Its Customs;* Woolf, *Fabric of Religious Life*, 139–45; Ta-Shma, "Minhagei Harhakat haNiddah," 280–88; and, most recently, Ben-Shaya, "Laws of Niddah."

84. Baumgarten, *Practicing Piety.* See also S. J. D. Cohen, "Menstruants and the Sacred"; S. J. D. Cohen, *Why Aren't Jewish Women Circumcised?*

85. Neta Bodner is currently preparing a book on this topic.

86. See Cohen, *Why Aren't Jewish Women Circumcised?* n. 82.

87. Eleazar b. Judah, *Sefer Rokeah*, no. 317, p. 195.

88. *Mahzor Vitry*, ed. Horowitz, 610, and parallels in *Sefer haPardes*, Hilkhot Niddah, p. 8.

89. Jacob b. Moses Moellin*, Shut Maharil haHadashot,* no. 93; Edward Fram, *My Dear Daughter.*

90. Amsterdam ROS.558, fol. 12v.

91. Sirat, "Les femmes juives," 14–23.

92. See the work of Sarit Shalev-Eyni, *Jews among Christian*, 45–47, and her discussion of the illustration from the Tripartite Mahzor there.

93. *Glossa ordinaria*, Gen. 3:17, col. 103.

94. Baumgarten, *Mothers and Children*, 106.

95. *Glossa ordinaria*, Gen. 3:17, col. 103. The commentary attributed to Procopius, the late antique Byzantine scholar, states, "Mariae typus Eva fuit."

96. Duby champions the position that all associations with women and sin refer to Eve; see his *Women of the Twelfth Century*; this is one of his central arguments.

97. BT Ketubbot 48a.

98. BT Ketubbot 48a; 61a; *Breshit rabbah*, Gen. 20:20; *Midrash Sekhel Tov*, Vayishlakh 34:6.

99. For a general discussion of this phenomenon, see Grossman, *Pious and Rebellious*, 212–30.

100. Ibid.

101. Meir b. Barukh of Rothenburg, *Responsa of Meir of Rothenburg* (Prague), ed. Blach, no. 81.

102. See Maharam, *She'elot uTeshuvot*, Crimona, no. 291; R. Yeruham, *Sefer Mesharim*, Venice, 1553, netiv 23, no. 5; R. Menahem Recanati, *Sefer Recanati*, no. 511; R. Isaac b. Moses, *Sefer Or Zaru'a* 3: Bava Kama, no. 161, quoting a case on which R. Simhah of Speyer ruled.

103. The ordinance (*takkanah)* of R. Peretz that relates to this issue does not include a biblical example, as that type of commentary is not typical of ordinances*,* but it does note that each woman should be treated "in accordance with her honor" (*lefi kevodah),* a phrase that alludes to talmudic discussion of rights that women merit as daughters of Eve. See Finkelstein, *Jewish Self-Government*, 216–17.

104. Deut. 25:11: "When men strive together one with another, and the wife of the one draws near to deliver her husband out of the hand of him that smites him and puts

forth her hand, and takes him by the secrets, *you shall cut off her hand*, your eyes shall have no pity" (italicized phrase quoted by *Sefer haNiyar*).

105. *Sefer haNiyar*, p. 166, *hagahah*.

106. Nelson, "Lay Readers of the Bible," 43–55.

107. Wain, "Nec Ancilla Nec Domina," 115.

108. Ibid., n. 8. See also Cohen, *"Be Fertile and Increase,"* 106–9. This connection is also evident in Geniza poetry. See Shmidman, "Epithalamia," 43.

109. These blessings first appear in the Talmud (BT Ketubbot 7b–8a), but they probably date from several centuries prior to the codification of that source. For an English translation of this text, see https://en.wikipedia.org/wiki/Sheva_Brachot.

110. *Mahzor Vitry*, ed. Horowitz circa 600.

111. Eleazar b. Judah, *Perushey Siddur haTefilah* 2: 734–37, esp. 736.

112. Salomon b. Samson of Worms, *Siddur*, 248.

113. It is noteworthy that other commentaries cite a different biblical event to explain these wedding customs, namely receiving the Torah at Mt. Sinai. See, for example, *Sefer Rokeah*, nos. 296, 353, as well as Samson b. Tzadok, *Sefer Tashbetz*, no. 463. See also *Sefer Tosafot haShalem*, 8: Ex. 19:6, no. 6.

114. *Sefer Tosafot haShalem*, Gen. 2:22, p. 113, no. 4.

115. *Sefer Tosafot haShalem*, Gen. 2:22, p. 113, no. 5.

116. Reynolds, *How Marriage Became One of the Sacraments*; Brooke, *Medieval Idea of Marriage*; Duby, *Women of the Twelfth Century*, 29–47.

117. The scholarship on this topic is nicely laid out in Wain, "Nec Ancilla Nec Domina," 108–14.

118. Reynolds, *Marriage in the Western Church*; Reynolds, *How Marriage Became One of the Sacraments*.

119. An unusual interpretation that ties Christian exegesis with the notion of Adam and Eve as a blessed couple can be found in the writings of R. Joseph Bekhor Shor (twelfth century, northern France), Gen. 2:18; 3:16–18. My thanks to Judah Galinsky, who pointed out this interpretation to me. Joseph explained that before the sin in Eden, Eve did not give birth, and he argued that the blessing to procreate was issued only after the sin. Before Eve and Adam were commanded to procreate, they were, according to his interpretation, a loving couple, helpmates and partners. He explained the idea of helpmate as "for company and assistance and not for procreation because as long as people were immortal, they did not need to be replaced." He then expounded that Eve was punished with birth because "until then she did not have to give birth as she was not supposed to die. But from now on she had to give birth, for they were mortal. If they did not procreate, the entire world would cease when they died." This understanding is unique among the medieval Jewish commentators.

120. The appearance of this formula was not widespread; other formulas, which call on the matriarchs (and patriarchs) rather than Adam and Eve, are discussed in the next chapter.

121. Trachtenberg, *Jewish Magic*, 168–69.

122. Baumgarten, *Mothers and Children*, 117–18.

123. Olsan and Jones, "Performative Rituals for Conception and Childbirth," 423.

124. Skemer, *Binding Words*, 236–50.

125. Baumgarten, "Ask the Midwives," 5.

126. Peter Comestor quotes a tradition concerning Eve and the Phoenix that can also be found in medieval Hebrew texts. See *Sefer haZikhronot*, 111–12; *Avot deRabbi Nathan* a, ch. 13; Rashi, Gen. 3:6; Peter Comestor, *Historia Scholastica*, 1072D. For parallels between Rashi and Peter Comestor, see Yassif, *Sefer haZikhronot*, 112; Shereshevsky, "Hebrew Traditions," 268–89. This tradition also appears in Rashi's commentary on Job 29:18; *Genesis Rabbah*, chap. 19; BT Sanhedrin 108b, and Rashi s.v. "Urshina." See also Morey, "Peter Comestor," 6–35; Hugh et al., *Interpretation of Scripture*; Curiá, *In Hebreo*. The comment of Joseph Bekhor Shor quoted earlier is an example of this type of comparison; see n. 119.

127. Novikoff, "'Plateas Publice Discurrentes,'" 45–63.

128. See the representation of this idea in art: Guldan, *Eva und Maria*; in literature: Boulton, *Sacred Fictions*, 84, 90; in theology: Flisfisch, "Eve-Mary Dichotomy," 37–46; Krahmer, "Adam, Eve, and Original Sin," 3–12; in drama: Fries, "Evolution of Eve," 1–16; in law: Delarun, "Clerical Gaze," 19–27. For some Jewish implications, see Koren, "Immaculate Sarah," 183–201.

129. Cohen, "'*Be Fertile*,'" 238; Benjamins, "Keeping Marriage Out," 93–106. The interpretation suggested by Joseph Bekhor Shor is along these lines. Despite this, as Peter Brown notes, all Christian wedding liturgies included a blessing for procreation modeled on God's address to Adam and Eve. Brown, *Body and Society*, 401.

130. The succession of Adam and Eve by Christ and Mary allowed this attitude. See Flood, *Representations of Eve*, 54–55.

131. Moulinier, "La pomme d'Eve et le corps d'Adam," 135–58.

132. As quoted in McCarthy, *Love, Sex and Marriage*, 39–40.

133. Karras, "Christianization of Medieval Marriage," 6–7; Reynolds, *Marriage in the Western Church*, 89–92, 371–84.

134. Cohen and Horowitz, "In Search of the Sacred," 225–50.

135. The Index of Medieval Art (https://ima.princeton.edu/) has hundreds of examples. See, for example, the church window from Saint Etienne in Mulhausen from 1340. In manuscripts, see MS Morgan 638, Old Testament Book, fol. 2r, from Paris, circa 1250; MS Morgan 140, fol. 5r; *Speculum humanae salvationis* from 1380, from Franconia; Morgan 730 fol. 10v, Book of Hours from Arras.

136. Jewish and Christian women shared many of the same jobs. See Herlihy, *Opera Muliebria*, 127–53; Dermer, "Jews" in the Tax Lists as per note 102.

137. Kogman-Appel, "Jewish Art and Non-Jewish Culture," 204–26, discusses this process in medieval Ashkenaz.

138. Flood attributes this reading and representation to Peter Comestor, who had close contacts with Jews. See Flood, *Representations of Eve*, 72 and note 126 above.

139. Yeruham b. Meshulam, *Sefer Toldot Adam veHava* (Venice, 1553), introduction, 2.

140. Fram, *My Dear Daughter*, 160–64; Altshul-Jeruschalmi, *Brantspigel*, 250–51. The premise of the entire treatise written for women were the three "women's commandments."

141. Fram, *My Dear Daughter*, 69.

142. Rivkah b. Meir, *Meneket Rivkah*, 153–54.

143. Ibid.

144. Ibid.

145. Ibid., introduction, 32–33.

146. *Tsena uRena*, Gen. 3.

147. See n. 17.

148. Jacob b. Isaac, *Tsena uRena*, Gen., 37–42.

149. *Sefer Tsene uRena*, 36–37.

150. Weissler, *Voices of the Matriarchs*, 62–63, 70, 97; Klirs, *Merit of Our Mothers*. The incorporation of Eve as one of the matriarchs is fascinating and merits further investigation.

151. Weissler, *Voices of the Matriarchs*, 68–73.

152. Translated by Klirs in *Merit of Our Mothers*, 126–27.

153. Fram, *My Dear Daughter*, 37–78.

154. http://www.steinheim-institut.de/cgi-bin/epidat?id=wls-730&lang=de.

155. Flood, *Representations of Eve*, 90–91; Fenster, ed., *Poems of Cupid*, 1: 604–16.

156. This idea appears, for example, in the exempla of Caesarius of Heisterbach, where a story recounts a servant who tries to argue he would not have sinned and then sins himself. See *Dialogus miraculorum*, IV: 75. About this story, see Polo de Beaulieu, "Dialogus Miraculorum," 203.

157. Sabar, "Mitzvot Hannah," 384–85, 388–413.

158. Sabar, "Mitzvot Hannah," 392–413. See, for example, the cover of Budapest, Jewish Museum 64.618, eighteenth century, Book of Blessings. More work needs to be done on this genre and its illuminations.

159. Sabar, "Mitzvot Hannah," 408.

160. See, for example, in Selnik's writings, Fram, *My Dear Daughter*, 250–51.

161. Salzer, "Adam, Eve, and Jewish Children," 396–411.

Chapter 2

Epigraph: National Library, Ms. Heb. 4° 681, fol. 7b–8a, fourteenth century. See BT Bava Batra 11a. Benjamin "the Righteous" (*haTzaddik*) was responsible for the communal charity fund. Once, during a drought, when there was no money in the fund, a mother of seven sons came to request charity. He explained to her that there was no money for her support, but after she pleaded with him, he gave her charity from his own money. Sometime later, Benjamin was ill and was about to die. The angels

came and advocated for him, reminding God of the charity he had given, and subsequently, he lived twenty-two more years. This story was well known in medieval
Europe. See *Avot deRabbi Nathan*, Nusah a, 3; and ibid., hosafah beit; *Yalkut Shimoni*, Prov. 10; *Yalkut Shimoni*, Ecc. 11.

1. Gen. 35:16–20.

2. 1 Samuel 1–2.

3. For the place of the matriarchs within the canon, see Ahuvia and Gribetz, "'The
Daughters of Israel,'" 1–27.

4. Throughout this chapter I refer to "collective memory." Research on this concept has
detailed the many ways in which a group preserves shared memory and, especially, the
patchwork nature of this type of memory. The work of Maurice Halbwachs,
On Collective Memory, is at the core of the perspective that I present. For a recent
review of this field, see Gensburger, "Halbwachs' Studies in Collective Memory,"
396–413. For medieval research on collective memory, see Geary, *Phantoms of
Remembrance*; his chapter 2 notes the importance of women in this process as well.

5. While *tekhines* are also liturgical, they differ from the *mi sheberakh* in that they are
private and typically recited by individuals on their own, often at home rather than
in a communal setting. For further discussion of this comparison, see Weissler,
Voices, 8–9, and the discussion at the end of this chapter.

6. Ya'ari's work appeared in several installments: "Tefillot" (1959): 118–30, 233–50;
"Tefillot," cont. (1961): 103–18. These articles were subject to responses by Fried,
"He'arot," 511–14; Daniel Cohen, "He'arot," 542–59.

7. Yaari, "Tefillot" (1959): 118–20.

8. Mishnah Ta'anit 2:4.

9. This is a standard High Holiday prayer in Ashkenaz.

10. Novick, *Piyyuṭ and Midrash*, explores this theme in the sixth chapter of his book,
169–90. He does not trace this phenomenon into the Middle Ages; rather, he focuses
on the period of classic *piyutim*.

11. This blessing cannot be found in the *Siddur of R. Sa'adiah Ga'on*. It appears in medieval manuscripts of *Seder R. Amram* but not in the earlier ones. See the Frumkin edition, 130, no. 46, and the discussion that follows. See the Goldschmidt edition, 59.

12. See, for example, MS Corpus Christi 133, fol. 100v; MS Cambridge Add. 3127, fol.
3b; Trinity College Library, Cambridge, England Ms. F 12 27, 48r. I thank Albert
Kohn for referring me to the Trinity College manuscript; MS Oxford, Can. Or. 70,
fol. 94b; MS Oxford Mich. 420, fol. 37b, 96a, 120a. Interestingly in this last manuscript, although the prayer appears three times, there are variations within it, including the names of the patriarchs. The prayer also appears in the rite of English
Jews, in the siddur that appears within Jacob b. Judah, *Etz Hayim*, 1:108. It is note-
worthy that most commentators on the siddur do not note this prayer at all. See
R. Samson of Worms, *Siddur*, 173–74, and the commentary from the siddur of
Hasidei Ashkenaz, 173–74; Eleazar b. Judah does not mention this blessing at all:
Perushey, 2: 560–61.

13. See *Seder Rav Amram Gaon*, ed. Frumkin, 2: 130. See Ya'ari, "Tefillot" (1959): 119.

14. Ya'ari, ibid.

15. For example, *Yekum purkan*, which endured as both a communal blessing and an individual blessing, like those recited for mother and child at the circumcision ceremony. These blessings were sometimes said in Aramaic at medieval Ashkenazic circumcision rituals, and it is interesting to see this mixed use of language. See *Seder Rav Amram Gaon*, ed. Frumkin, 2:400. For a discussion of their recitation in Ashkenaz, see Baumgarten, *Mothers and Children*, 77. See also Jacob and Gershom haGozrim, *Sefer Zikhron Brit*, 105, where he mentions that a blessing is recited for the infant's well-being in the names of Abraham, Isaac, and Jacob. This seems like a *mi sheberakh*, much like the variations discussed in this chapter. The medieval mahzorim and siddurim that include the circumcision blessings do not record such a blessing.

16. It is noteworthy there is no trace of these prayers in Geniza manuscripts.

17. Ta-Shma, *Early Ashkenazic Prayer*, 43–44. I have not found a specific affiliation to *Hasidei Ashkenaz* and over time doubt this affiliation more and more, see my "Who Was a Hasid."

18. Salfeld, *Martyrologium* contains a transcription of parts of this manuscript. Baumgarten, *Practicing Piety*, 103–37, analyzes some of the information that emerges from the manuscript concerning charitable giving.

19. Appears in Salfeld, *Martyrologium*, 86–87.

20. On *matnat yad* donations, see Zimmer, "Customs of Matnat Yad," 71–87.

21. On these customs, see also Galinsky, "Charity and Prayer," 163–74.

22. See n. 32.

23. For a discussion of this timing, see Baumgarten, *Practicing Piety*, 108–10.

24. See, for example, MS Parma Pal. 1904, fol. 35v, fourteenth-century siddur. See also MS Oxford Mich. 420, fol. 120a, from 1427.

25. There are some examples from the early modern period. See Baumgarten, *Practicing Piety*, 104–7.

26. Galinsky cites many of these comments: "Charity and Prayer," 163–74.

27. *Sefer Hasidim*, Parma, nos. 241–42.

28. Cambridge 3127 (1399), fol. 33b. This blessing also lists a different group of people who were cured, noting that Na'aman was cured from his leprosy by Elisha rather than Benjamin the *tzaddik*. Interestingly, these blessings appear twice, once as a note on an empty page (fol. 39b). On fol. 39b only the blessing for women appears.

29. See the examples that follow. And see MS Cambridge Add. 3127, fol. 33b.

30. MS NLI Heb. 4° 681, fol. 6b–7a.

31. Ibid.

32. See Ya'ari, "Tefillot mi sheberakh," for further examples. See also Baumgarten, *Mothers and Children*, 40. The figures mentioned in this blessing are each worthy of further investigation.

33. Ms NLI Heb 4° 681, fol. 6b–7a; Ms Cambridge Add. 3127, fol. 33b, 39a.

34. French siddurim refer to Israel rather than Jacob; see, for example, BNF MS Hebr. 634 fol. 61a.

35. See Ms NLI Heb 4° 681, fol. 6b–8a.

36. For examples of these blessings, see MS Munich 21, fol. 122r, a mahzor dated as thirteenth–fourteenth century; MS Munich 69, fol. 84r; MS Oxford Opp. 668, fol. 456a, 457a; MS Oxford Mich. 420, fol. 179a; MS Oxford Can. Or. 70, fol. 94b. I thank Gabriel Wasserman for his help on this matter..

37. I hope to write elsewhere about this wedding ritual. In the meantime, see Kaplan, "Rituals of Marriage," 273–300.

38. When writing this section, I often debated the correct verb: Was the blessing recited? Was it given to an individual? Until this day, in Yiddish and Hebrew the verb for this blessing is not "to say" but "to make." This is an indication of the ritual significance of the blessing.

39. For examples, MS Munich 21, fols. 278r and 278v; MS Berlin Or. 1224, fols. 174r and 174v.

40. Ya'ari, in his study of Simhat Torah, notes only much later examples for these blessings. Thus it would seem this is a nascent phenomenon here. See Ya'ari, *Toldot Hag Simhat Torah*, 132, 163, 256–57, where he dates the custom to the fifteenth century. It is evident that it was much earlier.

41. *Mahzor Vitry*, ed. Horowitz, 173; *Mahzor Vitry*, ed. Goldschmidt, 1:288, and, for a discussion of their differences, see Galinsky, "Charity and Prayer," n. 8. Meir b. Barukh of Rothenberg, Responsa, Berlin (1891), no. 371; Meir b. Barukh of Rothenberg, Responsa (Prague), Blach edition, no. 342.

42. Isaac b. Moses, *Sefer Or Zaru'a* 1: Hilkhot tefillah, no. 106.

43. See Shimon b. Yitzhak, *Piyutei*, 184–87. There is no *mi sheberakh* that routinely accompanies these poems in most manuscripts. These prayers are found in both German and northern French manuscripts. See also Fleischer, *Hebrew Liturgical Poetry*, 472; Fraenkel, "Introduction," *Mahzor Sukkot*, 42.

44. Ya'ari includes examples of each of these: "Tefillot" (1959): 128–30, 233–50. For an example containing blessings for the sick, women in childbirth, and those who pay taxes, see Ms Cambridge Trinity College Ms. F 12 27, 48r–v, Custom and prayer book, fifteenth century.

45. MS Vatican ebr. 323, fol. 112v, late thirteenth century.

46. *Sefer haMinhagim deBei Maharam b. Barukh meRothenburg*, ed. Elfenbein, 28. This is a fourteenth-century text.

47. Ms Leipzig, Universitatsbibliothek 1102, Kennicott 665, fol. 179a, fifteenth-century addition.

48. Goldschmidt mahzorim include these formulas. See, for example, *Mahzor Sukkot*, ed. Goldschmidt, 398–99.

49. See, for example, Gilat, "Two *Bakashot*," 54–58. Eleazar b. Judah, *Sefer Rokeah*, includes examples of other such personal prayers. See also MS BNF héb. 633, which includes dozens of such prayers. Although Colette Sirat described this manuscript

more than fifty years ago, this is an understudied phenomenon that requires further attention. See Sirat, "Un rituel juif," 7–40.

50. For the role of the patriarchs in daily Jewish liturgy, see Elbogen, *Jewish Liturgy*, 38; Novick, *Piyyut and Midrash*, 80–89, discusses the use of Abraham and of Leah. See also Gribetz, "Zekhut Imahot," 264–69.

51. See *Mahzor Sukkot*, ed. Goldschmidt and Fraenkel, p. 402–5.

52. About Eleazar Kallir and his poems, see Kallir, *Piyuṭim leRosh haShanah*, ed. Elitzur and Rand.

53. See *Mahzor Sukkot*, ed. Goldschmidt and Fraenkel, 476. This poem appears in multiple prayer books, often beautifully decorated. See, for example, MS Parma Pal. 2887, fol. 245r; Leipzig, Universitätsbibliothek, 1102, Kennicott 665, fol. 218r–v; Leipzig, Ms. B.H. fol. 3, 362v.

54. For examples of wedding liturgy, see *Mahzor Vitry* ed. Horowitz, 593–603. And see Einbinder, *Beautiful Death*, 7–9, for a brief discussion of the complexity of the poems.

55. See the discussion of this manuscript in Kogman-Appel, *Mahzor from Worms*.

56. Ms Vatican heb. 326 fol. 84b. I thank Gabriel Wasserman for referring me to this example.

57. Oxford Bod. Opp. 78, fol. 203v. The scribe, Benjamin b. Joseph compares himself to Abraham. This manuscript was written in Germany in the thirteenth century.

58. Paris BNF heb. 1032, fol. 30r, early fourteenth century.

59. The standard prayer appears already in Tractate Brakhot and can be found in a number of manuscripts from northern France and Germany; see, for example, MS Bibliothèque nationale héb. 633 fol. 252v; Vatican ebr. 329, fol. 177b; Parma Palatina 1265 fol. 19v, as well as in printed compilations. See, for example, *Sefer haOreh*, 1:121; *Mahzor Vitry*, ed. Horowitz, no. 529; Eliezer b. Nathan, *Sefer Ra'avan, Brakhot*, no. 199; Eliezer b. Joel haLevi, *Sefer Ra'avyah*, Massekhet Brakhot no. 146; Eleazar b. Judah of Worms, *Sefer Rokeah*, Hilkhot Brakhot, no. 343. This blessing deserves separate attention, and I hope to discuss it in a forthcoming publication.

60. For some examples, see Baumgarten, "Ask the Midwives."

61. See MS Paris, Bibliothèque nationale héb. 633, throughout the manuscript.

62. See McLaughlin, *Consorting with Saints*, 36. For the full text, see BNF Latin 818, fol. 183v. This is an eleventh-century manuscript.

63. See, for example, Fevrier, "Quelques aspects," 253–82.

64. For example, the work begun by Jean Sonet and continued by his students: Rézeau, *Les prières aux saints en Français*. Rézeau divides his volume into three types of prayers: those that have set forms according to the formal liturgy, those that have their own set form, and those that seem not to conform to a known pattern.

65. Franz, *Kirchlichen Benediktionen*, 197.

66. Elsakkers, "In Pain," 179–210; Franz, *Kirchlichen Benediktionen*, 198–201.

67. For the variations, see Elsakkers, "In Pain."

68. Elsakkers, "In Pain," 185–87.

69. Skemer, *Binding Words*, 250–59; Olsan and Jones, "Performative Rituals," 406–33.

70. Bohak, "Catching a Thief," 344–62.

71. Baumgarten, "Ask the Midwives," 16–17.

72. Gribetz, "Zekhut Imahot," 263–96, Gribetz shows that there is an amoraic tradition of calling out to the matriarchs, but that it is suppressed over time.

73. For additional comments on this epitaph, see: http://www.steinheim-institut.de /cgi-bin/epidat?id=wrm-151&lang=en.

74. For additional comments on this epitaph, see: http://www.steinheim-institut.de /cgi-bin/epidat?id=wrm-178&lang=en.

75. This appears in tombstones from Würzburg, and see Reiner, "From Paradise," 5–28.

76. See Baschet, "Medieval Abraham," 738–58; Baschet, *Le sein du père*. For the formulas recited at funerals, see Paxton, ed., *Death Ritual*, 138–39.

77. See Reiner, "From Paradise," 5–28. The matriarchs did continue, at least in cultural imagination, to greet women in Eden. See, for example, Fram, *My Dear Daughter*, 160–61.

78. See Reiner, "From Paradise," 5–28.

79. As should be evident, I am focusing on ritual implications. These stories were understood in a wide variety of other ways within different contexts. For example, in the Zoharic tradition, see Koren, "Immaculate Sarah," 183–201.

80. BT Bava Metzia 87a; *Sefer Tosafot haShalem*, Gen. 16:2, p. 123 no. 1 and no. 2.

81. *Sefer Tosafot haShalem*, Gen. 24:57, p. 278, no. 5, no. 13. See the discussion of amoraic discussion of this matter: Kanarek, *Biblical Narrative*, 67–106.

82. Brundage, *Law, Sex, and Christian Society*; Reynolds, *How Marriage Became One of the Sacraments*, 17, 647. Reynolds shows how the biblical stories played a role in post-Tridentine reforms as well (889–913).

83. The commentaries on Genesis focus on marriage and the marriage process, in some cases even when these are far from the topic they are commenting on. See, for example, *Sefer Tosafot haShalem*, Gen. 24:13, no. 4, no. 6, no. 7; Gen. 24: 57, no. 1; Gen. 24:58, no. 3, no. 5; Gen. 27:5, no. 1; Gen. 27:27, no. 5; Gen. 28:8, no. 1; Gen. 28:9, no. 1, no. 3; Gen. 28:1, no. 1.

84. *Sefer Tosafot haShalem*, Gen. 24:3, p. 256, no. 4, where Rebecca is depicted as beautiful, submissive, and wise; Gen. 27:5, p. 59, no. 2, where she is described as obedient.

85. For a discussion of this matter, see Hauptman, *Rereading the Rabbis*; Cohen, *Be Fertile*, 141–44.

86. Silvana Vecchio has outlined this tension at length. See " Good Wife."

87. This poem can be found in the compendium of wedding poems *Mahzor Vitry*, ed. Horowitz, 598. It is also commonly featured in prayer books that contain the wedding liturgy.

88. Ruth 4:11.

89. See, for example, in *Sefer haNiyar*, Hilkhot Kallah, no. 30. For a fascinating variant that was known in Spain and Provence and in medieval Ashkenaz that calls on Boaz

and Ruth when blessing a widow or widower, see Groner, *Berakhot shenishtak'u*, 241; MS Corpus Christi 133, fol. 328v.

90. For example, MS Parma Pal. 3134, fol. 336b–337a; MS Staatsbibliothek Berlin, Or. Fol. 1224, fol. 175b–76a.

91. *Mahzor Vitry*, ed. Horowitz, 597–98.

92. See, for example, Gen. 24: 21, Rashi, s.v. "vayeater."

93. Kushelevsky, *Tales in Context*, 295.

94. See ibid., 545–49.

95. This is a standard blessing. See the Galensian rite, *Liber Sacramentorum Gellonensis*, ed. A. Dumas, CCSL, 159, p. 413 and n. 84.

96. Franz, *Kirchlichen Benediktionen*, 2: 185.

97. The wedding ceremony took place on the steps of the church. See Brundage, *Law, Sex, and Christian Society*, 88. See also the general overview of symbolism in medieval Christian marriage: D'Avray, *Medieval Marriage: Symbolism and Society*; D'Avray, *Medieval Marriage Sermons*, 56, 110–13, 186–87.

98. *Corpus benedictionum pontificalium*, CCSL 162, p. 52, no. 115: "Benedicat Deus corpora vestra et animas vestras et det super vos benedictionem, sicut benedixit Abraham, Isaac et Iacob. Amen."

99. Ibid., p. 182, no. 450; p. 253, no. 963; *Corpus benedictionum pontificalium*, CCSL 162a, pars II, p. 416, no. 1020, p. 818, no. 2005. These examples come from Spanish and English manuscripts.

100. *Corpus benedictionum pontificalium* CCSL 162a, pars II, p. 735, no. 1798.

101. See Vecchio, "Good Wife."

102. *Corpus benedictionum pontificalium*; pars II, p. 735, no. 1798 : Omnipotens sempiterne Deus, qui primos parentes nostros Adam et Evam sua virtute creavit suaque bendictione sanctificavit et in sua societate copulavit, ipse corda et corpora vestra sanctificet et benedicat...Quique ad praeparandas Tobiae et Sarae nuptias Raphaelem angelum misit, ipse a supernis sedibus angelum suum sanctum mittat . . .

103. Ibid, p. 473, no. 1153: Deus, qui tegi Rebeccam paleo cum vidisset Usaac, Spiritu tuo docente, iussisti; qui habere mulierem super caput velamen per angelos paraecepisti. Dignare benedicere hanc famulam tuam Illam, quae nubendi animum gerit [Amen] . . . Respiciat ad Abraham patrem suum et ad Saram materem suam, atque similitudinem, matrem nubentium sanctorum atque fidelium liberorum procreation salvetur. [Amen]. Rebecca was seen as a symbol for religious life and spirit, D'Avray, *Medieval Marriage Sermons*, 187.

104. Greco and Rose, eds., *Le Ménagier de Paris*.

105. Ibid., 94–103.

106. For the literature about this book, see Grigsby, "Miroir des bonnes femmes," 458–81; Grigsby, "Miroir des bonnes femmes (Suite)," 30–51; Huot, "Writer's Mirror," 29–46.

107. About the *somme le roi*, see Lobrichon, *La Bible*; Riché and Lobrichon, eds., *Le Moyen Age*.

108. Grigsby, "Miroir des bonnes femmes," 463.

109. Ibid.

110. Ashley, "'Miroir des bonnes femmes,'" 86–105.

111. Robert de Blois, "Du chastoiement des dames," ed. Fox; Robert de Blois, "L'enseignment des princes," ed. Fox. Robert incorporates fewer biblical examples, but they are also evident in his instructions for princes. See *Robert de Blois*, ed. Fox, 24. It is noteworthy that there are similar manuals that do not include biblical figures, but they convey many of the same messages about proper conduct. See, for example, *Instructions of Saint Louis*, ed. O'Connell.

112. *Book of the Knight of the Tower*, ed. Offord.

113. Philippe de Mezieres, *Le livre de la vertu*.

114. Udry, "Robert de Blois," 90–102.

115. Grigsby, "Miroir des bonnes femmes," 465. For an overview of the content, see Burger, *Conduct Becoming*, 80–83.

116. Grigsby, "Miroir des bonnes femmes (Suite)," 33–34; Grigsby, "Miroir des bonnes femmes," 470.

117. Grigsby, "Miroir des bonnes femmes (Suite)," 33.

118. Augustine made this observation in his sermons: See *Sermons*, Sermon IV: 11 "It is this church that was represented by Rebecca the wife of Isaac," which is also echoed in the *Glossa ordinaria*, Gen. 24: 67 "Hanc Isaac in tabernaculo matris suae introduxit et uxorem accepit, quia in loco Synagogae de qua natus est Christum, Ecclesianm diligit." Bede states that Rebecca is the church: "*In Pentateuchum Commentarii, Expositio in primum librum Moysis*." These commentators consider her entry into Sarah's tent to be indicative of supersession. Peter Lombard and others echo these ideas as well. See Petrus Lombardus, *Commentarium in Psalmos*, Psalm 95 (96). See also D'Avray, *Medieval Marriage Sermons*, 187.

119. Jacobs-Pollez, "Education of Noble Girls."

120. See n. 74.

121. Kogman-Appel, "Pictorial Messages," 443–67.

122. Kogman-Appel, "Audiences," 99–143.

123. See *Tsena uRena*, Parashat Toldot.

124. Kogman-Appel, "Audiences of the Late Medieval Haggadah."

125. Eleazar b. Judah, *Perushey Tefillah*, 2: 512.

126. Much of the relevant literature is mentioned in the notes that follow.

127. Ta-Shma, "Ma'amad haNashim," 262–79; Grossman, *Pious and Rebellious*, 177–97; Har Shefi, *Women and Halakhah*, 214–331.

128. Baumgarten, *Practicing Piety*, 138–71; Baumgarten, *Mothers and Children*, 85–91.

129. Kanarfogel, "On the Nuances," 83–102.

130. Grossman, *Pious and Rebellious*, 177–97; Baumgarten, *Practicing Piety*, 138–71.

131. See Baumgarten, *Mothers and Children*, 85–91.

132. Howell, *Marriage Exchange*; Howell, "Gender of Europe's Commercial Economy," 519–38.

133. Baumgarten, "Towards a History," 98–109.

134. Baumgarten, *Mothers and Children*, chap. 2.

135. Jacob b. Moses Moellin, *Sefer Maharil: Minhagim*, Hilkhot Milah, no. 22.

136. In the illustration of Isaac's circumcision in the Regensburg Pentateuch (dated to 1300), women are portrayed entering the synagogue and passing the baby into the men's section rather than holding the infant during circumcision. Regensburg Pentateuch, IMJ B05.0009 180/052, fol. 18v, circa 1300.

137. Spiegel, "Woman as Ritual Circumcisor," 149–57. See the recent critique of this article by Kanarfogel, "On the Nuances," 97–99. I do not think his argument challenges the basic premise.

138. Weissler, *Voices*, 121–25; Fram, *My Dear Daughter*, 69–70.

139. Rivkah b. Meir Tiktiner, *Meneket Rivkah*, ed. Frauke von Rohden. This is the foundation of her book.

140. Klirs, *Merit*, 12–45. Compare Fram, *My Dear Daughter*, 161.

141. Klirs, *Merit*, 12–45.

142. Weissler, *Voices*, 126–46.

143. Ibid.; see chap. 1 as well. For candles in medieval culture, see Fraiman, "Sabbath Lamp," and, more recently, Lehmann, "Between Domestic and Urban Spaces."

144. See Gibson, "Blessings from Sun."

145. Klirs, *Merit*, 22.

146. Ibid., 23–24.

147. Weissler, *Voices*, 7.

148. Ibid.

Chapter 3

Epigraphs: *Tanna deVei Eliyahu Rabbah*, ed. Ish-Shalom, parashah 10.
Tombstone of Leah b. Asher, wife of Anschel Oppenheim, Worms, d. 1320: http://www.steinheim-institut.de/cgi-bin/epidat?id=wrm-153&lang=de. Leah is compared to Deborah and called woman and torch, meaning leader. See the German translation on the epidat website that also explains these references.

1. For more examples of such tombstones see the last section of this chapter.

2. Schroeder, *Deborah's Daughters*, chapters 1 and 2, 6–69.

3. Scholars of Josephus have quarreled over the extent to which his portrait is misogynist. See Roncace, "Josephus' (Real) Portraits," 250–59; Feldman, *Studies*, 153–62.

4. For Pseudo-Philo's treatment of this story, see *Liber antiquitatum biblicarum*, ed. Jacobson, pp. 145–53 (chs. 30–33); Brown, *No Longer Be Silent*, 39–93, and especially the comparison between Pseudo-Philo and Josephus (81–83); Halpern-Amaru, "Portraits of Women," 101–2.

5. See where I discuss *Sefer haZikhronot*, n. 44. The narrative therein was based to a large part on *Biblical Antiquities* but in this case provides a single paragraph in contrast to the lengthy late antique narratives.

6. BT *Megillah* 14a.

7. On the role of women making wicks, see Chapter 1. See also Weissler, *Voices*, 126–47; Baumgarten, *Mothers and Children*, 106–7.

8. BT *Megillah* 14a.

9. Ibid. Here the reference is to Huldah the Prophet.

10. Ibid. It is noteworthy that Josephus, *Antiquities*, V. 200–201, did the same. Josephus does not state whether this is a positive or a negative name, just its meaning. See Feldman, *Studies in Josephus' Rewritten Bible*, 49–62; Roncace, "Josephus' (Real) Portraits," 251.

11. BT *Pesahim* 66b.

12. Biblical Antiquities presents her as beautiful and hesitant. As Amaru states, Pseudo-Philo's Jael is meek. See Halpern-Amaru, "Portraits of Women," 101–2. For Josephus's portrayal, see Feldman, *Studies*, 160–61.

13. BT *Yebamot* 103a; BT *Nazir* 23b.

14. See also BT *Megillah* 15a, where she is presented as beautiful, an idea paralleled in Josephus and BT *Niddah* 55b, where Sisera is portrayed as nursing from her.

15. *Leviticus Rabbah*, ed. Margaliot, 23:10.

16. Schroeder, *Deborah's Daughters*, 3–4. A similar phenomenon is at work in the Babylonian Talmud's retelling of the story of Abigail, as is noted in Chapter 4.

17. *Yalkut Shimoni*, ed. Dov Hyman et al., 6: Jud. 4 and 5, remez 42–59.

18. *Tanna deVei Eliyahu*, parashah 10.

19. Here the word *eshet* means "wife" of rather than "maker."

20. Based on Jeremiah 11:20.

21. *Yalkut Shimoni*, Jud. 4, remez 42.

22. For example, *Sefer Hasidim Parma*. discusses the bad influence of a bad woman on a man. See no. 950, 1091. See also Yassif, ed., *Ninety-Nine Tales*, 152–56.

23. The midrash on the wife of On ben Pelet is remarkably similar to the story of Jael. On ben Pelet initially sided with Korah's challenge to Moses (Num. 16). According to the midrash, his wife ultimately prevented him from joining Korah and as a result saved his life. *Midrash Tanhuma* situates her in the family tent when she convinces On that he has nothing to gain by following this revolt she then blocks the entrance to their tent when Korah and his cronies call for him. She sat on their bed with her hair loose and spread out (rather than bound), hinting to the callers that they had interrupted an intimate moment that should not be disturbed. *Midrash Tanhuma*, Korah (Buber), 1; *Yalkut Shimoni*, Numbers 16, remez 750.

24. *Midrash Tanhuma*, Korah (Buber), 1.

25. Ibid.

26. Ibid.

27. *Tanna deVei Eliyahu*, parashah 10. See also *Yalkut Shimoni*, Jud. 4, remez 43.

28. According to amoraic traditions, Zebulun supported Issachar who studied Torah. In Deborah's song she suggests she is Issachar and Barak is Zebulun. See Jud. 5:15

29. The expression *Isha k'shera* is worthy of further study.

30. *Tanna deVei Eliyahu*, parashah 10. This is repeated in *Yalkut Shimoni*, Jud. 4, remez 42.

31. The date of the compilation is questioned by different scholars, and some date it as early as the third century. In addition the location of its compilation is unclear, with opinions ranging from Babylonia to Italy. For our purposes this is less important, although obviously of consequence. See the introduction by Meir Ish-Shalom, *Tanna deVei Eliyahu*, 44–91.

32. Ibid., 77.

33. Rashi, Jud 4:5, and R. Joseph Kara, Jud. 4:5, s.v. "vehi yoshevet," https://mg.alhatorah .org/Dual/R._Yosef_Kara/Shofetim/4.1#m7eon6.

34. Rashi, ibid.

35. This is based on his understanding of Jud. 5:8, "*ad shekamti*," but this appears only in the commentary on the Talmud and not in his biblical commentary.

36. The idea that she is nasty like a bee appears in *Yalkut Shimoni* on Judges but is not repeated elsewhere. See, for example, *Yalkut Shimoni*, Deut., Devarim 1: remez 795.

37. See, for example, Rashi, Jud. 4:21, s.v. "yated haohel"; "hamakevet."

38. Rashi, Jud. 5:24, s.v. "minashim baohel."

39. R. Joseph Kara, Jud. 4:5, s.v. "vehi yoshevet."Other northern French interpreters follow suit.

40. Jud. 4: 21 calls Jael's weapon a *makevet*, a mallet, according to the Jewish Publication Society translation. Jud. 5:26 translates the term "*halmut amelim*" as hammer. I have used hammer throughout for consistency.

41. See *Midrash Mishle*, Buber edition, parasha 31; *Yalkut Shimoni*, Jud. 5, remez 56; *Yalkut Shimoni*, Prov. 31, remez 964; This is also attributed to *Midrash Avkir.* but Amos Geula makes no note of it. See Geula, "Lost Aggadic Works."

42. R. Haim Paltiel, *Perushei R. Haim Paltiel*, Deut. 22:5.

43. Based on *Liber antiquitatum biblicarum*, chapter 33.

44. *Sefer haZikhronot*, 206.

45. In this case it is one of the only elements from the expansive story in *Biblical Antiquities* that is part of the *Sefer haZikhronot* narrative.

46. *Sefer haZikhronot*, 206.

47. Hieronymus, *Commentarium In Ezecheliem* 1.16.13.

48. For an excellent survey of the Christian sources, see Reardon, "Judge Deborah"; Schroeder, *Deborah's Daughters*.

49. Reardon, "Judge Deborah"; Schroeder, *Deborah's Daughters*, 19–21.

50. Reardon, "Judge Deborah"; Schroeder, *Deborah's Daughters*, 26.

51. Schroeder, *Deborah's Daughters*, 2–43.

52. See n. 48.

53. Schroeder, *Deborah's Daughters*, 62–67.

54. About these books, see Cockerell and Plummer, *Old Testament Miniatures*; Thomas, *Scènes de l'ancien testament illustrant*. About Psalters and their use, see Panayotova, "Illustrated Psalter," 247–71.

55. Schroeder, *Deborah's Daughters*, 34–36; Reardon, "Judge Deborah."

56. Schroeder, *Deborah's Daughters*, 49–55.

57. Ibid., 45.

58. For a discussion of the figure of the Maccabean mother and a comparison of Jewish and Christian attitudes toward her, see Baumgarten, "Jewish Conceptions of Motherhood," 149–65; Baumgarten and Kushelevsky, "From 'The Mother and Her Sons,'" 301, 313–21; Joslyn-Siemiatkoski, *Christian Memories*.

59. Quoted in Peter Abelard, *Letters*, 284; Peter Abelard, *Hymnarius Paraclitensis*, 2:258.

60. Schroeder, *Deborah's Daughters*, 45–46; see also Mews and Perry, "Peter Abelard, Heloise and Jewish Biblical Exegesis," 9.

61. Schroeder, *Deborah's Daughters*, 55–57.

62. Ibid., 59.

63. Ibid., 57–58.

64. A common idea when discussing biblical figures or saints.

65. As outlined by Schroeder, *Deborah's Daughters*, 47–48. Gratian explicitly discussed whether women could be judges.

66. Burger, *Conduct Becoming*, 81–82.

67. Albertus, *Valiant Woman*, 138.

68. See figures 3.4–3.7.

69. See *Glossa ordinaria*, Jud. 4, 179–80, in the interlinear gloss. For a summary of Christian interpretation, see Vrudny, *Friars, Scribes, and Corpses*, 130–33.

70. About the *Speculum*, see *Mirror of Salvation*, ed. Labriola and Smeltz, 9–11; *Medieval Mirror*, ed. Wilson and Wilson, 1–8.

71. About Rudolf, see Graeme Dunphy et al., *History as Literature*.

72. This returns to the theme underlined in the introduction that women were often educated by way of these figures; see also Saghy, "Master and Marcella," 127–38.

73. Reardon, "Judge Deborah."

74. Tosafot, BT Niddah 50a, s.v. "kol hakasher"; BT Bava Kamma, fol. 15a; BT Shevuot 30a and commentary there.

75. Isaac b. Moses, *Sefer Or Zaru'a, Piskei Bava Kamma*, 3: no. 93.

76. Meir b. Barukh of Rothenburg, *Shut Maharam*, Crimona edition, no. 29.

77. Mishnah, Sanhedrin 4:1.

78. See n. .

79. Furst, "Striving for Justice," outlines the roles women played in courts. Especially relevant is chapter 2. She demonstrates that women often had representatives. although they were active players outside the court; see, for example, 98–102.

80. Mordekhai, *Yebamot*, 45a; Asher b. Yehiel, *Tosafot*, Kiddushin 31a, s.v. "veasher tasim lifnehem,"

81. See *Mahzor Vitry*, ed. Horowitz, 463, where only men appear and Barak appears instead of Deborah; see also MS JTS 8092, fol. 77r. For a discussion of who wrote this commentary, see Ta-Shma, "Al Perush Avot," 507–8. For the purposes of my argument, it doesn't matter who the exact author of the commentary was.

82. Rashi, Jud. 5:15, s.v. "im Devorah" and this explanation is echoed by R. Joseph Kara ad locum as well.

83. BT Yoma 66b. This statement has been discussed by many scholars. The most relevant discussions for our purposes are Zolty, *And All Your Children*, 125; Baskin, "Some Parallels," 41–51; Grossman, *Pious and Rebellious*, 168–69.

84. They were killed by sword, by water, and by plague according to BT Yoma 66b, and Rashi, s.v. "ma'aseh ha'egel shavin," explains this.

85. *Sefer Hasidim Parma*, no. 1502. The entire passage is quoted in section on the pages that follow.

86. See Hauptman, *Rereading the Rabbis*, 22, 23, 43. Also compare with BT Sotah 21a.

87. This is the opinion of Ben Azzai in the talmudic discussion in Sotah.

88. *Sefer Hasidim Parma*, no. 1502.

89. Ibid., no. 1501.

90. This is not self-evident. A further comparison should be undertaken comparing between east and west. See, for example, Maimonides responsum concerning a female Torah teacher: Levine-Melammed, "He Said, She Said," 19–35.

91. Abelard and Heloise's story is one of the most famous in medieval western Christendom. For a précis, see Mews, *Abelard and Heloise*, 7–14.

92. Kanarfogel, *Jewish Education*, 10–11; Baskin, "Some Parallels."

93. For a discussion of this poem, see the concluding chapter of this volume.

94. See *Gezerot Ashkenaz veZarfat*, ed. Habermann, 167–68.

95. Ibid.

96. See MS Paris, BnF, Lat. 6220: "Livre de la taille de Paris pour l'an 1292"; Geraud, *Paris sous Philippe le Bel*.

97. Courtenay, "Parisian Grammar Schools," 209–10.

98. Jacobs-Pollez, "Role of the Mother," 15–27; Jacobs-Pollez, "Education of Noble Girls," 101–8.

99. Orme, *Medieval Children*, 237–72; Goering, "Thirteenth-Century English Parish," 208–22.

100. Kanarfogel, *Jewish Education*, 50–54, 57–58.

101. Kanarfogel, *Jewish Education*.

102. These tax lists were recently analyzed by Dermer, "Jews in the Tax Lists," 79–90. For an earlier analysis, see Loeb, "Le rôle des Juifs de Paris," 61–71.

103. This is often stated about women as if it in some ways diminishes their power or knowledge. Yet the same holds true for many men who were in positions of authority in the medieval world. They, too, were related to other powerful men and grew up in their households. In this way, their knowledge or power is no less or more theirs than their ancestors.

104. The list first appears in Berliner, and is repeated in Ta-Shma, "Ma'amad haNashim," 267–79; Grossman, *Pious and Rebellious*, 194–95.

105. See also Elias Bar-Levav, "Minhag yafeh," 47–85.

106. *Sefer Gezerot Ashkenaz ve Zarfat,* ed. Habermann, 168.

107. http://www.steinheim-institut.de/cgi-bin/epidat?id=wrm-903&lang=en.

108. http://www.steinheim-institut.de/cgi-bin/epidat?id=wrm-522&lang=en.

109. See Salfeld, *Martyrologium*, 36.

110. Elias Bar-Levav, "Minhag yafeh," 47–85, provides a detailed analysis of each of the sources she discusses.

111. *Hebräische Berichte*, ed. Haverkamp, 289.

112. Ephraim b. Jacob of Bonn, *Sefer Zekhirah*, 31. See the discussion of this figure in Einbinder, "Pucellina of Blois," 32–40.

113. The *Nürnberg memorbuch* includes a number of examples of such couples and women, as do a variety of responsa. See Baumgarten, *Practicing Piety*.

114. See http://www.steinheim-institut.de/cgi-bin/epidat?id=mz1-2210&lang=de; http://www.steinheim-institut.de/cgi-bin/epidat?id=wrm-1106&lang=de; http://www.steinheim-institut.de/cgi-bin/epidat?id=wrm-385&lang=de.

115. These inscriptions are analyzed and discussed in detail by Barzen, "Materialization of Memoria."

116. R. Meir b. Barukh died in 1293, three years before the *memorbuch* was created.

117. Lehnertz, "Margarete, Reynette, and Meide"; Aviya Doron has a number of such cases in her PhD in progress.

118. http://www.steinheim-institut.de/cgi-bin/epidat?id=mz1-2209&lang=de

119. http://www.steinheim-institut.de/cgi-bin/epidat?id=wrm-153&lang=de

120. This returns to the theme, as underlined in the introduction, that women were often educated by way of these figures; see also Saghy, "Master and Marcella," 127–38.

121. Kanarfogel, *Jewish Education*, 19–32.

122. Ibid.; tutors were the main method of education of boys, as Kanarfogel describes. Evidence from the Geniza indicates that girls often learned alongside boys in the schools. See Goitein, *Jewish Education*, 63–74.

123. Baumgarten and Frakes, *Introduction to Old Yiddish Literature*.

124. See Oren Roman, "Old-Yiddish Epics," whose edition is based on MS Parma 2513 from 1511. Roman, "Song of Deborah," 27–44. I thank Dr. Roman for his help on this matter.

125. Roman, "Old-Yiddish Epics," 2: 73–77, 189–95.

126. Ibid., 1: 111, 154.

127. According to Roman, the verse reads: "*Sie richtet Yisroel*," "*Kinder yisroel gingen zu ihr zu gerecht.*"

128. *Many Pious Women*, ed. Fox and Lewis, 62.

129. Ibid., 196–97.

130. Ibid.

131. Ibid., 197.

132. Ibid.

133. Ibid.

134. *Tsena uRena*, Ex. Beshalah.

135. Ibid.

136. Ibid.

137. Rashi., Jud. 4:19, s.v. "nod hehalav."

138. *Tsena uRena*, Ex. Beshalah.

139. Ibid.

140. This sentiment can be found in poetry recited on the seventh day of Passover, when the crossing of the Red Sea was commemorated. In his poem "I Patros," Shimon b. Isaac describes Deborah and Barak as being on par with Moses. It is telling that Deborah is not presented independently but only along with Barak. See Shimon b. Yitzhak, *Piyutei*, 39. About this poem, see Davidson, *Thesaurus*, 2628.

141. *Meneket Rivkah*, 118.

142. Ibid.

143. Ibid., 118–19.

144. Ibid.

145. Ibid.

146. Ibid., 101.

147. See the discussion in Chapter 4.

148. Hendele b. R. Mordekhai Oppenheim, Frankfurt am Main, d. 1695, http://www.steinheim-institut.de/cgi-bin/epidat?id=ffb-1509&lang=de.

149. Minkeleh b. Isaac, Frankfurt am Main, d. 1700, http://www.steinheim-institut.de/cgi-bin/epidat?id=ffb-141&lang=de.

150. http://www.steinheim-institut.de/cgi-bin/epidat?id=smk-36&lang=de.

151. Nuha b. Juda, Worms, d. 1683, http://www.steinheim-institut.de/cgi-bin/epidat?id=wrm-973&lang=de.

152. Sarah b. Yehiel, Hamburg-Altona, d. 1728, http://www.steinheim-institut.de/cgi-bin/epidat?id=hha-2981&lang=de.

153. Dina b. Nathan the Judge, Hamburg-Altona, d. 1735, http://www.steinheim-institut.de/cgi-bin/epidat?id=hha-1867&lang=de.

154. Hannah b. Joseph, Hamburg-Altona, d. 1737, http://www.steinheim-institut.de/cgi-bin/epidat?id=hha-1867&lang=de.

155. In Hamburg-Altona, these are Rebecca b. Joseph Hamel, Hamburg-Altona, d. 1764 [Glückel's daughter?], http://www.steinheim-institut.de/cgi-bin/epidat?id=hha-2286&lang=de; Rosche b. Bendit, Hamburg-Altona, d. 1775, http://www.steinheim-institut.de/cgi-bin/epidat?id=hha-1702&lang=de; Tzippora b. Moshe, Hamburg-Altona, d. 1782, http://www.steinheim-institut.de/cgi-bin/epidat?id=hha-651&lang=de. These women are joined by a woman from Trier (her name is illegible), 1766, http://www.steinheim-institut.de/cgi-bin/epidat?id=tri-333&lang=de; Dabrash of Worms, who died in 1736, http://www.steinheim-institut.de/cgi-bin/epidat?id=wrm-1218&lang=de ; and Rekhle, wife of Jacob of Worms, d. 1794, http://www.steinheim-institut.de/cgi-bin/epidat?id=wrm-1021&lang=de. All these epitaphs deserve further attention that is beyond the scope of this chapter.

156. http://www.steinheim-institut.de/cgi-bin/epidat?id=ffb-693&lang=de.

157. http://www.steinheim-institut.de/cgi-bin/epidat?id=hha-1475&lang=de.

158. http://www.steinheim-institut.de/cgi-bin/epidat?id=ffb-1591&lang=de.

159. http://www.steinheim-institut.de/cgi-bin/epidat?id=ffb-3027&lang=de.

160. http://www.steinheim-institut.de/cgi-bin/epidat?id=ffb-5841&lang=de.

161. For a discussion concerning the lack of female mystics in medieval Jewish culture, see Grossman, *Pious and Rebellious*, 277–80.

Chapter 4

Epigraph: This formula appears on many tombstones from Germany, entirely or in select portions (the opening or closing lines). I have collected only a small fraction of them and discuss them below. See n. 71.

1. For a discussion of gravestone inscriptions, see Greenblatt, *To Tell Their Children*, 181–227. For a detailed study of medieval tombstones, see the recent volume about grave markers in Würzburg: Müller et al., *Die Grabsteine*.

2. Various verses from Prov. 31 were included in a wide variety of common formulas for women.

3. Mark R. Cohen, *Poverty and Charity*, 83–90.

4. Gray, "Married Women," 204–5.

5. 1 Sam 25:2. For a discussion of "*tovat sekhel*," a phrase translated as "intelligent" in the modern JPS translation, see van Rensburg, "Intellect and/or Beauty," 112–17. As Sarah Ben-Reuven has noted, three women are described in the Bible as wise: the wise woman from Teko'a; the wise woman from Beit Ma'akhah, and Abigail. All three prevented bloodshed. "David bein Avigail veBatSheva," 244–45. See also Fischer, "Abigajil: Weisheit und Prophetie," 45–61.

6. For literature analyzing Abigail's figure in the Bible, see Bach, "Pleasure of Her Text," 41–58; Bach, *Women, Seduction, and Betrayal*; Garsiel, "Wit, Words and a Woman," 161–68; Donnet-Guez, "Modernité et independence," 29–48; Shraga Ben-Ayun, *David's Wives*, 87–158, esp. 137–57.

7. 2 Sam. 3:3; 1 Chronicles 3:1. Commentators in late antiquity and the medieval period alike viewed this son, Chileab, as especially righteous. See *Avot de Rabbi Nathan*, nusah A, hosafa B, ch. 2; BT Berakhot, 4a, Rashi s.v. "*mekhalim pnei Mefiboshet*." Rashi's commentary on 2 Sam. 3:3 and 1 Chronicles 3:1 attributed the reference in Prov. 23:15, "My son, if your mind gets wisdom," to Chileab.

8. As in the case of Deborah, the most relevant texts appear in a number of passages in the Talmud and Midrash, although once again Josephus includes Abigail and David's meeting in his *Antiquities* as well. In her analysis of Josephus's treatment of Abigail, Athalya Brenner argued that Josephus significantly reduced Abigail's role in this narrative, namely by abbreviating her speech: "Are We Amused?" 90–106. See

also Begg, "Abigail," 5–34. More recently, Michael Avioz has argued against this assessment: "Josephus's Retelling," 135–56. In any case, Josephus's writings were not included in the corpus available to medieval Jewish scholars.

9. BT Megillah 14b; some parallel passages to this discussion can be found in PT Sanhedrin, ch. 2.

10. Judith Baskin has discussed these passages: "Erotic Subversion," 227–44. See also Bodi, "Was Abigail a Scarlet Woman?" 67–73; Levine Katz, "Seven Prophetesses," 123–30.

11. Jerome, along with most of Christian commentators in late antiquity, ascribed the meaning "*patris meis exsultatio*" to the name Abigail. S. Eusebii Hieronymi Stridonensis, *PL* 23, *Liber de nominibus*, col. 811.

12. This quotation, as well as those that follow, are all from BT Megillah 14b.

13. It is noteworthy that David is presented as an authority on *Hilkhot Niddah* in other talmudic passages as well. See, for example, BT Avodah Zarah 24b. I thank Judah Galinsky for bringing this to my attention.

14. See Simon, *"Seek Peace and Pursue It,"* 177–217.

15. Bodi, "Was Abigail a Scarlet Woman?" 67–73.

16. BT Megillah 14b.

17. Modern scholars as well as ancient exegetes built on this comparison between Abigail and Bathsheba; see McKay, "Eshet Hayil," 257–80, especially 265–79 and the literature noted there; Shraga Ben-Ayun, *David's Wives*, 137–44.

18. BT Megillah 14 a–b.

19. Baskin, "Erotic Subversion," 227–44.

20. *Midrash Tanhuma*, ed. Buber, Toldot 6, 122–23.

21. See *Midrash Shmuel*, ed. Lifshitz, 78, lines 115–30.

22. See *Midrash Tadshe*, ed. Epstein, 170. About this midrash, see Reizel and Bazak, *Introduction to the Midrashic Literature*, 411–14.

23. For the history of this composition, see the introduction in *Midrash Tehillim haMekhune Shoher Tov*, ed. Buber, 3–9.

24. Ibid., Psalm 53, 144–45.

25. Joseph Kara, Samuel I, 25: 3, s.v. "and the woman was wise." I have relied here on the *Mikraot Gedolot*, 9: 1 Sam. 25:3. About Joseph Kara, see Grossman, *Early Sages of France*, 254–55, 311–18.

26. This commentary has been attributed to Judah Sirleon in early thirteenth-century Paris; and see Urbach, *Tosaphists*, 617–18.

27. Tosafot, BT Megillah 14b, s.v. *gilta shokah*.

28. Gray, "Married Women," 168–212. See also Katz, "Married Woman," 101–41.

29. BT Bava Kama 119a.

30. For a discussion of Jewish women's roles in the medieval economy, see Jordan, "Jews on Top," 39–57; Grossman, *Pious and Rebellious*, 147–53; Hoyle, "Bonds," 119–29, and in early modern Germany, Kaplan, "Because Our Wives Trade," 241–61.

31. Women's participation in family businesses is attested in seventeenth-century Germany by the well-documented life of Glückel of Hamel. She was an active partner alongside her husband in their business until his death, when she took the lead role and supervised the sons and sons-in-law who became her business partners; see Davis, *Women on the Margin*, 5–62; Turniansky, "Introduction." 39–44. Even though Glückel's family appears to illustrate an early modern pattern of Jewish family business that stems from medieval customs, the degree of continuity represented by their example still requires verification.

32. Agus, *Heroic Age*, 1: 256–419, contains sources that discuss economics and key roles held by women in business matters; Jordan, "Jews on Top," 39–56; Grossman, *Pious and Rebellious*, 117–22; Gray, "Married Women."

33. Eliezer b. Nathan, *Sefer Ra'avan*, response no. 115, and Eliezer b. Nathan, *Sefer Ra'avan*, Piskei Bava Kama, 191a.

34. See *Sefer Ra'avan*, Piskei Bava Kama, 191a, s.v. "but they take." And see Gray's discussion of these texts, "Married Women," 188–96.

35. For examples of women mentioned in narratives of persecution as women of means who excelled at business, one could note Marat Minna in the Crusade chronicles and Pucellina of Blois in the Blois event. See Grossman, *Pious and Rebellious*, 275; Einbinder, "Pucellina of Blois," 21–46.

36. See, for example, MS Paris héb. 326, fol. 71b, a collection of halakhot from the fourteenth century; Samson b. Tzadok, *Sefer Tashbetz*, no. 153; Asher b. Yehiel, *Shut haRosh*, no. 13, section 11. This is a more general phenomenon, relating to the role of the Talmud in thirteenth-century halakhic discourse. Fishman, *Becoming the People of the Talmud*, 121–181.

37. Isaac b. Moses, *Sefer Or Zaru'a*, Piskei Bava Kama, 3: no. 468.

38. Ibid.; Moses of Coucy, *Semag*, Aseh no. 162; Isaac of Corbeil, *Sefer 'Amudei Golah haNikra Semak*, no. 247.

39. Samson b. Tzadok, *Sefer Tashbetz*, no. 153.

40. Asher b. Yehiel, *Shut haRosh*, rule 13, no. 11.

41. Howell, "Gender," 519–38, has summarized recent scholarship.

42. Ibid, 522.

43. Fishman, *Becoming the People*, 147–54.

44. *Sefer Hasidim* has been the topic of much research during the past century. For an overview, see Marcus, *Piety and Society*; Marcus, "Introduction," 11–24; Soloveitchik, "Three Themes," 311–58; and the collection of articles in *Jewish Quarterly Review* 96 (2006) written in response to Soloveitchik, "Piety, Pietism," 455–93. Most recently see Baumgarten, Hollender and Shoham-Steiner, "Introduction."

45. *Sefer Hasidim Parma*, no. 1715. *Sefer Hasidim Bologna*, no. 1051. I thank Ivan Marcus for providing me with drafts of his translations of these passages, which were the basis for the translations that appear herein. I have altered his translations slightly.

46. Kaplan, *Patrons of the Poor*, 48–67.

47. *Sefer Hasidim Parma,* no. 844 (= *Sefer Hasidim Bologna,* no. 315). Here too I thank Ivan Marcus.

48. The relation between halakhah and medieval life (often called *realia* by some modern scholars) has been the subject of much research. See, for example, Ta-Shma, "Halakha and Reality," 315–29; Kanarfogel, "Halakha and Metziut," 193–224.

49. Jacob b. Moses Moellin, *Shut Maharil haHadashot,* no. 109.

50. See Gray's comments on this responsum, "Married Women," 2027.

51. *Sefer Hasidim Parma,* no. 670; *Sefer Hasidim Bologna,* no. 877.

52. Despite the distinction sometimes made between halakhists and figures such as Judah, who is often referred to as a hasid, it is noteworthy that he, too, was a legal decisor (*posek*); and see Kanarfogel, *Intellectual and Rabbinic Culture,* 44–45.

53. See Chapter 2; Baumgarten, *Practicing Piety,* 103–37.

54. Beda Venerabilis, *In Samuelem propheta allegorica expositio, PL* 91 Liber IV, 0687d–0688a, "*in operibus charitatis gloria praefulgidis, idem Pater exsultans affatur* (688d); and in later works: for example, Rabanus Maurus, *Commentaria in libros iv regum, PL* 109, librum primum, XXV: col. 64; Angelomus Luxonvensis, *Monachi errationes in libros Regum, PL* 115, Librum primum, XXV: col. 325; Rupertus Tuitiensis, *Opera omnia, PL* 168, Opus de gloria et honore filii hominis super Matthaeum, VII: col. 1452; Rupertus Tuitiensis, *Ad venerabilem ecclesiae, PL* 170, Liber secundus, VII, 39b; Godefridus Admontensis, *Homiliae dominicales, PL* 174, Homilia XLV, "de tempore paschali," col. 305a. The idea is echoed in Bernardus Clarvallensis, *Parabolae, PL* 183, parabola IV, "de Christo et ecclesia," col. 767d. This is a preliminary list of texts that discuss Abigail. I cite them here as they may be useful for future research.

55. Peter Abelard, *Letters,* 165.

56. I thank Sarah-Grace Heller for discussing this with me and look forward to her forthcoming book on the topic.

57. Abigail appears in ch. 36. For a discussion of the editions and the illustrations, see *Medieval Mirror,* ed. Wilson and Wilson.

58. I thank Dr. Leon Jacobowitz Efron, who brought to my attention that the colors Abigail is wearing in Fig. 4.2 typified the attire worn by urban matrons in fourteenth-century Germany.

59. Grigsby, "Miroir des bonnes femmes," 36.

60. Main, "Naming Children," 1–27; Ulrich, *Good Wives,* presents biblical women as female role models in colonial New England, focusing on Bathsheba, Jael, and Eve rather than Abigail.

61. Bleyerveld, *Hoe bedriechlijk dat die vrouwen zijn,* 180–84, 245–46; Bleyerveld, "Chaste, Obedient and Devout," 219–50.

62. Farmer, "Persuasive Voices," 517–43.

63. Ibid., 517.

64. Caesarius of Heisterbach, *Dialogus miraculorum*, 1: 351; this story is discussed and translated in Peter Biller, "Popular Religion," 134.

65. I note this because rabbis and preachers did not hold completely parallel roles. Nevertheless, communal rabbinic authorities often played more than one role within a community, both as legal authorities and as communal officials.

66. Shlomo Luria (Poland, 1510–73), *Yam shel Shlomo*, Tractate Bava Kama, 119a; Yehezkel Landau (Poland, 1713–93), *Noda be-Yehuda Tanina*, Yoreh De'ah, no. 158; Judah b. Israel Aszod (Hungary, 1794–188?), *Shut Ya'aleh Yehuda*, 2; *Even ha'Ezer*, Hoshen Mishpat, no. 43; Shlomo Gantzfried, *Kitzur Shulhan 'Arukh*, Yoreh De'ah, Hilkhot Tzedakah, no. 447, 459.

67. For a discussion of gravestone inscriptions, see Greenblatt, *To Tell Their Children*, 47–82. We look forward to the forthcoming publication of Michael Brocke's research on German cemeteries, some of which is already documented on the Steinheim website: http://www.steinheim-institut.de/cgi-bin/epidat. See Brocke and Müller, *Haus des Lebens* (esp. p. 76, for mention of Abigail). For a detailed study of medieval tombstones, see the recent volumes about grave markers in Würzburg (Müller et al. *Die Grabsteine vom jüdischen Friedhof*), where there is no mention of Abigail.

68. See http://www.steinheim-institut.de/cgi-bin/epidat. A search using the phrase "eshet hayil" results in hundreds of examples.

69. Various verses from Prov. 31 were included in a wide variety of common formulas for women in the early modern period. See http://www.steinheim-institut.de/cgi-bin/epidat, where most women's epitaphs include the phrase "woman of valor" with different formulas or without any other verses altogether.

70. The most recent epitaph I found is dated from 1881 (see n. 71). References to Abigail's charitable acts are found through the mid-nineteenth century. After that point tombstone inscriptions mention Abigail's modesty without making associations to charity.

71. All italics indicate biblical verses. See Dobrash Bachrach, d. 1736, in Lewysohn, *Nafshot Tzadikim*, #42, 79. Perl, wife of Jacob Hilb, 1777–1843, in *Der jüdische Friedhof Wankheim*, documented by Hüttenmeister, Stone no. 22, pp. 58–59; Dauphine Hertz (geb. Cantor), d. 1852, in Brocke and Pomeranz (eds.), *Steine wie Seelen*, 102; For a slightly different version of the formula following the mention of Abigail, see Rösche Neukamp, d. 1848, in Brocke, *Der jüdische Friedhof*, 72; also, an anonymous stone bears another variation on the formula, "here is a righteous and honest woman, charitable like Abigail and Sarah, her deeds were pleasant [. . .]," Brocke, *Der jüdische Friedhof*, 76–77; Gitel bat Oppenheim, d. 1777; Sarah bat Leser Bückeberg, d. 1800; Sarah bat Mordekhai Halle, d. 1816, in Gelderblom, *Die Juden von Hameln*, 210, 216, 218, and see the tombstones of Jetta, wife of Abraham, d. 1820 (221) and Hannah bat Salomon, d. 1844 (226) where only a portion of the formula appears. See also the Steinheim database, where the formula appears on tombstones until the mid-nineteenth century: Arolsen (1764, 3 examples from 1815–36); Bayreuth

(1881); Bingen (7 examples from 1825–39); Blieskastel (1836); Bonn-Schwarzrheindorf (1754); Detmold (1749); Dillingen-Diefflen (1870); Haigerloch (1844); Hamburg (1723, 1769, 1782, 1789, 1806); Hamburg-Altona (1815), Hammerstein (1732); Heilbronn (1843); Hildesheim (1760); Homburg (1832); Ilingen (1847, 1851, 1852); Jüchen-Garzweiler (1821); Krefeld (1852); Linnich (1821); Mönchengladbach-Odenkirchen (1798); Roermond, Oude kerkhof (1843); Preußisch Oldendorf (1772); Regensburg (1879); Rüthen (1847); Schermbeck (1801); Schmalkalden (1700, 1744, 1750–55, 1799); Sonderhausen (1836); Trier (1766); Worms (1658, 1736, 1736, 1749).

72. While Dobrash was named Deborah, the other women whose tombstones included this inscription show no commonality or link according to their variety of names.

73. Many epitaphs note the charity of the deceased without mention of Abigail, yet the association between her and charity is demonstrated over a long time frame and is therefore significant in my eyes.

74. Muneles, ed., *Ketovot*, no. 61, 161.

75. Although Abigail is not mentioned in this manual, the high level of familiarity with and ready access to biblical references assumed by its author (of her female readers) are of great relevance for this study; see *Meneket Rivkah*.

76. "Es sich trift das ain zadik hot ain bös weib. Un' der roscho ain vrumes di is ain grose znuo gewesen mit ire maasim" (Altschul-Jeruschalmi, *Brantspiegel*, 70).

77. See also the portrayal of Abigail in *Sefer Zekhirah*, a book of *segulot* written in the seventeenth century, where she is depicted seated in the fifth sphere in heaven, leading other women in prayer; cited by Hovav, *Maidens Love Thee*, 83.

78. *Birkat haMazon veZemirot*, fol. 27a in the original; p. 90 in the reproduction. I thank Albert Kohn for the reference to this booklet.

79. Interestingly, as is the norm in such books, this image appears elsewhere in the booklet as well (p. 53), providing instructions for prayers for the wine on the holiday of Shavuot and without any references to Abigail.

80. *Many Pious Women*, ed. Fox and Lewis, 226.

Chapter 5

1. For a detailed description of how these periods were calculated from the twelfth century in Europe, see Nothaft et al., *Medieval Latin Christian Texts*, 31–33; Carlebach, *Palaces of Time*, 6–27.

2. For an overview of astronomy in medieval Jewish culture, see Leicht, "Reception of Astrology," 201–34; Leicht, "Toward a History of Hebrew Astrological Literature," 255–91; Goldstein, "Astronomy among Jews," 136–46.

3. Mieke Bal has written the most notable work of scholarship on Jephthah's daughter in *Death and Dissymmetry*. For other interpretations, see Tapp, "Ideology of Expendability," 157–74; Fuchs, "Marginalization, Ambiguity, Silencing," 116–44; Brown, *No Longer Be Silent*, 93–109.

4. The story of Jephthah is read as the haftarah for *Hukat*. The choice is based on the shared discussion of fighting against Sihon the Amorite.

5. Many literary analyses have critiqued Jephthah's response as seeming to blame his daughter when he says: "You have brought me low; you have become my troubler" (Jud. 11:35).

6. For a survey of the classic interpretations of this story, see Valler, "Story of Jephthah's Daughter," 48–66, and Levenson, *Death and Resurrection*, 14–17. Also see n. 2.

7. For editions of the *Biblical Antiquities*, see *Pseudo-Philo*, ed. Jacobson; Harrington et al., *Les antiquités bibliques*; as well as Murphy, *Pseudo-Philo*, 166–69.

8. For a detailed discussion of this name, see Feldman, *Glory and Agony*, 208–14, who argues that it comes from the promise to sacrifice Jephthah's daughter and from the comparison between this narrative and the story of Hannah and Samuel. For a discussion of Pseudo-Philo's portrayal of Seila, see Brown, *No Longer Be Silent*; van der Horst, "Deborah and Seila," 111–17; Thompson, *Writing the Wrongs*, 106–11.

9. As *Pseudo-Philo*, ed. Jacobson, 961 notes this sentiment stands in contrast to the midrash, which portrays Jephthah's daughter protesting her imminent death.

10. *Pseudo-Philo*, ed. Jacobson, 40:6 and thus the source for her name, from *she'ol*, the underworld.

11. Ibid., 40:4.

12. BT Rosh Hashana 25b; see BT Sotah 8a for an example of the rabbi's negative assessment of Jephthah. See Valler, "Story of Jephthah's Daughter," for a full list of amoraic texts.

13. This is an anachronistic notion, since it assumes that the practice of revoking vows, which was well established by mishnaic and talmudic times, was operative in a similar way during the time of the judges.

14. Thus, for example, when discussing "And they have built the shrines of Topeth . . . to burn their sons and daughters in fire—which I never commanded, which never came to my mind" (Jeremiah 7:31), BT Ta'anit 4a and various midrashic sources (*Tanhuma*, Buber edition, Behukotai, no. 7, and parallels) interpret: "which I never commanded" as a reference to Jephthah's daughter and "which never came to my mind" in relation to Isaac. However, no expansion of this comparison follows, and this is the sole mention of Jephthah and Abraham together in the corpus of rabbinic literature. Jephthah is routinely discussed in association with Eleazar, Caleb, and Saul, for they all swore improper vows.

15. *Pseudo-Philo*, ed. Jacobson, 1:40:2, pp. 160–62.

16. Ibid., 161.

17. This is evident in one of the earliest known depictions of Jephthah's daughter, at the St. Catherine Monastery (Sinai Desert, dated to the sixth century). See Weitzmann, "Jephthah Panel," 341–58 and, more recently, Drewer, "Jephthah and His Daughter," 35–59.

18. Thompson, *Writing the Wrongs*, 125–36.

19. Alexiou and Dronke, "Lament," 819–69.

20. For similarities between Jephthah's daughter and Iphigenia (and other classical figures), see, for example, in Alexiou and Dronke, "Lament," 825–49. It is interesting to note the existence of a nonsacrificial tradition about Iphigenia, much like the nonsacrificial tradition about Jephthah's daughter. For Iphigenia, see Dowden, *Death*, 17 and 37. In some versions various animals are substituted for her, but in others she is placed in seclusion.

21. For a detailed history of the *Biblical Antiquities* in medieval western Christendom, see Smits, "Contribution," 197–216. For a summary of how ideas concerning Jephthah's daughter in the Augustine tradition were transmitted in medieval biblical exegesis, see Thompson, *Writing the Wrongs*, 133–44.

22. For a partial translation of this *planctus* into English, see Dronke, "Medieval Poetry," 840–45. For a full translation, see Peter Abelard, *Letters*, 284–88.

23. Dronke, "Medieval Poetry," 841, "*O Stupendam plus quam flendam virginem! O quam rarum illi virum similem!*"

24. Abelard emphasizes that her choice is all the more laudable for being carried out by a woman. This is one of the ways he emphasizes the glory she will achieve if she is sacrificed: "If he who refused a boy accepts a girl, think what a triumph it is for my sex . . . what a glory it is for me and for you!" Ibid., 842.

25. *Letters of Abelard and Héloise*, trans. Moncrieff, 158–59.

26. Rabanus Maurus, "On the Oblation of Children," translated by Boswell, *Kindness of Strangers*, 441–42. Rabanus Maurus quotes *Biblical Antiquities*.

27. Boswell, *Kindness of Strangers*, index, s.v. "Samuel," and, more recently, de Jong, *In Samuel's Image*.

28. "The woman worthy of solemn Mass" is the Maccabean mother of the seven martyred sons. See Peter Abelard, *Letters*, 284, n. 4. See also n. 87.

29. Ibid., 283–84. See Chapter 3 above, p. X.

30. Newman, *From Virile Woman*, 78–80.

31. Drewer, "Jephthah and His Daughter," 48–51.

32. *Glossa ordinaria, PL* 113:530; See also *Biblia latina cum glossa ordinaria*, 493.

33. Drewer, "Jephthah and His Daughter," 42–51.

34. Ibid., 49.

35. *Mirror of Salvation*, ed. Labriola and Smeltz.

36. Gibson, "Blessing," 139–57.

37. On the popularity of the *Speculum* see *Mirror of Salvation*, ed. Labriola and Smeltz, 5.

38. See *Medieval Mirror*, ed. Wilson and Wilson, 10.

39. Most notably, the *Glossa ordinaria, PL* 113, 530. For images of the Temple, see Harris, "Body as Temple," 233–56. Such depictions of Jephthah's daughter as a nun who endured a violent death are in contrast to earlier Byzantine imagery that often omitted the scene of her death; see Drewer, "Jephthah and His Daughter," 39–48.

40. Berman, "Medieval Monasticism," 228–56.

41. *Sefer haZikhronot*, ed. Yassif, 18–19, emphasizes that he refers to this book as *Sefer*

Toldot rather than *Divrei haYamim leYerahmiel*, although he does attribute the entire section to Yerahmiel.

42. Ibid., 27.

43. Ibid.

44. Ibid., 209–10.

45. Ibid.

46. Ibid.

47. Yerahmiel also modifies the wording of Seila's speech when she petitions the hills and rocks to mourn her death. According to *Biblical Antiquities*, she says: "But let my life not be taken in vain. May my words go forth to the heavens and my tears be written before the firmament, in order that a father not venture to sacrifice a daughter whom he has vowed and a ruler not let his only daughter be promised for sacrifice" (*Biblical Antiquities*, 40:5). Although Seila does repeat her critique that her father should never have sworn such a vow, she concludes by saying: "And let my life not be in vain—May my words be atoned in the heavens and my tears be encoded in the sky." By translating the opening word *sed* as "and" instead of "but," and *ut* as "because" rather than "in order," as in *Biblical Antiquities*, Yerahmiel's translation lacks the cautionary notion that such vows are unethical.

48. See the recent work of Ruth Nisse, which masterfully traces similar shared and lost traditions: *Jacob's Shipwreck*. Following *Biblical Antiquities* requires further research.

49. Alexiou and Dronke, "Lament," 849–63.

50. See Martha Himmelfarb "Mother of the Messiah," 369–90, on how these they may have been transmitted between cultures, despite the lack of textual evidence for mapping these traditions.

51. J. Cohen, *Sanctifying the Name of God*, 151–52. Davidovich-Eshed, "Desecrated Woman," 37–66.

52. See *Hebräische Berichte*, ed. Haverkamp, 424–34, esp. 431. Haverkamp identifies this place as Eller or Ellen.

53. Davidovich-Eshed, "Desecrated Woman," 37–66.

54. Ibid., 56–57, suggests that Jewish sources speak of some virgin deaths in similar terms to the consecration of nuns.

55. Marcus, *Jephthah and His Vow*.

56. Berman, "Medieval Monasticism," 232–38.

57. Abarbanel, *Perush*, 130.

58. This was noted in the ancient world as well. However, the records and customs I discuss appear specifically in medieval texts.

59. Carlebach, *Palaces of Time*, 6–27.

60. See Ta-Shma, "Danger of Drinking," 21–32, and the bibliography there.

61. *Teshuvot haGeonim*, no. 14 and *Sha'arei teshuva leGeonim*, no. 80. R. Judah heHasid also cites this explanation; see n. 71.

62. As Ta-Shma notes, "Danger of Drinking," 22, this explanation postdates R. Hai's

lifetime and can be situated in eleventh-century Spain, where it was dismissed as nonsense (*divrei havai*). See also Roth, "Al haTekufot," 69–74, where he reviews the literature on the custom.

63. Aptowizer, "Prohibition to Drink Water," 122–26; Klein, "On the Dangers," 87. Similar ideas are found in other customs. For example, Ta-Shma has shown that Ashkenazic Jews refrained from eating the third meal late on Sabbath afternoons for fear of the Angel of Death: Ta-Shma, "Beera shel Miriam," 251–70. See also Shoham-Steiner, "Virgin Mary," 75–91. Inbar Gabay-Zada, "Ritual." Notably, many of these traditions are also associated with women's customs.

64. Ta-Shma, "Danger of Drinking," 23. As Ta-Shma remarks, R. Abraham b. Hiyya considers this custom without merit and discourages its observance.

65. Ta-Shma agrees that this custom is best known from medieval Ashkenaz (ibid., 24).

66. Issues concerning *mayyim shelanu* (water that was left out overnight) are distinct but not unrelated.

67. Ta-Shma, "Danger of Drinking," 24–27.

68. See Dan, "Keta miSefer haKavod," n. 62.

69. *Sefer haKavod* is no longer extant as a book, but passages from this work appear in various manuscripts and printed volumes. The section quoted here appears in MS Paris héb. 1032, fol. 28b–29a. See Dan, "Keta miSefer haKavod," 118.

70. The report on this event in Num. 20:11 states that the waters came out (*yatzu*). However, this explanation relies on Ps. 78:20: "He struck the rock and waters flowed."

71. Published by Dan, "Keta miSefer haKavod," 118–20. I am thankful to Israel Yuval for introducing this source to me several years ago. R. Judah ends this explanation with the verse that begins: "The Lord protects the simple" (Ps. 116:6), which seems to imply a certain disregard for this custom. However, he also cites a number of other explanations, many of which are discussed in the pages that follow. His comments make clear that this custom was observed in his time and that he supported its observance.

72. Ta-Shma, "Danger of Drinking," 27. See also the detailed discussion of Jacob b. Samson's book on the calendar in Wartenberg, "Hebrew Calendrical Bookshelf," 100–109, esp. 105–7.

73. See Ta-Shma, "Danger of Drinking," 24–29, and the notes that follow the second section of this article. See also Ginzberg, *Legends*, 4: 44, 7: 203–4; Trachtenberg, *Jewish Magic*, 160, 257–58.

74. The other three biblical narratives that are associated with the *tekufot* also merit further study. They are less obscure, since the events attributed to Tammuz and Nisan are situated at these times of year, and the sacrifice of Isaac has been widely discussed.

75. On the addenda, see Ta-Shma, "Al kama inyanei Mahzor Vitry," 81–89.

76. *Mahzor Vitry*, ed. Horowitz, hashlama, no. 580 (p. 14 in the addenda). This psalm was also recited as a protection for women in childbirth. Aptowizer (see n. 63) dis-

cusses an Aramaic version in *Sefer Asufot* which is based on *Mahzor Vitry*. See also Wertheimer, *Ginzei Yerushalyim,* 3: 18b from a manuscript that originated in Frankfurt, 1619.

77. These passages suggest that Jews need not fear, but non-Jews have reason for concern. Moritz Güdemann has argued that this custom regarding water and the *tekufah* was practiced by both Jews and Christians, Güdemann, *Geschichte des Erziehungswesens,* 1: 210.

78. An interesting approach that is attributed to Maharil indicates that this custom was widely accepted in his day. While he does not contradict the assertion that water is safe during the *tekufah*, he also warns that one should not rely on miracles. Jacob b. Moses Moellin, *Sefer Maharil, hilkhot mayim delishat matzot*. For those who argued that Jews should not hesitate to use water during the *tekufah* see: R. Eleazar b. Judah, *Sefer Rokeah*, no. 275; R. Avraham Klausner, *Sefer minhagim,* no. 93. See also *Sefer Hasidim Parma*, no. 562; Trachtenberg, *Jewish Magic*, 258.

79. Ta-Shma has argued that this custom probably stemmed from fasts that were observed on these dates in antiquity: "Danger of Drinking," 31–32.

80. Roth, "Al haTekufot," 72.

81. For a standard medieval discussion of this comparison, see Auctor Incertus (In Hugonis de S. Victore dubia), "De filia Jephthe," cols. 323–34, esp. 324–25.

82. Spiegel, "Legend of Isaac's Slaying," 471–547.

83. Yuval, "Vengeance and Damnation," 33–90; J. Cohen, *Sanctifying the Name of God*, 150–52.

84. Auctor Incertus (Hugonis de St. Victore dubia), "De filia Jephthe," cols. 333–34; Martin Legionensis, *Sermones, PL* 208: 1144.

85. This practice and its explanation were known in early twentieth-century Eastern Europe. Notably, this custom was most actively practiced during the winter solstice, when Jephthah's daughter was memorialized; see Klein, "On the Dangers," 93, who suggests that some confused the *tekufah* in Tevet with customs that are related to *Nittel*.

86. For an example of such scorn, see Berger, ed., *Jewish-Christian Debate*, 27, 70.

87. Baumgarten, *Practicing Piety*, 202–7.

88. For a brief discussion of this story, see Baumgarten, *Mothers and Children*, 178–80; Bonfil, *Tra due mondi*, 3–11. See also G. D. Cohen, "Hannah and Her Seven Sons," 39–60. I discuss this story in my coauthored article, Baumgarten and Kushelevsky, "From 'The Mother and Her Sons,'" 273–300. See also the recent discussion of the popularity of *Jossipon* among medieval Ashkenazi Jews in the work of Nisse, *Jacob's Shipwreck*, 19–48.

89. Especially *Jossipon*, 1: 70–75 and *Sefer haZikhronot*, ed. Yassif, 351–54. See also Spiegel, "Legend of Isaac's Slaying," 476–77. He comments on the medieval inclination to enhance the biblical story lest this mother and her sons surpass Isaac in their deeds.

90. This comparison already appeared in the early rabbinic versions of this story, for example, *Lamentations rabbah*, Buber edition, no. 420.

91. Kushelevsky, *Tales in Context*.

92. The chronicle by Solomon bar Samson refers to the story of the mother of seven sons when recounting the story of Sarit; see *Sefer Gezerot Ashkenaz veTzarfat*, ed. Habermann, 47; *Hebräische Berichte*, ed. Haverkamp, 573. See also J. Cohen, *Sanctifying the Name*, 150–52.

93. The Maccabean mother was also an admired cultural model among medieval Christians. See Joslyn-Siemiatkoski, *Christian Memories*.

94. MS Parma Palatina 3057, fol. 169b. This manuscript was written in Germany, 1310.

95. G. D. Cohen, "Messianic Postures," 271–98; Yuval, "Vengeance and Damnation," 34–50; Soloveitchik, "Bein Hevel 'Arav leHevel Edom," 149–52.

96. Yuval, "Vengeance and Damnation," 63–73.

97. Abraham ibn Ezra, *Sefer haIbbur*, 3: Sod haIbbur, s.v. "vehaed hashevii."

98. For a detailed argument about the reasons Ibn Ezra wrote this composition, see Sittig, "*Sabbath Epistle* by Abraham Ibn Ezra," 217–18.

99. Abraham ibn Ezra, "Iggeret haShabbat," 164–65.

100. Ibid.

101. *Sefer Asufot*, a thirteenth-century miscellany from Germany, notes: "Anyone who drinks water during this time is harmed and their stomachs swell." See Aptowizer, "Prohibition to Drink Water," 124–25, who quotes the entire text.

102. R. David Abudraham, *Sefer Abudraham haShalem*, 311.

103. Ibid.

104. Nothaft et al., *Medieval Latin Christian Texts*, 75–76, 85, 158–59.

105. About John, see Nothaft, "John of Pulchro Rivo," 227–42; and for this passage, see the translation provided by Nothaft, *Medieval Latin Christian Texts*, 600.

106. Nothaft, *Medieval Latin Christian Texts*, 600–601.

107. Ta-Shma, "Danger of Drinking," 25–26. Water and its powers are also present in other Ashkenazi contexts. See, recently, Veltri, "Watermarks," 243–55.

108. Gabay-Zada, "Ritual"; Barzilay, "Well-Poisoning"; Soloveitchik, *Principles and Pressure*, 35–36. See also Leguay, *La pollution*, 24–27, 56–62; Clark, *English Alehouse*, 112. The rabbis also suggest that river water is safer than well water; see, for example, *Siddur Rashi*, no. 365, who attributes this to the waters' respective temperatures. However, later authorities argued that the danger stemmed from the *tekufah*; see R. Jacob Moellin, and R. Avraham Klausner, above n. 78, who both suggest that an iron object should be used to counter evil spirits.

109. Leguay, *La pollution*, 26–27.

110. Trachtenberg, *Jewish Magic*, 257. See also Frazer, *Golden Bough*, ii: 273; v: 246; x: 172, 205. I extend thanks to Elliott Horowitz z"l for this reference.

111. This explanation is attributed to *Sefer Alkoshi*. See Grossman, *Early Sages of France*, 420.

112. See notes 76 and 77.

113. See Hünnerkopf, "Brunnen," *Handwörterbuch des deutschen Aberglaubens* 2: 1677–79, 1683. The summer solstice, which was also observed as the birthday of John the

Baptist, was considered a day when all waters were blessed. If Jews viewed this this day with foreboding, they may have been inverting a local tradition. This subject requires further research. See Yuval, *Two Nations*, 191–93, and especially nn. 89–90. Similarly, Iberian New Christians are known to have observed this custom, especially near Christmas and during the summer solstice. This evidence suggests a need to reassess medieval Spanish rabbinical objections to this custom. See Stuczynski, *"Marrano Religion"?* I: 140–43.

114. Isserles and Nothaft, "Calendars Beyond Borders," 1–37; Stern, "Christian Calendars," 236–65; Baumgarten, "Shared and Contested Time," 262–64.

115. Baumgarten, "Shared and Contested Time."

116. Jacob b. Moses Moellin, *Sefer Maharil: Minhagim*, Hilkhot mayim delishat matza, no. 7. This custom is also mentioned by R. Abraham Klausner, see n. 78 and see Trachtenberg, *Jewish Magic*, 160.

117. For a summary of the powers ascribed to iron, see Löw, "Das Eisen," 25–55, esp. 50–52. In Christian culture, see Flint, *Rise of Magic*, 248, n. 167, 250,

118. Trachtenberg, *Jewish Magic*, 313, n. 14, cites references to this belief.

119. For further discussion of this custom as practiced by both Jewish and Christian women in childbirth, see Baumgarten, *Mothers and Children,* 49.

120. See nn. 99 and 102.

121. See Geary, *Phantoms of Remembrance*, 48–80, who discusses women as repositories of family memory. Perhaps one could apply this idea to everyday practices, such as those associated with the *tekufah*.

122. See Ta-Shma, "Be'era shel Miriam," 216, where he raises this as a possibility. See also Shoham-Steiner, "Virgin Mary"; Gabay-Zada, "Ritual."

123. Shoham-Steiner, "Virgin Mary."

124. Gabay-Zada, "Ritual."

125. Har Shefi, *Women and Halakha*, 74–75; See also Alexandre-Bidon, "Archéo-iconographie du puits," 519–43, and, especially, illustrations that portray many women by wells.

126. Wuttke, *Der deutsche Volksaberglaube*, 92–93. Connections between water and blood (and the soul) also abounded in the medieval world; for example, the custom of pouring water out of the window or door when someone died (Güdemann, *Geschichte des Erziehungswesens*, 1: 210), and its parallel among Christians (in Wuttke, *Der deutsche Volksaberglaube*, 145) and, as it appears in Burchard of Worms, *Corrector*: McNeill and Gamer, *Medieval Handbooks of Penance*, 334, no. 96, Burchard attributes this practice to women. It was believed that various elves, goddesses, and demons dwelled in rivers and wells, and many folkloric practices were observed with regard to them, especially by women. See Trachtenberg, *Jewish Magic*, n. 63, and Grimm, *Deutsche Mythologie*, 1: 484–500; 2: 165–71.

127. For example, in *Sefer haEvronot*, a book that was highly popular in the sixteenth and seventeenth centuries, which is attributed to Abraham b. Eliezer Blin. This volume survives in many manuscripts and printed versions, and all provide this explanation of

the custom; see *Sefer haEvronot*, (Zolkiew, 1805), 11b. The popularity of this tradition is also noted in works by various early modern converts who discuss the four *tekufot*. See Hirsch, *Sefer Megale Tekufot*, 7–9, where the story of Jephthah's daughter is presented in verse, as well as 17–20, for a discussion of medieval Spanish commentaries. I thank Yaacov Deutsch for this reference. See also Carlebach, *Palaces of Time*, 160–88.

128. See: E. N. Z. Roth, "Zutot miKetav Yad Nürnberg," *Yeda Am* 7 (25) (1961), 68–74.

129. Carlebach, *Palaces of Time*, 160–88.

Chapter 6

1. For a description of the event and the poem, see *Sefer Gezerot Ashkenaz veZarfat*, ed. Habermann, 164–68; Marcus, "Mothers, Martyrs and Moneymakers," 34–45; Baskin, "Dolce of Worms: Lives and Deaths," 429–37; Baskin, "Dolce of Worms: Women Saints," 39–70.

2. Eleazar is also known as a poet. For his poems, see Eleazar b. Judah, *Shirat HaRokeah*. For a general overview, see Urbach, *Tosaphists*, 409–11.

3. *Sefer Gezerot Ashkenaz veZarfat*, ed. Habermann, 165–69.

4. Marcus, "Mothers, Martyrs and Moneymakers," 34–42.

5. See the references to both her articles on this topic in n. 1.

6. For further discussion of Dulcia, see Grossman, *Pious and Rebellious*, 32, 120, 128, 163–80; Baumgarten, "Gender and Daily Life," 213–28.

7. Medieval tombstones do not often include the phrase until the fifteenth century. For example, on the tombstones from Worms, there are two examples of the phrase "women of valor" being used. In one case Marat Bruna b. Isaac (d. 1183 in Worms; http://www.steinheim-institut.de/cgi-bin/epidat?id=wrm-179&lang=en) is noted as "a woman of valor, an adornment to her house and a crown [of her husband]" (*eshet hayil, navat bayit veateret*). In the other case, of Gutlin b. Isaac (d. 1263 in Worms; http://www.steinheim-institut.de/cgi-bin/epidat?id=wrm-1023&lang=en). She is noted as "woman of valor, crown of her husband" (*eshet hayil, ateret ba'alah*). This phrase appears in Prov. 12:4 and is attributed to Sarah in a variety of midrashim, for example: *Genesis Rabbah*, ed. Theodor-Albeck; Lekh lekha; *Midrash Tanhuma*, ed. Buber, Hayei Sarah; *Midrash Shoher Tov*, ed. Buber, Psa. 59. The phrase "*navat bayit*," meaning housewife, originates in Ps. 68:13 but is not used as frequently. The expression is also used once in the Crusader chronicles; see *Hebräische Berichte*, ed. Haverkamp, 209, where the expression is also used to describe a woman from Worms. Not insignificantly, both tombstones postdate Dulcia's death. Other phrases on the tombstones echo phrases in the poem, which leads one to perhaps conclude that the poem was well known and imitated. This is a matter for a separate study. The phrase "*eshet hayil*" is also found on two tombstones from Würzburg from the thirteenth century; see Müller et al., *Grabsteine*, Leah, no. 1255, late thirteenth century; Blumah, no. 1297, late thirteenth century.

8. Alfonso, "Medieval Portrayals," 131–48.

9. I learned about the poems when I attended one of Dr. Granat's lectures. I thank Dr. Granat for sharing his sources with me. For his published work on women and medieval poetry, see Granat, "'Unto the Voice,'" 153–68.

10. *Liturgical Poems of Rabbi Yannai*, ed. Rabinovitz, 1:437; Shmidman, "Epithalamia," 692–97.

11. Recently, Michael Brocke has suggested there was a commemoration of their daughter Bellette, as well; see Brocke, "Bellette und ihr Pfeiler," 29–38.

12. See n. 1 and Elisheva Baumgarten, "Gender and Daily Life."

13. *Sefer Gezerot Ashkenaz veZarfat* ed. Habermann, 168–69.

14. Ibid.

15. Ibid., 147.

16. For a survey of this literature, see Cayam, "Fringe Benefits," 119–42; Har-Shefi, "Women and Halakha," 234–66; Baumgarten, *Practicing Piety*, 153–60.

17. For a discussion of Sabbath preparations, see Lehmann, "Between Domestic and Urban Spaces."

18. I hope to expand this direction in future publications. In the meantime, see my "Reflections of Everyday Jewish Life," 95–104.

19. See this volume, Introduction and Chapter 3.

20. See, for example, in the Crusade chronicles, where the women note their attendance and devotion to the Torah: *Hebräische Berichte*, ed. Haverkamp, 523.

21. Kushelevsky, *Tales in Context*.

22. For a formulation of this idea in a different medieval context, see Bourgain, "Circulation," 142.

23. Smalley, *Study of the Bible*, 25–26.

24. Elon, *Jewish Law*, 1: 212–16, 283–99, where the author explains different ways of deducing laws from biblical interpretation and also the extent to which the *amoraim* chose additional methods of interpreting the law. See also ibid., 2: 481–85; 3: 1020.

25. Eleazar b. Judah, *Sefer Rokeah*, no. 296, 353. For analysis of the Torah initiation ritual, see Marcus, *Rituals of Childhood*.

26. As explained by Elon. See n. 24.

27. Soloveitchik, *Use of Responsa*, 100–102; Soloveitchik, "Authority of Talmud," 70–100.

28. See Spiegel, *Last Trial*, and more recently a discussion of this topic in relation to *piyut* in Novick, *Piyyuṭ and Midrash*, 97–112.

29. Cover, "Supreme Court."

30. Kanarek, *Biblical Narrative*, 174.

31. Orsi, *Thank You, St. Jude*, 95–118; Orsi, *History and Presence*, 59–62.

32. Hopkin, *Voices of the People*, 12.

33. *Sefer Hasidim Parma*, no. 820.

34. *Sefer Hasidim Parma*, 820; see parallels: *Sefer Hasidim Bologna*, nos. 304, 305; MS JTS Boesky 45, no. 327.

35. See Gabay-Zada, "Ritual"; Shoham-Steiner, "Virgin Mary"; Ta-Shma, "Be'era shel

Miriam." I have not included Miriam in this book because of the work done by my student Gabay-Zada, which I hope will be published in the near future. Gabay-Zada demonstrates beautifully how Saturday night ritual practices corresponded with Christian veneration of the Virgin Mary and were both polemic and compatible with them. More recently, my student Hannah Teddy Schachter has been working on Esther and her significance for medieval queens. See her short article "The Queen and the Jews," 71–76.

36. Curiá, *In Hebreo*.

37. Weissler, *Voices*, 54–65.

38. Geary, *Phantoms of Remembrance*, 48–79.

39. Cubitt, "Folklore and Historiography," 204–11.

40. For examples of very local studies, see Haverkamp, "Martyrs in Rivalry"; Raspe, "When King Dagobert"; Raspe, "Sacred Space, Local History."

41. See the detailed essays in Beadle, ed., *Cambridge Companion to Medieval English Theatre*.

42. I have commented on this phenomenon in connection to stories at large: Baumgarten, "Tales in Context," 687–721.

43. Raspe, "Sacred Space, Local History."

44. Van Liere, *Introduction to the Medieval Bible*, 27–29.

45. See Shimon b. Yitzhak, *Piyutei* 1–24, esp. 11–16.

46. Shalev-Eyni, *Jews Among Christians*; Buda, "Animals and Gazing at Women," 136–64.

47. Shalev-Eyni, *Jews among Christians*, 43–47.

48. Buda, "Animals and Gazing at Women," 17.

49. https://jewishreviewofbooks.com/articles/3148/standing-at-sinai-in-medieval-germany/.

50. About this role, see Grossman, *Pious and Rebellious*, 180–85.

Bibliography

Manuscripts

Amsterdam
University of Amsterdam Library, Ros. 558, 1386, Prayers, Germany

Baltimore
Walters Museum, W72, first half of the thirteenth century, *Speculum virginum*, Germany

Berlin
Staatsbibliothek
Or. Fol. 1224, thirteenth-fourteenth century, Mahzor
Oct. 3150, 1689, *Sefer Evronot*, Germany

Budapest
Jewish Museum 64.618, 1739, Book of Blessings

Cambridge
Add. 3127, 1399, 1414, Mahzor, Ashkenaz
St. John's College, k. 26, 1270–1280, Psalter, England
Trinity College Ms. F 12 27, fifteenth century, Custom book, Germany

Copenhagen
National Library of Denmark and University Library, MS GKS 79 2, 1430, *Speculum humanae salvationis,* Germany

Darmstadt

Landesbibliothek, 2505, circa 1360, *Speculum humanae salvationis*, Cologne

Fulda

Hochschul und Landesbibliothek, As. 88, 1350–75, Rudolph von Ems, *Weltchronik*

Hamburg

State and University Library Carl von Ossietzky, Ms. 37, 1434, Mahzor, Germany

Jerusalem

Israel Museum

B46.04.0912 180/057, circa 1300, Birds' Head Haggadah, Germany

B05.0009 180/052, circa 1300, Pentateuch, Regensburg

National Library, Ms. Heb. 4° 681, fourteenth century, Prayers, Ashkenaz

Leipzig

Universitatsbibliothek

B.H. Duod. 43, fourteenth century, Piyutim, Germany

B.H. Fol. 3, thirteenth-fourteenth century, Mahzor, Germany

1102, Kennicott 665, fourteenth century, Mahzor, Germany

Vollers 1102, c. 1310, Mahzor Leipzig, Worms

London

British Library

Add. 11639, thirteenth century, Miscellany, northern France

Add. 22413, circa 1325, Tripartite Mahzor, Germany

David Sofer collection

Second Nürnberg Haggadah, c. 1470, Germany

Mainz

IR, Anon. 19, late thirteenth century, Memorbuch, currently privately owned

Manchester

John Rylands Library, Hebrew 31, fourteenth century, Customs

Munich

Staatsbibliothek

Cod. Hebr. 21, thirteenth–fourteenth century, Mahzor, Germany

Cod. Hebr. 69, fourteenth century, Mahzor, Germany

New York

Jewish Theological Seminary

Boesky 45, fourteenth-fifteenth century, *Sefer Hasidim,* Italy

8092, 1203, *Mahzor Vitry*, 1203, northern France

8219, fourteenth century, *Sefer Mitzvot Katan*

8972, 1295–1325, Siddur

Morgan Library

M43, 1210–1220, *Huntingfield Psalter,* England

M140, circa 1380, *Speculum humanae salvationis*, Franconia

M158, 1476, *Speculum humanae salvationis*, Basel

M268, circa 1380, Picture Bible, Germany

M385, fifteenth century, *Speculum humanae salvationis*, Flanders

M638, 1250, Bible of Saint Louis, Paris

M730, circa 1280, Book of Hours, Arras

M769, 1360, World Chronicle, Regensburg

M782, circa 1450, *Speculum humanae salvationis*, Augsburg

Oxford

Bodleian Libraries

Can. Or. 70, fourteenth century, Siddur

Mich. 420, 1427, Mahzor, Germany

Opp. 78, thirteenth century, Halakhic compilation, Germany

Opp. 339, 1347, Halakhic compilations, Germany

Opp. 613, fifteenth century, Calendar, northern Italy

Opp. 668, fourteenth century, Mahzor

Opp. Add. 34, fourteenth-fifteenth century, *Sefer Hasidim*, Germany

Corpus Christi College Library, 133, twelfth century, Siddur

Paris

Bibliothèque nationale

Héb. 326, thirteenth-fourteenth century, Prayers, Germany

Héb. 407, 1418, Calendric materials

Héb. 633, thirteenth century, Siddur, northern France

Héb. 634, twelfth-thirteenth century, Siddur, northern France

Héb.1032, fourteenth century, Customs

Lat. 818, eleventh century, Missal

Lat. 10525, circa 1270, St. Louis Psalter, Paris

Parma

Biblioteca Palatina

1265, fourteenth century, Siddur, Germany

1904, fourteenth century, Siddur

1912, fifteenth century, Grace after meals and songs

2513, 1510, Yiddish stories, Italy

2887, thirteenth century, Mahzor

3005, fourteenth century, Siddur, Germany

3057, circa 1310, Prayers, Germany

3134, fourteenth-fifteenth century, Mahzor, Italy

Vatican

ebr. 323, late thirteenth century, Siddur, Germany

ebr. 326, fourteenth century, Siddur, Germany

ebr. 329, thirteenth century, Siddur, Germany

Zurich

Jeselsohn 16, fourteenth century, Mahzor, Germany

Primary Sources

Aaron b. Jacob haCohen of Lunelle. *Orhot Hayim*. Ed. Elyakim Schlesinger. Berlin: Zvi Hirsch Itzckowski, 1902.

———. *Sefer Orhot Hayim*. Ed. Moses Schlesinger, 3 vols. Repr. Jerusalem: HaTehiya, 1955.

Abraham b. Azriel. *Sefer Arugat haBosem*. Ed. Ephraim Elimelekh Urbach. Jerusalem: Mekize Nirdamim, 1959–1963.

Abraham b. Eliezer Blin. *Sefer haEvronot*. Zolkiew, 1805.

Abraham Ibn Ezra. "Iggeret haShabbat." In *Sefer Kerem Hemed*. Ed. Samuel Leib Goldenberg. Prague: Landau, 1839, 4: 159–74.

———. "Sefer ha'Ibbur." In *Kitvei R. Avraham Ibn Ezra*. Jerusalem: Makor, 1970–72.

Abravanel, Isaac. *Perush al Neviim Rishonim*. Jerusalem: Torah veDa'at, 1965.

Albertus Magnus. *The Valiant Woman—De muliere forti: A Medieval Commentary on Proverbs 31:10–31—Especially Useful for Preachers*. Trans. Benedict M. Ashley and Dominic M. Holtz. Chicago: New Priory Press, 2013.

Altschul-Jeruschalmi, Moses Henochs. *Brantspigel*. Ed. and trans. S. Riedel. Frankfurt am Main: Peter Lang, 1993.

Amram Gaon. *Seder Rav Amram*. Ed. Daniel Goldschmidt. Jerusalem: Mossad haRav Kook, 1971.

———. *Seder Rav Amram Gaon*. Ed. Aryeh Leib Frumkin. 2 vols. Jerusalem: Zuckerman Press, 1912.

Angelomus Luxonvensis. "Monachi errationes in libros Regum." *Opera omnia*. Ed. Jacques-Paul Migne. Patrologiae cursus completus, series latina 115. Paris: J. P. Migne, 1852.

Asher b. Yehiel. *Shut haRosh*. Ed. Yitzhak Shlomo Yudelov. Jerusalem: Makhon Yerushalayim, 1994.

Aszod, Judah b. Israel, *Shut Ya'aleh Yehuda*, ed. Shimon Shlomo Goldberg. 3 vols. Sha'alavim: Makhon Shlomo Aumann, 2017–19.

Augustine. *Sermons (1–19) on the Old Testament*. Ed. John E. Rotelle, intro by Michele Pellegrino, trans. Edmund Hill. New York: New City Press, 1991.

Avot deRabbi Nathan, ed. Solomon Schechter. New York: Feldheim, 1967.

Barukh b. Isaac. *Sefer haTerumah*. Warsaw: Wenterhendler, 1897.

———. *Sefer haTerumah*. Ed. Ya'akov Kanievsky. Jerusalem: Makhon Yerushlayim, 2010.

Beda Venerabilis. "In Samuelem propheta allegorica expositio." *Opera omnia*. Ed. Jacques-Paul Migne. Patrologiae cursus completus, series latina 91. Paris: J. P. Migne, 1862.

Bernardus Clarvallensis. "Parabolae." *Opera omnia*. Ed. Joannis Mabillon. Patrologiae cursus completus, series latina 183. Paris: J. P. Migne, 1862.

Biblia latina cum glossa ordinaria, facsimile of Editio Princeps, Adolph Rusch, Strass-
bourg 1480/1481 glossae.net. *Biblia latina cum glossa ordinaria*, ed. Froehlich and
Gibson, Facsimile reproduction of the Editio Princeps of Adolph Rusch of Strasbourg 1480/81 ed. K. Froehlich and Margaret Gibson. Turnhout, 1992.

Birkat haMazon veZemirot, Prague 1514.

The Book of the Knight of the Tower. Ed. M. Y. Offord; trans. William Caxton. London:
Oxford University Press, 1971.

Burchardus Wormatiensis, Episcopi. "Decretorum." *Opera omnia*. Ed. Jacques-Paul Migne.
Patrologiae cursus completus, series latina 140. Paris: J. P. Migne, 1853.

Caesarii Heisterbacensis monachi., *Dialogus miraculorum*. Ed. Joseph Strange. 2 vols.
Bonn: J. M. Heberle, 1851.

Corpus benedictionum pontificalium. Ed. E. Moeller, Corpus Christianorum Series Latina
162. Turnhout: Brepols, 1971.

David Abudraham b. Joseph. *Sefer Abudraham*. Berlin: Zvi Hirsch Itzckowski, 1900;
repr. Jerusalem: Machon Even Yisroel, 1995.

Eleazar b. Judah. *Drasha lePesah*. Ed. Simcha Emanuel. Jerusalem: Mekize Nirdamin, 2006.

———. *Perushey Siddur haTefillah leRokeah*. Ed. Moshe Hershler and Yehudah A. Hershler. 2 vols. Jerusalem: Makhon haRav Hershler, 1992.

———. *Sefer Rokeah haGadol*. Jerusalem: S. Weinfeld, 1960.

———. *Shirat haRokeah*, ed. Yitzhak Meislish. Jerusalem, 1993.

Eleazar Kallir. *Piyuṭim leRosh haShanah*. Ed. Shulamith Elitzur and Michael Rand. Jerusalem: World Union of Jewish Studies, 2014.

Eliezer b. Joel haLevi. *Sefer Ra'aviah*. Berlin: Harry Fischel, 1914; repr. Jerusalem: Mekize
Nirdamim, 1983.

Eliezer b. Nathan. *Sefer Ra'avan*. Jerusalem: H. Vagshal, 1984.

Ephraim b. Jacob of Bonn. *Sefer Zekhirah*. Ed. Avraham M. Habermann. Jerusalem:
Bialik Institute, 1965.

Gantzfried, Shlomo. *Kitzur Shulhan 'Arukh*. Frankfurt: A. J. Hoffman, 1925–28.

Genesis Rabbah. Ed. Julius Theodor and Hanoch Albeck. 3 vols. Jerusalem: Wahrman
Books, 1965.

Glikl, Memoires, 1691–1719. Ed. Chava Turniyansky. Jerusalem: Merkaz Zalman Shazar,
2006.

Godefridus Admontensis. *Homiliae dominicales*. Ed. R. P. Bernardus Pezius. Patrologiae
cursus completus, series latina 174. Paris: J. P. Migne, 1854.

Haim b. Isaac. *Drashot Maharakh Or Zaru'a*. Ed. Yitzhak Shimshon Lange. Jerusalem:
Daf Hen, 1972.

Hebräische Berichte über die Judenverfolgungen während des Ersten Kreuzzugs. Ed. Eva
Haverkamp. Hanover: Hahn, 2005.

Hieronymus. *Commentariorum in Hiezechielem*. Ed. F. Glorie. Corpus Christianorum
Series Latina 75, Turnhout: Brepols, 1964.

Hirsch, Paul Wilhelm. *Sefer Megale Tekufot*: *Das ist Entdeckung derer Tekuphot, Oder das*

schädliche Blut, Welches über die Juden viermahl des Jahres kommet laut ihrer eigenen
luhot oder Calender. Berlin, 1717.

Hugh of Saint Victor et al. *Interpretation of Scripture: Practice. A Selection of Works of
Hugh, Andrew, and Richard of St. Victor, Peter Comestor, Robert of Melun, Maurice
of Sully and Leonius of Paris.* Ed. Franklin T. Harkins and Franciscus A. van Liere.
Turnhout: Brepols, 2015.

The Instructions of Saint Louis: A Critical Text. Ed. David O'Connell. Chapel Hill: UNC
Dept. of Romance Languages, 1979.

Isaac b. Joseph of Corbeil. *Sefer Amudei Golah haNikra Sefer Mitzvot Katan.* Kapost:
Israel Yafe, 1820; repr. Jerusalem, 1979.

Isaac b. Moses. *Sefer Or Zaru'a.* 4 parts. 2 vols. Zhitomir: Hil, 1862.

———. *Sefer Or Zaru'a.* Ed. Shalom Klein et al. 3 vols. Jerusalem: Makhon Yerushalayim, 2001–8.

Isaac b. Shlomo (Rashi). *Sefer haPardes.* Ed. H. L. Ehrenreich. Budapest: Katzbourg
Brothers, 1924.

Jacob and Gershom the Circumcisers (haGozrim). *Sefer Zikhron Brit.* Ed. Jacob Glass-
berg. Berlin: Zvi Hirsch Itzckowski, 1892.

Jacob b. Judah Hazzan of London. *The Etz Hayim.* Ed. Israel Brodie. 3 vols. Jerusalem:
Mossad haRav Kook, 1962.

Jacob b. Isaac. *Sefer Tsena uRena.* Amsterdam: Kasper Shein, 1703.

———. *Sefer Tsena uRena.* Trans. S. H. Hershkovitz. Bnei Brak, 1974.

Jacob b. Meir. *Sefer haYashar leRabbenu Tam.* Ed. Shimon Shlomo Schlesinger. Jerusalem: Kiryat Sefer, 1959.

Jacob b. Moses Moellin. *Shut Maharil haHadashot.* Ed. Yitzchok Satz. Jerusalem: Makhon
Yerushalayim, 1977.

———. *Sefer Maharil: Minhagim.* Ed. Shlomo Spitzer. Jerusalem: Makhon Yerushalayim,
1989.

Jean Beleth. *Summa de ecclesiasticis officiis.* Corpus Christianorum Continuatio Medievalis
41a. Ed. Herbert Douteil. Turnhout: Brepols, 1976.

Joseph Bekhor Shor. *Perushei R. Joseph Bekhor Shor al haTorah.* Ed. Yehoshafat Nevo.
Jerusalem: Mossad haRav Kook, 1994.

Joseph Kara, https://alhatorah.org/Commentators:R._Yosef_Kara's_Commentary_on
_Neviim_Rishonim.

Josephus Flavius. *Antiquities.* Ed. H. St. J. Thackeray. Cambridge, MA: Harvard University Press, 1984.

Jossipon. Ed. David Flusser. 4 vols. Jerusalem: Mossad Bialik, 1980.

Jousep Schammes. *Minhagim deKehillat Kodesh Wormeisa.* Ed. Benjamin Shlomo Ham-
burger and Eric Zimmer. 2 vols. Jerusalem: Makhon Yerushalayim, 1988.

Judah b. Samuel. *Perushei haTorah leRabbi Yehuda heHasid.* Ed. Isaac Samson Lange.
Jerusalem: Defus Hen, 1975.

———. Princeton University *Sefer Hasidim* Database (PUSHD). https://etc.princeton.edu
/sefer_hasidim.

———. *Sefer Hasidim*. Ed. Reuven Margaliot. Jerusalem: Mossad haRav Kook, 1957. (Bologna)

———. *Sefer Hasidim*. Ed. Judah Wistinetski. Frankfurt: M. A. Wahrmann, 1924. (Parma)

Lamentations Rabbah. Ed. Salomon Buber. Vilna: Defus Re'em, 1899.

Landau, Yehezkel. *Noda beYehuda*. Ashkelon: Makhon Yerushalayim, 1990–2008.

Le ménagier de Paris: A Medieval Household Book. Trans. Gina L. Greco and Christine M. Rose. Ithaca, NY: Cornell University Press, 2009.

Leviticus Rabbah. Ed. Reuven Margaliot. 2 vols. Jerusalem: JTS, 1993.

Liber sacramentorum Gellonensis. Ed. A. Dumas and J. Deshusses. Corpus Christianorum Series Latina 159, Turnhout: Brepols, 1971.

Luria, Shlomo. *Yam shel Shlomo*, Tractate Bava Kama. Bnei Brak: HaSafer, 1960.

Mahzor leYamim Nora'im. Ed. Daniel Goldschmidt. 2 vols. Jerusalem: Koren, 1970.

Mahzor Pesah. Ed. Jonah Fraenkel. Jerusalem: Koren, 1993.

Mahzor Shavuot. Ed. Jonah Fraenkel. Jerusalem: Koren, 2000.

Mahzor Sukkot, Shmini Atzeret veSimhat Tora. Ed. Daniel Goldschmidt and Jonah Fraenkel. Jerusalem: Koren, 1981.

Many Pious Women. Ed. and trans. Harry Fox and Justin Jaron Lewis. Berlin: De Gruyter, 2011.

A Medieval Mirror: Speculum Humanae Salvationis, 1324–1500. Ed. Adrian Wilson and Joyce Lancaster Wilson. Berkeley: University of California Press, 1984.

Meir b. Barukh of Rothenburg. *Responsa of Meir of Rothenburg* (Prague). Ed. Moshe Blach. Budapest, 1895; repr. Tel Aviv: Yahadut, 1985.

———. *Responsa of R. Meir of Rothenburg and His Colleagues*. Ed. Simcha Emanuel. Jerusalem: World Union of Jewish Studies, 2012.

———. *Sefer haMinhagim deBei Maharam b. Barukh meRothenburg*. Ed. I. Elfenbein. New York: Jewish Theological Seminary, 1929.

———. *She'elot uTeshuvot*. Crimona edition. Repr. Bnei Brak: Yahadut, 1986.

Meir b. Yekutiel Cohen. *Hagahot Maimoniyot*. In Maimonides, *Mishneh Torah*. Ed. Shabtai Frankel. 7 vols. Jerusalem: Frankel, 2005.

Midrash Sekhel Tov. Ed. Salomon Buber. New York: Menora, 1959.

Midrash Shmuel. Ed. Brakhyahu Lifshitz. Jerusalem: Makhon Schechter, 2009.

Midrash Tadshe or Braita deRabbi Pinhas ben Yair. In *Kadmoniyot haYehudim*. Ed. Abraham Epstein. Vienna: Lippa, 1887.

Midrash Tanhuma. Ed. Salomon Buber. 2 vols. Repr. New York: Hotza'at Sefer, 1946.

Midrash Tehillim haMekhune Shoher Tov. Ed. Salomon Buber. Repr. New York: Om, 1947.

Mikraot Gedolot, HaKeter, ed. M. Cohen. Ramat Gan: Bar Ilan University Press, 1993.

The Mirror of Salvation: Speculum Humanae Salvationis. An Edition of British Library Blockbook G.11784. Ed. Albert C. Labriola and John W. Smeltz. Pittsburgh: Duquesne University Press, 2002.

Moses b. Jacob of Coucy. *Sefer Mitzvot Gadol (Semag)*. 2 vols. Venice, 1547; repr. Jerusalem: Defus S. Monzon, 1961.

Moses b. Menahem of Zurich. *Sefer haSemak miZurich*. Ed. Isaac Jacob Har-Shoshanim. 3 vols. Jerusalem: Dfus Alef-Beit, 1973–88.

Moses Parnas. *Sefer haParnas*. Vilna: Katzenelinbogen, 1891.

Moshav Zekenim al haTorah. Ed. Saliman Sassoon. London: Honig and Sons, 1959.

Moshe haDarshan. *Breshit Rabbati*. Ed. Hanoch Albeck. Jerusalem: Mekitzei Nirdamim, 1940.

Nathan b. Yehiel. *Arukh haShalem*. Ed. Alexander Kohut. 8 vols. Vienna: Menorah, 1926.

Peter Abelard. *Hymnarius Paraclitensis*. Ed. and annotated by Joseph Szöverffy. 2 vols. Berlin: Classical Folia Editions, 1980.

Peter Abelard and Héloise, *Abelard and Heloise: The Letters and Other Writings*. Ed. William Levitan. Indianapolis: Hackett, 2007.

———. *The Letters of Abelard and Heloise*. Trans. and introduction by Betty Radice. New York: Penguin, 1974.

Petrus Comestor. *Historia scholastica*. Patrologiae cursus completus, series latina 198. Paris: J. P. Migne, 1855.

Petrus Lombardus. "Commentarium in Psalmos." *Opera omnia*. Patrologiae cursus completus, series latina 191. Paris: J. P. Migne, 1854.

Philippe de Mezieres. *Le livre de la vertu du sacrement de mariage*. Ed. Joan b. Williamson. Washington, DC: Catholic University of America, 1993.

Pseudo-Philo. *Liber antiquitatum biblicarum*. In *A Commentary on Pseudo-Philo's Liber Antiquitatum Biblicarum*. Ed. Howard Jacobson. 2 vols. Leiden: Brill, 1996.

Robert de Blois. "Du chastoiement des dames." In *Robert de Blois: Son oeuvre didactique et narrative*. Ed. John Howard Fox. Paris: Librairie Nizet, 1950.

———. "L'enseignement des princes." In *Robert de Blois: Son oeuvre didactique et narrative*. Ed. John Howard Fox. Paris: Librairie Nizet, 1950.

Rivkah b. Meir Tiktiner. *Meneket Rivkah: A Manual of Wisdom and Piety for Jewish Women*. Ed. Frauke von Rohden. Philadelphia: Jewish Publication Society, 2009.

Rabanus Maurus. "Commentaria in libros iv regum." *Opera omnia*. Ed. Jacques-Paul Migne. Patrologiae cursus completus, series latina 109. Paris: J. P. Migne, 1864.

Rupertus Tuitiensis. "Ad venerabilem ecclesiae." *Opera omnia*. Ed. Jacques-Paul Migne. Patrologiae cursus completus, series latina 170. Paris: J. P. Migne, 1854.

———. *Opera omnia*. Ed. Jacques-Paul Migne. Patrologiae cursus completus, series latina 168. Paris: J. P. Migne, 1854.

Samson b. Jacob of Worms. *Siddur Rabbenu Shlomo*. Ed. Moshe Hershler. Jerusalem: Hemed, 1972.

Samson b. Tzadok. *Sefer Tashbetz*. Ed. Shlomo Engel. Jerusalem: Makhon Yerushalayim, 2011.

Seder Eliyahu Rabbah and Seder Eliyahu Zutah (Tanna deVei Eliyahu). Ed. Meir Ish-Shalom. Wahrman Books, Jerusalem, 1969; repr. Vienna: Acjiasaf Verlag Warsaw, 1902.

Sefer Gezerot Ashkenaz veZarfat. Ed. Avraham M. Habermann. Jerusalem: Sifrei Tarshish, 1945.

Sefer haNiyar. Ed. Gershon Appel. New York: Sura, 1960.

Sefer haZikhronot, The Book of Memory That Is the Chronicle of Jerahme'el. Ed. Eli Yassif. Tel Aviv: Tel Aviv University Press, 2001.

Sefer Tosafot haShalem. Commentary on the Bible. Ed. Jacob Gellis et al. 12 vols. Jerusalem: Mif 'al Tosafot haShalem, 1982–2009.

Shimon b. Yitzhak, *Piyutei R. Shimon bar Yitzhak*, ed. Avraham M. Habermann. Jerusalem: Schocken Books, 1938.

Simha b. Samuel of Vitry. *Mahzor Vitry*. Ed. Simon haLevi Horowitz. Nuremberg: Mekize Nirdamim, 1892.

———. *Mahzor Vitry*. Ed. Arye Goldschmidt. 3 vols. Jerusalem: Makhon Otzar haPoskim, 2009.

Solomon b. Isaac. *Sefer haOrah (Ritualwerk Raschi)*. Ed. Salomon Buber. Lemberg: S. Buber, 1905.

Solomon b. Samson of Worms. *Siddur*. Ed. Moshe Hershler. Jerusalem: Hemed, 1971.

Speculum humanae salvationis. Ed. J. Lutz and P. Perdrizet. Leipzig, 1907.

Steinheim Database of Epitaphs. http://www.steinheim-institut.de:50580/cgi-bin/epidat.

Thomas de Chobham. *Summa confessorum*. Ed. F. Broomfield. Louvain: Editions Nauwelaerts, 1968.

Yalkut Shimoni. Ed. Dov Hyman. 7 vols. Jerusalem: Mossad haRav Kook, 1999.

Yannai. *The Liturgical Poems of Rabbi Yannai According to the Triennial Cycle of the Pentateuch and the Holidays*. Ed. Zvi M. Rabinovitz. 2 vols. Jerusalem: Bialik Institute, 1985.

Yeruham b. Meshulam. *Sefer Toldot Adam veHava*. Venice, 1553.

Secondary Sources

Agus, Irving A. (Irving Abraham). *The Heroic Age of Franco-German Jewry: The Jews of Germany and France of the Tenth and Eleventh Centuries, the Pioneers and Builders of Town-Life, Town-Government, and Institutions*. 2 vols. New York: Yeshiva University Press, 1969.

Ahuvia, Mika, and Sarit Kattan Gribetz. "'The Daughters of Israel': An Analysis of the Term in Late Ancient Jewish Sources." *Jewish Quarterly Review* 108 (2018): 1–27.

Alexandre-Bidon, Danièle. "Archéo-iconographie du puits au moyen âge." *Mélanges de l'école française de Rome, moyen âge* 104 (1992): 519–43.

Alexiou, Margaret, and Peter Dronke. "The Lament of Jephtha's Daughter: Themes, Traditions, Originality." *Studi Medievali* 12 (1971): 819–69.

Alfonso, Esperanza. "Medieval Portrayals of the Ideal Woman." *Journal of Medieval Iberian Studies* 3 (2011): 131–48.

Anderson, Gary. *The Genesis of Perfection: Adam and Eve in Jewish and Christian Imagination*. Louisville, KY: Westminster John Knox Press, 2010.

Appadurai, Arjun, ed. *The Social Life of Things: Commodities in Cultural Perspective.* Cambridge: Cambridge University Press, 1986.

Aptowizer, Avigdor. "Prohibition to Drink Water." *HaZofeh meEretz Hagar* 2 (1912): 122–26.

Arbel, Daphna. "Questions about Eve's Iniquity, Beauty and the Fall: The 'Primal Figure' in Ezekiel 28:11–19 and 'Genesis Rabbah' Traditions of Eve." *Journal of Biblical Literature* 124 (2005): 641–55.

Arnold, John. *Belief and Unbelief in Medieval Europe.* London: Hodder Arnold, 2005.

Ashley, Kathleen. "The 'Miroir des bonnes femmes': Not for Women Only?" In *Medieval Conduct*, ed. Kathleen Ashley and Robert L. A. Clark, 135–56. Minneapolis: University of Minnesota Press, 2001.

Assaf, Lilach. "Lovely Women and Sweet Men: Gendering the Name and Naming Practices in German-Jewish Communities (Thirteenth and Fourteenth Centuries)." In *Intricate Interfaith Networks in the Middle Ages: Quotidian Jewish-Christian Contacts*, ed. Ephraim Shoham-Steiner, 231–50. Turnhout: Brepols, 2016.

Avioz, Michael. "Josephus's retelling of the Story of David, Nabal and Abigail (1 Sam. 2)." In *Studies in Bible and Exegesis*, ed. M. Garsiel et al., 135–56. Ramat Gan: Bar Ilan University Press, 2011.

Bach, Alice. "The Pleasure of Her Text." *Union Seminary Quarterly Review* 43 (1989): 41–58.
———. *Women, Seduction, and Betrayal in the Biblical Narrative.* Cambridge: Cambridge University Press, 1997.

Bal, Mieke. *Death and Dissymmetry. The Politics of Coherence in the Book of Judges.* Chicago: University of Chicago Press, 1988.

Bar-Levav Elias, Leora. "Minhag yafeh lanashim shelanu: Pesikat halakhah al pi nashim beyemei habenayim." *Massekhet* 6 (2007): 47–85. [Hebrew]

Barzen, Rainer Josef. "Materialization of Memoria: Memory and Remembrance of Benefactors in Building Inscriptions in Medieval Ashkenaz." In *Visual and Material in Pre-modern Jewish Culture*, ed. Katrin Kogman-Appel et al. Forthcoming.

Barzilay, Tzafrir. "Well-Poisoning Accusations in Medieval Europe: 1250–1500." PhD diss., Columbia University, New York, 2017.

Baschet, Jerome. "Medieval Abraham: Between Fleshly Patriarch and Divine Father." *Modern Language Notes (MLN)* 108 (1993): 738–58.
———. *Le sein du père: Abraham et la paternité dans l'occident médiéval.* Paris: Gallimard, 2000.

Baskin, Judith R. "Dolce of Worms: The Lives and Deaths of an Exemplary Medieval Jewish Woman and Her Daughters." In *Judaism in Practice: From the Middle Ages through the Early Modern Period*, ed. Lawrence Fine, 429–37. Princeton: Princeton University Press, 2001.
———. "Dolce of Worms: Women Saints in Judaism." In *Women Saints in World Religions*, ed. Arvind Sharma, 39–70. Albany: State University of New York, 2000.
———. "Erotic Subversion : Undermining Female Agency in 'bMegillah' 10b–17a." *A Feminist Commentary on the Babylonian Talmud*, 227–44. Tübingen: Mohr Siebeck, 2007.

———. *Midrashic Women: Formations of the Feminine in Rabbinic Literature.* Hanover, NH: University Press of New England for Brandeis University Press, 2002.

———. "Some Parallels in the Education of Medieval Jewish and Christian Women." *Jewish History* 5 (1991): 41–51.

Baumgarten, Elisheva. "Ask the Midwives: A Hebrew Manual on Midwifery from Medieval Germany." *Social History of Medicine* 32 (2019): 712–33.

———. "Charitable like Abigail: The History of an Epitaph." *Jewish Quarterly Review* 105 (2015): 312–39.

———. "Towards a History of Medieval Jewish Women's Lives." In *Birkat Avraham.* Ed. Yosef Kaplan, 95–113. Jerusalem: Israel Academy of Science, 2019. [Hebrew]

———. "Gender and Daily Life in Jewish Communities." In *The Oxford Handbook of Women and Gender in Medieval Europe*, ed. Judith M. Bennett and Ruth Mazo Karras, 213–28. New York: Oxford University Press, 2013.

———. "Jewish Conceptions of Motherhood in Medieval Christian Europe: Dialogue and Difference." *Micrologus: Nature, Sciences and Medieval Societies* 17 (2009): 149–65.

———. *Mothers and Children: Jewish Family Life in Medieval Europe.* Princeton, NJ: Princeton University Press, 2004.

———. *Practicing Piety in Medieval Ashkenaz: Men, Women, and Everyday Religious Observance.* Philadelphia: University of Pennsylvania Press, 2014.

———. "Reflections of Everyday Jewish Life: Evidence from Medieval Cemeteries." In *Les vivants et les morts dans les sociétés médiévales*, 95–104. Paris: Éditions de la Sorbonne, 2018.

———. "Shared and Contested Time: Jews and the Christian Ritual Calendar in the Late Thirteenth Century." *Viator* 46 (2015): 253–76.

———. "A Tale of a Christian Matron and Sabbath Candles: Religious Difference, Material Culture and Gender in Thirteenth-Century Germany." *Jewish Studies Quarterly* 20 (2013): 83–99.

———. "Tales in Context: A Historical Approach." Epilogue in *Tales in Context: Sefer Ha-Ma'asim in Medieval Northern France: (Bodleian Library, University of Oxford, Ms. Bodl. Or. 135).* Ed. Rella Kushelevsky, Ruchie Avital, and Chaya Naor. 687–72. Detroit: Wayne State University Press, 2017.

———. "Who Was a Ḥasid or Ḥasidah in Medieval Ashkenaz? Reassessing the Social Implications of a Term." *Jewish History* 34 (2021): 125–54.

Baumgarten, Elisheva, Ephraim Shoham-Steiner, and Elisabeth Hollender. "Introduction: Sefer Ḥasidim—Book, Context, and Afterlife." *Jewish History* 34 (2021): 1–14.

Baumgarten, Elisheva, and Rella Kushelevsky. "From 'The Mother and Her Sons' to 'The Mother of the Sons' in Medieval Ashkenaz." *Zion* 71 (2006): 301–42. [Hebrew]

Baumgarten, Elisheva, Ruth Mazo Karras, and Katelyn Mesler. "Introduction." In *Entangled Histories. Knowledge, Authority and Jewish Culture in the Thirteenth Century*, ed. Elisheva Baumgarten, Ruth Mazo Karras, and Katelyn Mesler. 1–20. Philadelphia: University of Pennsylvania Press, 2017.

Beadle, Richard, ed. *The Cambridge Companion to Medieval English Theatre*. New York: Cambridge University Press, 1994.

Begg, Christopher T. "Abigail (1 Sam 25) According to Josephus." *Estudios Bíblicos* 54 (1996): 5–34.

Benarroch, Jonatan M. "'The Mystery of (Re)Incarnation and the Fallen Angels': The Reincarnations of Adam, Enoch, Metatron, (Jesus), and Joseph—An Anti-Christian Polemic in the Zohar." *Journal of Medieval Religious Cultures* 44 (2018): 117–47.

Benjamin, H. S. "Keeping Marriage Out of Paradise: The Creation of Man and Woman in Patristic Literature." In *The Creation of Man and Woman: Interpretations of the Biblical Narratives in Jewish and Christian Traditions*, ed. Gerard P. Luttikhuizen, 93–106. Boston: Brill, 2000.

Bennett, Judith M., and Ruth Mazo Karras, eds. *The Oxford Handbook of Women and Gender in Medieval Europe*. Oxford: Oxford University Press, 2013.

Ben-Reuven, Sarah. "David bein Avigail ve-BatSheva." *Beit Mikra* 27 (1982): 244–45. [Hebrew]

Ben-Shaya, Shulamit. "The Laws of Niddah in the Halakhic Works of France: From the School of Rashi until the Semak." PhD diss, Ramat Gan, Bar Ilan University, 2016. [Hebrew]

Berger, David, ed. *The Jewish-Christian Debate in the High Middle Ages: A Critical Edition of the Niẓẓaḥon Vetus with an Introduction, Translation, and Commentary*. Philadelphia: Jewish Publication Society of America, 1979.

Berman, Joshua. "Medieval Monasticism and the Evolution of Jewish Interpretation of the Story of Jephthah's Daughter." *Jewish Quarterly Review* 95 (2005): 228–56.

Biller, Peter. "Intellectuals and the Masses: Oxen and She-Asses in the Medieval Church." In *The Oxford Handbook of Medieval Christianity*, ed. John Arnold, 323–39. Oxford: Oxford University Press, 2014.

———. "Popular Religion in the Middle Ages." In *Companion to Historiography*, ed. Michael Bentley, 221–47. New York: Routledge, 1987.

Bleyerveld, Yvonne. "Chaste, Obedient and Devout: Biblical Women as Patterns of Female Virtue in Netherlandish and German Graphic Art, ca. 1500–1750." *Simiolus: Netherlands Quarterly for the History of Art* 28 (2000–2001): 219–50.

———. *Hoe bedriechlijck dat die vrouwen zijn. Vrouwenlisten in de beeldende kunst in de Nederlanden circa 1350–1650*. Leiden: Primavera Pers, 2000.

Bodi, Daniel. "Was Abigail a Scarlet Woman? A Point of Rabbinic Exegesis in Light of Comparative Material." In *Stimulation from Leiden: Collected Communications to the XVIIIth Congress of the International Organization for the Study of the Old Testament* (Leiden, 2004), ed. Herman M. Niemann and Matthias Augustin, 67–73. Frankfurt am Main: P. Lang, 2006.

Bogaert, Pierre, Christian Cannuyer, and Abbaye de Maredsous, eds. *Les bibles en Français: Histoire illustrée du moyen âge à nos jours*. Turnhout: Brepols, 1991.

Bohak, Gideon. *Ancient Jewish Magic: A History*. Cambridge: Cambridge University Press, 2008.

———. "Catching a Thief: The Jewish Trials of a Christian Ordeal." *Jewish Studies Quarterly* 13 (2006): 344–62.

Bonfil, Robert. *History and Folklore in a Medieval Jewish Chronicle: The Family Chronicle of Aḥimaʿaz ben Paltiel.* Leiden: Brill, 2009.

———. *Tra due mondi: Cultura ebraica e cultura cristiana nel Medioevo.* Naples: Ligouri, 1996.

Boswell, John. *The Kindness of Strangers: The Abandonment of Children in Western Europe from Late Antiquity to the Renaissance.* New York: Pantheon Books, 1988.

Boulton, Maureen Barry McCann. *Sacred Fictions of Medieval France: Narrative Theology in the Lives of Christ and the Virgin, 1150–1500.* Rochester, NY: D. S. Brewer, 2015.

Boureau, Alain. *The Lord's First Night: The Myth of the Droit de Cuissage.* Chicago: University of Chicago Press, 1998.

Bourgain, Pascale. "The Circulation of Texts in Manuscript Culture." In *The Medieval Manuscript Book: Cultural Approaches,* ed. Michael James Johnston and Michael Van Dussen, 140–59. Cambridge: Cambridge University Press, 2015.

Boynton, Susan. "The Bible and the Liturgy." In *The Practice of the Bible in the Middle Ages,* ed. Susan Boynton and Diane J. Reilly, 10–33. New York: Columbia University Press, 2011.

Boynton, Susan, and Diane J. Reilly, eds. *The Practice of the Bible in the Middle Ages: Production, Reception, and Performance in Western Christianity.* New York: Columbia University Press, 2011.

Brenner, Athalya. "Are We Amused? Small and Big Differences in Josephus' Representations of Biblical Female Figures in Jewish Antiquities 1–8." In *Are We Amused? Humor About Women in the Biblical Worlds,* ed. Athalya Brenner, 90–106. London: T&T Clark International, 2003.

Britnell, R. H., ed. *Pragmatic Literacy, East and West, 1200–1330.* Woodbridge: Boydell Press, 1997.

Brocke, Michael. "Bellette und ihr Pfeiler in der Wormser Frauensynagoge." *Der Wormsgau. Wissenschaftliche Zeitschrift der Stadt Worms und des Altertumsvereins Worms* 33 (2017): 29–38.

———. *Der jüdische Friedhof in Soest. Eine Dolumentation in Text und Bild.* Soest: Westfälische Verlagsbuchhandlung Mocker & Jahn, 1993.

Brocke, Michael, and Christiane E. Müller. *Haus des Lebens: Jüdische Friedhöfe in Deutschland.* Leipzig: Reclam, 2001.

Brocke, Michael, and Aubrey Pomeranz, eds. *Steine wie Seelen: Der alte jüdische Friedhof Krefeld Grabmale und Inschriften.* Krefeld: Stadt Krefeld, 2003.

Brooke, Christopher Nugent Lawrence. *The Medieval Idea of Marriage.* Oxford: Oxford University Press, 1991.

Brown, Cheryl Anne. *No Longer Be Silent: First Century Jewish Portraits of Biblical Women.* Louisville, KY: Westminster John Knox Press, 1992.

Brown, Peter. *The Body and Society: Men, Women, and Sexual Renunciation in Early Christianity.* New York: Columbia University Press, 1988.

Brundage, James A. *Law, Sex, and Christian Society in Medieval Europe*. Chicago: University of Chicago Press, 1987.

Buc, Philippe. *L'ambiguïté du livre: Prince, pouvoir, et peuple dans les commentaires de la Bible au moyen âge*. Paris: Beauchesne, 1994.

———. "David's Adultery with Bathsheba and the Healing Power of Capetian Kings." *Viator* 24 (1993): 101–20.

———. "Pouvoir royal et commentaires de la bible (1150–1350)." *Annales. Histoire, Sciences Sociales* 44 (1989): 691–713.

Buda, Zsofia. "Animals and Gazing at Women: Zoocephalic Figures in the Tripartite Mahzor." In *Animal Diversities*, ed. Gerhard Jaritz and Alice Mathea Choyke, 136–64. Krems: Medium Aevum Quotidianum, 2005.

Burger, Glenn. *Conduct Becoming: Good Wives and Husbands in the Later Middle Ages*. Philadelphia: University of Pennsylvania Press, 2018.

Bynum, Caroline W. *Metamorphosis and Identity*. New York: Zone Books, 2001.

Carlebach, Elisheva. *Palaces of Time: Jewish Calendar and Culture in Early Modern Europe*. Cambridge, MA: Belknap Press of Harvard University Press, 2011.

Cayam, Aviva. "Fringe Benefits: Women and 'Tzitzit.'" In *Jewish Legal Writings by Women*, ed. Micah D. Halpern and Chana Safrai, 119–42. Jerusalem: Urim, 1988:

Chapin, Elizabeth. *Les villes de foires de Champagne: Des origines au début du XIVe siècle*. Paris: Champion, 1937.

Chazan, Robert. *In the Year 1096: The First Crusade and the Jews*. Philadelphia: Jewish Publication Society, 1996.

———. *The Jews of Medieval Western Christendom, 1000–1500*. Cambridge: Cambridge University Press, 2006.

Clark, Peter. *The English Alehouse: A Social History, 1200–1830*. London: Longman, 1983.

Cockerell, Sydney Carlyle, and John Plummer. *Old Testament Miniatures: A Medieval Picture Book with 283 Paintings from the Creation to the Story of David*. New York: G. Braziller, 1969.

Cohen, Daniel. "He'arot." *Kiryat Sefer* 40 (1965): 542–59. [Hebrew]

Cohen, Esther, and Elliott Horowitz. "In Search of the Sacred: Jews, Christians and Rituals of Marriage in the Later Middle Ages." *Journal of Medieval and Renaissance Studies* 20 (1990): 225–50.

Cohen, Gerson D. "Hannah and Her Seven Sons in Hebrew Literature." In Cohen, *Studies in the Variety of Rabbinic Cultures*, 39–60. Philadelphia: Jewish Publication Society, 1991.

———. "Messianic Postures of Ashkenazim and Sephardim." In Cohen, *Studies in the Variety of Rabbinic Cultures*. 271–97. Philadelphia: Jewish Publication Society, 1991.

Cohen, Jeremy. *"Be Fertile and Increase, Fill the Earth and Master It": The Ancient and Medieval Career of a Biblical Text*. Ithaca, NY: Cornell University Press, 1989.

———. *Living Letters of the Law: Ideas of the Jew in Medieval Christianity*. Berkeley: University of California Press, 1999.

———. *Sanctifying the Name of God: Jewish Martyrs and Jewish Memories of the First Crusade*. Philadelphia: University of Pennsylvania Press, 2004.

Cohen, Mark R. *Poverty and Charity in the Jewish Community of Medieval Egypt*. Princeton, NJ: Princeton University Press, 2005.

———. *The Voice of the Poor in the Middle Ages: An Anthology of Documents from the Cairo Geniza*. Princeton, NJ: Princeton University Press, 2005.

Cohen, Shaye J. D. "Menstruants and the Sacred in Judaism and Christianity." In *Women's History and Ancient History*, ed. Sarah b. Pomeroy, 273–99. Chapel Hill: University of North Carolina Press, 1991.

———. *Why Aren't Jewish Women Circumcised? Gender and Covenant in Judaism*. Berkeley: University of California Press, 2005.

Courtenay, William J. "Parisian Grammar Schools and Teachers in the Long Fourteenth Century." *Viator* 49 (2018): 199–249.

Cover, Robert M. "The Supreme Court, 1982 Term—Foreword: Nomos and Narrative. (1983)." *Faculty Scholarship Series*. Paper 2705.

Cubitt, Catherine. "Folklore and Historiography: Oral Stories and the Writing of Anglo-Saxon History." In *Narrative and History in the Early Medieval West*, ed. Elizabeth M. Tyler and Ross Balzaretti, 189–223. Turnhout: Brepols, 2006.

Cuffel, Alexandra. *Gendering Disgust in Medieval Religious Polemic*. Notre Dame, IN: University of Notre Dame Press, 2007.

Curiá, Montse Leyra. *In Hebreo: The Victorine Exegesis of the Bible in the Light of Its Northern-French Jewish Sources*. Turnhout: Brepols, 2017.

D'Avray, D. L. *Medieval Marriage Sermons: Mass Communication in a Culture Without Print*. New York: Oxford University Press, 2001.

———. *Medieval Marriage: Symbolism and Society*. Oxford: Oxford University Press, 2005.

Dan, Joseph. "Keta miSefer haKavod leRabbi Judah heHasid." *Sinai* 71 (1972): 118. [Hebrew]

Danielou, Jean. *The Bible and the Liturgy*. 2 vols. Notre Dame, IN: University of Notre Dame Press, 1956.

Darnton, Robert. "Peasants Tell Tales: The Meaning of Mother Goose." In *The Great Cat Massacre and Other Episodes in French Cultural History*, 260–61. New York: Basic Books, 1984.

Davidovich-Eshed, Avital. "Desecrated Woman: The Female Body as a Site of Cultural Conflict—Rereading the Story of the Murder of Sarit from a Hebrew Chronicle of 1096." *Jerusalem Studies in Hebrew Literature* 27 (2014): 37–66. [Hebrew]

Davidson, Israel. *Thesaurus of Medieval Hebrew Poetry*. 4 vols. New York: Ktav, 1970.

Davis, Natalie Zemon. *Women on the Margins: Three Seventeenth-Century Lives*. Cambridge, Mass: Harvard University Press, 1997.

de Certeau, Michel. *The Practice of Everyday Life*. Berkeley: University of California Press, 1984.

de Jong, Mayke. *In Samuel's Image. Child Oblation in the Early Medieval West*. Leiden: E. J. Brill, 1996.

De Visscher, Eva. *Reading the Rabbis: Christian Hebraism in the Works of Herbert of Bosham*. Leiden: Brill, 2014.

Delarun, Jacques. "The Clerical Gaze." In *History of Women in the West: Silences of the Middle Ages*, ed. Christiane Klapisch-Zuber, 23–30. Cambridge, MA: Harvard University Press, 1992.

Dermer, Nureet. "The Jews in the Tax Lists (*Taille*) of Late 13th Century Paris: The Socio-economic and Cultural Lives of Jewish Men and Women in Christian Neighborhoods." Master's thesis, Hebrew University of Jerusalem, 2018.

Doležalová, Lucie, and Tamás Visi, eds. *Retelling the Bible: Literary, Historical, and Social Contexts*. Frankfurt am Main: Peter Lang, 2011.

Donnet-Guez, Brigitte. "Modernité et indépendance d'Abigail dans la littérature biblique (1 Sam 25) et post biblique." *Tsafon* 54 (2007–2008): 29–48.

Dowden, Ken. *Death and the Maiden: Girls' Initiation Rites in Greek Mythology*. London: Routledge, 1989.

Drewer, Lois. "Jephthah and His Daughter in Medieval Art: Ambiguities of Heroism and Sacrifice." In *Insights and Interpretations. Studies in Celebration of the Eighty-fifth Anniversary of the Index of Christian Art*, ed. Colum Hourihane, 35–59. Princeton, NJ: Princeton University Press, 2002.

Dronke, Peter. "Medieval Poetry I: Abélard." *The Listener* 74 (Nov. 25, 1965): 840–45.

Dronzek, Anna. "Gendered Theories of Education in Fifteenth-Century Conduct Books." In *Medieval Conduct*, ed. Kathleen Ashley and Robert L. A. Clark, 135–59. Minneapolis: University of Minnesota Press, 2001.

Duby, Georges. *Women of the Twelfth Century*. 3 vols. Chicago: University of Chicago Press, 1997.

Dunphy, Graeme R. *History as Literature: German World Chronicles of the Thirteenth Century in Verse, Excerpts from: Rudolf von Ems, Weltchronik*. Kalamazoo, MI: Medieval Institute Publications, 2003.

Dyer, Joseph. "The Bible in the Medieval Liturgy, 600–1300." In *The New Cambridge History of the Bible,* ed. Richard Marsden and E. Ann Matter, 659–79. Cambridge: Cambridge University Press, 2013.

Edwards, Katie, ed., *Rethinking Biblical Literacy*. London ; New York: Bloomsbury, T&T Clark, 2015.

Ehrenschwendtner, Marie-Luise. "Literacy and the Bible." In *The New Cambridge History of the Bible*. Ed. Richard Marsden and E. Ann Matter, 704–21. Cambridge: Cambridge University Press, 2013.

Einbinder, Susan L. *Beautiful Death: Jewish Poetry and Martyrdom in Medieval France*. Princeton, NJ: Princeton University Press, 2002.

———. "Pucellina of Blois: Romantic Myths and Narrative Conventions." *Jewish History* 12 (1998): 29–46.

———. "The Troyes Laments: Jewish Martyrology in Hebrew and Old French." *Viator* 30 (1999): 201–30.

Elbogen, Ismar. *Jewish Liturgy: A Comprehensive History*. Philadelphia: Jewish Publication Society, 1993.

Elon, Menaḥem. *Jewish Law: History, Sources, Principles—HaMishpat haIvri*. 4 vols. Trans. Bernard Auerbach. Philadelphia: Jewish Publication Society, 1994.

Elsakkers, Marianne. "In Pain You Shall Bear Children (Gen. 3:16): Medieval Prayers for Safe Delivery." In *Women and Miracle Stories: A Multidisciplinary Exploration*, ed. Anne-Marie Korte, 179–210. Leiden: Brill, 2001.

Epstein, Marc Michael. *The Medieval Haggadah: Art, Narrative, and Religious Imagination*. New Haven, CT: Yale University Press, 2011.

———. "Standing at Sinai in Medieval Germany." In https://jewishreviewofbooks.com /articles/3148/standing-at-sinai-in-medieval-germany/

Farmer, Sharon A. "Persuasive Voices: Clerical Images of Medieval Wives." *Speculum* 61 (1986): 517–43.

———. *The Silk Industries of Medieval Paris: Artisanal Migration, Technological Innovation, and Gendered Experience*. Philadelphia: University of Pennsylvania Press, 2017.

Feldman, Louis H. *Studies in Josephus' Rewritten Bible*. Supplements to the *Journal for the Study of Judaism*, v. 58. Leiden: Brill, 1998.

Feldman, Yael S. *Glory and Agony: Isaac's Sacrifice and National Narrative*. Stanford, CA: Stanford University Press, 2010.

Fenster, Thelma S. ed., *Poems of Cupid, God of Love: Editions and Translations*. Leiden: Brill, 1990.

Fevrier, Paul-Albert. "Quelques aspects de la prière pour les morts." In *La prière au Moyen-Age: Littérature et civilisation*, ed. CUER MA, 253–82. Aix-en-Provence, Paris: CUER MA, Université de Provence; H. Champion, 1981.

Finkelstein, Louis. *Jewish Self-Government in the Middle Ages*. New York: Jewish Theological Seminary of America, 1924.

Fischer, Irmtraud. "Abigajil: Weisheit und Prophetie in einer Person vereint." In *Auf den Spuren der schriftgelehrten Weisen. Festschrift für Johannes Marböck anlässlich seiner Emeritierung*, ed. Irmtraud Fischer, Ursula Rapp, and Johannes Schiller, 45–61. Berlin: de Gruyter, 2003.

Fishbane, Michael A. *Biblical Myth and Rabbinic Mythmaking*. Oxford: Oxford University Press, 2003.

Fisher, Esther. "'His Yetzer Is External, Her Yetzer Is Internal': Gendered Aspects of Sexual Desire in Rabbinic Literature." PhD diss. Bar Ilan University, Ramat Gan, 2014. [Hebrew]

Fishman, Talya. *Becoming the People of the Talmud: Oral Torah as Written Tradition in Medieval Jewish Cultures*. Philadelphia: University of Pennsylvania Press, 2011.

Fleischer, Ezra. *Hebrew Liturgical Poetry in the Middle Ages*. Jerusalem: Magnes Press, 2007.

Flint, Valerie. *The Rise of Magic in Early Medieval Europe*. Oxford: Clarendon Press, 1991.

Flisfisch, María Isabel. "The Eve-Mary Dichotomy in the 'Symphonia' of Hildegard of Bingen." In *The Voice of Silence: Women's Literacy in a Men's Church*, ed. Thérèse de Hemptinne and María Eugenia Góngora, 37–46. Turnhout: Brepols, 2004.

Flood, John. *Representations of Eve in Antiquity and the English Middle Ages*, New York: Routledge, 2011.

Fossier, Robert. *The Axe and the Oath: Ordinary Life in the Middle Ages*. Princeton, NJ: Princeton University Press, 2010.

Fourquin, Guy. *Les campagnes de la région Parisienne à la fin du moyen âge*. Paris: Presses universitaires, 1964.

Fox, John Howard. *Robert de Blois: Son oeuvre didactique et narrative*. Paris: Librairie nizet, 1950.

Fraiman, Susan Nashman. "The Sabbath Lamp: Development of the Implements and Customs for Lighting the Sabbath Lights among the Jews of Ashkenaz." PhD diss., Hebrew University, 2013.

Frakes, Jerome C. and Jean Baumgarten. *Introduction to Old Yiddish Literature*. Oxford, New York: Oxford University Press, 2005.

Fram, Edward. *My Dear Daughter: Rabbi Benjamin Slonik and the Education of Jewish Women in Sixteenth-Century Poland*. Cincinnati, OH: Hebrew Union College Press, 2007.

Franklin-Brown, Mary. *Reading the World: Encyclopedic Writing in the Scholastic Age*. Chicago: University of Chicago Press, 2012.

Franz, Adolf. *Die Kirchlichen Benediktionen im Mittlealter*. 2 vols. Freiburg: Herder, 1909.

Frazer, James G. *The Golden Bough. A Study in Magic and Religion*. 2 vols. London: Macmillan, 1914.

Fried, Nathan. "He'arot." *Kiryat Sefer* 37 (1962): 511–14. [Hebrew]

Fries, Maureen. "The Evolution of Eve in Medieval French and English Drama." *Studies in Philology* 99 (2002): 1–16.

Fuchs, Esther. "Marginalization, Ambiguity, Silencing. The Story of Jephthah's Daughter." In *A Feminist Companion to Judges*, ed. Athalya Brenner, 116–44. Sheffield: JSOT Press, 1993.

Fudeman, Kirsten Anne. *Vernacular Voices: Language and Identity in Medieval French Jewish Communities*. Philadelphia: University of Pennsylvania Press, 2010.

Funkenstein, Amos. "Changes in the Patterns of Christian Anti-Jewish Polemics in the 12th Century." *Zion* 33 (1968): 125–44. [Hebrew]

————. *Perceptions of Jewish History*. Berkeley: University of California Press, 1993.

Furst, Rachel. "Striving for Justice: A History of Women and Litigation in the Jewish Courts of Medieval Ashkenaz." PhD diss., Hebrew University of Jerusalem, 2014.

Gabay-Zada, Inbar. "The Ritual of Miriam's Well and the Jews of Ashkenaz and Provence: 11th–14th Centuries." Master's thesis, Bar Ilan University, 2017.

Galinsky, Judah D. "Charity and Prayer in the Ashkenazic Synagogue: The Medieval Yizkor." In *VeHinneh Rivka Yotzet: Essays in Honor of Rivka Dagan*, 163–74. Jerusalem: Dagan Family, 2017. [Hebrew]

———. "Custom, Ordinance or Commandment? The Evolution of the Medieval Monetary-Tithe in Ashkenaz." *Journal of Jewish Studies* 62 (2011): 203–32.

Garsiel, Moshe. "Wit, Words and a Woman: 1 Samuel 25." In *On Humour and the Comic in the Hebrew Bible*, ed. Yehuda T. Raddai and Athalya Brenner, 161–68. Sheffield: Almond Press, 1990.

Geary, Patrick J. *Phantoms of Remembrance: Memory and Oblivion at the End of the First Millennium*. Princeton, NJ: Princeton University Press, 1994.

Gelderblom, Bernhard. *Die Juden von Hameln, von ihren Anfängen im 13. Jahrhundert bis zu ihrer Vernichtung durch das NS-Regime*. Holzminden: J. Mitzkat, 2011.

Gensburger, Sarah. "Halbwachs' Studies in Collective Memory: A Founding Text for Contemporary 'Memory Studies'?" *Journal of Classical Sociology* 16 (2016): 396–413.

Géraud, Hercule. *Paris sous Philippe-le-Bel*. Paris: Crapelet, 1837.

Geula, Amos. "Lost Aggadic Works Known Only from Ashkenaz: Midrash Abkir, Midrash Esfa and Devarim Zuta." PhD diss., Hebrew University of Jerusalem, 2006. [Hebrew]

Gibson, Gail McMurray. "Blessing from Sun and Moon: Churching as Women's Theater." In *Bodies and Disciplines: Intersections of Literature and History in Fifteenth-Century England*, ed. Barbara A. Hanawalt and David Wallace, 139–57. Minneapolis: University of Minnesota Press, 1996.

Gilat, Yitzhak D. "Two Bakashot of Moses of Coucy." *Tarbiz* 28 (1959): 54–58. [Hebrew]

Ginzberg, Louis. *The Legends of the Jews*. 7 vols. Philadelphia: Jewish Publication Society of America, 1910.

Goering, Joseph. "The Thirteenth-Century English Parish." In *Educating People of Faith*, ed. John Van Engen. 208–22. Grand Rapids, MI: Eerdmans, 2004.

Goetz, Hans-Werner and Steven W. Rowan. *Life in the Middle Ages: From the Seventh to the Thirteenth Century*. Notre Dame, IN: University of Notre Dame Press, 1993.

Goitein, Shlomo Dov. *Jewish Education in Muslim Countries*. Jerusalem: Makhon Ben Zvi, 1962. [Hebrew]

———. *A Mediterranean Society*. 6 vols. Berkeley: University of California Press, 1967–93.

Goldstein, Bernard R. "Astronomy among Jews in the Middle Ages." In *Science in Medieval Jewish Cultures*, ed. Gad Freudenthal, 136–46. Cambridge: Cambridge University Press, 2011.

Golinkin, David. *The Status of Women in Jewish Law: Responsa*. Jerusalem: Center for Women in Jewish Law at the Schechter Institute of Jewish Studies, 2012.

Goodwin, Deborah L. *Take Hold of the Robe of a Jew: Herbert of Bosham's Christian Hebraism*. Leiden: Brill, 2006.

Goody, Jack. *The Power of the Written Tradition*. Washington, DC: Smithsonian Institution Press, 2000.

Granat, Yehoshua. "'Unto the Voice of the Girl's Songs': On Singing Women in Medieval Hebrew Poetry (The Andalusian School and Its Offshoots)." In *Mirkamim: Studies in Honor of Galit Hasan-Rokem*, ed. Hagar Solomon and Avigdor Shinan, 153–68. Jerusalem: Magnes Press, 2013. [Hebrew]

Gray, Alyssa M. "Married Women and Tsedaqah in Medieval Jewish Law: Gender and the Discourse of Legal Obligation." *Jewish Law Association Studies* 17 (2007): 168–212.

Greenblatt, Rachel L. *To Tell Their Children: Jewish Communal Memory in Early Modern Prague*. Stanford, CA: Stanford University Press, 2013.

Gregg, Robert C. *Shared Stories, Rival Tellings: Early Encounters of Jews, Christians, and Muslims*. Oxford: Oxford University Press, 2015.

Gribetz, Sarit Kattan. "Zekhut Imahot: Mothers, Fathers, and Ancestral Merit in Rabbinic Sources." *Journal for the Study of Judaism* 49 (2018): 263–96.

Grigsby, John L. "Miroir des bonnes femmes." *Romania* 82 (1952): 458–81.

———. "Miroir des bonnes femmes (Suite)." *Romania* 83 (1953): 30–51.

Grimm, Jacob. *Deutsche Mythologie*. Repr., fourth ed. Graz: Akademische Druck-u Verlagsanstalt, 1953.

Groner, Tzvi. *Berakhot shenishtak'u*. Jerusalem: Mossad haRav Kook, 2003. [Hebrew]

Grossman, Avraham. *The Early Sages of France: Their Lives, Leadership and Works*. Jerusalem: Magnes Press, 1995. [Hebrew]

———. *The Early Sages of Germany: Their Lives, Leadership and Works*. Jerusalem: Magnes Press, 1981. [Hebrew]

———. *Pious and Rebellious: Jewish Women in Medieval Europe*. Trans. Jonathan Chipman. Hanover, NH: Brandeis University Press, 2004.

Gubrium Jaber F., and James A. Holstein. *Analyzing Narrative Reality*. London: Sage, 2009.

Güdemann, Moritz. *Geschichte des Erziehungswesens und der Cultur der Juden in Frankreich und Deutschland*. 3 vols. Vienna: Holder, 1880.

Guldan, Ernst. *Eva und Maria. Eine Antithese als Bildmotiv*. Graz-Cologne: Verlag Hermann Böhlaus Nachf, 1966.

Halbwachs, Maurice. *On Collective Memory*. Chicago: University of Chicago Press, 1992.

Halpern-Amaru, Betsy. "Portraits of Women in Pseudo-Philo's Biblical Antiquities." In *"Women Like This": New Perspectives on Jewish Women in the Greco-Roman World*, ed. Amy-Jill Levine, 85–106. Atlanta, GA: Scholars Press, 1991.

Hamilton, Sarah. *Church and People in the Medieval West, 900–1200*, Harlow: Pearson, 2013.

Har Shefi, Bitkha. "Women and Halakhah in the Years 1050–1350." PhD diss., Hebrew University of Jerusalem, Jerusalem, 2002. [Hebrew]

Harrington, Daniel J., et al. *Les antiquités bibliques*. Paris: Éditions du Cerf, 1976.

Harris, Jennifer A. "The Body as Temple in the High Middle Ages." In *Sacrifice in Religious Experience*, ed. Albert I. Baumgarten, 233–56. Leiden: Brill, 2002.

Hasan-Rokem, Galit. "Ecotypes: Theory of the Lived and Narrated Experience." *Narrative Culture* 3 (2016): 110–37.

Hauptman, Judith. *Rereading the Rabbis: A Woman's Voice*. Boulder, CO: Westview Press, 1998.

Haverkamp, Alfred. "Jews and Urban Life: Bonds and Relationships." In *The Jews of Europe in the Middle Ages (Tenth to Fifteenth Centuries)*, ed. Karin Birk, Werner Transier, and Markus Wener, 55–69. Ostfildern: Hatje Cantz, 2004.

Haverkamp, Alfred, ed. *Geschichte der Juden im Mittelalter von der Nordsee bis zu den Südalpen: Kommentiertes Kartenwerk.* Hanover: Hahnsche Buchhandlung, 2002.

Haverkamp, Eva. "Martyrs in Rivalry: The 1096 Jewish Martyrs and the Thebean Legion." *Jewish History* 23 (2009): 319–42.

Herlihy, David. *Opera Muliebria: Women and Work in Medieval Europe.* New York: McGraw-Hill, 1990.

Himmelfarb, Martha. "The Mother of the Messiah in the Talmud Yerushalmi and Sefer Zerubbabel." In *The Talmud Yerushalmi and Graeco-Roman Culture,* ed. Peter Schäfer and Catherine Hezser, 3: 369–90. Tübingen: Mohr Siebeck, 2002.

Hoffman, Lawrence A. *Covenant of Blood: Circumcision and Gender in Rabbinic Judaism.* Chicago: University of Chicago Press, 1996.

Hoffman-Krayer, Eduard, ed. *Handwörterbuch des deutschen Aberglaubens.* 10 vols. Leipzig: M. Ruhl, 1925–1927.

Holo, Joshua. *Byzantine Jewry in the Mediterranean Economy.* Cambridge: Cambridge University Press, 2009.

Hopkin, David M. "The Ecotype, Or a Modest Proposal to Reconnect Social and Cultural History." In *Exploring Cultural History: Essays in Honour of Peter Burke,* ed. Melissa Calaresu et al., 31–54. Farnham: Ashgate, 2010.

———. *Voices of the People in Nineteenth-Century France.* Cambridge: Cambridge University Press, 2012

Hovav, Yemima. *Maidens Love Thee.* Jerusalem: Dinur Center for Jewish History Research, 2009. [Hebrew]

Howell, Martha. "The Gender of Europe's Commercial Economy, 1200–1700." *Gender & History* 20 (2008): 519–38.

———. *The Marriage Exchange: Property, Social Place, and Gender in Cities of the Low Countries, 1300–1550.* Chicago: University of Chicago Press, 1998.

Hoyle, Victoria. "The Bonds that Bind: Money Lending between Anglo-Jewish and Christian women in the Plea Rolls of the Exchequer of the Jews, 1218–1280." *Journal of Medieval History* 34 (2008): 119–29.

Hünnerkopf, R. "Brunnen." *Handwörterbuch des deutschen Aberglaubens.* In *Der deutsche Volksaberglaube der Gegenwart,* ed. Eduard Hoffman-Krayer, 2: 1677–79. Leipzig: M. Ruhl, 1925.

Huot, Sylvia. "The Writer's Mirror: Watriquet de Couvin and the Development of the Author-Centered Book." In *Across Boundaries: The Book in Culture and Commerce,* ed. Bill Bell, Jonquil Bevan, and Philip Bennett, 29–46. Winchester: St. Paul's Bibliographies, 2000.

Hüttenmeister, Frowald Gil, Elke Maier, and Jan Maier. *Die jüdische Friedhof Wankheim.* dokumentiert von Frowald Gil Hüttenmeister in Zusammenarbeit mit Elke Maier und Jan Maier. Stuttgart: K. Theiss, 1995.

Isserles, Justine, and C. Philipp E. Nothaft. "Calendars Beyond Borders: Exchange of Calendrical Knowledge Between Jews and Christians in Medieval Europe (12th–15th Century)." *Medieval Encounters* 20 (2014): 1–37.

Jacobs-Pollez, Rebecca J. "The Education of Noble Girls in Medieval France: Vincent of
Beauvais and *De eruditione filiorum nobilium*." PhD diss., University of Missouri-
Columbia, 2012.

———. "The Role of the Mother in Vincent of Beauvais' *De eruditione filiorum nobilium*."
Proceedings of the Western Society for French History 38 (January 2010): 15–27.

Jager, Eric. "Did Eve Invent Writing? Script and the Fall in 'The Adam Books.'" *Studies
in Philology* 93 (1996): 229–50.

Johnson, Rebecca Wynne. "Praying for Deliverance: Childbirth and the Cult of the
Saints in the Late Medieval Mediterranean." PhD diss., Princeton University, 2015.

Jordan, William C. *The French Monarchy and the Jews: From Philip Augustus to the Last
Capetians*. Philadelphia: University of Pennsylvania Press, 1989.

———. "Jews on Top: Women and the Availability of Consumption Loans in Northern
France in the Mid-Thirteenth Century." *Journal of Jewish Studies* 29 (1978): 39–57.

Joselit, Jenna Weissman. *Set in Stone: America's Embrace of the Ten Commandments*. New
York: Oxford University Press, 2017.

Joslyn-Siemiatkoski, Daniel. *Christian Memories of the Maccabean Martyrs*. New York:
Palgrave Macmillan, 2009.

Kanarek, Jane L. *Biblical Narrative and the Formation of Rabbinic Law*. New York: Cambridge University Press, 2014.

Kanarfogel, Ephraim. "Halakha and Metziut (Realia) in Medieval Ashkenaz: Surveying
the Parameters and Defining the Limits." *Jewish Law Annual* 14 (2003): 193–224.

———. *The Intellectual and Rabbinic Culture of Medieval Ashkenaz*. Detroit: Wayne University Press, 2012.

———. *Jewish Education and Society in the High Middle Ages*. Detroit: Wayne State University Press, 1992.

———. "On the Nuances of Reading Tosafist Literature and Other Medieval Rabbinic
Texts for Trends in Religious Observance." *Jewish History* 31 (2017): 83–102.

Kaplan, Debra. "'Because Our Wives Trade and Do Business with Our Goods': Gender,
Work, and Jewish-Christian Relations." In *New Perspectives on Jewish-Christian Rela-
tions*, ed. Elisheva Carlebach, Jacob J. Schachter, and David Berger, 241–61. Leiden:
Brill, 2011.

———. *The Patrons and Their Poor: Jewish Community and Public Charity in Early Modern Germany*. Philadelphia: University of Pennsylvania Press, 2020.

———. "Rituals of Marriage and Communal Prestige: The *Breileft* in Medieval and Early
Modern Germany." *Jewish History* 29 (2015): 273–300.

Karras, Ruth Mazo. "The Christianization of Medieval Marriage." In *Christianity and
Culture in the Middle Ages: Essays to Honor John Van Engen*, ed. David Charles Mengel
and Lisa Wolverton, 3–24. Notre Dame, IN: University of Notre Dame Press, 2015.

———. *Thou Art the Man: The Masculinity of David in the Christian and Jewish Middle
Ages*. Philadelphia: University of Pennsylvania Press, 2021.

Katz, Maidi S. "'The Married Woman and her Expense Account': A Study of Women's Ownership and Use of Marital Property in Jewish Law." *Jewish Law Annual* 13 (2000–2001): 101–41.

Klein, A. I. "On the Dangers of Drinking Water During the *Tekufah* and the Means to Avoid It." In *Jubilee Volume in Honour of Prof. Bernhard Heller on the Occasion of His Seventieth Birthday*, ed. Alexander Scheiber, 86–100. Budapest: Scheiber, 1942. [Hebrew]

Kleinberg, Aviad M. *Flesh Made Word: Saints' Stories and the Western Imagination*. Cambridge, MA: Belknap Press of Harvard University Press, 2008.

Klepper, Deeana Copeland. *The Insight of Unbelievers: Nicholas of Lyra and Christian Reading of Jewish Text in the Later Middle Ages*. Philadelphia: University of Pennsylvania Press, 2007.

Klirs, Tracy Guren. *Merit of Our Mothers*. Cincinnati, OH: Hebrew Union College, 1992.

Kogman-Appel, Katrin. "The Audiences of the Late Medieval Haggadah." In *Patronage, Production, and Transmission of Texts in Medieval and Early Modern Jewish Cultures*, ed. Esperanza Alfonso and Jonathan P. Decter, 99–143. Turnhout: Brepols, 2014.

———. "Jewish Art and Non-Jewish Culture: The Dynamics of Artistic Borrowing in Medieval Hebrew Manuscript Illumination." *Jewish History* 15 (2001): 187–234.

———. *A Mahzor from Worms: Art and Religion in a Medieval Jewish Community*. Cambridge, MA: Harvard University Press, 2012.

———. "Pictorial Messages in Medieval Illuminated Hebrew Books." In *Jewish Manuscript Cultures: New Perspectives*, ed. Irina Wandrey, 443–67. Berlin: De Gruyter, 2017.

Koopmans, Rachel. *Wonderful to Relate: Miracle Stories and Miracle Collecting in High Medieval England*. Philadelphia: University of Pennsylvania Press, 2011.

Koren, Sharon. "Immaculate Sarah: Echoes of the Eve/Mary Dichotomy in the Zohar." *Viator: Medieval and Renaissance Studies* 41 (2010): 183–201.

Krahmer, Shawn Madison. "Adam, Eve, and Original Sin in the Works of Bernard of Clairvaux." *Cistercian Studies Quarterly: An International Review of the Monastic and Contemplative Spiritual Tradition* 37 (2002): 3–12.

Kushelevsky, Rella. *Penalties and Temptations*. Jerusalem: Magnes Press, 2010. [Hebrew]
———. *Tales in Context: Sefer Ha-Ma'asim in Medieval Northern France*. Detroit, MI: Wayne State University Press, 2017.

Kvam, Kirsten, Linda S. Schearing, and Valarie H. Ziegler, eds. *Eve and Adam: Jewish, Christian, and Muslim Readings on Genesis and Gender*. Bloomington: Indiana University Press, 1999.

Langer, Ruth. "Biblical Texts in Jewish Prayers: Their History and Function." In *Jewish and Christian Liturgy and Worship: New Insights into Its History and Interaction*, ed. Albert Gerhards and Clemens Leonhard, 63–90. Leiden: Brill, 2007.

Leguay, Jean-Pierre. *La pollution au moyen âge dans le royaume de France et dans les grands fiefs*. Gisserot-Histoire. Paris: Gisserot, 1999.

Lehmann, Ariella. "Between Domestic and Urban Spaces: Preparing for Shabbat in Ashkenazic Communities, 13th–15th Centuries." *Jewish Studies Quarterly* 28 (2021), forthcoming.

———. Lehnertz, Andreas. "The Erfurt *Judeneid* between Pragmatism and Ritual: Some Aspects of Christian and Jewish Oath-Taking in Medieval Germany." In *Ritual Objects in Ritual Contexts*. Erfurter Schriften zur Jüdischen Geschichte 6, ed. Claudia Bergmann and Maria Stürzebecher, 12–31. Jena, Quedlingburg; Bussert and Stadeler, 2020.

———. "Margarete, Reynette, and Meide: Three Jewish Women from Koblenz in the 14th Century Archbishopric of Trier." *Jewish Studies Quarterly* 28 (2021), forthcoming.

Leicht, Reimund. "The Reception of Astrology in Medieval Ashkenazi Culture." *Aleph* 13 (2013): 201–34.

———. "Toward a History of Hebrew Astrological Literature: A Bibliographical Survey." In *Science in Medieval Jewish Cultures*, ed. Gad Freudenthal, 255–91. New York: Cambridge University Press, 2011.

Levenson, Jon D. *The Death and Resurrection of the Beloved Son: The Transformation of Child Sacrifice in Judaism and Christianity.* New Haven, CT: Yale University Press, 1993.

Levine Katz, Yael. "Seven Prophetesses and Seven Sefirot: A Consideration of Kabbalistic Interpretation." *Da'at* 44 (2000): 123–30. [Hebrew]

Lewysohn, Ludwig. *Nefashot Tzadikim, Sechzig Epitaphien von Grabstein des israelitisches Friedhofes zu Worms.* Frankfurt am Main: Baer, 1855.

Lobrichon, Guy. *La Bible au moyen age.* Les Médiévistes Français 3. Paris: Picard, 2003.

Loeb, Isidore. "Le rôle des juifs de Paris en 1296 et 1297." *Revue des études juives* 1(1880): 61–71.

Lourdaux, W. and D. Verhelst, eds. *The Bible and Medieval Culture.* Leuven: Leuven University Press, 1979.

Löw, Immanuel. "Das Eisen." *Monatsschrift für die Geschichte und Wissenschaft des Judenthums* 81 (1937): 25–55.

Luttikhuizen, Gerard P., ed. *The Creation of Man and Woman: Interpretations of the Biblical Narratives in Jewish and Christian Traditions.* Leiden: Brill, 2000.

Mack, Hananel. *The Mystery of Rabbi Moshe HaDarshan.* Jerusalem: Mossad Bialik, 2010. [Hebrew]

Magdalino, Paul, and Robert S. Nelson, eds. *The Old Testament in Byzantium.* Dumbarton Oaks Byzantine Symposia and Colloquia. Washington, DC: Dumbarton Oaks Research Library and Collection, distributed by Harvard University Press, 2010.

Main, Gloria L. "Naming Children in Early New England." *Journal of Interdisciplinary History* 27 (1996): 1–27.

Malkiel, David Joshua. *Reconstructing Ashkenaz: The Human Face of Franco-German Jewry, 1000–1250.* Stanford, CA: Stanford University Press, 2009.

Marcus, David. *Jephthah and His Vow.* Lubbock: Texas Tech Press, 1986.

Marcus, Ivan G. "Introduction." In *The Religious and Social Ideas of the Jewish Pietists in Medieval Germany: Collected Essays*, ed. Ivan Marcus, 11–24. Jerusalem: Zalman Shazar Center for Jewish History, 1986. [Hebrew]

———. "A Jewish-Christian Symbiosis: The Culture of Early Ashkenaz." In *Cultures of Jews: A New History,* ed. David Biale, 449–516. New York: Schocken Books, 2002.

———. "Mothers, Martyrs and Moneymakers: Some Jewish Women in Medieval Europe." *Conservative Judaism* 38 (1986): 34–45.

———. *Piety and Society: The Jewish Pietists of Medieval Germany.* Leiden: Brill, 1981.

———. *Rituals of Childhood. Jewish Acculturation in Medieval Europe.* New Haven: Yale University Press, 1996.

Marsden, Richard, and E. Ann Matter, eds. *The New Cambridge History of the Bible.* Cambridge: Cambridge University Press, 2013.

McAuliffe, Jane Dammen, Barry Walfish, and Joseph Ward Goering, eds. *With Reverence for the Word: Medieval Scriptural Exegesis in Judaism, Christianity, and Islam.* Oxford: Oxford University Press, 2010.

McCarthy, Conor, ed., *Love, Sex and Marriage in the Middle Ages: A Sourcebook.* London: Routledge, 2004.

McKay, Heather A. "Eshet Hayil or Ishah Zarah: Jewish Readings of Abigail and Bathsheba, Both Ancient and Modern." In *Jewish Ways of Reading the Bible*, ed. George J. Brooke, 257–80. Oxford: Oxford University Press on behalf of the University of Manchester, 2000.

McKendrick, Scot, and Kathleen Doyle. *The Art of the Bible.* New York: Thames & Hudson, 2016.

McLaughlin, Megan. *Consorting with Saints: Prayer for the Dead in Early Medieval France.* Ithaca, NY: Cornell University Press, 1994.

McNeill, John T., and Helena M. Gamer. *Medieval Handbooks of Penance: A Translation of the Principal Libra Poenitentiales.* Records of Western Civilization Series. New York: Columbia University Press, 1990.

Medick, Hans. "Turning Global? Microhistory in Extension." *Historische Anthropologie* 24, no. 2 (2016): https://doi.org/10.7788/ha-2016-0206.

Meens, Rob. "The Uses of the Old Testament in Early Medieval Canon Law: The Collectio Vetus Gallica and the Collectio Hibernensis." In *The Uses of the Past in the Early Middle Ages*, ed. Yitzhak Hen and Matthew Innes, 67–77. Cambridge: Cambridge University Press, 2000.

Melammed, Renée Levine. "He Said, She Said: A Woman Teacher in Twelfth-Century Cairo." *Association of Jewish Studies Review* 22 (1997): 19–35.

Mendelson, Sara Heller, and Patricia Crawford. *Women in Early Modern England, 1550–1720.* Oxford: Oxford University Press, 1998.

Mews, C. J. *Abelard and Heloise.* Great Medieval Thinkers. Oxford: Oxford University Press, 2005.

Mews, C. J. and Micha Perry, "Peter Abelard, Heloise and Jewish Biblical Exegesis." *Journal of Ecclesiastical History* 62 (2011): 3–19.

Morey, James H. "Peter Comestor, Biblical Paraphrase, and the Medieval Popular Bible." *Speculum* 68 (1993): 6–35.

Moulinier, Laurence. "La pomme d'Eve et le corps d'Adam." *Micrologus* 45 (2012): 135–58.

Muessig, Carolyn. "Sermon, Preacher and Society in the Middle Ages." *Journal of Medieval History* 28 (2002): 73–91.

Muir, Lynette R. *The Biblical Drama of Medieval Europe.* Cambridge: Cambridge University Press, 1997.

Müller, Karl-Heinz, Simon Schwarzfuchs, and Rami Reiner. *Die Grabsteine vom jüdischen Friedhof in Würzburg aus der Zeit vor dem Schwarzen Tod. (1147–1346).* Würzburg: Gesellschaft für Fränkische Geschichte, 2011.

Muneles, Otto. *Ketovot miBeit ha'Almin haYehudi bePrague.* Jerusalem: Israel Academy of Science, 1955.

Murphy, Frederick J. *Pseudo-Philo: Rewriting the Bible.* New York: Oxford University Press, 1993.

Nedkvitne, Arnved. *The Social Consequences of Literacy in Medieval Scandinavia.* Turnhout: Brepols, 2004.

Nelson, Janet L. "Lay Readers of the Bible in the Carolingian Ninth Century." In *Reading the Bible in the Middle Ages,* ed. Janet L. Nelson, 43–55. London: Bloomsbury Academic, 2015.

Newman, Barbara. *From Virile Woman to WomanChrist: Studies in Medieval Religion and Literature.* Philadelphia: University of Pennsylvania Press, 1995.

Nisse, Ruth. *Jacob's Shipwreck: Diaspora, Translation, and Jewish-Christian Relations in Medieval England.* Ithaca, NY: Cornell University Press, 2017.

Nothaft, C. Philipp E. "John of Pulchro Rivo and John of Saxony: A *Mise Au Point.*" *Journal for the History of Astronomy* 45, no. 2 (May 2014): 227–42.

Nothaft, C. Philipp E., et al. *Medieval Latin Christian Texts on the Jewish Calendar: A Study with Five Editions and Translations.* Leiden: Brill, 2014.

Novick, Tzvi. *Piyyut and Midrash: Form, Genre, and History.* Göttingen: Vanderhock and Ruprecht, 2019.

Novikoff, Alex. "'Plateas Publice Discurrentes': Performance and the Audio-Visual Jew in the Age of Pope Innocent III." In *Jews and Muslims under the Fourth Lateran Council,* ed. Marie-Thérèse Champagne and Irven M. Resnick, 45–63. Turnhout: Brepols, 2019.

Olsan, Lea T. "Charms and Prayers in Medieval Medical Theory and Practice." *Social History of Medicine* 16 (2003): 343–66.

Olsan, Lea T., and Peter Murray Jones. "Performative Rituals for Conception and Childbirth in England, 900–1500." *Bulletin of the History of Medicine* 89 (2015): 406–3.

Olszowy-Schlanger, Judith. "Learning to Read and Write in Medieval Egypt: Children's Exercise Books from the Cairo Geniza." *Journal of Semitic Studies* 48 (2003): 47–69.

Orme, Nicholas. *Medieval Children.* New Haven: Yale University Press, 2001.

Orsi, Robert A. *History and Presence.* Cambridge, MA: Belknap Press of Harvard University Press, 2016.

———. *Thank You, St. Jude: Women's Devotion to the Patron Saint of Hopeless Causes.* New Haven, CT: Yale University Press, 1996.

Panayotova, Stella. "The Illustrated Psalter: Luxury and Practical Use." In *The Practice of the Bible in the Middle Ages*, ed. Susan Boynton and Diane J. Reilly, 247–71. New York: Columbia University Press, 2011.

Paxton, Frederick S., ed. *The Death Ritual at Cluny in the Central Middle Ages: Le rituel de la mort à Cluny au moyen âge central*. Turnhout: Brepols, 2013.

Perry, Micha, and Rebekka Voss. "Approaching Shared Heroes: Cultural Transfer and Transnational Jewish History." *Jewish History* 30 (2016): 1–13.

Poleg, Eyal. "Interpretation of Hebrew Names in Theory and in Practice." In *Form and Function in the Late Medieval Bible*, ed. Eyal Poleg and Laura Light, 217–36. Leiden: Brill, 2013.

———. "'A Ladder Set Up on Earth': The Bible in Medieval Sermons." In *The Practice of the Bible in the Middle Ages*, ed. Susan Boynton and Diane J. Reilly, 205–27. New York: Columbia University Press, 2011.

Poleg, Eyal, and Laura Light, eds. *Form and Function in the Late Medieval Bible*. Leiden: Brill, 2013.

Polo de Beaulieu, Marie Anne. "*Dialogus Miraculorum*: The Initial Source of Inspiration for Johannes Gobi the Younger's *Scala Coeli*?" In *The Art of Cistercian Persuasion in the Middle Ages and Beyond: Caesarius of Heisterbach's* Dialogue on Miracles *and Its Reception*, ed. Victoria Smirnova, Marie Anne Polo de Beaulieu, and Jacques Berlioz, 183–210. Leiden: Brill, 2015.

Raspe, Lucia. *Jüdische Hagiographie im mittelalterlichen Aschkenas*. Tübingen: Mohr Siebeck, 2006.

———. "On Men and Women Reading Yiddish: Between Manuscript and Print." *Jewish Studies Quarterly* 26 (2019): 199–202.

———. "Sacred Space, Local History, and Diasporic Identity: The Graves of the Righteous in Medieval and Early Modern Ashkenaz." In *Jewish Studies at the Crossroads of Anthropology and History: Authority, Diaspora, Tradition*, ed. Ra'anan S. Boustan, Oren Kosansky, and Marina Rustow, 147–63. Philadelphia: University of Pennsylvania Press, 2011.

———. "When King Dagobert Came to Halle: Place and Displacement in Medieval Jewish Legend." *Jewish Studies Quarterly* 20 (2013): 146–58.

Reardon, Patrick Henry. "Judge Deborah: The Hebrew Prophetess in Christian Tradition." *Touchstone* 13 (2000): http://www.touchstonemag.com/archives/article.php?id=13-03-018-f.

Reif, Stefan C. "Use of the Bible." In *Problems with Prayers: Studies in the Textual History of Early Rabbinic Liturgy*, ed. Stefan C. Reif, 71–92. Berlin: W. de Gruyter, 2006.

Reiner, Avraham (Rami). "Bible and Politics: A Correspondence between Rabbenu Tam and the Authorities of Champagne." In *Entangled Histories: Knowledge, Authority, and Jewish Culture in the Thirteenth Century*, ed. Elisheva Baumgarten, Ruth Mazo Karras, and Katelyn Mesler, 59–72. Philadelphia: University of Pennsylvania Press, 2017.

———. "From 'Paradise' to the 'Bonds of Life': Blessings for the Dead on Tombstones in Medieval Ashkenaz." *Zion* 76 (2011): 5–28. [Hebrew]

Reiner, Elhanan. "From Joshua to Jesus: The Transformation of a Biblical Story to a Local Myth: A Chapter in the Religious Life of the Galilean Jew." In *Sharing the Sacred; Religious Contacts and Conflicts in the Holy Land, First-Fifteenth Centuries CE*, ed. Arieh Kofsky and Guy G. Stroumsa. 223–71. Jerusalem: Yad Izhak Ben-Zvi, 1998.

Reizel, Anat, and Amnon Bazaḳ. *Introduction to the Midrashic Literature*. Alon Shevut: Tevunot—Mikhlelet Herzog, 2011.

Reynolds, Philip Lyndon. *How Marriage Became One of the Sacraments: The Sacramental Theology of Marriage from Its Medieval Origins to the Council of Trent*. Cambridge: Cambridge University Press, 2016.

———. *Marriage in the Western Church: The Christianization of Marriage during the Patristic and Early Medieval Periods*. Leiden: E. J. Brill, 1994.

Rézeau, Pierre. *Les prières aux saints en français à la fin du moyen âge*. Geneva: Librarie Droz, 1982.

Riché, Pierre, and Guy Lobrichon, eds. *Le moyen âge et la Bible*. Bible de Tous Les Temps 4. Paris: Beauchesne, 1984.

Ricœur, Paul, and Emerson Buchanan. *The Symbolism of Evil*. Boston: Beacon Press, 1969.

Roman, Oren. "The Old-Yiddish Epics on the Book of Joshua and on the Book of Judges." PhD diss., Hebrew University of Jerusalem, 2014.

———. "The Song of Deborah in Sefer Shoftim (Mantua 1564)." In *Early Modern Yiddish Poetry*, ed. Shlomo Berger, 27–44. Amsterdam: Menasseh ben Israel Institute, 2009.

Roncace, Mark. "Josephus' (Real) Portraits of Deborah and Gideon: A Reading of 'Antiquities' 5.198–232." *Journal for the Study of Judaism in the Persian, Hellenistic, and Roman Period* 31 (2000): 247–74.

Roth, Ernst. "Al haTekufot." *Yeda' 'Am* 7, no. 25 (1961): 69–74. [Hebrew]

———. "Educating Jewish Children on Shavuot." *Yeda' 'Am* 11 (1966): 9–12. [Hebrew]

———. "Zutot miKetav Yad Nürnberg." *Yeda' 'Am* 7, no. 25 (1961): 61–69. [Hebrew]

Rubenstein, Jeffrey L. *Stories of the Babylonian Talmud*. Baltimore: Johns Hopkins University Press, 2010.

Rublack, Ulinka. "Pregnancy, Childbirth and the Female Body in Early Modern Germany." *Past & Present* 150 (1996): 84–110.

Sa'ar, Ortal-Paz. *Jewish Love Magic: From Late Antiquity to the Middle Ages*. Leiden: Brill, 2017.

Sabar, Shalom. "Mitzvot Hannah: Visual Depictions of the 'Three Women's Commandments' among the Jews of Europe from the Middle Ages to Late Nineteenth Century." *Jerusalem Studies in Hebrew Folklore* (2013): 383–413. [Hebrew]

Saghy, Marianne. "The Master and Marcella: Saint Jerome Retells the Bible to Women." In *Retelling the Bible: Literary, Historical, and Social Contexts*, ed. Lucie Doležalová and Tamás Visi, 127–38. Bern: Peter Lang, 2011.

Salfeld, Sigmund. *Das Martyrologium des Nürnberger Memorbuches*. Berlin: L. Simion, 1898.

Salzer, Dorothea M. "Adam, Eve, and Jewish Children: Rewriting the Creation of Eve for the Jewish Young at the Beginning of Jewish Modernization." *Jewish Quarterly Review* 106 (2016): 396–411.

Saperstein, Marc. *"Your Voice like a Ram's Horn": Themes and Texts in Traditional Jewish Preaching*. Monographs of the Hebrew Union College, no. 18. Cincinnati, OH: Hebrew Union College Press, 1996.

Schachter, Hannah Teddy. "The Queen and the Jews." In *In and Out, Between and Beyond: Jewish Daily Life in Medieval Europe*, ed. Elisheva Baumgarten and Ido Noy, 71–76. Jerusalem: Hebrew University of Jerusalem, 2021.

Schäfer, Peter. *Mirror of His Beauty: Feminine Images of God from the Bible to the Early Kabbalah*. Princeton, NJ: Princeton University Press, 2002.

Schearing, Linda S., and Valarie H. Ziegler. *Enticed by Eden: How Western Culture Uses, Confuses, (and Sometimes Abuses) Adam and Eve*. Waco, TX: Baylor University Press, 2013.

Schroeder, Joy A. *Deborah's Daughters: Gender Politics and Biblical Interpretation*. New York: Oxford University Press, 2014.

Scott, Joan Wallach. *Gender and the Politics of History*. New York: Columbia University Press, 1988.

Sed-Rajna, Gabrielle. *The Hebrew Bible in Medieval Illuminated Manuscripts*. New York: Rizzoli, 1987.

Shacham-Rosby, Channa. "Elijah the Prophet in Medieval Franco-German (Ashkenazi) Jewish Culture." PhD diss., Be'er Sheva, Ben Gurion University, 2018. [Hebrew].

Shalev-Eyni, Sarit. *Jews Among Christians: Hebrew Book Illumination from Lake Constance*. London: Harvey Miller, 2010.

Shereshevsky, Esra. "Hebrew Traditions in Peter Comestor's 'Historia Scholastica': I. Genesis." *Jewish Quarterly Review* 59 (1969): 268–89.

Shinners, John Raymond, ed. "A Litany of the Saints." In *Medieval Popular Religion, 1000–1500: A Reader*. 2nd ed., 303–6. North York: University of Toronto Press, 2007.

Shmidman, Avi. "Epithalamia for the Grace after Meals from the Cairo Geniza." MA thesis, Bar Ilan University, 2005. [Hebrew]

Shoham-Steiner, Ephraim. *On the Margins of a Minority: Leprosy, Madness, and Disability among the Jews of Medieval Europe*. Detroit, MI: Wayne State University Press, 2014.

———. "The Virgin Mary, Miriam, and Jewish Reactions to Marian Devotion in the High Middle Ages." *Association of Jewish Studies Review* 37 (2013): 75–91.

Shraga Ben-Ayun, Chaya. *David's Wives—Michal, Abigail, Bathsheba*. Tel Aviv: Sifre hemed, 2005. [Hebrew]

Signer, Michael A. "The *Glossa Ordinaria* and the Transmission of Medieval Anti-Judaism." In *A Distinct Voice: Medieval Studies in Honor of Leonard E. Boyle, O.P.*, ed. Jacqueline Brown and William P. Stoneman, 591–605. Notre Dame, IN: University of Notre Dame Press, 1997.

———. "God's Love for Israel: Apologetic and Hermeneutical Strategies in Twelfth-Century Biblical Exegesis." In *Jews and Christians in Twelfth-Century Europe*, ed. Michael A. Signer and John Van Engen, 123–49. Notre Dame, IN: University of Notre Dame Press, 2001.

Simon, Uriel. *"Seek Peace and Pursue It": Topical Issues in the Light of the Bible, The Bible in the Light of Topical Issues.* Tel Aviv: Miskal Publishing, 2002. [Hebrew]

Simon-Shoshan, Moshe. *Stories of the Law: Narrative Discourse and the Construction of Authority in the Mishnah.* New York: Oxford University Press, 2012.

Sirat, Colette. "Les femmes juives et l'écriture au Moyen Age." *Les nouveaux cahiers* 101 (1990): 14–23.

———. "Un rituel juif de France: Le manuscrit hébreu 633 de la bibliothèque nationale de Paris." *Revue des études juives* 119 (1961): 7–40.

———. "Hannah bat Menahem Zion Finished Her Copy of the Sefer Mitzwot Katan." In *Bibliotheca Rosenthaliana: Treasures of Jewish Booklore—Marking the 200th Anniversary of the Birth of Leeser Rosenthal, 1794–1994,* ed. Adri K. Offenberg, Emile G. L. Schrijver et al., 37–62. Amsterdam: Amsterdam University Press, 1997.

Sittig, Anna C. Kineret. "The Sabbath Epistle by Abraham Ibn Ezra." In *Time, Astronomy and Calendars in the Jewish Tradition,* ed. Sacha Stern and Charles Burnett, 209–19. Leiden: Brill, 2014.

Skemer, Don C. *Binding Words: Textual Amulets in the Middle Ages.* University Park: Pennsylvania State University Press, 2006.

Smalley, Beryl. *The Study of the Bible in the Middle Ages.* Oxford: Basil Blackwell, 1952.

Smith, Lesley. "Continuity and Change in the Study of the Bible: The Ten Commandments in Christian Exegesis." In *Jews and Christians in Thirteenth Century France,* ed. Elisheva Baumgarten and Judah D. Galinsky, 17–30. New York: Palgrave Macmillan, 2015.

———. *The Glossa Ordinaria: The Making of a Medieval Bible Commentary.* Leiden: Brill, 2009.

———. *The Ten Commandments: Interpreting the Bible in the Medieval World.* Leiden: Brill, 2014.

Smits, Edmé R. "A Contribution to the History of Pseudo-Philo's *Liber Antiquitatum Biblicarum* in the Middle Ages." *Journal for the Study of Judaism* 23 (1992): 197–216.

Smoller, Laura A. "'Popular' Religious Culture(s)." In *Oxford Handbook of Medieval Christianity,* ed. John Arnold, 340–56. Oxford: Oxford University Press, 2014.

Soloveitchik, Haym. "The Authority of the Babylonian Talmud and the Use of Biblical Verses and Aggadah in Early Ashkenaz." In *Collected Essays* II, ed. Haym Soloveitchik, 70–100. Oxford: Littman Library, 2014.

———. "Bein Hevel 'Arav leHevel Edom." In *Sanctity of Life and Martyrdom: Studies in Memory of Amir Yekutiel,* ed. Isaiah M. Gafni and Aviezer Ravitzky, 149–52. Jerusalem: Zalman Shazar Center for Jewish History, 1992. [Hebrew]

———. "On Deviance. A Reply to David Malkiel." In *Collected Essays* I, ed. Haym Soloveitchik, 283–93. Oxford: Littman Library, 2013.

———. "Piety, Pietism and German Pietism : 'Sefer Hasidim I' and the Influence of 'Hasidei Ashkenaz.'" *Jewish Quarterly Review* 92 (2002): 455–93.

———. *Principles and Pressures: Jewish Trade in Gentile Wine in the Middle Ages.* Tel Aviv: Am Oved, 2003. [Hebrew]

———. "Review Essay *of Olam Ke-Minhago Noheg.*" *Association of Jewish Studies Review* 23 (1998): 223–25.

———. "The 'Third Yeshivah of Bavel' and the Cultural Origins of Ashkenaz: A Proposal." In *Collected Essays* II, ed. Haym Soloveitchik, 150–215. Oxford: Littman Library, 2014.

———. "Three Themes in the 'Sefer Hasidim.'" *Association of Jewish Studies Review* 1 (1976): 311–58.

———. *The Use of Responsa as Historical Source.* Jerusalem: Merkaz Shazar, 1990. [Hebrew]

Southern, Richard W. *Saint Anselm: A Portrait in a Landscape.* Cambridge: Cambridge University Press, 1990.

Spellberg, D. A. "Writing the Unwritten Life of the Islamic Eve: Menstruation and the Demonization of Motherhood." *International Journal of Middle East Studies* 28 (1996): 305–24.

Spiegel, Shalom. "The Legend of Isaac's Slaying and Resurrection." In *Alexander Marx Jubilee Volume*, ed. Saul Lieberman, Hebrew volume, 471–547. New York: Jewish Theological Seminary of America, 1950. [Hebrew]

———. *The Last Trial.* New York: Pantheon Books, 1967.

Spiegel, Shlomo. "Woman as Ritual Circumcisor." *Sidra* 5 (1989):149–57. [Hebrew]

Stern, Sacha. "Christian Calendars in Medieval Hebrew Manuscripts." *Medieval Encounters* 22 (2016): 236–65.

Strauss, David L. "Pat 'Akum in Medieval France and Germany." Master's thesis, Revel Graduate School, Yeshiva University, 1979.

Stuczynski, Claude. "A 'Marrano Religion'? The Religious Behavior of the New Christians of Bragança Convicted by the Coimbra Inquisition in the Sixteenth Century (1541–1605)." 2 vols. PhD diss., Bar-Ilan University, Ramat Gan, 2005. [Hebrew]

Tanner, Norman, and Sethina Watson. "Least of the Laity: The Minimum Requirements for a Medieval Christian." *Journal of Medieval History* 32 (2006): 395–423.

Tapp, Ann M. "An Ideology of Expendability: Virgin Daughter Sacrifice in Genesis 19.1–11, Judges 11.30–39 and 19.22–26." In *Anti-Covenant: Counter Reading Women's Lives in the Hebrew Bible*, ed. Mieke Bal, 157–74. Sheffield: Almond Press, 1989.

Ta-Shma, Israel M. "Al Kama Inyanei Mahzor Vitry." *'Alei Sefer* 11 (1984): 81–89. [Hebrew]

———. "Al Perush Avot shebeMahzor Vitry." *Kiryat Sefer* 42 (1967): 507–8. [Hebrew]

———. "Beera shel Miriam: Gilgulei Minhag Ashkenaz beSeudah Shlishit shel Shabbat." In *Early Franco-German Ritual and Custom*, 201–20. Jerusalem: Hebrew University/ Magnes Press, 1992. [Hebrew]

———. "The Danger of Drinking Water During the Tequfa—The History of an Idea." *Jerusalem Studies in Jewish Folklore* (1995): 21–32. [Hebrew]

———. *The Early Ashkenazic Prayer: Literary and Historical Aspects.* Jerusalem: Magnes Press, 2003. [Hebrew]

———. *Early Franco-German Ritual and Custom.* Jerusalem: Magnes Press, 1992. [Hebrew]

———. "Halakha and Reality—The Tosafist Experience." In *Rashi et la culture juive en France du Nord au moyen âge*, ed. Gilbert Dahan, Gerard Nahon, and Elie Nicolas, 315–29. Paris: E. Peters, 1997.

———. "Ma'amad haNashim haMitnadvot leKayem Mitzvot 'Aseh shehaZman Graman." In *Ritual, Custom, and Reality in Franco-Germany, 1000–1350,* 262–79. Jerusalem: Hebrew University/Magnes Press, 1996. [Hebrew]

———. "Minhagei Harhakat haNiddah beAshkenaz haKeduma: HaHayyim vehaSifrut." In *Ritual, Custom, and Reality in Franco-Germany, 1000–1350,* 280–9. Jerusalem: Hebrew University/Magnes Press, 1996. [Hebrew]

———. "Ner shel Kavod." In *Early Franco-German Ritual and Custom.* 125–35. Jerusalem: Magnes Press, 1992. [Hebrew]

Thomas, Marcel. *Scènes de l'ancien testament illustrant le psautier de Saint Louis.* Graz: Akademische Druck- u. Verlagsanstalt, 1970.

Thompson, John Lee. *Writing the Wrongs: Women of the Old Testament among Biblical Commentators from Philo through the Reformation.* Oxford: Oxford University Press, 2001.

Toch, Michael. *The Economic History of European Jews: Late Antiquity and Early Middle Ages.* Leiden: Brill, 2013.

Touitou, Elazar. *Exegesis in Perpetual Motion: Studies in the Pentateuchal Commentary of Rabbi Samuel b. Meir.* Ramat-Gan: Bar-Ilan University Press, 2003. [Hebrew]

Trachtenberg, Joshua. *Jewish Magic and Superstition: A Study in Folk Religion.* Philadelphia: Jewish Publication Society, 1939.

Tubul, Meirav. "Excluding Women from the Cemetery: Halachic versus Kabbalistic Rulings." *Hebrew Union College Annual* 78 (2007): *47–65. [Hebrew]

Turniansky, Chava. "Introduction." *Glikl: Zikhronot 1691–1719.* Jerusalem: Zalman Shazar Center for Jewish History, 2008. [Hebrew]

———. "Women and Books in Early Modern Europe." *Israel Academy of Sciences Newsletter* (Dec. 2009): 7–10. [Hebrew]

Udry, Susan. "Robert de Blois and Geoffroy de La Tour Landry on Feminine Beauty: Two Late Medieval French Conduct Books for Women." *Essays in Medieval Studies* 19 (2002): 90–102.

Ulrich, Laurel Thatcher. *Good Wives: Image and Reality in the Lives of Women in Northern New England, 1650–1750.* New York: Oxford University Press, 1983.

Urbach, Ephraim Elimelech. *The Tosaphists: Their History, Writings and Methods.* 4th ed. Jerusalem: Bialik Institute, 1980. [Hebrew]

Valler, Shulamith. "The Story of Jephthah's Daughter in the Midrash." In *The Feminist Companion to the Bible,* Second Series, ed. Athalya Brenner, 48–66. Sheffield: Sheffield Academic Press, 1999.

van Bekkum, Wouter Jacques. "Eve and the Matriarchs: Aspects of Woman Typology in Genesis." In *The Creation of Man and Woman: Interpretations of the Biblical Narratives in Jewish and Christian* Traditions, ed. Gerard P. Luttikhuizen, 128–39. Leiden: Brill, 2000.

van der Horst, Pieter W. "Deborah and Seila in Pseudo-Philo's Liber Antiquitatum Biblicarum." In *Messiah and Christos: Studies in the Jewish Origins of Christianity; Pre-*

sented to David Flusser on the Occasion of His Seventy-fifth Birthday, ed. Itamar Gruenwald, Shaul Shaked, and Guy Stroumsa, 111–17. Tübingen: Mohr Siebeck, 1992.

Van Liere, Franciscus A. An Introduction to the Medieval Bible. New York: Cambridge University Press, 2014.

van Rensburg, Johannes F. "Intellect and/or Beauty: A Portrait of Women in the Old Testament and Extra Biblical Literature." Journal for Semiotics 11 (2002): 112–17.

Vansina, Jan. Oral Tradition as History. Madison: University of Wisconsin Press, 1985.

Vecchio, Silvana. "The Good Wife." In History of Women in the West, vol. 2: Silences of the Middle Ages, ed. Christiane Klapisch-Zuber. Cambridge, MA: Belknap Press of Harvard University Press, 1998.

Veltri, Giuseppe. "Watermarks in MS. Munich Hebr. 95." In Jewish Studies Between the Disciplines: Papers in Honor of Peter Schäfer on the Occasion of His Sixtieth Birthday, ed. Klaus Hermann, Margarete Schlüter, and Giuseppe Veltri, 243–55. Leiden: Brill, 2003.

Veyne, Paul, Bread and Circuses: Historical Sociology and Political Pluralism, trans. Brian Pearce. London: A. Lane, 1990.

Vitz, Evelyn Birge. "Liturgy as Education in the Middle Ages." In Medieval Education, ed. Ronald b. Begley and Joseph W. Kotersky, 20–34. New York: Fordham University Press, 2009.

Vrudny, Kimberly J. Friars, Scribes, and Corpses: A Marian Confraternal Reading of the Mirror of Human Salvation (Speculum Humanae Salvationis). Paris: Peeters, 2010.

Wain, Gemma Louise. "'Nec Ancilla Nec Domina': Representations of Eve in the Twelfth Century." PhD diss., Durham University, 2012.

Wartenberg, Ilana. "The Hebrew Calendrical Bookshelf of the Early Twelfth Century: The Cases of Abraham bar Hiyya and Jacob Bar Samson." In Time, Astronomy and Calendars in the Jewish Tradition, ed. Sacha Stern and Charles Burnett, 97–112. Leiden: Brill, 2014.

Weinstein, Roni. Marriage Rituals Italian Style: A Historical Anthropological Perspective on Early Modern Italian Jews. Leiden: Brill, 2004.

Weissler, Chava. Voices of the Matriarchs: Listening to the Prayers of Early Modern Women. Boston: Beacon Press, 1998.

Weitzmann, Kurt. "The Jephthah Panel in the Bema of the Church of St. Catherine's Monastery on Mount Sinai." Dumbarton Oaks Papers 18 (1964): 341–58.

Wertheimer, Shlomo Aharon. Ginzei Yerushalayim. 3 vols. Jerusalem: Wertheimer, 1896. [Hebrew].

Williams, John, ed. Imaging the Early Medieval Bible. University Park: Pennsylvania State University Press, 1999.

Wimpfheimer, Barry S. Narrating the Law: A Poetics of Talmudic Legal Stories. Philadelphia: University of Pennsylvania Press, 2011.

Woolf, Jeffrey R. The Fabric of Religious Life in Medieval Ashkenaz (1000–1300): Creating Sacred Communities. Leiden: Brill, 2015.

Wuttke, Adolf. Der deutsche Volksaberglaube der Gegenwart. Leipzig: M. Ruhl, 1925.

Ya'ari, Avraham. "Tefillot mi sheberakh: Hishtalshelutan, minhagehen venushaotehen."
    Kiryat Sefer 33 (1959):118–30, 233–50; cont. *Kiryat Sefer* 36 (1961): 103–18. [Hebrew]
———. *Toldot Hag Simhat Torah.* Jerusalem: Mossad haRav Kook, 1998. [Hebrew]
Yassif, Eli. *The Hebrew Folktale: History, Genre, Meaning.* Folklore Studies in Translation.
    Bloomington: Indiana University Press, 1999.
———. "The Hebrew Story in the Middle Ages: An Introduction." *Jewish Studies Quar-
    terly* 20 (2013): 3–8.
———, ed. *Me'ah Sipurim Ḥaser Eḥad: Agadot Ketav Yad Yerushalayim baFolḳlor
    haYehudi shel Yeme ha-Benayim (Ninety-nine Tales: The Jerusalem Manuscript Cycle of
    Legends in Medieval Jewish Folklore).* Tel Aviv: Tel Aviv University, 2013. [Hebrew]
Yuval, Israel J. "Heilige Städte, Heilige Gemeinden: Mainz als das Jerusalem Deutschlands,
    Aschkenaz." In *Jüdische Gemeinden und Organisationsformen von der Antike bis zur Gegen-
    wart,* ed. Robert Jütte and Abraham Kustermann, 91–101. Cologne: Oldenbourg, 1996.
———. *Two Nations in Your Womb: Perceptions of Jews and Christians in Late Antiquity,* trans.
    Barbara Harshav and Jonathan Chipman. Berkeley: University of California Press, 2006.
———. "Vengeance and Damnation, Blood and Defamation: From Jewish Martyrdom to
    Blood Libel Accusation." *Zion* 58 (1993): 33–90. [Hebrew]
Zacher, Samantha. *Rewriting the Old Testament in Anglo-Saxon Verse: Becoming the Chosen
    People.* New York: Bloomsbury Academic, 2014.
Zieman, Katherine. *Singing the New Song: Literacy and Liturgy in Late Medieval England.*
    Philadelphia: University of Pennsylvania Press, 2008.
Zimmer, Eric. *Society and Its Customs: Studies in the History and Metamorphosis of Jewish
    Customs.* Jerusalem: Zalman Shazar Center for Jewish History, 1996. [Hebrew]
Zimmer, Yitzhak (Eric). "The Customs of Matnat Yad and Hazkarat Neshamot." In *Lo
    Yasur Shevet miYehudah: Hanhagah, Rabanut uKehilah beToldot Yiśra'el, Mehkarim
    Mugashim leProf. Shim'on Shvartsfuḳs,* ed. Joseph Hacker and Yaron Harel, 71–87.
    Jerusalem: Bialik Institute, 2011. [Hebrew]
Zolty, Shoshana Pantel. *And All Your Children Shall Be Learned: Women and the Study of
    Torah in Jewish Law and History.* Northvale, NJ: J. Aronson, 1993.

Index

Index

Index

Acknowledgments

The idea for this book originated during my graduate studies, when I was first pointed to a passage about Jephthah's daughter by Israel Yuval, and it has evolved slowly over time. Since then my debts of gratitude have accumulated, and it is with deep appreciation that I now acknowledge the institutions and individuals that have contributed to this study. While this writing has been reviewed and improved along the way, any and all mistakes in this volume are mine alone.

At the completion of the first monograph I have written from start to finish since joining the faculty of the Hebrew University of Jerusalem, I want to take this special opportunity to thank my colleagues in my two academic homes—the Department of Jewish History and Contemporary Jewry and the Department of History— for their friendship and collegiality. I am delighted and honored to be a member of the Faculty of Humanities at the Hebrew University. I also gratefully acknowledge the support of the Dora Schwartz Fund at the Jack, Joseph and Morton Mandel Institute of Jewish Studies at The Hebrew University of Jerusalem.

Parts of this book appeared in preliminary form in print. An initial attempt to discuss some of this material appeared as "'Like Adam and Eve': Biblical Models and Jewish Daily Life in Medieval Christian Europe," *Irish*

Theological Quarterly 83, (2018), 44–61. Preliminary versions of chapters four and five appeared in the *Jewish Quarterly Review*: "Charitable Like Abigail: The History of an Epitaph", *Jewish Quarterly Review* 105 (2015): 312–39; "Remember that Glorious Girl: Jephthah's Daughter in Medieval Jewish Culture", *Jewish Quarterly Review* 97 (2007): 180–209. The Israel Science Foundation (Grant no. 646/14) provided the initial funding that allowed me to turn disparate examples into a book. This research developed and took shape in conjunction within my ongoing project, *Beyond the Elite: Jewish Daily Life in Medieval Europe* (European Research Council Grant no. 681507). This collegial framework for considering daily life and different methodologies for accessing the minds and practices of medieval Jews led to many of my conclusions and formulations. I thank André Rothschild, my research assistant during the early phase of my ISF grant, and I am especially grateful to the *Beyond the Elite* research team: Tzafrir Barzilay, Neta Bodner, Adi Namia-Cohen, Nureet Dermer, Aviya Doron, Miri Fenton, Annika Funke, Etelle Kalaora, Albert Kohn, Ariella Lehmann, Andreas Lehnertz, Eyal Levinson, Ido Noy, Erez Rochman, Hannah (Teddy) Schachter and Amit Shafran. This scholarly enterprise —my own and our team's—would not be possible without the assistance of Audrey Fingherman Zabari, who deserves the greatest appreciation of all.

The process of transforming a panoply of ideas into a cohesive monograph took place in 2017–18, when I was the George William Cottrell Jr. Member at the Institute for Advanced Study in Princeton. I am deeply grateful to IAS for this opportunity and support during that academic year in Princeton. The medieval group, led by Patrick Geary, provided engaging interlocutors for conversation. The institute provided a home for concentrated work, and its library staff enabled me access to every imaginable book and article. I extend thanks to Marcia Tucker, Kirstie Venanzi, Cecilia Kornish, and Karen Downing for their help obtaining these materials; and, to Brett Savage, Alexis May, and Uta Nitschke-Joseph for their assistance scanning and organizing them. I also want to express my gratitude to Marian Zelazny, who made all matters easier. Studying Talmud with Sheila Kurtzer in Princeton and being a regular guest at Dan and Sheila's house made the year a memorable experience and added to this volume in many ways as well.

My project began and culminated in Jerusalem, particularly at the Hebrew University: often in the Judaica reading room at the National Library, during 2016–17 at the Israel Institute for Advanced Studies, and most recently in the offices of our *Beyond the Elite* team, where students, local colleagues, and friends were regularly present. Colleagues from elsewhere in Israel and abroad were ever ready for consultation by email and, when possible, in person. My appreciation goes to Michael Brocke, Elisheva Carlebach, Naama Cohen-Hanegbi, Yaacob Dweck, Simcha Emanuel, Elisabeth Hollender, Ephraim Kanarfogel, Debra Kaplan, Sharon Koren, Ivan Marcus, Renée Levine Melammed, Micha Perry, Rami Reiner, Oren Roman, Moshe Rosman, Pinchas Roth, Danny Schwartz, Ephraim Shoham-Steiner, David Shyovitz, Daniella Talmon-Heller, Paola Tartakoff, Israel Yuval, and Oded Zinger for their collegiality and scholarship.

Two colleagues deserve special mention. Judah Galinsky has brought consistent interest to this project. Over the years he has referred me to numerous sources and read multiple drafts. Tova Ganzel has been a partner for conversation and a dear friend. I am indebted to them both for their friendship and erudition.

Parts of this study made up my talks for the Brettler Lecture Series, at the invitation of the Pardes Institute of Jewish Studies (Jerusalem) in 2015. In 2018, after completing a full draft manuscript, I presented significant portions of this work as the Arffa Scholar at Yale University. Sections of this study were also incorporated in papers as well as conference presentations in Berkeley, Berlin, Frankfurt, Jerusalem, New York, Tel Aviv, Toronto, and Washington, DC. I am grateful to my hosts and audiences for these opportunities and for their insightful questions.

Some of the mentors who accompanied the early stages of my academic career have continued in that capacity. Robert Bonfil, my doctoral advisor, continues to be a dear teacher and advisor. Shulamith Shahar has accompanied me since I was a graduate student, and she greeted this project with enthusiasm. She has followed it with consistent encouragement and excellent comments throughout, often serving as a sounding board for fresh ideas and first drafts. The role Caroline Walker Bynum holds is unlike any other. Since we met in Spring 2000, I have been fortunate to learn from her, professionally and personally. Her reading of this manuscript led me to reconsider and revise significant points. I am grateful for her ongoing insistence that I always push myself harder. I have truly been blessed with teachers who exemplify the qualities of the finest scholarship and of admirable human beings, and I thank each of them for their shining example.

I was thrilled when the University of Pennsylvania Press accepted this book for publication, and I thank the series editors, Steven Weitzman, Shaul Magid and Francesca Trivellato, for including my scholarship in the Jewish

Culture and Contexts Series yet once more. From our first discussion of this topic, Jerry Singerman, the senior Humanities editor, was enthusiastic about this monograph; I am grateful for his advice throughout this process and for his patience and wisdom. His vision of what this book could become was a driving force and an inspiration. I also thank the Penn Press staff for all of their assistance and especially the copyeditor, Mindy Brown, and Noreen O'Connor-Abel. The readers for the University of Pennsylvania Press deserve special acknowledgment. Above and beyond reading this volume for the press, Ruth Mazo Karras (and her work) has served as a model over the past decade. I thank Ruth for her invaluable comments and her help. The second reader pushed me to reexamine the articulation of certain assertions and offered important criticism. I appreciate the time and thought that went into this reading of the manuscript, and I hope the reader finds it much improved. I am fortunate to have had two such insightful readers. Susan Oren has accompanied the preparation of this book in its final form, and as always, her sage advice and insight as an editor have helped me to refine my prose and ideas.

Last but not least, this book came into being amid the caring support of my family—my parents, Albert and Rita Baumgarten; and my sisters, Shoshana, Margalit, and Naama, and their families. My parents each read and heard passages along the way, and my whole family provided encouragement throughout. My husband, Yaacov Deutsch, a scholar in his own right, was a partner in conversation throughout this process, reading drafts and hearing ideas. Without his dedication, confidence, and love, this project would not have been completed. All that has become mine during these nearly three decades of our shared life is also his. Our children—Yonatan and Ruth, Ayelet and Eli, Nitzan, and Amir—provide the balance and love that make work worthwhile, and I cherish them each for being who they are. The expansion of our family to include Eli and Ruth, together with Nomi and Yitzhak and their children, heightens the pertinence of examining the stories we tell to define ourselves and guide our daily practices.

As this study developed and I recognized that storytelling and related praxis were at its heart, I thought repeatedly of those who told me the stories and taught me the practices that have shaped me. I dedicate this book to my parents, Al and Rita Baumgarten, with love and gratitude. It is my hope that the stories and practices I learned from them will continue to accompany our children (their grandchildren) and their future families.